PRAISE FOR *THE 3rd ALTERNATIVE*

"You can 'get' Stephen Covey's message in five pages—or less. But I dearly hope you will carefully read and apply *every* page. Stephen has given us a precious gift, but, like most profound ideas, it is the daily, conscious practice that can or will transform your life."

—Tom Peters, author of *The Brand You 50*
and *Re-imagine: Business Excellence in a Disruptive Age*

"In this book, Covey reaches out way beyond his familiar domain, to the universe, and has come up with a social vaccine capable of addressing if not resolving the existential agonies and angst that we all face as individuals, as well as the organizations and societies that we work and live in. In this Olympiad vault, Covey has written his most ambitious and hopeful book, in my own view—a masterpiece to benefit all of us doing our best to live in peace and justice in this messy world."

—Warren Bennis, Distinguished Professor of Management,
University of Southern California, and author of the memoir *Still Surprised*

"A most compelling approach for addressing the most challenging issues of the day. It is an inarguable formula for success in the corporate world and beyond."

—Douglas R. Conant, retired CEO, Campbell Soup Company,
and *New York Times* bestselling author

"Dr. Covey has done it again. *The 3rd Alternative* is not only powerful reading, it answers some of life's most challenging questions. A must-read for all future leaders."

—Jon M. Huntsman, Sr.,
executive chairman and founder of Huntsman Corporation

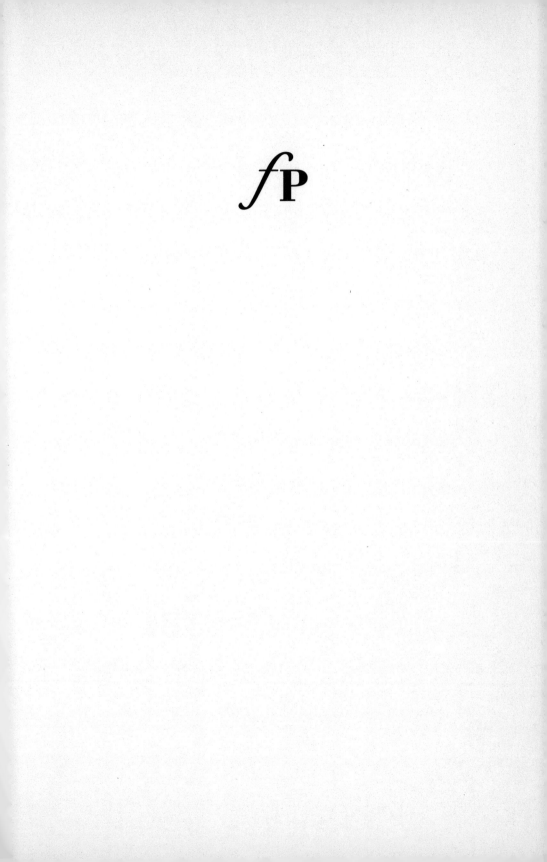

ALSO BY STEPHEN R. COVEY

The 8th Habit
The Leader in Me
The 7 Habits of Highly Effective People
Predictable Results of Unpredictable Times
Great Work, Great Career
The 7 Habits of Highly Effective Families
Living the 7 Habits
The Nature of Leadership
First Things First
Principle-Centered Leadership

ALSO FROM FRANKLINCOVEY CO.

The 7 Habits of Highly Effective Teens
The 7 Habits of Highly Effective Teens Personal Workbook
The 7 Habits of Highly Effective Teens Journal
Life Matters
businessThink
What Matters Most
The 10 Natural Laws of Successful Time and Life Management
The Power Principle
Breakthrough Factor

The 3rd Alternative

Solving Life's Most Difficult Problems

Stephen R. Covey

with Breck England

Free Press

New York   London   Toronto   Sydney   New Delhi

Free Press
A Division of Simon & Schuster, Inc.
1230 Avenue of the Americas
New York, NY 10020

First Free Press hardcover edition October 2011

FREE PRESS and colophon are trademarks of Simon & Schuster, Inc.

For information about special discounts for bulk purchases,
please contact Simon & Schuster Special Sales at
1-866-506-1949 or business@simonandschuster.com.

The Simon & Schuster Speakers Bureau can bring authors to your live event.
For more information or to book an event, contact the Simon & Schuster Speakers
Bureau at 1-866-248-3049 or visit our website at www.simonspeakers.com.

Designed by Carla Jayne Jones

Manufactured in the United States of America

10 9 8 7 6 5 4 3 2 1

Library of Congress control no.: 2011033731

ISBN 978-1-4516-2626-1
ISBN 978-1-4516-2628-5 (ebook)

Contents

In the case of all things which have several parts, the whole is something beside the parts.
—*Aristotle*

Synergy is the only word in our language that means behavior of whole systems unpredicted by the separately observed behaviors of any of the system's separate parts or any subassembly of the system's parts.
—*Buckminster Fuller*

Synergy: a mutually advantageous conjunction or compatibility of distinct business participants or elements.
—*Webster's Dictionary*

The emergent is unlike its components insofar as these are incommensurable, and it cannot be reduced to their sum or their difference.
—*G. H. Lewes*

Synergy is when the whole is greater than the sum of the parts.
—*Fourth-grade student, A. B. Combs Elementary School, Raleigh, North Carolina*

To my wife and eternal friend, Sandra—
full of life, light, and courageous hope

The 3rd
Alternative

1

The Transition Point

Life is full of problems. Problems that seem impossible to solve. Personal problems. Family problems. Problems at work, in our neighborhoods, and in the world at large.

Perhaps you're in a marriage that started off great, but now you can barely stand each other. You may have estranged relationships with your parents, siblings, or children. It could be that you feel overwhelmed and out of balance at work, always trying to do more with less. Or maybe, like so many others, you are tired of our litigious society, in which people are so quick to sue you don't dare make a move. We worry about crime and its drag on our society. We see politicians going at it and getting nowhere. We watch the news at night and lose hope that the perpetual conflicts between people and nations will ever be resolved.

So we lose hope, give up, or settle for a compromise that doesn't feel so good in the end.

That's why I've longed to write this book.

It's about a principle so fundamental that I believe it can transform your life and the whole world. It is the highest and most important insight I have garnered from studying those people who lead truly effective lives.

Basically, it's the key to solving life's most difficult problems.

All people suffer adversities, mostly in silence. Most soldier on bravely in the face of their problems, working and hoping for a better future. For many, terror is just under the surface. Some of these terrors are physical, some psychological, but all are very real.

If you understand and live by the principle in this book, you may not only conquer your problems, but you may go on to build a future for yourself that's better than you ever imagined possible. I did not discover this principle—it's eternal. But for those who apply it to the challenges they face, it's no understatement to say that it may be the greatest discovery of their lives.

My book *The 7 Habits of Highly Effective People* leads up to it. Of all the principles in that book, I called it "the most catalytic, the most empowering, the most unifying, and the most exciting." In *The 7 Habits,* I was able to deal with this principle in only a general way; but in this book, I invite you to explore it with me much more broadly and deeply. If you pay the price to truly understand it, you'll never think the same way again. You'll find yourself approaching your most difficult challenges in life in an entirely new, exponentially more effective way.

I'm profoundly excited to share with you stories about some rare people who have grasped this principle. They are not only problem solvers but also creators of the new future we all dream of. Among many, you'll read about

- A father who rescued his troubled daughter from years of despair and near suicide in one surprising evening.
- A young man in India who is solving the problem of electric power for millions of poor people—at virtually no cost.
- A police chief who cut the juvenile crime rate in a major Canadian city by half.
- A woman who is bringing New York's polluted harbor back to life—again at almost no cost.
- A husband and wife who once could hardly speak to each other and now laugh together about those difficult days.
- The judge who brought a quick, peaceful end to the biggest environmental lawsuit in American history—without setting foot in a courtroom.
- The principal of a high school for migrant workers' children who raised the graduation rate from a dismal 30 percent to 90 percent and tripled his students' basic skill levels—without spending any more money.

- A single mother and her teenager who went from bitter confrontation to renewed understanding and affection.
- A doctor who cures virtually all his patients of a deadly disease at a fraction of the price other doctors charge.
- The team that transformed Times Square from a cesspool of violence and filth to the top tourist attraction in North America.

Let me emphasize: none of these is a celebrity with lots of money and influence. All are, for the most part, ordinary people who are successfully applying this supreme principle to their toughest problems. And so can you.

I can hear you thinking, "Well, I'm not trying to do anything heroic like those people. I've got my own problems, and they're big to me. I'm tired, and I just want to find a solution that works."

Believe me, there's nothing in this book that isn't both global *and* personal. The principle applies equally well to a single mother trying her hardest to raise a restless teenager as to a head of state trying to stop a war.

You can apply this principle to

- A serious conflict at work with your boss or co-workers.
- A marriage with "irreconcilable differences."
- A dispute with your child's school.
- A situation that has put you in financial trouble.
- A critical decision you have to make on your job.
- A battle over some issue in your neighborhood or community.
- Family members who quarrel chronically—or won't speak to each other at all.
- A weight problem.
- A job that doesn't satisfy you.
- A child who won't "launch."
- A knotty problem you need to solve for a customer.
- An issue that might drag you into court.

I have taught the underlying principle of this book for more than forty years to literally hundreds of thousands of people. I've taught it to young schoolchildren, to rooms full of corporate CEOs, to graduating students, to heads of state in some thirty countries, and to everyone in between. I've approached all of them in virtually the same way. I have written this book to apply equally well to a playground, a battlefield, a boardroom, a legislative chamber, or a family kitchen.

I belong to a world leadership group seeking to build a better relationship between the West and the Islamic community. It includes a former U.S. secretary of state, prominent imams and rabbis, global business leaders, and experts on conflict resolution. At our first meeting, it became obvious that everyone had an agenda. It was all rather formal and cool, and you could just feel the tension. That was on a Sunday.

I asked permission from the group to teach them one principle before we went any further, and they graciously agreed. So I taught them the message of this book.

By Tuesday night the whole atmosphere had changed. The private agendas had been shelved. We had arrived at an exciting resolution that we had never anticipated. The people in the room were filled with respect and love for one another—you could see it, and you could feel it. The former secretary of state whispered to me, "I've never seen anything so powerful. What you've done here could totally revolutionize international diplomacy." More on this later.

As I said, you don't have to be a global diplomat to put this principle to work on your own challenges. Recently we surveyed people around the world to find out what their top challenges were personally, on the job, and in the world at large. It was not a representative sample; we just wanted to find out what different people had to say. The 7,834 people who responded were from every continent and from every level of every kind of organization.

- *In their personal lives.* The challenge they feel most personally is the pressure of overwork, coupled with job dissatisfaction. Many are having relationship problems. Typically, one middle manager from Europe writes, "I get stressed, feeling burned out, and don't have time and energy to do things for me." Another says, "My family is going wrong and it tips everything else out of balance."
- *On the job.* Of course, people's top job concerns are always scarce capital and profits. But many are also worried about losing ground in the global game: "We are very much stuck in our 100-year tradition. . . . We're becoming more irrelevant every day. . . . Too little use is made of creativity and entrepreneurship." From

Africa, a top manager wrote, "I was working for an international company, but I resigned last year. I left because I could no longer find meaning in what I was doing."

- *In the world.* From our respondents' viewpoint, the top three challenges we face as a human family are war and terrorism, poverty, and the slow destruction of the environment. An Asian middle manager struck a pleading tone: "Our country belongs to one of the poorest in Asia. This is the battle cry among [us] where the majority of our population lives in poverty. There is a lack of employment, poor education, infrastructure facilities are hardly available, huge debt, poor governance, and corruption is rampant."[1]

This is a snapshot view of how our friends and neighbors are feeling. They might list different challenges tomorrow, but I suspect we'd see only variations on the same sorts of pain.

Under these mounting pressures, we fight each other more. The twentieth century was an age of impersonal war, but the twenty-first seems like an age of personal malice. The rage thermometer is way up. Families quarrel, co-workers contend, cyber bullies terrorize, courts are jammed, and fanatics murder the innocent. Contemptuous "commentators" swamp the media—the more outrageous their attacks, the more money they make.

This rising fever of contention can make us ill. "I'm deeply disturbed by the ways in which all of our cultures are demonizing the Other. . . . The worst eras in human history start like this, with negative otherizing. And then they morph into violent extremism," says the wellness expert Elizabeth Lesser.[2] We know too well where this sort of thing leads.

So how *do* we resolve our most divisive conflicts and solve our most difficult problems?

- Do we go on the warpath, determined that we *won't* take it anymore, but we *will* take it out on our "enemies"?

---

1 Access the full survey report, "The 3rd Alternative: The Most Serious Challenges," at http://www.The3rdAlternative.com.
2 Elizabeth Lesser, "Take the 'Other' to Lunch," *dotsub.com*, no date, http://dotsub.com/view/6581098e-8c0d-4ec0-938d-23a6cb9500eb/viewTranscript/eng.

- Do we play the victim, helplessly waiting for someone to save us?
- Do we take positive thinking to the extreme and slip into a pleasant state of denial?
- Do we sit back stoically, with no real hope that things will ever get better? Deep down, do we believe that all the prescriptions are just placebos anyway?
- Do we keep plugging away, like most people of goodwill, doing what we've always done in the slim hope that things will *somehow* get better?

No matter what approach we take to our problems, natural consequences will follow. War begets war, victims become dependent, reality crushes people in denial, cynics contribute nothing. And if we keep doing the same things we've always done, hoping that *this* time the results will be different, we are not facing reality. Albert Einstein reportedly said, "The significant problems we have cannot be solved at the same level of thinking with which we created them."

To solve our most difficult problems, we must radically change our thinking—and that's what this book is about.

As you read, you will find yourself poised on a transition point between your past, whatever it has been, and a future you have never imagined until now. You will discover within yourself a talent for change. You will think about your problems in an entirely revolutionary way. You will develop new mental reflexes that will propel you through barriers others find insurmountable.

You will be able to see from that transition point a new future for yourself—and the years ahead might be not at all what you expected. Instead of halting into an inevitable future of diminishing capacity riddled with problems, you can start now to fulfill your hunger for a life "in crescendo" that is always fresh and meaningful and filled with extraordinary contributions—right to the end.

By recentering your life on the principle of this book, you will find a surprising way forward into that future.

The 3rd Alternative

2

The 3rd Alternative: The Principle, Paradigm, and Process of Synergy

There is a way to solve the toughest problems we face, even those that look unsolvable. There is a path that cuts through nearly all life's dilemmas and deep divisions. There is a way forward. It's not your way, and it's not my way. It's a higher way. It's a better way than any of us have thought of before.

I call it "the 3rd Alternative."

Most conflicts have two sides. We are used to thinking in terms of "my team" against "your team." My team is good, your team is bad, or at least "less good." My team is right and just; your team is wrong and perhaps even unjust. My motives are pure; yours are mixed at best. It's my party, my team, my country, my child, my company, my opinion, my side against yours. In each case, there are 2 Alternatives.

Almost everyone identifies with one alternative or the other. That's why we have liberals against conservatives, Republicans against Democrats, workers against management, lawyer against lawyer, children against parents, Tories against Labour, teachers against administrators, college against town, rural against urban, environmentalists against developers, white against

The 3rd Alternative

Our Way

My Way

Your Way

The 3rd Alternative. Most conflicts are two-sided. The 1st Alternative is my way, the 2nd Alternative is your way. By synergizing, we can go on to a 3rd Alternative—our way, a higher and better way to resolve the conflict.

black, religion against science, buyer against seller, plaintiff against defendant, emerging nations against developed nations, spouse against spouse, socialists against capitalists, and believers against nonbelievers. It's why we have racism and prejudice and war.

Each of the two alternatives is deeply rooted in a certain mind-set. For example, the mind-set of the environmentalist is formed by appreciation for the delicate beauty and balance of nature. The mind-set of the developer is formed by a desire to see communities grow and economic opportunities increase. Each side usually sees itself as virtuous and rational and the other side as lacking virtue or common sense.

The deep roots of my mind-set entwine with my very identity. If I say I'm an environmentalist or a conservative or a teacher, I'm describing more than what I believe and value—I'm describing *who I am*. So when you attack my side, you attack me and my self-image. At the extreme, identity conflicts can intensify into warfare.

Given that 2-Alternative thinking is so deeply embedded in so many of us, how can we ever get past it? Usually we don't. We either keep fighting or go for a shaky compromise. That's why we face so many frustrating impasses. The problem, however, is usually not in the merits of the "side" we belong to but in *how we think*. The real problem is in our mental paradigms.

The word "paradigm" means a pattern or model of thinking that influences how we behave. It's like a map that helps us decide which direction to go. The map we *see* determines what we *do*, and what we *do* determines the results we *get*. If we shift paradigms, our behavior and results change as well.

For example, when the tomato was first brought to Europe from the Americas, a French botanist identified it as the dreaded "wolfpeach" spoken of by ancient scholars. Eating a tomato would cause twitching, foaming at

See-Do-Get. Our paradigms govern our behavior, which in turn governs the consequences of our actions. We GET results based on what we DO, and what we DO depends on how we SEE the world around us.

the mouth, and death, he warned. So early European colonists in America wouldn't touch it, although they grew it in their gardens as a decorative plant. At the same time, one of the most dangerous diseases the colonists faced was scurvy, brought on by the lack of vitamin C—which is plentiful in tomatoes. The cure was right in their gardens, but they died because of a flawed paradigm.

After a century or so, the paradigm shifted as new information came out. The Italians and Spanish began eating tomatoes. Thomas Jefferson reportedly grew them and promoted their use as food. Today the tomato is the most popular of vegetables. Now we *see* tomatoes as healthful, we *do* eat them, and we *get* healthy. That is the power of a paradigm shift.

If I am an environmentalist, and my paradigm, or mental map, shows only a beautiful untouched forest, I will want to preserve it. If you as a developer have a mental map that shows only underground oil deposits, you will want to drill for oil. Both paradigms might be accurate. Yes, there is a pristine forest on the land, but the oil deposits are there too. The problem is that neither mental map is *complete*—and never can be. As it turns out, the foliage of the tomato plant *is* poisonous, so in part the anti-tomato paradigm was correct. Though some mental maps may be more complete than others, no map is ever truly complete because the map is not the terrain itself. As D. H. Lawrence said, "Every half-truth at length produces the contradiction of itself in the opposite half-truth."

If I see only the mental map of the 1st Alternative—my *own* incomplete map—then the only way to solve the problem is to persuade you to shift your paradigm or even force you to accept my alternative. It's also the only way to preserve my self-image: I must win and you must lose.

If, on the other hand, I throw away my map and follow yours—the 2nd Alternative—I face the same problem. You can't guarantee that your mental map is complete either, so I could pay a terrible price for following your map. You might win, but I could lose.

We could combine maps, and that helps. We would have a more inclusive map that takes into account both our perspectives. I would understand your perspective, and you would understand mine. That is progress. Even so, we might be left with incompatible goals. I still don't want the forest to be touched, and you still want to drill for oil in the forest. My thorough understanding of your map might lead me to fight you even harder.

But then we get to the exciting part. That happens when I look at you and say, "Maybe we can come up with a better solution than either one of us has in mind. *Would you be willing to look for a 3rd Alternative we haven't even thought of yet?*" Hardly anyone ever asks that question, yet it is the key not just to resolving conflicts but also to transforming the future.

The Principle of Synergy

We get to the 3rd Alternative through a process called synergy. Synergy is what happens when one plus one equals ten or a hundred or even a thousand! It's the mighty result when two or more respectful human beings determine together to go beyond their preconceived ideas to meet a great challenge. It's about the passion, the energy, the ingenuity, the excitement of creating a new reality that is far better than the old reality.

Synergy is not the same thing as compromise. In a compromise, one plus one equals one and a half at best. Everybody loses something. Synergy is not just *resolving* a conflict. When we get to synergy, we *transcend* the conflict. We go beyond it to something new, something that excites everyone with fresh promise and transforms the future. Synergy is better than my way *or* your way. It's our way.

Synergy is an idea almost no one understands. One reason for this is that it's been cheapened by widespread misuse. In business, "synergy" is often cynically used as a nice word for mergers or acquisitions that take place just to boost a stock price. In my experience, if you want to make someone's eyes roll, just throw the word "synergy" at them. That's because many people have never really experienced even a moderate degree of synergy. And if they ever hear the word spoken, it's often by manipulators who distort the idea. As a friend said, "When I hear the word 'synergy' used by people wearing suits, I know my retirement fund is in danger." People don't trust this word. Their leaders have scripted them into a defensive mind-set, into believing that all the talk about "creative, collaborative, cooperative synergy" is just code for "Here's a new way for us to exploit you." And minds on the defensive are neither creative nor cooperative.

Yet synergy is a miracle. It is all around us. It is a fundamental principle at work throughout the natural world. Redwood trees intermingle their roots to stand strong against the wind and grow to incredible heights. Green algae and fungus united in the lichen colonize and thrive on bare rock where

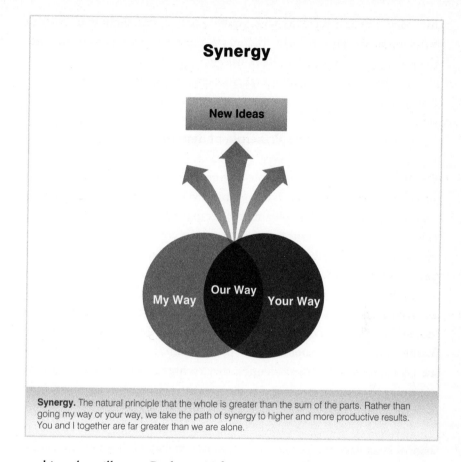

Synergy. The natural principle that the whole is greater than the sum of the parts. Rather than going my way or your way, we take the path of synergy to higher and more productive results. You and I together are far greater than we are alone.

nothing else will grow. Birds in a V formation can fly nearly twice as far as a lone bird because of the updraft created by the flapping of their wings. If you put two pieces of wood together, they will carry exponentially more weight than each piece can bear separately. Tiny particles in a water drop work together to create a snowflake that is absolutely unlike any other snowflake. In all these cases, the whole is greater than the sum of the parts.

One plus one equals two—except in a synergistic situation. For example, a machine that can exert 60,000 pounds per square inch (PSI) on a bar of iron will break it. A bar of chromium of the same size will break at about 70,000 PSI. A bar of nickel will break at about 80,000 PSI. Added up, that's 210,000 PSI. Therefore, if mixed into one bar, iron, chromium, and nickel will withstand 210,000 PSI, right?

Wrong. If I mix iron, chromium, and nickel in certain proportions, the resulting bar of metal will withstand 300,000 PSI! Subtracting 210,000 PSI from 300,000 PSI, we're left with 90,000 pounds of strength that seems to have appeared from nowhere. The metals together are 43 percent stronger than they are separately. And that's *synergy*.[1]

This extra strength is what makes jet engines possible. The tremendous heat and pressure of a jet would melt a weaker metal. But chrome-nickel steel can take temperatures much higher than ordinary steel can handle.

The same synergy principle is true of human beings. They can do things together that no one would predict based on their individual strengths.

Music is a wonderful example of human synergy. Rhythms, melodies, harmonies, and individual styles combine to create new textures, richness, and musical depth. Musicologists tell us that for most of human history music was an improvisational art; people simply played or sang together whatever the moment called for. Writing music down in a fixed form is a recent development. Even today, some of the most compelling music, like jazz, is improvised.

A musical chord is made up of several notes played at once. The notes do not lose their individual character, but together they create a synergy—a harmony—that single notes cannot produce. Like musical notes, synergistic people do not lose their identity; they combine their strengths with the strengths of others to produce a result far greater than anything either could achieve alone.

In sports, it's called chemistry. Great sports teams enjoy the kind of synergy or chemistry that can beat other teams made up of showboating grandstanders with more talented individuals but no synergy. You can't foretell based on the athletic skills of each player how the team will turn out. The performance of a great team far surpasses the sum of the individual skills of the players.

The supreme example of human synergy is, of course, the family. Every child is a "3rd Alternative," a distinctive human being endowed with capabilities that have never existed before and will never be duplicated. Those capabilities cannot be predicted by adding up the capabilities of the parents. The particular combination of human endowments in that child is unique in the universe, and the creative potential of the child is exponentially great. The great Pablo Casals said, "The child must know that he is a miracle, that

---

1 This example comes from R. Buckminster Fuller, *Synergetics–Explorations in the Geometry of Thinking* (New York: Macmillan, 1975), 6.

since the beginning of the world there hasn't been, and until the end of the world there will not be, another child like him."

Synergy is the very essence of the family. Every family member contributes a different flavor to the mix. What happens when a child smiles at her mother is more than just symbiosis—more than just living together and profiting from one another. As my friend Colin Hall says, synergy may be just another word for love.

Myriad examples like these illustrate the power of synergy to transform the world. But it can also transform your work and your life. Without synergy, your work will stagnate. You're not going to grow, and you're not going to improve. Market competition and technological change have intensified to such a point that if you don't have a mind-set of positive synergy, you could quickly become history in your marketplace. No synergy, no growth. You will be caught in a vicious downward spiral of price cutting until you have no business left. On the other hand, if you develop the mind-set of positive synergy, you can be perpetually at the cutting edge, in a virtuous cycle upward, toward more growth and influence.

There is also such a thing as negative synergy. This happens when the vicious cycle is accelerated by emerging forces. For example, smoking causes lung cancer. Asbestos also causes lung cancer. If you smoke *and* breathe asbestos, your chance of getting lung cancer is far greater than the two individual rates added together. If you're not deliberately engaged in positive synergy, you might find yourself trapped in negative synergy.

Positive synergy is nonincremental. You can improve a product through a steady continuous-improvement process, but you're not likely to invent a new product. Synergy is not only the answer to human conflict; it is also the principle that underlies the creation of every truly new thing in the world. It's the key to quantum leaps in productivity. It's the driving mental force behind all genuine creativity.

Consider a few cases—at national, personal, and organizational levels—where synergy has changed the game.

Creative Nonviolence

When I met Arun Gandhi, grandson of the legendary Mahatma Gandhi, he told me his insights about his grandfather's life:

> *Ironically, if it hadn't been for racism and prejudice, we may not have had a Gandhi. See, it was the challenge, the conflict. He may have been just another successful lawyer who had made a lot of money. But, because of prejudice in South Africa, he was subjected to humiliation within a week of his arrival. He was thrown off a train because of the color of his skin. And it humiliated him so much that he sat on the platform of the station all night, wondering what he could do to gain justice. His first response was one of anger. He was so angry that he wanted eye-for-eye justice. He wanted to respond violently to the people that humiliated him. But he stopped himself, and said "That's not right." It was not going to bring him justice. It might make him feel good for the moment, but it wasn't going to get him any justice. It would just perpetuate the cycle of conflict.*
>
> *From that point onward, he developed the philosophy of nonviolence and practiced it in his life, as well as in his search for justice in South Africa. He ended up staying in that country for twenty-two years. And then he went and led the movement of India. And that movement ended up with an independent country, something that no one would have ever envisioned.[1]*

Gandhi is one of my heroes. He was not perfect, and he did not accomplish all his goals. But he learned synergy within himself. He invented a 3rd Alternative: *creative nonviolence*. He transcended 2-Alternative thinking. He was not going to run away, and he wasn't going to fight. That's what animals do; when cornered, they fight or they flee. That's also what 2-Alternative thinkers do. They fight or they flee.

Gandhi changed the lives of over three hundred million people using synergy. Today there are more than a billion people in India. It's a tremendous place. You can just feel the energy, the economic and spiritual vigor of that great, independent people.

---

1 Quoted in Stephen R. Covey, "The Mission Statement That Changed the World," *The Stephen R. Covey Community*, http://www.stevencovey.com/blog/?=14.

The Music Class

A woman we'll call Nadia could see that her little daughter was crying as she came out of school carrying her violin case. The eight-year-old sobbed to her mother that her teacher would not allow any more music in class. All that night Nadia, a trained violinist herself, became more and more angry—she couldn't sleep thinking about the disappointment on her daughter's face— and carefully planned a tirade to let loose on that teacher.

But in the morning Nadia thought better of it and decided to find out exactly what was going on at the school before launching her attack. She went early to see the teacher before class. "My daughter loves the violin," she said, "and I'm wondering what has happened that the children can no longer practice at school." To her surprise, the teacher began to cry. "There is no more time for music," she explained. "We must spend all of our time on basics like reading and mathematics." It was a government order.

For an instant Nadia considered an attack on the government, but then she said, "There must be a way for the children to learn music *and* their basic skills." The teacher blinked for a moment. "Of course, music *is* mathematical." At this, Nadia's brain began to whir. What if the basics could be taught *through* music? She stared at the teacher, and both began to laugh because both had the same thought at once. The next hour's rush of ideas was almost magical.

Soon Nadia was volunteering what time she could in her daughter's class. Together, she and the teacher taught every subject using music. The students did fractions with not only numbers but also notes of music (two eighth notes equal a quarter note). Reading poems was much easier when the children could sing them. History came alive as the children studied great composers and their times and played their music. They even learned a bit of different foreign languages by singing folk songs from other countries.

The synergy between the musical parent and the teacher was as important as the synergy between music and the basics. The students learned both— and quickly. Soon other teachers and parents wanted to try it. In time, even the government got interested in this 3rd Alternative.

Total Quality

When in the 1940s the management professor W. Edwards Deming tried to convince American industrialists of the need to increase the quality of their products, they opted instead to mortgage their future by cutting R&D and focusing on short-term profits. This is 2-Alternative thinking: you can have high quality or you can have low costs, but not both. Everybody knew that. In America the demand for short-term profits produced constant pressure to cut corners on quality, and a vicious cycle was born. A mind-set developed: *What can we get away with? How shoddy can we make this product before the customer rebels?*

Rejected in America, Deming went to Japan. Essentially Deming taught that defects creep into any manufacturing process, and defects will drive customers away; therefore, the goal of manufacturing should be to continuously reduce the defect rate. Japanese industrialists combined Deming's idea with their own *kanban* philosophy, which puts control of manufacturing in the hands of the workers. *Kanban* means "marketplace"; workers on the factory floor get to choose parts like a shopper in a grocery store. The pressure is always to produce better parts. The result of this combination of ideas was a new thing in the world, a 3rd Alternative: "Total Quality Management," the aim of which was to continually improve quality while continually decreasing costs. A mind-set developed: *How can this product be improved?*

Meanwhile American manufacturers, plagued by the 2-Alternative mind-set, struggled to compete against ever more reliable and affordable Japanese cars and electronics. Over time, this vicious cycle had a crippling effect on America's heavy manufacturing.

2-Alternative Thinking

As these examples show, the lack of a 3rd Alternative mind-set is the great obstacle to synergy. People with the 2-Alternative mind-set on a given issue can't get to synergy until they admit synergy is even possible. 2-Alternative thinkers see only competition, never cooperation; it's always "us versus them." 2-Alternative thinkers see only false dilemmas; it's always "my way or the highway." 2-Alternative thinkers suffer from a kind of color blindness; they can see only blue or yellow, never green.

2-Alternative thinking is everywhere. Its most extreme manifestation is war, but short of that it means engaging in some "Great Debate." We see it in liberals who stop their ears when conservatives talk, and vice versa. We see it in business leaders who sacrifice the long-term interests of the com-

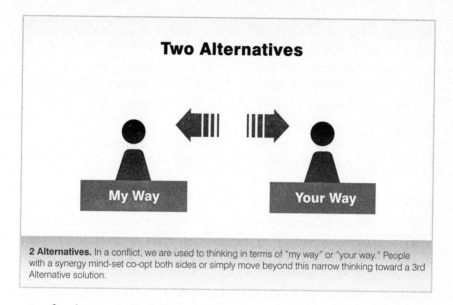

2 Alternatives. In a conflict, we are used to thinking in terms of "my way" or "your way." People with a synergy mind-set co-opt both sides or simply move beyond this narrow thinking toward a 3rd Alternative solution.

pany for short-term gain, but also in those who insist they are "long-term visionaries" while the company collapses around them because they refuse to consider the short term. We see it in the religious person who rejects science and the scientist who sees no value in religion. (In one London university the scientists won't even eat lunch in the faculty dining room when the theologians are there!)

2-Alternative thinkers often can't *see* other people as individual human beings—only their ideologies. They don't value different points of view, so they don't try to understand them. They might make a phony show of respect, but they don't really want to listen; they want to manipulate. They're on the offensive because they are insecure: their territory, their self-image, their very identity is at stake. Ultimately their strategy for dealing with differences is "search and destroy." For these people, one plus one equals zero or less. Synergy can't thrive in that environment.

You might be asking, "Is it possible to get to synergy with everyone?" It would be very hard with cognitively or emotionally impaired people who lack impulse control. Of course, you can't synergize with a psychopath. But most people are just people. The insidious problem with 2-Alternative thinking is the bipolar trap we perfectly ordinary, rational people easily fall into. It looks like the illustration on page 20: "People on my side are [choose from column A]. People on your side are [choose from column B]."

A	B
Good	Evil
Generous	Heartless
Intelligent	Stupid
Wise	Foolish
Reasonable	Irrational
Virtuous	Vicious
Flexible	Liars
Geniuses	Idiots
Patriots	Traitors
The Best People in the World	The Worst People in the World

I used to think most adults were above this sort of thing, that they understood the complexity of the world we live in. Watching the media these days, and the people who make a very good living at promoting 2-Alternative thinking, I'm not so sure.

Additionally, 2-Alternative thinking vexes us when we confront a dilemma, which is defined as a problem that seems to have no satisfactory solution. I hear about such problems all the time, and so do you. A teacher says, "I can't work with this student, but I can't give up on her either." A business leader says, "We can't grow this business without more capital, but we can't get capital unless we grow the business—it's a classic catch-22." A politician says, "We can't afford to provide quality medical care for everyone, nor can we let people suffer if they can't pay." A sales director says, "My two top salespeople badmouth and undermine each other constantly. But without them, we'd lose our best accounts." A wife says of her husband, "I can't live with him, and I can't live without him."

The Horns of a Dilemma

It can be agonizing to feel you have only two equally awful alternatives. The ancient Greeks thought of it as being caught on the "horns of a dilemma" because it was like facing a charging bull: regardless of which horn catches you, it runs you through.

In the face of such dilemmas, the insecurity of the 2-Alternative thinker is understandable. Some people throw up their hands and surrender. Others pounce on one "horn" of the dilemma and drag everyone else along. So obsessed with being right, they make a great show of defending their rightness even while bleeding from the wound. Still others select a horn to die on because they feel they must; they can see no 3rd Alternative.

Too often we fail to recognize when we're confronting a *false* dilemma—which is too bad, because in fact most dilemmas are false. We see them everywhere. Surveys ask, "Are you for the Republican or the Democratic solution? Do you favor or oppose legalizing drugs? Is it right or wrong to use animals for research? Are you for us or against us?" Such questions don't allow us to think past 2 Alternatives (which is usually what the questioner intends!). Except to 2-Alternative thinkers, there are almost always options beyond the two extremes of a dilemma. We seldom ask ourselves if there's a better answer—a 3rd Alternative. No pollster will *ever* ask you that question.

The Great Middle

One debilitating response to 2-Alternative thinking is to stop hoping. In any Great Debate, there is a "Great Middle" of people who don't identify with either pole. They are generally turned off by extremes of 2-Alternative thinking. They believe in teamwork and collaboration and seeing the other side's point of view, but they don't see possibilities of 3rd Alternatives. They don't really believe there are real *solutions* to a conflict with the boss, a bad marriage, a lawsuit, or between Israel and Palestine. They're the ones who say, "We don't get along. We're not compatible. There's no solution."

They do believe in compromise, and see compromise as the best they can hope for. Compromise has a good reputation, and it's probably prevented many problems from getting worse. According to dictionaries, both parties in a compromise "concede, sacrifice, or surrender" some of their own interests in order to get to an arrangement. This is called a "lose-lose" situation—the opposite of a "win-win" situation. People might walk away from a compromise satisfied but never delighted. The relationship is weakened, and too often the dispute just flares up again.

Because they live in a lose-lose world, people in the Great Middle don't hope for much. They are often the ones who plug away at their jobs year after year but contribute little of themselves and their potential. They tend to see life through an outdated Industrial Age lens. Their job is to show up and mechanically fulfill a job description, not to transform their world or create a new future. They are good players but not game changers. No one asks anything else of them. Of course, their skepticism is an understandable defense against 2-Alternative thinking. "A plague on both your houses" is their silent response when caught in a turf war at work or a battle between family members. And their guard goes up immediately with a leadership change or a new strategy. "Out with the old ways, in with the new. We're going to be a lean, high-performance organization!" To them, this is code for "Don't you agree that it would be a good thing for you to give up your benefits/take a salary cut/do the jobs of two people so our bottom line will look better? Don't you agree that everyone should have to give up a little?" Of course they agree. They are never consulted, they are viewed as inter-changeable parts, and they learned long ago not to be hopeful.

Often, therefore, a sad consequence for the Great Middle is the me-tastasizing cancer of cynicism. Anyone with enthusiasm is suspect. There's contempt for new ideas. And when they hear the word "synergy," they have an allergic reaction. They have never experienced true synergy.

The Paradigms of Synergy

As we've seen, those who get past 2-Alternative thinking and go on to the synergy mind-set—people like Gandhi and Deming and Nadia, the musical parent—are rare but highly influential, creative, and productive. They auto-matically assume that every dilemma is false. They are the paradigm shifters, the innovators, the game changers.

If we want to join them, to go on to 3rd Alternative thinking, we have to shift our paradigms in four significant ways. (See figure on page 23.) Please know right now that these four paradigm shifts are not easy. They are coun-terintuitive. They will lead us away from egotism and toward authentic re-spect for others. They will divert us from the need to find the "right" answer all the time because we will be searching for the "better" answer. They will lead us down unpredictable pathways, for no one knows beforehand what a 3rd Alternative will look like.

The chart on page 24 contrasts the four paradigms of common, garden-variety 2-Alternative thinking with the paradigms of 3rd Alternative think-

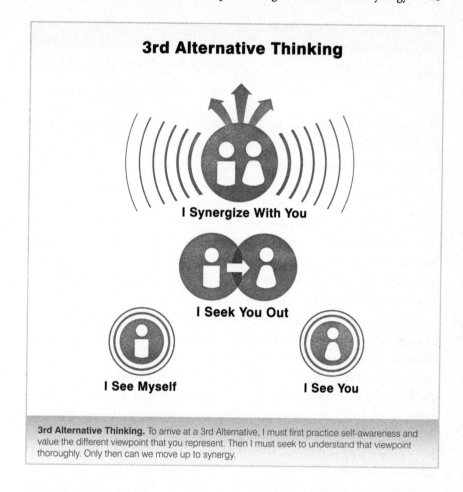

3rd Alternative Thinking

I Synergize With You

I Seek You Out

I See Myself   I See You

3rd Alternative Thinking. To arrive at a 3rd Alternative, I must first practice self-awareness and value the different viewpoint that you represent. Then I must seek to understand that viewpoint thoroughly. Only then can we move up to synergy.

ing. You can see that 2-Alternative thinking moves further and further away from creative solutions at each stage. Without the paradigms of 3rd Alternative thinking, creative solutions are impossible. One paradigm is the foundation for the next, so the sequence of paradigms is important. Why is this so?

Psychologists tell us that the first condition for healing and growth is "genuineness, realness, or congruence." The less we ourselves put up a front or façade, the greater the chance of getting to synergy. Thus the first paradigm is "I See Myself." It means I am self-aware—I have searched my own heart for my motives, my uncertainties, and my biases. I have examined my own assumptions. I am ready to be authentic with you.

The second condition is accepting, caring for, and prizing *you*. Carl

	2-Alternative Thinking	3rd Alternative Thinking
1	I see only my "side."	I see my self–independent of my "side."
2	I stereotype you.	I see you—as a human being, not as just a representative of your "side."
3	I defend myself against you because you're wrong.	I seek you out because you see things differently.
4	I attack you. We make war on each other.	I synergize with you. Together we create an amazing future that no one could have foreseen.

Rogers, one of my favorite authors and a hero of mine, calls this attitude "unconditional positive regard," an outgoing, positive feeling toward you because I value you as a whole human being and not as a set of attitudes, behaviors, or beliefs. You are not a *thing* to me, you are a person. "I See You" as a sister, a brother, a child of God.

The third condition is empathic understanding, which can't happen until I have accepted the first two paradigms. Empathy means getting into and really understanding where the other person is coming from. Empathy is rare; you and I neither give nor get it very often. Instead, as Rogers says, "we offer another type of understanding which is very different: 'I understand what is wrong with you.'" By contrast, the effective paradigm is "I Seek You Out" in order to fully grasp what is in your heart, mind, and soul, not in order to pass judgment on you. New ideas breathe best in an atmosphere of authentic mutual understanding.

We have to meet the first three conditions to get to the fourth condition. Then we can learn and grow together toward a true "win-win" solution that is new to both of us. "I Synergize With You" only when I have genuine positive regard for you *and* for myself and understand clearly what is going on in your heart and mind. "I Synergize With You" only when I get past the scarcity mind-set that there are only two possible alternatives and one of them is *wrong*. "I Synergize With You" only when I adopt the abundance mind-set that there are infinite rewarding, exciting, creative alternatives we haven't even thought of yet.[1]

Let's take a closer look at each of these paradigms.

---

1 For more about the conditions that promote growing, creative relationships, see Carl Rogers, *On Becoming a Person* (New York: Houghton Mifflin Harcourt, 1995), 61–63.

Paradigm 1: I See Myself

This first paradigm is about seeing myself as a unique human being capable of independent judgment and action.

What do I see when I look in the mirror? Do I see a thoughtful, respectful, principled, and open-minded person? Or do I see a person who knows all the answers and holds in contempt the people on the "other side" of the conflict? Do I think for myself, or has the thinking been done for me?

I am not merely "my side" of a controversy. I am more than the sum of my prejudices, party, and preconceptions. My thoughts are not predetermined by my family, my culture, or my company. I am not, to paraphrase George Bernard Shaw, a selfish little clod of grievances complaining that the world will not fall in line with my—or "our"—way of thinking. I can

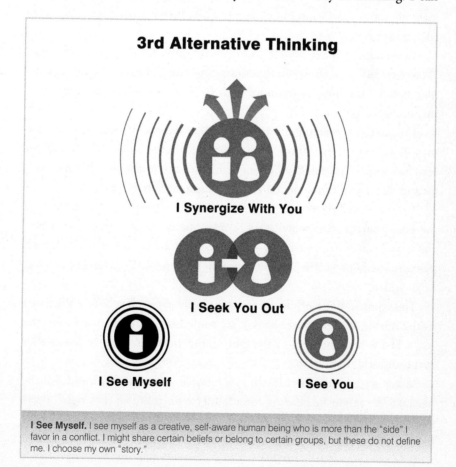

3rd Alternative Thinking

I Synergize With You

I Seek You Out

I See Myself   I See You

I See Myself. I see myself as a creative, self-aware human being who is more than the "side" I favor in a conflict. I might share certain beliefs or belong to certain groups, but these do not define me. I choose my own "story."

	I See Myself	I See My "Side"
SEE	I see myself as a creative, self-aware human being who is more than the "side" I favor. I might share certain beliefs or belong to certain groups. But these do not define me. My thinking comes from inside out.	I see myself in terms of the group I belong to: my "side," my party, my company, my country, my gender, my race. I define myself as a Conservative, a Working Guy, a Feminist, or a Gangster instead of as an individual. My thinking comes from the outside in.
DO	I think about what I think. I challenge my own assumptions as well as other people's.	I think what my group thinks. I am right—why would I challenge my assumptions?
GET	Creative engagement with other people.	Destructive conflicts with other people.

mentally stand apart from myself and evaluate how my paradigms are influencing my actions.

The paradigm "I See Myself" contrasts sharply with the typical paradigm "I See My 'Side,'" as shown in the contrasting boxes in figure 10. In any conflict, how we *see* things determines what we *do*, and what we *do* determines the results we *get*.

The ineffective paradigm is to see myself as *defined* by something outside myself; as a result, everything I value comes from the outside. To be *defined* is to be fixed or limited. But human beings are free to choose what they will be and do; this is fundamental to being human. When a person says she's an environmentalist, she really means that she shares some beliefs about the environment with some other people. She certainly doesn't mean that she is *only* an environmentalist—she's also a woman, someone's daughter, perhaps a wife or girlfriend. She may also be a musician, a lawyer, a cook, or an athlete.

The point is, none of these roles completely *defines* her. When she looks in the mirror, if she is wise she will see something more than the roles she plays. She will see her *self*—a thoughtful, independent, creative personality that transcends definition.

When a leader defines himself as a rational, practical, hardheaded businessman, he might be heading for a fall. He can make all the "right" decisions according to the assumptions of his MBA culture and still go bust. It happens every day, and there's nothing new in it. More than two thousand companies have made it to the Fortune 500 since the 1950s; the vast majority of them are gone. We have seen for ourselves how fragile this hardheaded thinking can be in the economic calamities of the past few years. Observers like the eminent business professor Henry Mintzberg worry that an arrogant MBA culture is at the root of a cycle of repeated financial meltdowns.[1]

To a great extent, of course, we feel defined by our culture. We tend to dress, talk, eat, play, and think like the people we identify with. It doesn't matter if we're business executives, ballet dancers, priests, politicians, or police officers. We wear the uniform. We listen to the pundits. We see the movies. And we talk the talk.

The philosopher Owen Flanagan puts it this way: "We are born into families and communities with an image of persons already in place. We have no say about the location in space of images into which we are born. The image antedates us, often by centuries. . . . Once we reach an age where we do have some control, we work from the image, from the story that is already deeply absorbed, a story line that is already part of our self-image."[2] We can become stout defenders of that self-image even as it becomes less and less about ourselves and more and more about an externally imposed image.

The Real Identity Theft

We hear a lot about identity theft when someone takes your wallet and pretends to be you and uses your credit cards. But the more serious identity theft is to get swallowed up in other people's definitions of you. You get so immersed in the external agendas, the cultural story, the political and social pressures, that you lose the sense of who you are and what you could do in life. I call this "the real identity theft." This identity theft is very real and going on all of the time simply because people do not distinguish between their own mind and the mind of the culture.

Our politicians are becoming paralyzed by identity theft. Even those with the best intentions, who start out with a free mind and high integrity, allow their identity to be taken from them. The force of 2-Alternative think-

1 Henry Mintzberg, "A Crisis of Management, Not Economics," *Globe and Mail* (Toronto), March 31, 2009.
2 Owen J. Flanagan, *The Problem of the Soul* (New York: Basic Books, 2002), 30.

ing, rather than their independent judgment, drives their behavior. As a former U.S. congressman says, "They cluster helplessly behind partisan lines. It's begun to seem as though there's no way out."[1]

When man created the mirror, he began to lose his soul. He became more concerned with his image than with his self. Thus, he tells himself a story that aligns with the social image:

"I hate these political meetings, but as a good party member I should be here."

"There's that guy from the other party. His turn to speak. I don't know why they waste their time."

"How can people believe stuff like that? Why can't they use a little common sense? I'm just a straightforward, commonsense guy. Why can't they be like me? Are they blind?"

"Well, he made some sense there. But wait—he can't be making sense! That's not possible. He's from the other side."

"I don't know how such a sensible guy can be so wrongheaded."

It can be a blow to our cultural self-image to recognize value in a countercultural image. ("You mean we don't have all right and truth on our side? There might be some on the other side?") Still, each of us has the power to transcend our cultural image of ourselves. We can rise above the uniforms we wear, our conventional opinions, and all the other symbols of sameness.

For one thing, we are not preprogrammed machines. Unlike a car or a clock or a computer, we each have the distinctively human endowment to see beyond our cultural programming. We are self-aware. This awareness means that we can stand mentally outside of ourselves and evaluate our beliefs and our actions. *We can think about what we think.* We can challenge

1 Lee H. Hamilton, "We Can Reconcile Polarized Politics," *JournalStar.com*, December 3, 2010, http://journalstar.com/news/opinion/editorial/columnists/article_bf62ba78 -9073-5d13-b19e-ef5a66ea2465.html.

our assumptions. A machine can't do this. As self-aware human beings, we are free to make our own choices, we are creative, and we have a conscience. This understanding about ourselves gives us confidence.

For another thing, we can never completely see ourselves by ourselves. When we look in a mirror, we can see only part of ourselves. We have blind spots. 2-Alternative thinkers who face conflict rarely question their own programming. They rely on cultural assumptions that seem thoroughly rational to them but are always already deficient. Synergy will cause us to learn not only about others, but also about ourselves—it's inevitable. This understanding gives us humility.

If I truly see myself, I also see my cultural tendencies. I see where I need to be complemented because I'm incomplete. I see the pressures on me. I see the expectations others have of me, and I see my true motives.

But I can also see beyond my own culture. I see where I can contribute because I have a unique perspective. I see the influence I can have. I see myself not as a victim of circumstances, but as a creator of the future.

When you think about it, those who really *see* themselves understand this creative paradox—that they are both limited and unlimited. They don't mistake their mental map for the actual territory. They know they have blind spots as well as boundless potential. Therefore, they can be both humble and confident at the same time.

Most conflicts arise from a poor understanding of this paradox about ourselves. Those who are too sure of themselves lack self-awareness. Failing to realize that their own perspective is *always* limited, they insist on having their way. ("I've been around long enough to know when I'm right.") Inevitably, they get weak results and often hurt people in the process. On the other hand, those who dwell on their limitations become dependent. They see themselves as victims and fail to make the contribution they are capable of.

I call this paradox *creative* because only those who recognize that they don't have the answers ever go looking for answers, and only those who recognize their own potential have the courage and confidence to go looking. As Eliezer Yudkowsky, a researcher of artificial intelligence, says, "The first step in obtaining a third alternative is deciding to look for one."

My son David has looked for the 3rd Alternative all his life. Here's what he has to say about it:

The 3rd Alternative is the foundation for all your interactions. It's how everybody ought to think. My father ingraining that in my mind has been the single greatest lesson I've taken from him.

When I was in college, I was trying to get into a certain class I needed to graduate, and heard the standard line: "I'm sorry, we're full, you can't get in." So I talked to my dad and asked him what I should do. He said, "Persist! Come up with a 3rd Alternative. If they say there's no room, tell them you'll bring your own chair or you'll stand up the whole time. Tell them you're going to be in that class regardless. Tell them you know other people will drop out, and that you're more committed than those other people and you're going to show your commitment." And I got into the class!

As a kid, I thought the 3rd Alternative concept was totally wild, seriously bold. But when I started to apply it, I was amazed at the power of persistently finding a way to get done what I needed to do.

One time I got a really bad grade in a health class. The teacher gave us this unbelievably difficult final that shocked everybody. So I went to my dad and said, "What do I do? I can't have a grade like this on my record." He told me to talk to the professor and find a way to get an A. So I went to the teacher and said, "I really did poorly on the final like a lot of other people, but there must be something I can do to get a better grade than this." He gave me all the standard nos, but I persisted, and at last he asked me, "What do you do for exercise?" I told him I was a runner on the track-and-field team. He said, "If you can run the four hundred meters in less than fifty-five seconds, I'll give you an A minus." At that time I was running the 400 in fifty-two seconds—this health professor was obviously out of date on what was a fast time. I had my friend time me and I easily ran it in fifty-two and got an A minus out of the class. It was a case of being persistent and going for a 3rd Alternative.

Because I grew up with this idea of always seeking the 3rd Alternative, it became part of me. It's not about being pushy or rude or obnoxious, but I don't easily take "no" for an answer. There's always a 3rd Alternative.

David's experiences are simple examples of how we can see within ourselves the seeds of the 3rd Alternative. He himself is an example of how we can redefine who we are by changing the story we tell ourselves about ourselves.

The Most Important Power We Have

Our paradigms and cultural conditioning make up the story of our lives. Each has a beginning, a plot, and characters. There may even be heroes and villains. Countless subplots make up the big plot. There are crucial twists and turns in the narrative. And, most crucially, there is conflict. No conflict, no story. Every great story turns on a struggle of some kind: a hero against a villain, a race against time, a character against her conscience, a man against his own limits. Secretly, we see ourselves as the hero of our own story (or, in some dark and often profound instances, as our own enemy). A 2-Alternative thinker plays the role of the put-upon protagonist locked in combat with the antagonist.

But there is a third voice in the story that is neither the hero nor the villain. This is the voice that *tells* the story. If we are truly self-aware, we realize that we are not just characters in our own story but also the narrator. We are not just written, we are the writer too.

My story is only a part of much bigger stories—stories of a family, a community, and a whole culture. I might have limited influence on how those stories evolve, but I am very much in control of how *my* story goes. I am free to tell my own story. There is wisdom in this observation by the journalist David Brooks:

> Among all the things we don't control, we do have some control over our stories. We do have a conscious say in selecting the narrative we will use to make sense of the world. Individual responsibility is contained in the act of selecting and constantly revising the master narrative we tell about ourselves.
>
> The stories we select help us, in turn, to interpret the world. They guide us to pay attention to certain things and ignore other things. They lead us to see certain things as sacred and other things as disgusting. They are the frameworks that shape our desires and goals. So while story selection may seem vague and intellectual, it's actually very powerful. The most important power we have is the power to help select the lens through which we see reality.[1]

My son David often tells the story about taking his own chair to the college class. He uses it to illustrate how simple and powerful 3rd Alternative

1 David Brooks, "The Rush to Therapy," *New York Times*, November 9, 2009.

thinking can be. But at a deeper level, this little story is an important subplot of the larger story he tells himself *about* himself—that he is not a victim, that he is not limited by 2-Alternative thinking, that he is in charge of what Brooks calls "the master narrative" of his life.

In the plot conflicts of our lives, we are not merely "characters." We are also the narrators, the ones who choose how the story unfolds. I have met so many people who lack this simple insight and feel trapped inside some nightmarish conflict as if they were helpless to change the story. I have seen battling wives and husbands each proclaiming his or her own heroism in dealing with that villain, all the time ignoring the fact that they are not just in the story but also creators of the story! They protest that they are no longer in love, and are astonished when I point out that they are both perfectly free to love one another if they choose. The notion of being "in love" is purely passive; the notion of "loving" is active—it's a verb. Love "the feeling" is the fruit of love "the verb." People have the power to do loving things *for* each other just as they have the power to do hateful things *to* each other. *They*—not someone else—write the script.

I said earlier that our lives are stories in that they all have a beginning. A story also has a middle and an end. Most of us are somewhere in the middle of the story. We get to decide how the story ends.

The 3rd Alternative always starts with myself. It comes from the inside out, from the innermost part of myself, from a foundation of confidence and humility. It comes from the paradigm of self-awareness, which enables me to stand outside myself and observe and weigh my own prejudices and biases. It comes from the recognition that I write my own story and a willingness to rewrite it if necessary—because I want it to end *well*.

Think about it—deeply. If you're involved in a conflict situation, ask yourself:

- What's my story? Do I need to change the script?
- Where might I have blind spots about myself?
- How has my cultural programming influenced my thinking?
- What are my real motives?
- Are my assumptions accurate?
- In what ways are my assumptions incomplete?
- Am I contributing to an outcome—an end to the story—that I really want?

Paradigm 2: I See You

The second paradigm is about seeing others as people instead of things.

When we look at others, what do we see? Do we see an individual, or do we see age, gender, race, politics, religion, disability, national origin, or sexual orientation? Do we see a member of an "out group" or an "in group"? Or do we really see the uniqueness, the power, the gifts of every diverse individual?

Perhaps we don't really see *them* as much as we see our own ideas, preconceived notions, and maybe even biases *about* them.

We all know when someone is "putting on," when we are dealing with the person himself or with a fake front. The question is, *Am I that kind of person? Or am I one who looks upon others with genuine, authentic respect?*

The paradigm "I See You" contrasts sharply with the typical paradigm

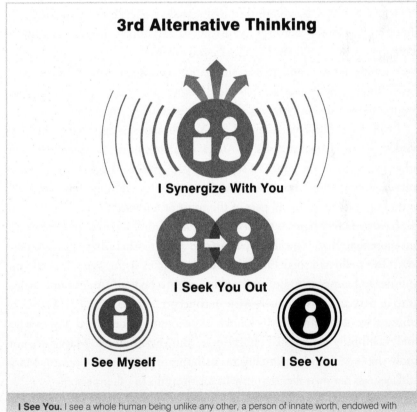

3rd Alternative Thinking

I Synergize With You

I Seek You Out

I See Myself

I See You

I See You. I see a whole human being unlike any other, a person of innate worth, endowed with talents, passions, and strengths that are irreplaceable. You are more than your "side" in a conflict. You deserve dignity and my respect.

	I See You	I Stereotype You
SEE	I see a whole human being endowed with innate worth, talents, passions, and strengths that are unique in the universe. You are more than your "side." You deserve dignity and respect.	I see the group you belong to: your "side," your party, your gender, your nationality, your company, your race. You are a symbol, a "thing," a Liberal, a Boss, a Hispanic, or a Muslim instead of a unique person.
DO	I demonstrate authentic respect for you.	I ignore you or fake respect for you.
GET	An atmosphere of synergy where we are much stronger together than separately.	An atmosphere of hostility. We are weakened by our divisions and antagonisms for each other.

"I Stereotype You," as shown in the contrasting boxes in the chart above. Remember, what we *see* determines what we *do*, and what we *do* determines the results we *get*.

The "I See You" paradigm is fundamentally a question of character. It is about human love, generosity, inclusiveness, and honest intent. With the "I Stereotype You" paradigm, I cannot be fully trusted to keep your interests as well as mine at heart, and no 3rd Alternative is possible. When I look at you, I see only the representative of a side. I might behave correctly toward you, but my show of respect for you as a person is actually counterfeit.

I call the effective paradigm "I See You" because of an insight from the wisdom of the Bantu peoples of Africa. In that culture, people greet each other by saying "I see you." To say "I see you" means "I acknowledge your unique individuality." It is to say, "My humanity is caught up, is inextricably bound up, in yours." It's all part of the spirit of *Ubuntu*.

Ubuntu is very hard to translate. It means something like "personhood," but more than that, it means "a person depends on other persons to be a person." The wellness expert Elizabeth Lesser explains it this way: "I need you in order to be me, and you need me in order to be you." An example helps us to understand this uniquely African concept: "A phrase such as 'Mary has Ubuntu' would mean Mary is known to be a caring, concerned person who abides faithfully in all social obligations." But there's more: "Mary does not know she is beautiful, or intelligent, or humorous, without Ubuntu. Mary understands her own identity only in relationship to other persons."[1]

---

1 Michael Battle and Desmond Tutu, *Ubuntu: I in You and You in Me* (New York: Church Publishing, 2009), 3.

Another way to understand *Ubuntu* is by its opposite: stereotyping. To stereotype is to eliminate from the picture the things that make us singular individuals. We say, "Yeah, he's a sales guy—aggressive, pushy." "She's one of those self-absorbed types—always thinking everything revolves around her." "He's a type-A personality." "He's a jerk." "He's a finance guy." "What do you expect? He's a quitter." "She's one of those who are always running for CEO." We're unable to see these people as individuals, not as types.

In the spirit of *Ubuntu*, to really see other people is to welcome the gifts only they can bring: their talents, intelligence, experiences, wisdom, and differences of perspective. In an *Ubuntu* society, travelers don't need to carry provisions; their needs will be met by gifts from those they encounter on the way. But these tangible gifts are only tokens of the much greater gift of self. If we refuse the gift of self or devalue it, we are no longer free to benefit from one another's capabilities.

In explaining the meaning of *Ubuntu*, Orland Bishop, director of the Shade Tree Multicultural Foundation in Watts, California, talks about what we lose when we don't really see each other: "Our present civilization has taken away freedoms from human beings, not because one culture oppresses another, but because we have lost the imagination of what sight means, of what these inner capacities really mean."[1]

The spirit of *Ubuntu* is essential to 3rd Alternative thinking. In a conflict situation, unless I see you as more than a symbol of the opposition, I can never get to synergy with you. The spirit of *Ubuntu* is more than just the notion that I should behave respectfully toward you. It means that my humanity is tied up in yours—that when I act in a way that dehumanizes you, I also dehumanize myself. Why? Because when I reduce you to the status of a *thing*, I do the same to myself.

Recently, a friend was driving down a city street when another motorist began honking and waving at her. She slowed down, thinking there was something wrong with her car. But the other driver sped up close to her, shouted obscenities at her about a certain politician, and nearly ran her off the road. Then she realized she had on her car a bumper sticker that favored the politician. To the angry driver, she was no longer another human being; she was a *thing*, a bumper sticker, a hated symbol.

---

1 Orland Bishop, "Sawubona," http://www.youtube.com/watch?v=2IjUkVZRPK8&feature =related. Accessed November 22, 2010.

The angry man dehumanized my friend. But in the process, he diminished his own humanity as well. He probably has a house, a job, a family. There are probably people who love him. But in that moment of choice, he became less than human, nothing more than the blunt instrument of an ideology.

This dehumanizing of others—what we often refer to as stereotyping—starts from a deep insecurity within the self. This is also where conflict begins. Psychologists know that most of us tend to remember negative things about others more than positive things. "We hold people responsible for their bad behaviors and don't give them credit for their good ones," says Oscar Ybarra, the eminent psychologist. He believes this happens because seeing others in a negative light helps us to feel superior to them. Ybarra has found that when people begin with a healthy, realistic regard for themselves, the negative memories fade away.[1] That's why the paradigm "I See Myself" precedes the paradigm "I See You."

People Are Not Things

In his famous book *I and Thou,* the great philosopher Martin Buber taught that we too often relate to each other as objects, not as people. An object is an *It*, but a person is a *Thou*. If I treat a person as an It, as an object to be used for my own purposes, I too become an It, no longer a living person but a machine. The relationship between "I and It" is not the same as the relationship between "I and Thou." "The mankind of mere *It* that is imagined . . . has nothing in common with a living mankind," Buber says. "If a man lets it have the mastery, the continually growing world of *It* overruns him and robs him of the reality of his own *I*."

By reducing other people to the status of things, we think we can better control them. That's why companies refer to their employees by the ironic term "human resources," as though they were just another liability on the balance sheet, like taxes or accounts payable. That's why most people in most organizations are seen only in terms of their function, even though they possess far more creativity, resourcefulness, ingenuity, intelligence, and talent than their jobs require or even allow! The opportunity cost of seeing people only as things is very high. No balance sheet shows the astonishing size of the locked-up potential of people and their capacities.

---

1 David J. Schneider, *The Psychology of Stereotyping* (New York: Guilford Press, 2004), 145.

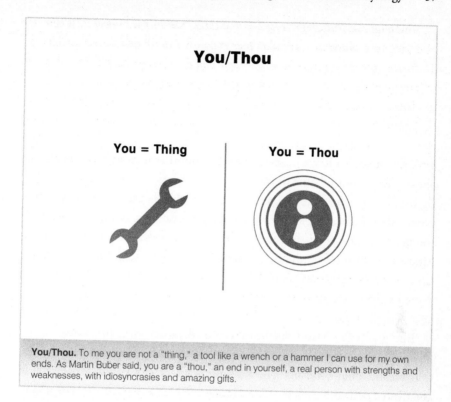

You/Thou

You = Thing   **You = Thou**

You/Thou. To me you are not a "thing," a tool like a wrench or a hammer I can use for my own ends. As Martin Buber said, you are a "thou," an end in yourself, a real person with strengths and weaknesses, with idiosyncrasies and amazing gifts.

By contrast, Buber says, "If I face a human being as my *Thou* . . . he is not a thing among things."[1]

Buber uses the term "Thou" because it suggests more than just surface respect; it also evokes reverence for another person. It suggests intimacy, openness, and trust. To see another as an "it" suggests remoteness and indifference. It encourages exploitation.

I feel genuinely sorry for those who don't feel that reverence. To come to understand another—without the urge to control or manipulate—is to enter sacred territory and is deeply enriching. Carl Rogers eloquently describes what this experience means to him:

One of the most satisfying feelings I know . . . comes from my appreciating [an] individual in the same way that I appreciate a sunset. People are just as wonderful as sunsets if I can let them be. In fact, perhaps the

---

1 Martin Buber, *I and Thou* (New York: Simon & Schuster, 2000), 23, 28, 54.

reason we can truly appreciate a sunset is that we cannot control it. When I look at a sunset as I did the other evening, I don't find myself saying, "Soften the orange a little on the right hand corner, and put a bit more purple along the base, and use a little more pink in the cloud color." I don't do that. I don't try to control a sunset. I watch it with awe as it unfolds.[1]

Losing that sense of awe in the presence of another human being might be one of the greatest of human tragedies.

In 1964 the freedom fighter Nelson Mandela began serving a twenty-seven-year sentence in South Africa's desolate Robben Island prison. As a young lawyer, he had rebelled against the apartheid system that repressed black Africans like himself. "A thousand slights, a thousand indignities and a thousand unremembered moments produced in me an anger, a rebelliousness, a desire to fight the system that imprisoned my people," he explains.[2] In prison he experienced more of the same, and at first he grew even more bitter.

But gradually, Mandela's heart changed. Years after his release from prison, I had a personal visit with him. I asked him, "How long did it take to overcome your bitterness toward your warders, those who tortured you and treated you with such profound indignity?" He answered, "It took about four years." I asked him why the change of heart, and he said, "They would talk about their relationships with each other, about their families, and I came to realize they too were victims of the apartheid system."

One young guard, Christo Brand, described his personal journey as follows: "When I started on Robben Island I was told that the men we guarded were no better than animals. Some warders hated the prisoners and were very cruel."[3] But then he was assigned to supervise Nelson Mandela. "When I came to the prison, Nelson Mandela was already 60. He was down-to-earth and courteous. He treated me with respect and my respect for him grew. After a while, even though he was a prisoner, a friendship grew."

This friendship transformed Christo Brand's life. He began to do favors for Mandela, smuggling bread to him and bringing him messages. He even

---

1 Carl Rogers, *A Way of Being* (New York: Houghton Mifflin Harcourt, 1995), 22.
2 Nelson Mandela, *In His Own Words* (New York: Hachette Digital, 2003), xxxii.
3 "Christo Brand," *The Forgiveness Project,* http://theforgivenessproject.com/stories/christo
   -brand-vusumzi-mcongo-south-africa/. Accessed November 23, 2010.

broke rules to allow Mandela to meet and hold his infant grandson. "Mandela was worried that I would get caught and be punished. He wrote to my wife telling her that I must continue my studies. Even as a prisoner he was encouraging a warder to study."

Mandela became devoted to Brand's young son, Riaan, who was allowed to visit him and grew to love him like a grandfather. In later years, when Mandela was president of South Africa, his education fund awarded a scholarship to Riaan.[1]

For both Nelson Mandela and Christo Brand, their relationship moved from "I-It" to "I-Thou." The young man who saw black Africans as animals came to love the old prisoner and to oppose the apartheid system. The old man who had seen whites as his enemies became fond of the young guard. It was just one stage of what Mandela calls his "long walk to freedom" from his own prejudices.

Mandela writes, "It was during those long and lonely years that my hunger for the freedom of my own people became a hunger for the freedom of all people, white and black. I knew as well as I knew anything that the oppressor must be liberated just as surely as the oppressed. . . . The oppressed and the oppressor alike are robbed of their humanity."[2] Because of this kind of insight, his people would say that Mandela has *Ubuntu*.

These transformations happen when relationships become authentically personal. Mandela and Brand came to see each other as *persons* instead of as representatives of the hated opposition. When we at last truly *see* one another, as Archbishop Desmond Tutu says, "we catch a glimpse of the better thing . . . when the world is galvanized by a spirit of compassion and an amazing outpouring of generosity; when for a little while we are bound together by bonds of a caring humanity."[3] This is the power of the "I See You" paradigm.

When I embrace the "I See You" paradigm, my respect for you is authentic, not faked. I see *you,* not your side of the conflict. I know your story is rich and complex and packed with awe-inspiring insights. In the "I See You"

---

1 Andrew Meldrum, "The Guard Who Really Was Mandela's Friend," *Observer* (London), May 20, 2007, http://www.guardian.co.uk/world/2007/may/20/nelsonmandela. Accessed November 23, 2010.

2 Nelson Mandela, *Long Walk to Freedom* (New York: Holt, Rinehart and Winston, 2000), p. 544.

3 Desmond Tutu, *No Future Without Forgiveness* (New York: Doubleday, 1999), 265.

paradigm, you and I together are uniquely powerful because your strengths and my strengths complement each other. There's no combination like us anywhere else. We can move to a 3rd Alternative together. This is not possible if we operate under the paradigm of stereotyping.

In the "I See You" paradigm, I have *Ubuntu;* I have a wide circle of empathy. If I truly see *you,* I'm predisposed to understand you, to feel what you feel, and thus to minimize conflict and maximize synergy with you. By contrast, if you stand outside my circle of empathy, I can't feel what you feel or see as you see, and neither you nor I can ever be as strong or insightful or innovative as we could be together.

I encourage you to take this paradigm seriously in your personal life. Think of one or two people—a colleague, a friend, a family member—who needs to be *seen.* You know what I mean by that. Do they have reason to think you devalue them, ignore them, or fake respect for them? Do you talk about them behind their back? Do you see them as symbols, or do you see them as real people full of strengths and weaknesses, idiosyncrasies and inconsistencies, amazing gifts and terrific blind spots—just like you?

Paradigm 3: I Seek You Out

This paradigm is about deliberately seeking out conflicting views instead of avoiding or defending yourself against them.

The best response to someone who doesn't see things your way is to say, "You disagree? I need to listen to you!" And mean it.

The best leaders don't deny or repress conflict. They see it as an opportunity to move forward. They know there is no growth, no discovery, no innovation—and indeed no peace—unless the provocative questions are brought out into the open and dealt with honestly.

Instead of ignoring, demoting, or firing a person who disagrees, the effective leader goes to him and says, "If a person of your intelligence and competence and commitment disagrees with me, then there must be something to your disagreement that I don't understand, and I need to understand it. You have a perspective, a frame of reference I need to look at."

I call this paradigm "I Seek You Out" to express the strong shift in thinking that the 3rd Alternative requires. When faced with someone who disagrees with me, like everyone else I automatically go on the defensive. That's

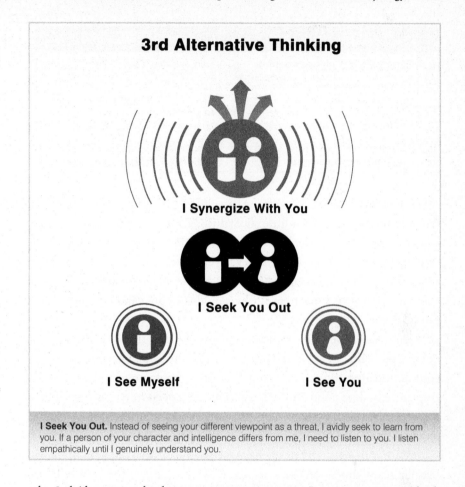

3rd Alternative Thinking

I Synergize With You

I Seek You Out

I See Myself   I See You

I Seek You Out. Instead of seeing your different viewpoint as a threat, I avidly seek to learn from you. If a person of your character and intelligence differs from me, I need to listen to you. I listen empathically until I genuinely understand you.

why 3rd Alternative thinking is so counterintuitive. It urges me to put a high value on people who differ from me instead of throwing up defensive walls.

The paradigm "I Seek You Out" contrasts sharply with the paradigm "I Defend Myself Against You," as shown in the contrasting boxes in the chart on page 42. Remember, what we *see* determines what we *do*, and what we *do* determines the results we *get*.

My very identity is caught up in my opinions, my ideas, my instincts, and, yes, my prejudices; that's why the preceding paradigms must be "I See Myself" and "I See You." 3rd Alternative thinking requires the deep inner security that comes from a realistic view of myself and from an appreciation for the exceptional gifts and perspectives that you bring. The defensive mentality is the opposite: it feeds on insecurity and self-delusion, and it dehumanizes people who are different.

	I Seek You Out	I Defend Myself Against You
SEE	Other viewpoints—different "slices of truth"—are not only desirable but essential.	Other viewpoints are wrong—or at best not very useful.
DO	I say, "You see things differently—I need to listen to you!" Then I listen empathically until I genuinely understand how you see things.	I say, "You see things differently—you are a threat." If I can't persuade you, I ignore, avoid, or actively oppose you.
GET	A broader, more inclusive view of the problem that enables a more robust solution.	A narrow, exclusive view of the problem that leads to a defective solution.

"I Seek You Out" starts with the principle that truth is complicated and that everybody likely has a little slice of it. "Truth is never pure and rarely simple," said Oscar Wilde. No one has it all. 3rd Alternative thinkers recognize that the more slices of truth they have, the more they see things as they really are. So these thinkers *deliberately* seek out different slices of truth. If you have truth that I don't have, why wouldn't I come and find you so you can teach me?

Let me emphasize how radical a shift in thinking this is. It sees conflict not as a problem but as an opportunity. It sees strong disagreement as an avenue for learning, not as a brick wall. The many books on negotiation always emphasize finding points you can agree on, areas of common interest. This is important. But it is perhaps even more important to explore and capitalize on the differences.

It's not only natural, but essential for people to have different opinions. I've said many times over the years that if two people have the same opinion, one of them is unnecessary. A world without difference would be a world of sameness where no progress is possible. Still, instead of valuing these differences, we defend ourselves against them because we believe our identity is under threat. People laboring under the defensive mind-set put up walls around themselves to shore up their position instead of moving forward.

Walls

One of the discouraging things about how we deal with conflict is that cement wall of opinion. Historically, we've seen the figurative walls between people turn into real walls. We saw it in Berlin between the capitalist and the communist worlds. We see it in the Middle East between the Israelis and Palestinians. We can't move forward as long as the walls are up, until at least one of us is willing to seek out the other and truly understand the other.

These walls are made of piles of unthinking clichés. Political clichés are, of course, the most transparent form of manipulation, but you'll find hackneyed arguments everywhere, at work and at home. The same accusations-as-arguments go on year after year, producing lots of heat among the 2-Alternative thinkers but dismally low light for everybody else:

"Tax-and-spend liberal!"
"Heartless conservative!"
"Soft on crime!"
"Racist warmonger!"
"Weak-kneed flip-flopper!"
"Fat-cat pawn of the military-industrial complex!"
"If we elect you, the terrorists win!"
"If we elect you, the rich get richer and the poor get thrown under
     the bus!"
"Socialist!"
"Fascist!"

In Jonathan Swift's *Gulliver's Travels,* we meet a strange group called the Laputans, who are the ruling elite in their country. They have decided that actually talking with one another takes too much effort, so they carry around sacks filled with symbols that they just flash at each other when they meet. "I have often beheld two of these sages," says Gulliver, "who open their sacks, and hold conversation for an hour together, then put up their implements and take their leave."[1] Of course, Swift was making fun of government and business leaders who toss out the same stale talking points over and over as substitutes for authentic communication.

Today an increasingly venomous tone is creeping into these acts of non-communication. We seem to be at an all-time low for civility in discourse. There's anger, division, frustration, and polarization. Even at the highest levels of government, where mutual respect once reigned, we hear time and again of outbursts instead of dialogue. 2-Alternative thinking is becoming poisonous.

On the internet, on cable TV's so-called news, on the radio waves of every nation, demagogues have found a short cut to wealth by cheering and cursing people into opposing camps. Some of these demagogues see them-

---

1 Jonathan Swift, *Gulliver's Travels* (London: Bibliolis Books, 2010), 186.

selves as martyrs, some are clearly just self-serving profiteers, but many are in the business of whipping up hatred for anyone who differs with them. By their simple-minded "us against them" mentality, as Professor Ronald Arnett says, they "give the illusion of sharpness of perception, when in reality there is a refusal to gain new insights by listening to the other's viewpoint."[1]

With the internet, we have a newfound power to form tribes, as the entrepreneur Seth Godin points out.[2] It's a wonderful thing. Everyone from Stoic philosophers to Ukrainian folk dancers can connect and explore their common interests together. But there is a menacing side to this new tribalism: people clustering only with like-minded people. Two people asking Google the same question will get two different answers because the sophisticated search engine already knows the kind of answers they each want to hear. Ironically, even as the opportunities for hearing many voices proliferate on the internet, people immobilized behind digital walls withdraw from any contact or consideration of different viewpoints. They become like the Laputans, nodding vigorously at one another's banalities, stopping their ears at anything else.

The Talking Stick

For years now I have been troubled by these agents of hostility and fragmentation. I have tried to counter them by teaching the paradigm "I Seek You Out." I've met with more than thirty heads of state and countless corporate and government leaders. I've met with schoolchildren from Singapore to South Carolina. And I always teach the same thing, what I call "Talking Stick Communication."

For centuries, Native Americans have used the Talking Stick at their council gatherings to designate who has the right to speak. As long as the speaker holds the stick, no one may interrupt until the speaker feels heard and understood. Once a noble group of Native American leaders awarded me a traditional Talking Stick, which I cherish. (They also renamed me

1 Ronald C. Arnett, *Communication and Community: Implications of Martin Buber's Dialogue* (Carbondale: Southern Illinois University Press, 1986), 34.
2 Seth Godin, "The Tribes We Lead," http://www.ted.com/talks/seth_godin_on_the_tribes_we_lead.html. Accessed November 20, 2010.

The Talking Stick. An ancient Native American tradition, the Talking Stick is a symbol of peaceful communication. So long as the speaker holds the stick in hand, no one may interrupt until the speaker feels heard and understood.

"Bald Eagle" in the same ceremony!) The symbolism of the Talking Stick is well worth considering:

> *Whoever holds the Talking Stick has within his hands the sacred power of words. Only he can speak while he holds the stick; the other council members must remain silent. The eagle feather tied to the Talking Stick gives him the courage and wisdom to speak truthfully and wisely. The rabbit fur on the end of the stick reminds him that his words must come from his heart and that they must be soft and warm. The blue stone will remind him that the Great Spirit hears the message of his heart as well as the words he speaks. The shell, iridescent and ever changing, reminds him that all creation changes—the days, the seasons, the years—and people and situations change, too. The four colors of beads—yellow for the sunrise (east), red for the sunset (west), white for the snow (north) and green for the earth (south)—are symbolic of the powers of the universe he has*

in his hands at the moment to speak what is in his heart. Attached to the
stick are strands of hair from the great buffalo. He who speaks may do so
with the power and strength of this great animal.[1]

This description of a Cherokee Talking Stick sums up beautifully what I have
tried to teach. The Talking Stick is not about winning arguments but about
hearing the story and understanding the heart of a person. It requires courage, wisdom, and the tempering of truth with compassion. Nothing is more
crucial in the global culture of the twenty-first century than to understand
others rather than try to dominate them. Talking Stick communication is a
moral necessity in our time.

The Talking Stick is central to what is known as the talking circle, convened by the elders to discuss and deal with important problems and decisions. By custom, the circle is not a debating society. Dr. Carol Locust
describes it this way: "The circle is to allow each person to speak their truth
in a place of confidence and safety. . . . No one is more prominent than any
other person, all are equal and there is no beginning and no end, so that all
words spoken are accepted and respected on an equal basis."

The origins of the talking circle are lost in time but find expression in
the founding myth of the Iroquois Confederation. For centuries the five nations of the lower Great Lakes region of North America fought bloody wars
among themselves, each tribe seeking a dominant position. Perhaps as early
as the twelfth century CE a young outsider known to legend as Deganawi-
dah, the Peacemaker, came among the nations and transformed everything.

The story goes that the Peacemaker sought out a bloodthirsty warrior who
lived by violence, who was so terrifying and isolated from others that no one
had even given him a name. One night the Peacemaker stole up to the name-
less warrior's lodge and climbed to the top of it, where smoke from his fire
escaped through a hole. Inside the warrior was brooding over a boiling kettle.
Seeing the face of the stranger reflected up at him from the depths of the water,
he was struck by its beauty and began to meditate on the evil of his ways.

When the stranger came down from the roof and entered the hut, the
warrior embraced him. "I was surprised that there was a man looking up
from the bottom of the pot. His personal beauty amazed me greatly. . . .

---

1 Carol Locust, "The Talking Stick," *Acacia Artisans: Stories and Facts,* http://www.acaciart
.com/stories/archive6.html. Accessed October 10, 2010.

I came to the conclusion that it was perhaps I myself who was looking up from there. At that time I thought, 'My custom of killing human beings is not fitting.'"

He unburdened himself to the stranger. He told his story, and the stranger listened respectfully. Finally the warrior said, "So now then I have finished. Now in turn it rests with you. I in turn will listen to whatever message you bring."

The Peacemaker told him, "Now you have changed the very pattern of your life. Now a new frame of mind has come to you, namely Righteousness and Peace." Together they looked again into the water and saw how much alike they were. The Peacemaker gave the warrior a name, Hiawatha, and the two men together "waged an intellectual and spiritual battle of many years' duration" to unite the Mohawks, Oneidas, Onondagas, Cayugas, and Senecas into what is known today as the Iroquois Confederation.[1]

Called by some "the oldest living participatory democracy in the world," the Confederation began as a 3rd Alternative to unceasing war on one hand and enslavement to the strongest tribe on the other. The Five Nations never again made war on each other. The Iroquois constitutional system, known as the Great Law of Peace, persists to this day, governed by a council of clan chiefs, with most decisions made by consensus in which each representative has an equal voice.[2] Though important, this council deals only with major issues, while most local questions are dealt with by tribal councils in a unique federal system of government. Interestingly, women's councils have veto power over the decisions of male leaders.

Although historians disagree about the extent of its influence, the Iroquois Confederacy appears to have provided a model for the creation of the United States. Decades before the American Revolution, Benjamin Franklin first proposed a similar union of the British colonies in America. He was impressed at the ingenious Iroquois "scheme of Union": "It has subsisted Ages, and appears indissoluble." If they could do it, Franklin asked, why couldn't the colonies?[3]

1 William Nelson Fenton, *The Great Law and the Longhouse: A Political History of the Iroquois Confederacy* (Norman, OK: University of Oklahoma Press, 1998), 90–91.
2 *Encyclopedia of the Haudenosaunee (Iroquois Confederacy)*, ed. Bruce Elliott Johansen and Barbara Alice Mann (Westport, CT: Greenwood Publishing Group), 246.
3 Cited in Susan Kalter, *Benjamin Franklin, Pennsylvania, and the First Nations* (Champaign: University of Illinois Press, 2006), 28.

This is the great legacy of that first talking circle, born in that moment when Hiawatha saw himself and his brother reflected in the water. The result, as the Peacemaker said, was a "new frame of mind"—the paradigms "I See Myself" and "I See You"—that "changed the very pattern" of Hiawatha's life. To spread this new frame of mind among the nations, the two men practiced the further paradigm "I Seek You Out," convening talking circles wherever they went, building toward the Great Law of Peace among the Five Nations. The Talking Stick became the icon of the Great Law of Peace.

For nearly a millennium, the Five Nations have lived in peace with each other; at the same time the so-called civilized West has been raising war and mass killing to a science.

Empathizing

The essence of Talking Stick communication is empathic listening, as psychologists would say. I've devoted much of my life to teaching empathic listening because it is the very key to peace and to synergy. It is not just another technique for manipulating others. Hiawatha gave vent to all his loneliness and rage and guilt because the Peacemaker was willing to seek him out and listen to his heart as well as his words. Only after freeing himself of this burden was Hiawatha open to hearing the message of the Peacemaker: "So now then I have finished. I in turn will listen to whatever message you bring."

What is empathy? I like this definition from the Israeli philosopher Khen Lampert: "Empathy happens when we find ourselves . . . in the mind of the other. We observe reality through her eyes, feel her emotions, share in her pain."[1] A capacity for empathy seems to be hardwired into us: even newborns cry at the sound of other babies' crying.

Empathy differs from sympathy, which is about agreeing with or coming over to the other person's side in a conflict. To listen empathically does not mean we agree with the other person's point of view. It does mean that we try to *see* that point of view. It means listening for both the content and the emotion the other person is expressing so that we can stand in her shoes and know what it feels like.

I liken empathic listening to giving people "psychological air." If you were suffocating right at this moment, you wouldn't care about anything except getting air—now! But once you get your breath, the need has been

---

1 Khen Lampert, *Traditions of Compassion* (New York: Palgrave-Macmillan, 2006), 157.

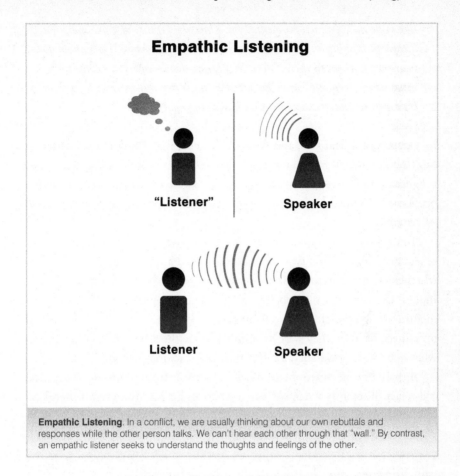

Empathic Listening

"Listener"   Speaker

Listener   Speaker

Empathic Listening. In a conflict, we are usually thinking about our own rebuttals and responses while the other person talks. We can't hear each other through that "wall." By contrast, an empathic listener seeks to understand the thoughts and feelings of the other.

satisfied. Like the need for air, the greatest psychological need of a human being is to be understood and valued.

When you listen with empathy to another person, you give that person psychological air. Once that vital need is met, you can then focus on problem solving. In a conflicted world, so many people feel unheard, disenfranchised, frustrated at being ignored or misrepresented. That person who steps forward to listen—to really listen—carries a key that unlocks a suffocating mental prison. Listen to Carl Rogers describe the response of those who genuinely feel understood:

> *Almost always, when a person realizes he has been deeply heard, his eyes moisten. I think in some real sense he is weeping for joy. It is as though he were saying, "Thank God, somebody heard me. Someone knows what it's*

*like to be me." In such moments I have had the fantasy of a prisoner in a
dungeon, tapping out day after day a Morse code message, "Does anybody
hear me? Is anybody there?" And finally one day he hears some faint tap-
pings which spell out "Yes." By that one simple response he is released from
his loneliness; he has become a human being again.*[1]

I seek you out, I hear you, and the walls come down. Think of the impact on
our troubled marriages, on our legal disputes, on our political battles, on the
toughest conflicts we face when we can at last say, "Thank God, somebody
hears me." The psychic tension drains away and we can move on to a 3rd
Alternative.

The ability to feel what another feels is native to us. In the early 1990s
researchers discovered a type of brain cell called a "mirror neuron" that fires
whether we perform an action ourselves or see another person perform it.
Italian scientists first noticed this phenomenon in monkeys. While experimenting to see which brain cells light up when their test monkey reached
for a piece of food, they were astounded to see the same brain cells light up
when the monkey watched *another* monkey reaching for food.

Apparently the mirror neurons can tell hostile from innocent moves. The
cells react differently when we watch a person lift his arm, even if there's no
way to know whether the person intends to comb his hair or grab a club to
knock us down. The same neurons fire whether we smile ourselves or someone smiles at us. By seeing a smile, we feel the smile. By seeing pain, we feel
pain. These neurons can *feel* what the other person feels.[2]

If the capacity for empathy is natural to us and has such a profound impact, why is it so rare? Because the competing paradigms are strong. In her
fine study *Empathy and the Novel,* Suzann Keen observes that "the desire for
dominance, division, and hierarchal relationships" weakens empathy. Conven-
tionally, an empathic person is a "bleeding heart" who believes naïvely that understanding people will change them.[3] Hardheaded realists are not empathic.

But when you consider the natural consequences of imposing "dominance, division, and hierarchy" on human beings, you have to ask yourself

---

1 Rogers, *A Way of Being,* 10.
2 I am indebted to Dr. Joseph G. Cramer of the Department of Pediatrics, University of
  Utah, for this information.
3 Suzann Keen, *Empathy and the Novel* (Oxford: Oxford University Press, 2007), 151.

who the *real* realists are. If I seek to dominate and divide people, forcing them into categories, I will inevitably breed resistance. There will be no "I-Thou," only "I-It." I will get conflict instead of creativity.

Another barrier to empathy, as Rogers says, "is our very natural tendency to judge, to evaluate, to approve, or disapprove the statement of another person." He gives an example: "As you leave a lecture, one of the statements you are likely to hear is, 'I didn't like that man's talk.' Now how do you respond? Almost invariably your reply will be either approval or disapproval of the attitude expressed. Either you respond, 'I didn't either,' or else you reply 'Oh, I thought it was really good.' In other words, your primary reaction is to evaluate what has just been said to you, to evaluate it from your point of view." [1] This sort of exchange is usually harmless, but the sharper the conflict, the more judgmental we become and the less likely we are to empathize. When disagreement touches on deep beliefs or identity issues, empathy often disappears entirely. That's why empathic listening is counterintuitive unless we make it a habit, as I've taught for many years: "Seek *first* to understand, *then* to be understood." Not the other way around.

To make empathic listening a habit, we must be deliberate about it. When I hear someone who disagrees with me, I walk up to him and say, "You see things differently. I need to listen to you." The more I do this, the more comfortable it becomes and the more I learn. I enjoy the exchanges.

In response to the person who "didn't like that man's talk," as an empathic listener I will say, "Tell me more." If the point at issue is minor, I'll gain some insight. If the issue is one I really care about and I *first* seek to understand the other person's point of view, she will then be more likely to hear *my* point of view.

But you say, "I'm a good listener. I'm fair. I'm open." Chances are that you haven't been listening empathically. If you're like most of us, you are formulating your answers while I'm talking. Can I really be free and open with you if you automatically counter everything I say? If you're trying to communicate with your daughter, will she open herself up to you if you judge or contradict or laugh at her points? If you're the boss, can the people who work for you really talk to you and expect to be understood?

---

1 Carl Rogers, "Communication: Its Blocking and Its Facilitation," http://www.redwoods
.edu/instruct/jjohnston/English1A/readings/rhetoricandthinking/communicationitsblock
ingitsfacilitation.htm. Accessed October 23, 2010.

The next time you get in a discussion, try this experiment: each person can speak only after he or she has stated the ideas *and* feelings of the previous speaker to that person's satisfaction. The first thing you'll find out is that it isn't as easy as it sounds. It's one thing to restate another person's ideas, but to capture *feelings* is tough. If you keep trying, however, you'll arrive at empathy. You'll find out what it's like to stand in the other person's shoes and to see the world as he sees it.

The techniques of active listening—mirroring feelings, repeating ideas, refraining from judging or commenting—are widely known and helpful. But to be an empathic listener, you need to just sit back, be quiet, and pay attention. Of course, if you're the kind of person whose face gets red when you don't like what you're hearing, this can be a challenge.

By far the greater challenge is to adopt the *mind-set* of empathy. If you seek me out because I differ from you, if in your positive regard for me you sincerely want to understand what I think, why I think it, and how I feel about it, you'll be amazed at how fast I'll open up to you. Active listening techniques might get in the way of empathic listening. And if I sense that you're only pretending to be interested in my viewpoint, I will deeply resent your using active listening techniques as just another attempt at manipulation.

In the end, empathy enlarges your own thinking. When your spouse or your co-worker or your friend really opens up to you and becomes transparent to you, he injects his views into yours. His truths now belong to you as well. Because she valued the truth so much and understood how limited she was, the political philosopher Hannah Arendt taught herself how to get past those limits into the minds of others. She wrote, "To think with an enlarged mentality means that one trains one's imagination to go visiting."[1] And the Dalai Lama often says that those with whom he is in conflict are his most important teachers.[2]

You might be thinking, "But won't empathic listening drag out the conflict? Do I really have to hear it all again? Doesn't it just make things worse? I don't have time for this!" These questions reveal your paradigm. If you think you've heard it all before, you're mistaken. Unless you've figuratively

---

1 Hannah Arendt and Ronald Beiner, *Lectures on Kant's Political Philosophy* (Chicago: University of Chicago Press, 1989), 43.
2 Cited in Marc Gopin, *Healing the Heart of Conflict* (Emmaus, PA: Rodale, 2004), 237.

given me the Talking Stick—unless you've understood me and my feelings so well that you could make my argument for me—you haven't actually heard anything.

And as for dragging out the conflict, I've found invariably that the quickest way to a solution is empathic listening. The time you invest in understanding my mind and heart is nothing compared to the time and resources you would waste fighting me. In the United States alone, 1.2 million lawyers charge approximately $71 billion a year for their services—and this number doesn't even include the financial judgments they win in court. How much of that time and money could be spared if people sought to understand one another openly and honestly?

On a personal level, how many years are wasted in conflicted marriages and other relationships because empathy is lacking? Empathic listening takes time, but nothing like the time it takes to restore frayed or broken ties, to live with repressed and unresolved problems.

In 2010, in the midst of a divisive national debate over a new health-care law, the president of the United States and the leaders of Congress decided to talk out their opposing opinions on television. It was a rare and fascinating experience to watch the interchange at the highest levels of government that usually takes place behind closed doors. It was also incredibly revealing.

I acknowledge that synergy can be harder to get to when many, many people are involved. But it has been done often, and it usually happens when a few people step outside the insanity and decide to go for a better way. That didn't happen this time. Both sides spoke with intelligence and persuasive skill. They told horror stories about people who couldn't get help, about extravagant costs and outrageous wrongs. They laughed and cried at gross inefficiencies and inequities. They made sharp points about the shortcomings of their opponents' philosophies. By the impressive information they had at their command, you could tell they had clearly done their homework.

But at the end you could just feel the frustration of the two sides. Despite all their skillful appeals to logic, to data, to emotion, they had made not one micrometer of progress in resolving their conflict. Even allowing for the fact that they all knew they were on camera and that it had been an exercise in political gamesmanship, you could still sense the hollowness, the disappointment they all felt that the walls between them showed no signs of coming down.

What was missing? Their paradigms were wrong, and I'm not talking about their political paradigms. It was clear that they saw themselves and each other merely as representatives of a side, not as thinking, reasoning, creative individuals capable of independent judgment. As a result, there was no attempt whatever at empathic listening. They were simply not interested in *understanding* each other's stories so that they could learn from one another and move toward a 3rd Alternative.

I am not saying there should be no debate, that people shouldn't argue things out.

Within the polarized paradigms of our society, we often assume that the whole point of an argument is to win—to beat the other side. Just try that on your friends and family and see how far you get toward a loving and creative relationship. For a 3rd Alternative thinker, the goal is not victory but *transformation,* for everyone on all sides. As we learn from each other, we naturally change our views, sometimes radically.

In the paradigm "I Seek You Out," I argue with you to try out ideas, not to impose them. I use argument as a vehicle for learning, not as a weapon. My purpose is not to score points on you in the weary old game of one-upmanship but to *change* the game.

In the paradigm "I Seek You Out," I listen to you to understand your slices of truth, not to scout out holes in your argument to use against you. Rogers explains, "The only reality I can possibly know is the world as I perceive it. . . . The only reality you can possibly know is the world as you perceive it. . . . And the only certainty is that those perceived realities are different. There are as many 'real worlds' as there are people!"[1] Unless I have the whole truth myself (which, I'm sorry to say, isn't likely), I can only benefit from your truth. I'm not going to learn much if I hear only myself talking. Consider this thought from the philosopher John Stuart Mill:

Not the violent conflict between parts of the truth, but the quiet suppression of half of it, is the formidable evil; there is always hope when people are forced to listen to both sides; it is when they attend only to one that errors harden into prejudices, and truth itself ceases to have the effect of truth.[2]

---

1 Rogers, *A Way of Being,* 102.
2 John Stuart Mill, *On Liberty and Other Essays* (Lawrence, KS: Digireads.com, 2010), 35.

In the paradigm "I Seek You Out," I take a terrible, delightful risk. If I really come to understand how you feel, to see things as you see them, I'm in danger of changing my own point of view! If I'm honest, it's unlikely I will see things as I did before, nor is it desirable. If you don't influence my thinking, then I have cause to worry about my own closed-mindedness. Indeed for my own good I need to hear your truth. As Carl Rogers says, my paradigm should not be "I care for you because you are the same as I" but "I prize and treasure you because you are different from me." [1]

Making Robust Decisions

Now you might be saying to yourself, "All this talk about empathy seems not only softhearted but also softheaded. Sure, I'm willing to listen, I don't want to be disrespectful, but I know my own mind. I don't need other people telling me what to think."

My response is that there is nothing at all softheaded about empathic listening; in fact, it's a very practical thing to do. You're in trouble if you *don't* do it. Anyone in the workplace who doesn't listen well is headed for a fall. Business punishes leaders who don't make robust decisions, and robust decisions depend on a thorough understanding of the viewpoints of customers, suppliers, team members, other departments, innovators, investors—in short, of all stakeholders. A robust decision is defined as "the best possible choice found by eliminating all the uncertainty possible." [2] And the only way to minimize uncertainty is to hear people out.

For example, some years ago leaders of a multinational food company decided to cut production costs by purchasing apple-juice concentrate from a new, lower-price supplier. The executives included only their financial people in the decision, excluding the R&D director who was supposed to be in charge of product development. The astounded R&D director, a research scientist, tried to warn his bosses that the new product contained no apple juice at all—it was just sugar water—but the bosses were so delighted with the $250,000 a year they were saving that they laughed off the man as "naïve and impractical." Eventually a day came when the executives went to jail and

---

1 Rogers, *A Way of Being*, 105.
2 David G. Ullman, *Making Robust Decisions* (Bloomington, IN: Trafford, 2006), 35.

paid $25 million in fines—an amount equal to a hundred years of the dollars they supposedly saved by serving up a fraudulent product.[1]

So who is "naïve and impractical"? Those who seek out different viewpoints with the intent to understand, or those who don't?

Defective decisions like these are made every day by business people who can't or won't listen empathically. But the same weakness helps explain failed decisions in every part of life: at home, in the community, within governments, between parents and children. The refusal to listen breeds conflict instead of creativity, weakness instead of robustness. The great irony? Those who worry that empathic listening makes them appear weak are the very ones who make the weakest decisions.

I know of a couple with three grown children. This is a good family, ordinary in every way and full of life and spirit. The father did a good deal of traveling for his work while his daughter and two boys were growing up. His relationship with them was sound and safe, but he just wasn't around very much. Everything was fine until his teenage daughter started having behavioral problems at school and then with the law.

Each time she got in trouble, her anxious, time-conscious father would sit down with her and try to talk through the problem—maybe a little impatiently. They would go around on the same issues every time: "I'm too fat, I'm too ugly." "No, you're not, you're beautiful to me." "You have to say that, you're my dad." "I wouldn't say it if it wasn't true." "Yes, you would." "Do you think I'd lie to you?" And the discussion would turn to the question of the father's honesty. Or he would tell her a story from his own youth, like the one about how he grew up with skinny arms and shoulders and everyone made fun of him. "Is that supposed to make me feel better?" she would say.

Things would calm down, he'd leave town, and the cycle would start again. He was on a trip when his wife rang him to say their daughter had disappeared. Frantically, he caught a plane home and the family fretted for days while the search went on. At last she turned up in a runaway shelter in another city, and the parents collected her. She was silent all the way home. The father, a kind man and genuinely baffled, poured out his heart to her about how much she'd been missed, how frightening it had been not to

1 Marianne M. Jennings, ed., *Business Ethics: Case Studies and Selected Readings* (Florence, KY: Cengage Learning, 2008), 216–17.

know where she was. He told her stories about friends of his who had been troubled as youths but were now sturdy grownups.

That night he and his wife talked things through. "I do not know what to do about her," he confessed. His wife replied, "You might try listening to her." "What do you mean? I listen to her constantly. It's getting to be all I do when I'm home."

His wife gave him a half smile. "Go and listen to her. Don't talk. Don't talk. Just listen."

He sat down with his daughter, who was still silent, and asked her, "Would you like to talk?" She shook her head, but he stayed where he was, silent as well. It was getting dark before she finally spoke. "I just don't want to live anymore."

Alarmed, he fought the urge to protest this and said softly, "You don't want to live anymore." This was followed by about five minutes of silence— the longest five minutes of his life, he later said.

"I'm just not happy, Dad. I don't like anything about myself. I want it to be over."

"You're not happy at all," he breathed.

The girl began to cry. In fact, she began to sob intensely, trying to talk at the same time, words flowing like a flood. It was as if a dam had burst. She talked into the early morning hours, he said hardly ten words, and the next day things looked hopeful. Where before he was giving her only sympathy, at last he had discovered empathy.

This was only the first "psychological airing" of many over the next few hard adolescent years, but the young girl is now a woman, calm and confident of herself and her father's love for her. That he would seek her out, that he would value the outpourings of her heart instead of imposing his version of reality on her, helped give her a robust foundation for life.

I encourage you to take this paradigm to heart: "I Seek You Out." Think about your own stressed and strung-out moments in your relationships with others. When tensions are high and confidence is low, when the next step doesn't look clear at all, when a wall has gone up, try an experiment with empathy.

- Go to the other side and say, "You see things differently. I need to listen to you."
- Pay the price to understand. Give your full attention. Don't

multitask while you're listening. Don't judge, evaluate, analyze, advise, toss in your footnotes, commiserate, critique, or quarrel. The speakers don't need you on their side. All they need is your positive regard for *them*.

- Be quiet. You don't have to provide an answer, a verdict, a solution, or a "fix." Free yourself from all that pressure. Just sit back and listen.

- Speak only to keep the flow going. Say things like "Tell me more," "Go on," or just "Hm."

- Pay close attention to emotions. Affirm feelings: "You must feel (sorry, angry, hurt, worn out, anxious, disappointed, baffled, confused, betrayed, unsure, suspicious, skeptical, worried, frustrated) about this."

- Use a Talking Stick—literally or figuratively—if that will help.

- Remember, you're listening to a story. When you go to a movie, you don't interrupt and argue with the story and talk back to the screen. (If you do, you'll be asked to leave—and good riddance!) You're involved, your sense of reality is suspended, you're almost in a trance.

- Be ready to learn. If you're open, you'll gain insights that will light up your own mind and complement your own perspective. Changing your viewpoint due to more data is natural—it is not a sign of weakness.

- Make sure you really do understand. If necessary, tell the story back to the storyteller. Restate what you thought you heard. Talk about the feelings you perceived. Ask if he feels that you have thoroughly understood where he's coming from. If not, try again until he is satisfied.

- Show some gratitude. It's a great compliment to be invited into the mind and heart of another human being. And it's a real benefit to you because you've grasped a slice of truth you didn't understand before. As John Stuart Mill said, "If there are any persons who contest a received opinion, let us thank them for it, open our minds to listen to them, and rejoice that there is someone to do for us what we otherwise ought." [1]

---

1 Mill, *On Liberty and Other Essays*, 31.

Do you see how to let "psychological air" into a conflict? At some point in the experiment, don't be surprised if the other parties change their attitude toward you and want to hear *you* out too. If you've paid the price to truly understand them, then they're ready to hear your story. When that happens, you're really on your way to a 3rd Alternative.

Paradigm 4: I Synergize With You

This last paradigm is about going for a solution that's better than anyone has thought of before, rather than getting caught up in the cycle of attacking one another.

I call this paradigm "I Synergize With You." As we've seen, synergy is the

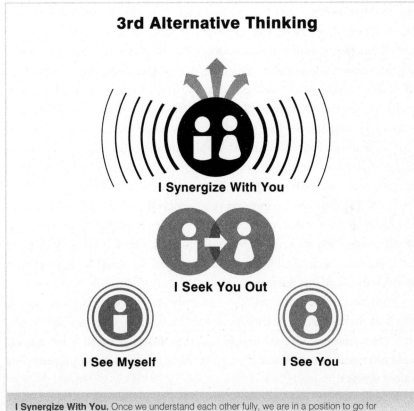

3rd Alternative Thinking

I Synergize With You

I Seek You Out

I See Myself   I See You

I Synergize With You. Once we understand each other fully, we are in a position to go for synergy, to find a solution that is better than anything we've come up with individually. Synergy is rapid, creative, collaborative problem solving.

	I Synergize With You	I Attack You
SEE	1 + 1 equals 10 or 100 or 1000!	1 + 1 equals 0 or less!
DO	I look for the 3rd Alternative. I ask: "Are you willing to go for a solution that is better than either one of us has in mind?"	I look for a Fight. I insist on my own narrow solution. I make sure the other side loses, although in the end I might have to compromise.
GET	What are the benefits of finding the 3rd Alternative?	What are the costs of contempt for others? To a business? To a nation? To a family?

process of actually creating the 3rd Alternative. It's about the passion, the energy, the inventiveness, the excitement of creating a new reality that is far better than the old reality. That's why I also call this *the paradigm of creation*.

The chart above illustrates how the paradigm of synergy contrasts with the paradigm of attack. The mind-set "I Attack You" is the logical conclusion to the mind-sets "I Stereotype You" and "I Defend Myself Against You." This is the paradigm of destruction—of relationships, of partnerships, companies, families, organizations, nations—indeed of the future. If I have this mind-set about you, you're a stereotype, not a *person* I can *see*. You stand for an ideology that I can't tolerate because you're just plain *wrong*. Or you're a wife or husband or partner or family member who threatens my identity, my very self-worth. So if I see you that way, what do I say? "I'll get even with you." "There's no room for both of us—it's either you or me."

I can pity you, I can try to convert you to my point of view, but ultimately you are merely a representation of something I can't live with, so I defend myself against you by ignoring you, mocking you, or undermining you. The final stage is the direct attack: I have to take you down. It's not enough for me to win; you must lose. One plus one equals zero, because we're playing a zero-sum game. And what results do we get? You and I together cannot produce anything but warfare.

With the attack mind-set, the best possible endgame is compromise, which by definition means we both lose something. Compromise is one plus one equals one and a half. Compromise is not synergy. It has a good reputation, and people think it's a great thing to get to a compromise, but it's not synergy.

By contrast, the opposite mind-set, "I Synergize With You," is the logical conclusion to the mind-sets "I See Myself," "I See You," and "I Seek You Out." Recall that everything starts with authentic respect for myself and for you: I meet you, I don't use you, to paraphrase Martin Buber. The next stage is enthusiastic empathy, a genuine determination to seek out and understand all the slices of truth available. I can't go on to synergy until everyone feels completely understood in terms of both content and emotion. Professor Horacio Falcao of the international business school INSEAD describes it this way: "I show by my own behavior that you don't have to fear me. Therefore, you don't have to defend yourself because I'm not attacking you. You therefore don't have to resist and you don't have to bring your power to the table because I'm not bringing mine."[1]

Now ask yourself: What are the costs of the attack mind-set to your business? To your nation? To your family? On the other hand, what are the benefits to your business of the synergy mind-set dedicated to finding the 3rd Alternative? To your nation? To your family?

You can answer these questions for yourself. But consider what would have happened if, on that fateful night at a South African train station, Mohandas Gandhi had surrendered to the attack mind-set? What would have been the consequences for himself and ultimately for the future of India? On a totally different level, what would have happened if Nadia, the parent so upset at the discontinuation of music in her daughter's school, had launched a blazing attack on the teacher instead of synergizing with her? And on a different level yet, what if Japanese manufacturers had treated W. Edwards Deming as a foreign intruder and attacked him with cultural antibodies?

The Japanese word for the attack paradigm is *kiai*. In the martial arts, this term refers to total and intense focus of strength on blocking or destroying an enemy and is symbolized by an explosive shout. The opposite, synergy paradigm is called *aiki*. This term refers to openness of mind, a nonconfrontational alignment of your strength with your opponent's strength. The revolutionary martial art based on synergy is called *aiki-do*, or "the way of peace." In aikido, you defuse the conflict by blending your strength with the strength of your opponent to produce, paradoxically, much more power. Fortunately, Japanese industry met the American Deming with an aikido mind-set, and the results were historic.

According to the prominent aikido master Richard Moon, "The most important thing in aikido is that we never oppose someone else's force. The way

---

1 Horacio Falcao, "Negotiating to Win," *INSEAD Knowledge*, April 16, 2010, http://knowledge.insead.edu/strategy-value-negotiation-100419.cfm?vid=404.

that is applied in conflict resolution is that we never oppose someone else's beliefs, or someone else's ideas. . . . We want to learn more about what they are thinking, we want to learn more about their energy, their spirit, and when we do that, we can get playful and move with it and it can change the situation." [1]

Never lose sight of the fact that true synergy requires *aiki* rather than *kiai,* the mind-set of authentic respect and empathy instead of the mind-set of blocking and attacking.

The Process of Synergy

After the lack of a proper mind-set, the second obstacle to synergy is a lack of skill. Synergy is the process that gets to the 3rd Alternative, and you need to know how that process works. Up to now I've been talking about the essential *character* of a synergistic person and have examined the paradigms that make up 3rd Alternative thinking. From here on, I'll talk about the *skills* of a synergistic person.

Children practice synergy naturally. We are born with the paradigm of creation. A friend tells me he watched his two young boys and their friends build a whole city out of a couple of food boxes, some windfall cherries (these were the people), a pile of rocks, and a banana peel (this was the king's palace). They told each other an elaborate story about this great civilization, inventing it as they went along. They introduced politics, wars, economics, love, jealousy, and passion into their story.

Children are natural world makers. As we grow up and specialize through school and work, we often mislay the skills we once used to create worlds. But those skills are never lost. Sometimes people surprise themselves when they arrive at a 3rd Alternative out of necessity. A crisis can force 3rd Alternative thinking, as in the events surrounding the accident on *Apollo 13*, the ill-fated April 1970 mission to the moon. After an explosion onboard, the three astronauts found themselves slowly asphyxiating inside the crippled spaceship because of carbon dioxide buildup from their own lungs. Loss of electrical power forced the astronauts to move from the command module of the ship into the lunar landing module, which was not designed to

---

1 Cited in Lisa Schirch, *Ritual and Symbol in Peacebuilding* (Sterling, VA: Kumarian Press, 2005), 91.

support three breathing human beings. The carbon dioxide filters gradually depleted, and that meant slow death. There were plenty of fresh cube-shaped filters available in the command module, but they were incompatible with the lunar module's system, which required cylinder-shaped filters. It was the classic 2-Alternative problem of fitting a square peg into a round hole.

"Failure is *not* an option!" vowed Gene Kranz, the mission director on the ground. A 3rd Alternative had to be found. So from materials available to the astronauts—plastic wrap, duct tape, cardboard, rubber hoses—the technicians on the ground rapidly constructed a mailbox-like contraption that would connect the mismatched filters. The specs for this makeshift solution were radioed to the astronauts. They built it, and it worked.

In this case, the 3rd Alternative originated under the pressure of a life-or-death situation, which is of course extreme. But what can we learn from the synergizing done by the Apollo mission team? We learn that 3rd Alternatives can come quickly. We also learn that we can create 3rd Alternatives out of the resources we have; we don't always need more or different resources. We learn once again that most dilemmas are false dilemmas. Most of all, we learn that people profoundly committed to one another can achieve miraculous synergies.

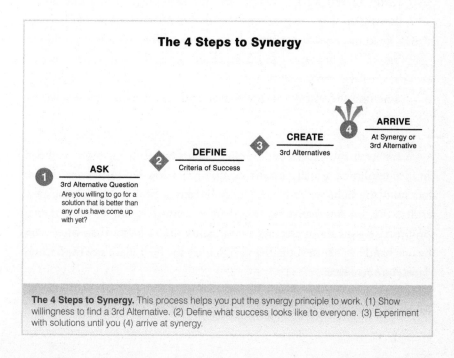

The 4 Steps to Synergy

ARRIVE
At Synergy or
3rd Alternative

CREATE
3rd Alternatives

DEFINE
Criteria of Success

ASK
3rd Alternative Question
Are you willing to go for a
solution that is better than
any of us have come up
with yet?

The 4 Steps to Synergy. This process helps you put the synergy principle to work. (1) Show willingness to find a 3rd Alternative. (2) Define what success looks like to everyone. (3) Experiment with solutions until you (4) arrive at synergy.

We've seen that sometimes a crisis forces synergy. But I don't need a crisis to get to synergy. If I start with the right mind-set, I can get to synergy on purpose by following four steps.

4 Steps to Synergy

1. I ask you: "Are you willing to go for a solution that is better than any of us have come up with yet?" This one revolutionary question can disarm defensiveness because I am not asking you to give up your idea. Not at all. I'm simply asking if we can look for a 3rd Alternative that is *better* than my idea *or* your idea. It begins as a thought experiment, nothing more.

2. Then I ask you something like this: "What would *better* look like?" The idea is to come up with a clear vision of the job to be done, a list of criteria for a successful outcome that would delight us both—criteria that move beyond our entrenched demands.

3. Once these criteria are up on the wall, we start experimenting with possible solutions that will meet the criteria. We create prototypes, we brainstorm new frameworks, we turn our thinking upside down. We suspend judgment for the time. Later, I'll describe several ways of doing this, but all synergy depends on allowing ourselves to experiment with radical possibilities.

4. We know when we've arrived at synergy by the excitement in the room. The hesitation and conflict are gone. We keep working at it until we experience that burst of creative dynamism that represents a successful 3rd Alternative, and we recognize it when we see it.

There are many experts in "conflict resolution." But for most of them, conflict resolution usually means negotiating a low-level accommodation that stops the fight without necessarily breaking through to amazing new results. The 3rd Alternative is more than an armistice, and far more than a compromise—it's about creating a new reality that is better than what's "on the one hand" *or* "on the other hand." Neither the First Place nor the Second Place. A *Third* Place.

Let's go a little more deeply into how these steps to synergy play out in real life.

Step 1: Ask the 3rd Alternative Question

The first step in the synergy process is to ask the 3rd Alternative Question: "Are you willing to go for a solution that is better than either one of us has in mind?"

This question changes everything. If the answer is yes, suddenly there's no need for negotiation, which only lures us toward compromise. If the answer is yes, the tension goes out of the conflict. In a low-trust situation, the "yes" might be very hesitant, even grudging. But it's the first step away from the hardened position and toward the promising solution.

Asking this question sincerely requires me to retrain my own thinking. I must no longer see myself as the objective, right-thinking source of all wisdom. I must think within the paradigms of mutual respect and valuing the differences. I must, as we have seen, understand the paradoxical principle that two people can disagree and both be right at the same time.

Further, I must see myself as more than just a representative of a side. I am more than my grievances, my position, my ideology, my team, my company, or my party. I am not a victim of the past. I am a whole person, a unique individual, capable of shaping my own destiny. I can choose a different future. I must also be willing to suspend my own preconceived notions of a solution. (Note that I said "be willing to.") I must be open to possibilities *I* never thought of. I must be ready to go where the process takes me, because synergy is by nature unpredictable.

> *"Would you be willing to go for a better solution?"*
>
> *"Yes, but I don't see what it could be, and I won't compromise."*
>
> *"I'm not asking you to compromise. I'm asking if you are willing to work with me to create something better than you or I had in mind. It doesn't exist yet. We'll create it together."*

Without these paradigms in place, I will never be able to ask the 3rd Alternative Question and mean it. I will never be able to get beyond the limits of my mental conditioning.

But what if the other side of the conflict doesn't think that way? What if their paradigms are distrustful, disrespectful, and purely partisan?

When I ask them the 3rd Alternative Question, they'll probably be disarmed by it. They will be surprised that I'm willing to open myself up to new possibilities. Often they are intrigued and curious, maybe even wondering what I'm up to. But if I have always acted from the motive of respect and truly sought to understand the interests and positions of the other party, the response will usually be "Yes, of course," however hesitant. Remember, if I haven't given them their day in court by deeply understanding them, they might well reject any overture from me toward a new solution. And they would be justified in doing so.

In my own experience, the results in almost every case have been astounding. I've seen agonizing conflicts years in the making resolved in a matter of hours. Not only have problems been solved, but relationships have been strengthened. I know of bitter courtroom fights that suddenly end when the two sides truly come to understand one another and seek something better than just beating up on each other.

Remember that when you ask the 3rd Alternative Question, you are not asking others to give up their ideas or positions. You are performing a thought experiment together, asking "what if." You are both suspending your positions for the sake of the experiment.

Winning is fun. But there is more than one way to win. Life isn't a tennis game in which only one player gets to jump the net. It's even more exciting when both sides win, when they create a new reality that delights them both. That's why the synergy process begins with the question "Would you be interested in going for a win-win solution that both of us feel really good about?"

Step 2: Define Criteria of Success

Aren't you often surprised by the things people fight over? Frequently the point of conflict is petty. Countries go to war over tiny, useless patches of land. Husbands and wives divorce over whose turn it is to clean up after dinner. Companies go bankrupt battling over trifles.

But the point of conflict is usually not "the point." Generally, much deeper issues underlie destructive conflicts. To paraphrase my friend Professor Clayton M. Christensen, the real job to be done is not to resolve the point of conflict but to change the paradigm that led to the conflict in the first place.

When Palestinians come together to protest a new Israeli settlement, the settlement itself is certainly not the issue. The real job to be done is to change hearts. The deeper conflict in the Middle East that goes back decades if not centuries is about principles that people hold fast in their hearts, like fairness and justice. A conflict of the heart can be the toughest and most intractable conflict.

Remember that in Japanese the synergistic mind-set is *aiki,* the blending of strengths to create a harmonious result. In a conflict of principles, you cannot simply reject the principles of the other. Usually, ironically, you *share* those principles. Certainly both Israelis and Palestinians or Turkish and Greek Cypriots or Catholics and Protestants in Northern Ireland can and do appeal to the principle of basic fairness in justifying their positions. The key to resolving the conflict is to move to a new and better application of the shared principle, the *aiki* mind-set at work. Both sides draw strength from their commitment to that shared principle by taking it to a totally new level.

Assuming that we already deeply understand each other's stories, slices of truth, we are now free to satisfy our deepest needs and desires in creating an entirely new vision that will be a victory for both of us. We put this synergistic mind-set to work by defining the criteria of success. The word *criterion* comes from the Greek and means "a means of compliance with a principle or a standard." In a conflict, we all want a great outcome. The question is, what does a great outcome look like?

Here's a simple example of this step: A public-park supervisor was frustrated. A park in his small city faced possible closure because of funding cuts. There was also a chronic conflict between dog owners who wanted to exercise their pets in the park and others who objected to the noise and the mess. Of course, none of them wanted to see the park close. All were willing to go for a 3rd Alternative, so they met and drew up a list of success criteria:

- The park must stay open with adequate funding.
- People and dogs must be safe in the park.
- The park must be kept clean.
- There must be no excessive noise in the park.

Everyone agreed on these simple criteria. They all joined in on the job to be done: finding a 3rd Alternative that would help everyone to win: the park officials, the public, the taxpayers, and the dogs. Later, we'll see how this turned out.

This synergy process has been used to create entire nations. When the original confederation government of the United States proved unworkable, the people's representatives gathered to design a new set of criteria of success: the Constitution of 1787. More recently, consider the unusual case of the Republic of Mauritius. This small island in the Indian Ocean, home to more than a million people of African, European, Indian, and Southeast Asian ancestry, is a remarkable example of synergy. Here adherents of every major religion, speaking dozens of languages and celebrating many different ethnic traditions, combine in a prosperous, harmonious culture unlike any other in the world. When Mauritius gained its independence from Britain in 1968, limited resources and ethnic differences threatened the viability and peace of the island. With an Indian majority, non-Indians feared being underrepresented and marginalized. Some experts predicted that Mauritius would self-destruct in a volatile stew of politics, religion, and race—as have so many other societies. But with a synergistic approach and an underlying commitment to celebrate differences, Mauritians crafted a constitution to give voice to everyone in the country. This was an essential criterion of success. When elections are held, most parliamentary seats go to those elected—but eight seats are reserved for "best losers." This guarantees balanced representation for minorities and a voice for them. What a novel 3rd Alternative this is!

Another issue arose because there were so many religions and cultures on Mauritius that it was always someone's holiday. So much celebrating went on that it was actually hard to get work done, but no group wanted to give up its festival. So a criterion was defined: If one person celebrates, we all celebrate. Mauritius now sets aside certain days each year as religious holidays that the whole country observes. Everyone honors the Christian Easter, the Muslim Eid, and the Hindu Diwali. Mauritians love celebrating each other's holidays, and it creates a rich sense of appreciation, respect, and love for each other and the community.

By defining novel, shared criteria of a successful society, Mauritius has escaped the deep conflicts that grip many other ethnically diverse nations. Mauritians aren't perfect, they have significant social problems, but this is a true success story. They succeeded not by abandoning the principle of fairness or by restricting it within a narrow, self-interested framework, but by *leveraging* it in novel and robust new ways. They don't just coexist—they *thrive* together. As the Mauritian leader Navin Ramgoolam says, "All of us came on different ships from different continents. Now we are all on the same boat." [1]

---

1 "Beyond Beaches and Palm Trees," *Economist*, October 2008; Joseph Stiglitz, "The Mauritius Miracle, or How to Make a Big Success of a Small Economy," *Guardian* (Manchester), March 7, 2011, http://www.guardian.co.uk/commentisfree/2011/mar/07/mauritius-healthcare-education.

To get to synergy, we need a robust set of criteria that represent success to as many stakeholders as possible. And we need it as early as possible. If we exclude important criteria, we end up having to tear down our solution and rework it because it does not represent true synergy. We save ourselves a lot of grief if we can start with a comprehensive set of success criteria.

Your criteria of success might take many forms. You might have a powerful mission statement that sums up your highest aspirations; if you fail to achieve that mission, nothing else matters very much. Or your criteria might be less ambitious than that. If you're building a house, you'll have a blueprint. If you're programming a computer app, you'll have a list of specs and a wireframe. If you're running a company, you'll have a strategic plan. You might have a code of values to live up to. In any case, you should have a clear end in mind before you move to synergy; otherwise you're just asking for chaos.

The mantra of synergy is this: *As many ideas from as many people as possible as early as possible.*

Take for instance the innovation philosophy at Procter & Gamble, perhaps the most successful consumer-product company in the world. The source of dozens of world-class brands, including Crest toothpaste, Tide, Gillette, Herbal Essences shampoo, Pampers, and Bounce, the P&G innovation team always starts with a firm goal and clear criteria of success. For example, some years ago consumer research showed that people wanted whiter teeth but didn't want to pay dentists the high price required for whitening. So the P&G team went to work defining the criteria of a successful solution. They invited to the party dental experts from Crest, bleach experts from Tide, adhesive experts from their long history with thermoplastics, and many others. This diverse team put the criteria on the wall: the product would be affordable, easy to apply, quick to show results, manufactured at high speed, and packaged for long shelf life. Many technical criteria rounded out the list. With these criteria of success in mind, the team created Whitestrips, which became a blockbuster product for P&G.[1]

This effort contrasts starkly with the experience of one of our European pharmaceutical clients who several years ago tried to put on the market a drug that would reduce high blood pressure. When they applied for ap-

---

1 A.G. Lafley and Ram Charan, *The Game Changer* (New York: Random House, 2008), 240–41.

proval to sell the drug in the United States, the Food and Drug Administration turned down their application. The drug required a twice-daily dosage, and the FDA pointed out that competing drugs already on the market required only a once-daily dosage. The twice-a-day dosage doubled the risk to the consumer of overdose or underdose; therefore, the drug could not be marketed in the United States.

It was a crushing blow to the company. Furthermore, when the news got back to headquarters in Europe, the sales director of the company said, "Why didn't you include us in the planning? We could have told you that such a drug wouldn't meet FDA requirements." A criterion of success in the U.S. market is a once-daily dosage, but the development team didn't know that. By failing to include important stakeholders in setting criteria of success, the firm created a drug that was not robust enough to survive in the marketplace.

Although the synergy process takes us places we can't anticipate, that doesn't mean we start with no destination in mind. The synergy process is about *how* to get to the place we all want to get to. Setting criteria of success helps us define what that place will be like. The criteria help us to better understand where we are now so that we will be going in the right direction. Without criteria of success, it's easy to start climbing a ladder together only to discover it's leaning against the wrong wall and every step just gets us closer to the wrong place.

You're probably wondering, "What if someone insists on criteria that are unacceptable to others?" This possibility is less likely if we've done the work of Paradigm 3, of truly understanding one another; then we will know what is and isn't a "win" for each party. The real question is, "Are we willing to look for criteria that allow us *all* to win? Criteria that we haven't thought of yet?" A "yes" permits us to dig deeper.

Beyond Fairness

Nonnegotiable criteria almost always come out of an issue of fairness or justice. "It's not fair, it's not equitable, it's not just, it's not respectful." There are no more basic human cries than these, whether in the schoolyard or the marketplace or a courtroom or the United Nations. In my opinion, however, the challenge for a 3rd Alternative thinker is to come up with criteria that are *more* than fair, that go *beyond* the principle of fairness. How do we do that?

Many conflicts, if not most, arise over the issue of fairness. People everywhere have some notion of whether or not they're being treated fairly. In trying to understand the idea of fairness, economists over the years have experimented with what they call the Ultimatum Game. In this game, one person is the Proposer and the other the Responder. The Proposer receives ten one-dollar bills. He or she then gets to offer any number of bills to the Responder, who is then free to accept or reject the offer. The catch is that both players must end the game with money; if they don't, the one with the money must return it.

If both players were robots, the reasoning goes, the ultrarational Proposer would offer only one dollar to the Responder, who would then rationally accept it, and both would have money. But human beings don't play that way. Usually the Proposer offers the Responder five dollars, which the Responder accepts, and both end up with equal amounts of money. Fair enough. Intriguingly, though, when the Proposer offers the Responder too little, the Responder often refuses to accept *any* money because it's not fair, and so both players lose out. This result might seem irrational, but it demonstrates the power of the principle of fairness.

This game has been tried with hundreds of groups worldwide, from London bankers to shepherds in the mountains of Peru. Although the results vary *within* cultures, there is little variation *between* cultures. All cultures have an innate sense of fairness.

But, as the Ultimatum Game shows, fairness is usually in the eye of the beholder: what's fair in my eyes might be unfair in yours. That's why 3rd Alternative thinking has to transcend the principle of fairness. The problem with the Ultimatum Game is that it artificially imposes *scarcity* on the players. In the game, there are only ten one-dollar bills to be shared. Given the rules, no matter how the game is played, the Proposer loses. He or she *must* give up some money. By contrast, in the real world neither party has to lose because the ten dollars can be leveraged. In the real world, the principle is not *scarcity* but *abundance*—there is no limit to the wealth that can be created. And there is a wealth of ways to get there. As a 3rd Alternative, the players could form a partnership and invest the cash for a healthy return or make a down payment on a business that generates far more cash for both of them. The 3rd Alternative mentality escapes the artificial limits of the 1st and 2nd Alternatives, which usually drive us to a tug of war in which fairness is the key issue.

Frankly, as 3rd Alternative thinkers, we are not very interested in fairness; we are far more interested in synergy. For us, a merely fair or just or equitable solution is not enough. We want more. If we want only what's fair, we haven't arrived at the 3rd Alternative mentality.

I like this observation by Charles H. Green, the founder and CEO of Trusted Advisor Associates: "The demand for 'fairness' can be the enemy of trust. Mutual trust is founded on reciprocity, which requires we reach out to value the other side. . . . If we spend our energy negotiating who gets 49 and who gets 51, we kill trust in our quest for 'fairness.'"[1] Therefore, making a list of criteria can become a strained exercise that just leads to more conflict. You don't have to hammer down every single nail; often, the best thing to do is simply to ask, "What does success look like?" Then write down the quick, obvious answers.

Whenever you're going for the 3rd Alternative, try making a list of criteria of success. To come up with the criteria, ask yourself these questions:

- Is everyone involved in setting the criteria? Are we getting as many ideas from as many people as possible?
- What outcomes do we *really* want? What is the *real* job to be done?
- What outcomes would be "wins" for everyone?
- Are we looking past our entrenched demands to something better?

When everyone is satisfied with the answers, you're ready to create 3rd Alternatives. Later, when you select your course of action, you can go back and ask which alternative best meets your criteria of success.

Step 3. Create 3rd Alternatives

Thinking back on my years of working with people around the world, I can say that the highlights have always been synergistic. It usually starts when someone shows the courage to tell a truth that really needs to be told. Then others feel they too can be authentic, and eventually empathy leads on to synergy. This is the lesson of the Iroquois Confederation. When one man, the Peacemaker, was brave enough to seek out his adversary and really listen, it was the beginning of the transformation of that culture from war to peace.

---

1 Charles H. Green, "Get Beyond Fairness," http://trustedadvisor.com/trustmatters/91/
  Trust-Tip-16-Get-Beyond-Fairness.

It takes only one person—you—to start the cycle of synergy. It begins when you're willing to say to others "You see things differently. I need to listen to you." Once everyone feels heard, then you can ask, "Are you willing to go for a 3rd Alternative?" If the answer is yes, you can start experimenting with possible solutions that will meet your criteria of success.

Please note that I said "solutions," plural. The search for a 3rd Alternative almost always involves many possible alternatives. We create models, we throw old things together in new ways, we turn our thinking upside down. We work in a freewheeling mode, confident about the abundance of solutions. We suspend judgment until that exciting moment when we all know we've arrived at synergy.

In this book, you'll see many ways of creating 3rd Alternatives, but all synergy depends on giving ourselves permission to experiment freely, richly, almost without limits. When I say this to people, they all agree in principle, but most people simply won't give themselves that kind of freedom. That might sound ironic in our time, when everyone claims to worship new ideas and our technologies move forward at light speed. Still, the culture of most work teams and organizations is profoundly starchy—and this is true worldwide. Anybody who wants to try synergy is taking an awful, wonderful risk.

Because we are looking for an entirely new solution, we must be willing to let go *entirely* of our position to make room for the creative conception of a third way. We must be willing to be made vulnerable in the "letting go." It can be very hard: all of our instincts tell us to fight (or flee) when we face opposition. That's why it's so crucial to pause and deliberately choose to seek the 3rd Alternative. According to the law of synergy, *There is always a better way.*

Where Do 3rd Alternatives Come From?
Where do we go to find 3rd Alternatives? What is the wellspring of synergy? The writer Amy Tan speaks of the sources of synergy as "hints from the universe, the arrival of luck, the ghost of my grandmother, accidents."[1] In other words, the insights that produce a 3rd Alternative can be universal and personal, random and jarring. But they are always new, exciting, and extraordinarily productive.

---

1 Amy Tan, "Creativity," TED.com, April 2008, http://www.ted.com/talks/lang/eng/amy _tan_on_creativity.html.

The concept of the 3rd Alternative is very ancient. Hindu sages and Greek philosophers alike knew that the truly revolutionary ideas arise not from debates but from dialogues between people with different perspectives. The Dialogues of Plato embody a search for new truths, not an attempt to persuade others of settled truths. The Buddha taught that we will never find enlightenment in an atmosphere of anger, ill will, or craving for power. He spoke of a "perfect vision" that goes beyond the narrow formula "I'm right and you're wrong." The German philosopher Hegel used the word *aufhebung* ("overriding") to describe that instant of insight that overrides all prior assumptions. He saw how the 1st Alternative (the thesis) and the 2nd Alternative (the antithesis) can combine to produce a 3rd Alternative: a synthesis. Practitioners of Zen seek the moment of *kensho,* a flash of understanding that makes all our petty arguments irrelevant.

The great philosopher Immanuel Kant was fascinated by the 3rd Alternative. The 2-Alternative thinkers of his time squabbled over religion and science, just as they do today, but Kant wanted to get past the fight toward a higher view of both. He said:

> *I do not approach reasonable objections with the intention merely of refuting them, but that in thinking them over I always weave them into my judgments, and afford them the opportunity of overturning all my most cherished beliefs. I entertain the hope that by thus viewing my judgments impartially from the standpoint of others some* third view *that will improve upon my previous insight may be obtainable.*[1]

The greatest minds of history are the ones who advance the world toward a 3rd Alternative. They are called the "seminal" thinkers because they sow a new seed of understanding that blossoms into entirely new ways of seeing the world. Our universities ought to be the seedbeds of 3rd Alternatives. But synergy is not solely the property of "great minds." We all benefit from simple synergies whenever we combine forces. Try tying your shoe with one hand and you'll see how useful synergy can be. One child can't reach even one apple on a tree, but if another child stands on his shoulders, the two of them can pick all the apples they want. Together they win it all; separately they lose it all.

---

1 Quoted in Arendt and Beiner, *Lectures on Kant's Political Philosophy,* 42. Emphasis mine.

Sometimes the 3rd Alternative comes from combining elements of two opposing arguments. In some cases, you can leverage ideas from the conflicting sides to come up with an entirely new solution. For example, surrender and resistance are opposites. Resistance is typically violent; surrender is nonviolent. But Gandhi and, following him, Martin Luther King Jr. combined the two ideas into the 3rd Alternative of nonviolent resistance, a concept that has led to the freedom of whole peoples.

Even when he was a college student, King's teachers noticed his ability to do synergistic thinking. "Regardless of subject matter, King never tired of moving from a one-sided thesis to an also one-sided antithesis and finally to a more coherent synthesis beyond both," one of them recalls. King was an unusually effective 3rd Alternative thinker in conflict situations. In a room where people were near to "crawling across the table and slitting each other's throats, King would just sit there until it would come to an end." While some saw his passivity as a flaw, others could see that his habit of silent listening was part of his creative thinking process. A friend of his said, " 'He had a remarkable facility for sitting through long, contentious meetings and then summarizing what everybody had said and synthesizing that' into a conclusion that appealed to all." He would often challenge somebody to "express as radical a view as possible and somebody to express as conservative a view as possible." It was almost like a game.[1] Empathic listening and synergistic solutions went hand in hand for Martin Luther King Jr.

Synergy can come from deliberately combining forces or leveraging opposing forces. But often the most interesting 3rd Alternatives happen when people make odd, unexpected connections.

Take the example of the little, underfunded city park threatened with closure and fought over by dog owners and their opponents. Although everyone concerned agreed on an outcome—a beautiful, clean, permanent park for both pet owners and their neighbors—they had no idea how to get there. So they started looking for 3rd Alternatives. No one remembers who came up with the odd idea of a dog cemetery, but it turned out to be the key to saving and renewing the park. It didn't take up much space, allowed people to honor the memory of their pets who enjoyed the park, and provided much-needed cash to keep the park open. Pet owners donate money

---

1 David J. Garrow, *Bearing the Cross: Martin Luther King, Jr., and the Southern Christian Leadership Conference* (New York: Harper Collins, 2004), 46, 464.

for paving stones, gardens, and trees. An off-leash area allows dogs to roam freely, and their owners self-police the park to keep it clean. So the dogs saved the park, and everyone is delighted with this 3rd Alternative.

Sometimes a simple 3rd Alternative cuts through a far more complex puzzle. In 1992 a frightening new type of cholera raged through India. Politicians and health workers pointed fingers at each other, fighting over the expense and difficulty of purifying water in the hardest-hit areas of the country. While they argued, an Indian scientist, Ashok Gadgil, was thinking about how to decontaminate water without costly chemicals or boiling, which required large amounts of fuel. He knew that ultraviolet radiation destroys bacteria, so he took the cover off a standard fluorescent lightbulb and held it over a basin of infected water. In a short time, the UV rays completely decontaminated the water.

While others fought about politics and research funding and infrastructural investments, Gadgil introduced a UV water purifier that can run off a car battery. Now widely used around the world, Gadgil's method can decontaminate a ton of water for about half a cent.

Ashok Gadgil shows us that 3rd Alternatives can come from making extraordinary connections with the ordinary and the everyday. Genius is not required, nor vast research outlays, but a different kind of thinking *is* required. As the Nobel Prize winner Albert Szent-Györgyi once said, "Discovery consists of seeing what everybody has seen and thinking what nobody has thought."

The origin of the computer is a particularly good example of how those unlikely connections work. In the eighteenth century, the silk makers of Lyons, France, struggled with the costly errors that marred their patterned silk. A young silk worker named Basile Bouchon knew that these errors crept in because the pattern had to be reset each time the drawloom was raised. It was a tedious and mistake-prone process.

Bouchon's father was an organ builder. At some point, the young man made a connection between silk-weaving patterns and the paper template his father used as a guide for boring holes into organ pipes. Bouchon punched holes in a piece of cardboard and used it to guide the needles of his drawloom so that the pattern stayed consistent. His invention of the punch card automated the textile industry, which in turn touched off the Industrial Revolution.

A century later, Herman Hollerith, a twenty-one-year-old engineer working for the U.S. Census Bureau, learned about punch cards. It occurred to him that, like the needles of a loom, electric wires could connect through the holes in a punch card, so he built a card machine for tabulating census data. Until then, it had taken as long as eight years to complete the census by hand. Used for the first time in the 1890 census, Hollerith's punch-card machine cut the process to a few months. To manufacture his tabulating machines, Hollerith started a little company; today it is known as IBM. Over the next fifty years the electronic computer evolved from Hollerith's basic concept. Looking at a computer today, you can't easily picture the unlikely links among organ pipes, silk looms, and the U.S. census that gave rise to it. But these are the kinds of accidental associations that make synergy happen.

You're probably saying, "Fine, but those connections were made over centuries. We need solutions now!"

Naturally, you can't force connections like these, but you can create an environment where they're more likely to take place. You can speed up the process and foster odd, unexpected connections that give rise to wild, wonderful ideas.

Consider just one example. A classic political, environmental, and humanitarian conflict arose in the twentieth century over attempts to wipe out malaria. Prevalent in tropical countries, this cruel killer sickens more than 250 million people a year and takes a million lives, mostly children and the elderly. Malaria is spread by the anopheles mosquito; when it bites, it injects a deadly parasite into the bloodstream.

For a while in midcentury, insecticides like DDT controlled the mosquitoes, and malaria deaths dropped. Then scientists became alarmed that DDT was killing off not only the pests but also birds and other wildlife and possibly causing cancer in humans. In 1962 Rachel Carson's pivotal book *Silent Spring* raised the alarm that chemical pesticides might be poisoning the environment for all living things. Eventually DDT was virtually banned and malaria roared back to life.

Politicians and scientists took sides. Some argued that the DDT ban caused unnecessary deaths and that the benefits of DDT far outweighed the risks. Others argued that DDT was dangerous and that the mosquitoes were developing resistance to the insecticide anyway. While the 2-Alternative thinkers were scoring debating points on each other, the Bill and Melinda Gates Foundation asked experts from many different backgrounds to get together and come up with new alternatives for stopping malaria. The group included medical researchers, an insect physiologist, software engineers, an astrophysicist, and even a rocket scientist. In the spirit of synergy, the alternatives flew.

It was the rocket scientist who suggested using lasers to shoot down the mosquitoes. Everyone rolled their eyes and laughed, but the idea gained speed. Optical engineers experimented with blue lasers from ordinary DVD players. Programmers created software to guide the lasers. An inventor named 3ric Johanson (that's right, 3ric) put it all together with parts acquired on eBay. The result? A "WMD" (Weapon of Mosquito Destruction) that zaps anopheles mosquitoes out of the sky. Harmless to humans and wildlife, the laser is so finely calibrated that it can spot a mosquito by its wing vibrations and bring it down with a tiny burst of light. Perimeter fences equipped with such lasers are capable of defending entire villages from malaria.

The anti-mosquito laser fence is just one wild idea among many. The Gates Foundation team has also proposed mutating the mosquito to drive out the malaria parasite, tricking the mosquito with fake targets, or genetically altering the parasite itself. And that's just the beginning.[1] The fight between the pro- and anti-DDT forces seems so unimaginative in contrast to the creative power of this team determined to find a 3rd Alternative—or many such alternatives.

What have we learned about the wellspring of synergy? We know that we won't find it in the strained atmosphere of 2-Alternative thinking. We know that it helps to disengage our minds from the day-to-day routine. We know that it requires a willingness to look for something completely new. We know that it takes empathic listening and a genuine openness to divergent ideas.

All of this is true—and there's also something more, something wild and unfathomable about the human brain that we can tap into. It's found in the magnificent reality of billions upon billions of neural links. Our minds are *designed* to make strange, unexpected, even bizarre connections that can lead to almost magical insights. The more we are able to draw upon this vast capacity we each have, the more fully we will be able to visualize, to synthesize,

---

1 Lisa Zyga, "Scientists Build Anti-Mosquito Laser," *physorg.com*, March 16, 2009, http://www.physorg.com/news156423566.html; Jennifer 8 Lee, "Using Lasers to Zap Mosquitoes," *New York Times*, February 12, 2010, http://bits.blogs.nytimes.com/2010/02/12/using-lasers-to-zap-mosquitoes/.

to transcend time and present circumstances and arrive at the wellspring of synergy.

Now let's see how we can consciously create the environment for this kind of experience.

The Magic Theater

In Hermann Hesse's famous novel *Steppenwolf*, the main character, Harry, feels trapped in a stifling, 2-Alternative world. He chafes at the conventional life he is forced to lead, where all the thinking has been done, and longs for something more. One day he meets a mysterious musician who takes him to a secret room called the "Magic Theater." The sign on the door says, "For Madmen Only. Price of Admittance: Your Mind."

Inside the Magic Theater, within "an inexhaustible world of doors and magic mirrors," Harry sees infinitely refracted images, some joyful, others extravagant and dark. He envisions many possible lives for himself and feels an exhilarating sense of freedom: "The very air had a charm. The warmth embedded me and wafted me on." He talks about "losing the sense of time." He learns that every human being is a "manifold world, a constellated heaven, a chaos of forms, of states and stages, of inheritances and potentialities." Most of all, Harry learns how to laugh—at his own wild visions and those of others.[1]

The best environment for finding the 3rd Alternative is a "Magic Theater" where all possibilities are on the table, where everyone can contribute, and where no idea is out of bounds. It's a free-for-all. People lose their egotism and pride of authorship of their ideas because all ideas in this room are tentative. They can propose a solution one minute and turn around and propose exactly the opposite solution the next; nobody cares about being consistent.

Ralph Waldo Emerson said, "A foolish consistency is the hobgoblin of little minds." What he meant is that we shouldn't feel shackled to our ideas—why not dump them if we can think of better ones? In the Magic Theater you don't win any points for being consistent. No idea is final. All ideas are welcome, even—and perhaps especially—crazy ideas. After all, how many great inventions started out as somebody's crazy idea? So people laugh

---

1 Hermann Hesse, *Steppenwolf* (New York: Macmillan, 2002), 59, 164–65, 205.

a lot at each other and at themselves in the Magic Theater, which is just as it should be.

Entering the Magic Theater requires a temporary paradigm shift. We suspend judgment. We're not there to debate, critique, or finalize anything; all of that comes later. It's more play than work, more of a start than a finish, more proposing than resolving. It's a place for building models and knocking them down and starting over again. In the Magic Theater, as Hesse says, "A thousand possibilities await us."

Any place can be a Magic Theater, although some teams and organizations who really value creativity designate space for this kind of work. Wherever it's done, you get everyone together and follow these ground rules:

- Play at it. It's not "for real." Everybody knows it's a game.
- Avoid closure. Avoid agreement or consensus. Avoid the temptation to lock down a solution.
- Avoid judging others' ideas—or your own. Suggest whatever comes to mind; nobody's going to hold you to it. Don't just get out of the box—*leap* out of it.
- Make models. Draw pictures on whiteboards, sketch diagrams, build mockups, write rough drafts. Show what you think instead of telling it; play it out so everyone can see what you have in mind.
- Turn ideas on their heads. Reverse the conventional wisdom, no matter how upside-down it sounds: "What if we made roads out of rubber and tires out of cement?" (That question actually led to the development of rubberized asphalt. The rubber from old tires is mixed with asphalt to significantly cut road noise on highways.)
- Work fast. Set a time limit so the energy in the room stays high and creative thinking flows rapidly.
- Breed lots of ideas. Abundance is the theme. Thinking should thrive, bloom, and burgeon. Sketches should cover the walls. You can't predict which offhand insight might lead to a 3rd Alternative. If the Magic Theater doesn't look like a jungle of ideas when you've finished, you haven't been synergizing.

The Magic Theater sounds a little like brainstorming, which many people are familiar with. But I've found that most brainstorming sessions are too tame to produce anything new. We come up with a few halting ideas, choose one, adjourn, and think we've been creative. But we can't do this kind of work with the wrong paradigm—one that's judgmental, slow, self-defensive. It's the paradigm that matters. We have to be willing to live just for a while in a room "for madmen only."

All of this may be uncomfortable for you at first, but the more you experiment with these ground rules, the more eager you'll be to see what happens. You'll feel the way a creative artist feels because the 3rd Alternative is going to be strikingly original and distinctive. Most artists tell us that they don't know what their creation will be like until they create it. Said Max Weber, a pioneer modern painter, "In carrying on my own humble creative effort, I depend greatly upon that which I do not yet know, and upon that which I have not yet done."[1]

Now, of course, the Magic Theater is worldwide. Seeking the 3rd Alternative no longer depends on being face to face in the Magic Theater, not to mention in formal meetings. With social networking, devices like tablets and mobile phones, and wireless connections from Manhattan to Sydney, from remote Peruvian villages to the base camp on Mt. Everest, our ability to synergize with people worldwide has absolutely exploded. People are linking their minds virtually around our toughest challenges, sharing insights from personal and professional experience, data from actual research, their own innovative ideas. The online phenomenon is synergy on a cosmic scale.

Now you can throw out an important question and get the whole world to synergize with you. The beauty of online synergy is that you don't have to be present—it moves on without you. If the issue is real enough and you have the right community, your great question will create its own viral movement, spawning new ideas, unexpected insights, 3rd Alternatives—and more provocative questions. Even if you discover a good answer to your question, other people keep exploring it and it grows way beyond you.

You'll hear skeptics mock the Magic Theater. They can't tolerate it. They'll try to make you feel like a fool for suggesting it. Secretly, they're afraid of it; they think their dignity is in danger. But they are wrong. The best place to stimulate synergy is a laboratory, real or virtual, governed by the ground rules listed earlier. Only in such a laboratory could the Gates Foundation anti-malaria team come up with dodgy ideas like shooting down mosquitoes

1 Carl Rogers, *On Becoming a Person* (New York: Houghton Mifflin, 1995), 23.

with lasers. And who knows how many children will eventually owe their lives to that team? Albert Einstein was not joking when he said, "If at first the idea is not absurd, then there is no hope for it."

Most business leaders put a high premium on creativity. In a landmark survey conducted in 2010 for IBM, fifteen hundred CEOs in sixty nations and thirty-three industries singled out creativity as the "number one leadership competency of the future."[1] Every leader wants her people to be creative. But creativity, as Edward de Bono, a leader in the field, has said, cannot be "brought about by vague exhortation." It requires a "deliberate and practical procedure."[2] As you should be able to tell by now, the 3rd Alternative process looks simple and freewheeling, but it is not undisciplined. For business, 3rd Alternative thinking is clearly a best practice.

But this is not true only for business. For any group using the Magic Theater paradigm, creativity can explode. Defensive energy goes down and creative energy goes up. Carl Rogers confirms this:

> I have found that if I can help bring about a climate marked by genuineness, prizing, and understanding, then exciting things happen. Persons and groups in such a climate move away from rigidity and toward flexibility . . . away from being predictable toward an unpredictable creativity.[3]

Step 4: Arrive at Synergy

How do we know when we've arrived at a 3rd Alternative?

We know the 3rd Alternative by the excitement in the room. The sulking, the defensiveness, the reticence are all gone. A burst of creative dynamism accompanies a 3rd Alternative, and we recognize it when we feel it. We speak of "quantum leaps" in our understanding, of "peak experiences," of being "in the flow." The thrill of discovery is in the air, a childlike delight in seeing something precious that was just out of sight. We can't wait to tell people about what we've found. The author Bolivar J. Bueno reflects on the adven-

---

1 Austin Carr, "The Most Important Leadership Competency for CEOs? Creativity," *Fast Company*, May 18, 2010, http://www.fastcompany.com/1648943/creativity-the-most -important-leadership-quality-for-ceos-study.

2 Edward de Bono, *Lateral Thinking: Creativity Step by Step* (New York: HarperCollins, 1973), 7.

3 Rogers, *A Way of Being*, 43.

ture of synergy: "Children love to play hide and seek—there's joy in finding something that's hidden. As we grow up, that longing for surprise never really goes away. We like to discover hidden treasures—it's the stuff that we want to share with others."[1]

We know the 3rd Alternative when we are no longer interested in old fights and old assumptions. The new alternative overtakes and overwhelms us with its simplicity and elegance. We change our thinking fundamentally. The new alternative is not a compromise, whereby everyone gives up something to get an agreement while the resentment lingers. The 3rd Alternative transforms our relationships with old adversaries—we suddenly become partners in discovery instead of enemies on a battlefield.

We know the 3rd Alternative when we feel inspired by it. All at once we see clearly. We wonder why we never saw it before. When properly understood, synergy is the highest activity in all life—the true test and manifestation of our potential as individuals, families, teams, and organizations. I believe the lack of synergy is one of the great tragedies in life, because so much potential remains untapped, completely undeveloped and unused. Ineffective people live day after day with unused potential. They experience synergy only in small, peripheral ways in their lives. By contrast, synergy focuses our unique talents, insights, and diversity of perspectives on the toughest challenges. The results can be almost miraculous. We create new alternatives—answers that were never there before—that serve our greatest needs.

We know the 3rd Alternative because it works really well. It's not an incremental improvement, but a fundamental breakthrough, a quantum leap forward. Whole products, services, companies, and even industries erupt from it. It sprouts new sciences, technologies, and even cultures. It revolutionizes relationships. It can be unbelievably valuable to the people who come up with it, usually because it delights the rest of the world.

So how do we recognize the 3rd Alternative? It's the one that meets our criteria of success. It does the job that needs to be done. It embodies the outcome we all want. It changes the game. It enables everyone to win.

In short, the paradigm "I Synergize With You" takes us beyond war to peace—not just to an absence of conflict, but to a blossoming of new possibilities. It leverages differences instead of rejecting them. It includes an abundance mentality, the conviction that there is plenty of everything to be

---

1 Bolivar J. Bueno, *Why We Talk* (Kingston, NY: Creative Crayon Publishers, 2007), 109.

discovered and shared: solutions, prestige, profits, recognition, possibilities. The opposite of the attack paradigm, it is the paradigm of creativity.

It might be a little misleading to call the moment of synergy a "step" in the process of arriving at a 3rd Alternative. It might better be called a "stumble" or a "leap." It's startling and unpredictable, to say the least. And there are no guarantees that we'll arrive at all. But the rewards are so great that we keep working at it until we get there; we couldn't possibly settle for anything less.

Going for the 3rd Alternative in Your World

In this book you will get to know many people—ordinary people, workers, doctors, police officers, sales reps, artists, teachers, parents—in addition to business, education, and government leaders who have chosen not to settle for anything less than the 3rd Alternative. You'll see how many of them have gone beyond what looks like hopeless conflict to create a new future for themselves and the rest of us. Each story is an invitation to you to go for the 3rd Alternative in dealing with your own challenges and opportunities.

A caution: As I say, these stories can be enormously helpful. An individual or organization might for a season be a shining example of 3rd Alternatives, but then might stray and become a glaring nonexample. People have weaknesses and are not consistent in their principles. Visionary, synergistic leaders leave and people with very different paradigms take their places. Directions change. The point of these stories is not to hold up any particular person or organization but to illustrate the principle and process of synergy. Learn from success. Learn from failure. Keep your eye on the principle and you will soon grasp the transformative power of the 3rd Alternative in every important domain of your life:

The chapter "The 3rd Alternative at Work" is about discovering 3rd Alternative solutions in the workplace. You'll see how you can prosper in your work and your business as you become a synergistic partner with others.

"The 3rd Alternative at Home" is about having a positive, supportive, creative family in a world of conflicted families, where our most precious relationships are threatened.

"The 3rd Alternative at School" is about getting past the bickering over education and moving on to transform the lives of our children, to help them become 3rd Alternative thinkers who will in turn transform the future for all of us.

"The 3rd Alternative and the Law" is about changing our culture of litigation into a culture of understanding, empathy, and synergy, putting to better use the staggering energy and treasure we waste on fighting each other in court.

"The 3rd Alternative in Society" is about overcoming the disintegrating forces in our communities. It's about finding 3rd Alternatives for tough issues like crime, disease, environmental degradation, and poverty.

"The 3rd Alternative in the World" is about rising above the wearisome, worsening quarrels that threaten to tear our world apart. You'll meet some remarkable people who have taken on the incomparable role of peacemaker—the highest expression of synergy.

The final chapter "A 3rd Alternative Life" is about "living in crescendo." To me, this means that my most exciting synergistic experiences await me, that my most important contribution is always ahead of me. I'll get quite personal with you. I am approaching my eightieth year and could easily retire, but I don't plan to retire to a life of leisure. Rather, I see my life becoming more and more meaningful.

In the end, the search for the 3rd Alternative is our greatest opportunity to change our mind-set and stop the unproductive wrangling that takes us nowhere, to open our minds and listen to each other and rejoice at the new lives we can create for ourselves. What else but 3rd Alternative thinking can ever produce the striking new solutions we so desperately need for our toughest challenges? Our highly politicized, conflict-ridden way of thinking has so far failed to relieve the world of poverty, disease, and slavery of so many kinds. The 3rd Alternative is not just a "best practice"—it is a moral imperative.

TEACH TO LEARN

The best way to learn from this book is to teach it to someone else. Everybody knows that the teacher learns far more than the student. So find someone—a co-worker, a friend, a family member—and teach him or her the insights you've gained. Ask the provocative questions here or come up with your own.

- Define the principle of synergy. What does nature teach us about the power of synergy? Why is synergy fundamentally important to both your personal and professional growth?
- What are the limitations of 2-Alternative thinking? In what ways does it keep us from finding solutions to hard problems?
- Explain the concept of the 3rd Alternative. Describe instances in your life or the lives of others when you've seen people reach a genuine 3rd Alternative.
- Describe how our mental paradigms govern our behavior and the results we get in life.
- Why do people find their way to the "Great Middle"? How does 2-Alternative thinking lead to skepticism and cynicism?
- Explain the paradigms of 3rd Alternative thinking: I See Myself, I See You, I Seek You Out, I Synergize With You. Why must they be in this sequence?
- What is "the real identity theft"?
- Define the spirit of *Ubuntu*. How does it differ from stereotyping? What does the story of Nelson Mandela's prison guard teach us about overcoming the obstacles to synergy?
- Explain the rules of Talking Stick communication. How does it lead us to synergy?
- Try using Talking Stick communication with a person you need to understand better—a friend, a co-worker, or a family member. How does it work for you?
- What is the 3rd Alternative Question? Explain the steps of the 3rd Alternative process.

- What is the Magic Theater? How do the rules of the Magic Theater help us arrive at synergy?

TRY IT

On the follow pages, you'll find a "4 Steps to Synergy" planning tool and a user guide for the tool. Use this tool to experiment with creating 3rd Alternatives for the following scenarios, or come up with your own.

- The neighbors want to build an outdoor shed on their property that will block your view of a beautiful pine forest.
- Your spouse/partner has been offered an enviable new job with a rapidly expanding company, but it requires a move to a different city. You don't really want to move and leave your own job and friends.
- You have a serious ongoing disagreement with a school or teacher whose methods and approach you don't approve of.
- You love your job at a small company that might be forced to let you and your co-workers go because of a lack of business.

4 STEPS TO **SYNERGY**

1 Ask the 3rd Alternative Question:

"Are you willing to go for a solution that is better than any of us have come up with yet?" If yes, go on to step 2.

2 Define Criteria of Success

List in this space the characteristics of a solution that would delight everyone. What does success look like? What is the real job to be done? What would be a "win-win" for all concerned?

3 Create 3rd Alternatives

In this space (or other spaces) create models, draw pictures, borrow ideas, turn your thinking upside down. Work quickly and creatively. Suspend all judgment until that exciting moment when you know you've arrived at synergy.

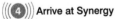 4 Arrive at Synergy

Describe here your 3rd Alternative and, if you want, how you intend to put it into practice.

USER GUIDE TO THE 4 STEPS TO SYNERGY TOOL

> **The 4 Steps to Synergy.** This process helps you put the synergy principle to work. (1) Show willingness to find a 3rd Alternative. (2) Define what success looks like to everyone. (3) Experiment with solutions until you (4) arrive at synergy. Listen empathically to others throughout the process.

How to Get to Synergy

1 Ask the 3rd Alternative Question

In a conflict or creative situation, this question helps everyone move past firm positions or preconceived ideas toward developing a third position.

2 Define Criteria of Success

List characteristics or write a paragraph describing what a successful outcome would look like to everyone. Answer these questions as you go:

- Is everyone involved in setting the criteria? Are we getting as many ideas from as many people as possible?
- What outcomes do we really want? What is the real job to be done?
- What outcomes would be "wins" for everyone?
- Are we looking past our entrenched demands to something better?

3 Create 3rd Alternative

Follow these guidelines:

- Play at it. It's not "for real." Everybody knows it's a game.
- Avoid closure, premature agreement, or consensus.
- Avoid judging others' ideas—or your own.
- Make models. Draw pictures on whiteboards, sketch diagrams, build mockups, write rough drafts.
- Turn ideas on their heads. Reverse the conventional wisdom.
- Work fast. Set a time limit to keep energy and ideas flowing rapidly.
- Breed lots of ideas. You can't predict which offhand insight might lead to a 3rd Alternative.

((4)) Arrive at Synergy

You recognize the 3rd Alternative by the sense of excitement and inspiration in the room. The old conflict is abandoned. The new alternative meets the criteria of success. Caution: Avoid mistaking compromise for synergy. Compromise breeds satisfaction but not delight. Compromise means everyone loses something; synergy means everyone wins.

The 3rd Alternative at Work

3

The 3rd Alternative at Work

A man will be imprisoned in a room with a door that's unlocked and opens inwards, as long as it does not occur to him to pull rather than push.
—*Ludwig Wittgenstein*

We live in a time when walls are falling. We are seeing the rise of the borderless economy. With technology, we are seeing the end of the artificial walls that imprison the human mind. But the most challenging walls remain: the walls between people. These walls are mostly invisible, but they form barriers to trust, communication, and creativity. In today's workplace, we simply can't afford these walls. Imagine the incalculable cost to people and organizations when sales and marketing don't get along, when there is mistrust between labor and management, or when people feel they can't be open and honest, resulting in office politics, backbiting, and micromanaging.

The key to tearing down these walls is the internal strength to think "we," not "me." When we listen to understand, when we deeply believe in 3rd Alternatives—that there is truly something better just waiting to be created—marvelous things can happen. They can happen in your organization. They can happen in any relationship.

Everyone knows that the workplace is full of walls. There are walls between teams, departments, divisions, and functions. There are walls between the creative types and the accounting types. There are walls between the executives and the workers. There are walls between the organization and its customers. It's only natural to want to defend our walls, and that's why we have conflict in the workplace. The defensive 2-Alternative mind-set is the problem.

Viewed more positively, an organization is full of conflict because it has a job to do, and every creative, thoughtful, talented, exceptional human being in the organization has different insights into how to do that job. Those insights are contradictory, baffling, quirky, and inconsistent; they can also be useful or even brilliant.

Some organizations tolerate conflict better than others; some are conflict-averse; some are downright abusive. But most try to "manage" conflict. Managers take courses on how to avert and control and resolve conflict because we live by the premise that conflict is to be avoided if possible, controlled if unavoidable, and resolved quickly so that harmony can reign again. Books on conflict resolution treat it like a passing storm that you hope to get through with as little damage as possible.

But the problem with conflict in the workplace is not that it exists, but that we have the wrong paradigm about it. The 2-Alternative response to conflict is "fight or flight," while the synergistic response is welcome, delight, engagement, discovery. For example:

- An employee speaks to the boss about some "stupid thing" the company's been doing. What a typical boss hears is called "a complaint." What a synergistic boss hears is called "an idea."
- A team member says to a project manager, "Suppose we did this thing a little differently?" What the typical project manager thinks is "She is trying to tell me how to do my job." What the synergistic project manager thinks is "I need to listen to her."
- A worker says to his team leader, "I just can't work with so-and-so." What the typical team leader thinks is "Here we go again with the personality conflicts." What the synergistic team leader thinks is "Here's a cry for help."
- A guy from corporate headquarters shows up and says, "I'm here to help you." A typical mental response? "Great, they don't think I can do this job. Well, I'll teach this guy a lesson." The synergistic mental response? "Great, what can I learn from this guy?"

These typical responses are rooted in the paradigm that sees difference as a threat. Usually, we either fight over our differences or flee from them because we have a defensive paradigm born of insecurity. We see it in the CEO who smooths over disagreements in meetings. We see it in the project team that walks out of the room in outrage when their plans are questioned. We see it in the petulant sales manager who runs the region by the philosophy "my way or the highway."

Such people can't see that conflict is a sign of life. Conflicts usually arise when people are actually *thinking* about their work. When I talk about the "gift of conflict," people look sideways at me, but what I mean is that thoughtful people will *always* differ from each other—and that if they care enough to express their differences with passion, that's an offering that ought to be accepted eagerly.

One of the most effective business leaders I know often starts meetings with a provocative question: "What if we could change the product line tomorrow?" "What if the problem we're in business to solve doesn't even exist?" "What one thing, if we did it better, would change everything?" "How is our company like Enron?" "What am I in denial about?" His purpose is to provoke conflict—not dry lightning, but disputes with juice that energize the minds of his team. His meeting room becomes a Magic Theater. Because his team is used to this, they've become very good at productive conflict. "I don't want people sitting around me nodding sagely when I speak," he says. "I want to see heads going back and forth, not up and down. I want to hear people *think*. I want to see sparks." And then he listens intensely. He can wear you out just by listening to you.

The 2 Alternatives: Fight or Flight

Contrast this 3rd Alternative leader with 2-Alternative leaders. They either fight or flee.

The first example is of a leader who fights. An accomplished executive took over as CEO of one of the largest media firms in the world. By many accounts, he was not a listener and marginalized those who didn't agree with him. Employees of the company felt demeaned, reporting that they were constantly told how stupid they were. Apparently he was good at picking fights. His style was to stay on the offensive all the time. After six months, he was fired. Everyone knew he was smart, but his intellect could not make up for the absence of respect and empathy.

Now consider this example of a leader who flees. He's the president of a well-known household-goods company. My colleague who worked closely with this president for a while has this to say about him:

> *He came in making grand pronouncements about growing the company, but after ten years, the share price hasn't budged. He still makes grand pronouncements about his vision for the future. Now no one listens. Not just because of the lack of performance, but also because he doesn't listen to anyone else. He is, as they say, "conflict-averse." Disagreements are frowned on. He doesn't like confrontations—"Not my style," he says. He's a great guy and a terrific friend, but no one can ask hard questions in his presence. They sit at his feet and listen to him think aloud about his grand vision for growing the company, mostly the latest and greatest strategic notions from the last business book he's read. But there are no sparks. Meanwhile, I sit there not daring to ask the question on my mind: "Why don't we just make better products?"*

Some theorists of conflict resolution advise us to separate the *issue* at conflict from the *emotion* of conflict. I don't believe this is possible. At the foods company, the issue about product quality *cannot* be extracted from the emotions of the president. With this man, to question his approach to the business is to question his identity and self-worth. He is not sufficiently self-aware to listen empathically to his team members.

Issue-driven conflicts are almost always emotional conflicts too. Unfortunately, most companies are so trapped in Industrial Age thinking that it still takes a lot of courage for workers to question their supervisors. They're afraid. Will they be ignored? Will they look stupid? Will they unintentionally make the boss look stupid? Will they get slapped down, figuratively or even literally? Will they make an enemy of the boss? Will they lose their jobs? If the emotional investment is too risky, a fearful silence reigns. Business leaders often mistake the smiling, nodding faces around them for harmony and consensus. This can be a fatal error.

All conflict is laden with emotion. What you might think of as a simple conflict over salary, for example, is actually tied up with deep fears and aspirations. Suppose you are a woman, a supervisor, and a male worker comes

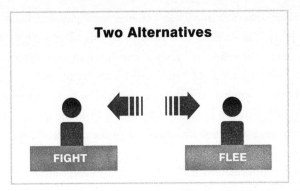

to you unhappy about his pay. You may well be facing a person simmering with conflicted emotions. His salary is a symbol of his self-worth, of his standing with his family and friends. This meeting is very hard for him—it's taken courage just to be here. He doesn't want to cause trouble or look weak in your eyes; on the other hand he might feel slighted or even angry. To complicate things, his male ego is probably involved. You won't see his whole story in his face or hear it in his words—just know that there *is* a story.

If you're a 2 Alternative supervisor, you have only two options: fight or flight. If you choose flight, you surrender and give him what he wants. Conflict theorists call this "accommodation," and it usually just creates more problems. If you choose flight you're being unfair to the other workers, you've created a bad precedent, and you've raised this worker's expectations for the next salary talk.

Or you can choose to fight. There are various ways:

- You can minimize him: "You're getting paid the same as everybody else." This answer turns him into a machine: he's a worker unit just like all the other worker units.
- You can butter him up: "You're such a valued employee and we wish so much we could do more." This answer might reduce the tension a bit, but it's the kind of phony blather that in most languages is usually characterized by an expletive.
- You can compete with him: "I've never had to ask for a raise. They come my way because I'm a team player." In this condescending battle of the biographies, you will win not because your story is more compelling but because you have more power.

- You can compromise: "I can't change your pay, but I can let you leave a half-hour early on Fridays." In this kind of fight, both of you lose. The employer loses a half-hour of the employee's services, and the employee never gets what he needs. Compromise is always a pinched and narrow thing. The assumption is there's only so much pie on the table, and if you get more, I get less. Compromise is the polite outcome of scarcity thinking.

If he gets emotional, you can follow the typical advice and tell him, "Let's just stick to the issue," which does nothing to resolve the emotion. As much as you'd like to, you can't just "stick to the issue." Oh, you can reach a modus vivendi, but the emotions involved are nonnegotiable. A reckoning will come.

The 3rd Alternative: Synergy

If you're a 3rd Alternative supervisor, you'll neither flee nor fight. You'll look for something better, a solution that will provide your employee with a huge emotional payoff and create for the firm new and significant value.

A friend of mine explained how a 3rd Alternative leader dealt with exactly this situation in his life:

I was new at the job and had come in hoping for a better salary. I settled for something a lot less than I'd hoped for just to get in the door. But after a couple of months, it was clear that my family was struggling. We couldn't get by because of some medical expenses. Besides that, I felt more and more that I was getting paid too little for the work I was doing. So I took a real risk and went to talk to the big boss about a raise. I didn't know her very well and she didn't know me. I had no real track record yet with that company.

But she invited me into her office and I explained why I was there. I was kind of surprised when she said, "Tell me more." I told her about my family situation. She just listened, and I talked quite a lot about what I'd been doing for the firm. She asked me what I thought about the company, its customers, its products. It was odd. We had this long conversation that I thought was going to be about my pay, but instead it was about me—

how I was doing, what I thought, what I'd learned in my few months at the company.

Then she asked me about a certain customer I'd been working with. She wanted to know my ideas for expanding our business with that client, and I actually did have some thoughts that I shared.

A couple days later, she invited me back into her office. Three or four other people joined us, and she had put up on a whiteboard my ideas for this client. We had quite the discussion, and a lot more discussions after that. I was excited. Finally, they offered me an expanded job with higher pay and responsibility for a new level of service to this important client.

For my friend, these discussions were just the beginning of a swift rise in that company; he eventually became a partner to the "big boss."

I've rarely heard of a wiser leader than this woman. She had a fine capacity for 3rd Alternative thinking. How easy it would have been for her either to fight my friend off or just to give in to his request. Instead, she sensed the possibility of a dramatic win-win. Rather than haggling over the existing pie, she could envision the prospect of a much bigger pie. She suspected that combining my friend's needs and energies with the client's needs might well produce growth for everyone. The eventual result was a whole new line of business and a partner who increased his worth to the company every year. From what I know of this young man's contribution to his firm, he was ultimately responsible for doubling its size.

Consider how this woman led her team to a 3rd Alternative:

- First, she took time to listen empathically. She wanted to understand her young employee's issue and his feelings about it. On the face of it, she wanted to know why his salary bothered him. But more deeply, she wanted to grasp what he was all about and what he could bring to the company that would pay off for everyone, not just for him.
- Then she sought him out. She brought him back again and again, explored his thinking and involved other thinkers. She valued his distinctive gifts and insights.
- Finally, the group arrived at synergy: new services, new products, new ways of meeting the needs of an important client, and beyond that the needs of a new segment of clients.

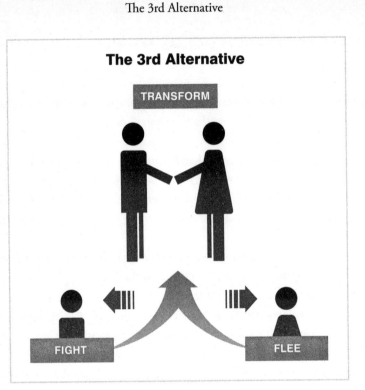

All of this came about because the boss has the *habit* of reaching for the 3rd Alternative whenever the opportunity arises. An employee comes in with a complaint and she sees a chance to build her business. She sees conflict as fertile ground instead of battleground.

Most thinkers about conflict resolution treat a conflict as a transaction. It's about dividing up the pie. You can either accommodate or confront your opponent. You can give away the pie or you can fight over it, and there are techniques and tricks to gain an advantage. But divide it as you will—in the end, it's the same pie.

By contrast, the 3rd Alternative is to *transform* the situation. It's about making a new pie that's bigger and better—perhaps exponentially bigger and better. Where most conflict resolution is transactional, the 3rd Alternative is transformational.

If I find myself caught up in a conflict at work, I mustn't fall automatically into the defensive mind-set. This is crucial, but it's also highly counter-intuitive. The natural, unthinking response to a challenge is to fight or flee.

This is what animals do out of instinct; they have only the 2 Alternatives. But mature human beings can choose a 3rd Alternative.

Remember the first paradigm of synergy: "I See *Myself*." I have the power to stand outside myself and think about my own thoughts and feelings. I can examine my own motives: "Why am I caught up in this? Am I being egocentric? Do I need attention or affirmation? Do I feel my status is being threatened? Or am I genuinely concerned about this issue?" If I am already sure of my own self-worth, if I already feel confident about my own contribution and capability, I don't need to defend myself against you. I can express myself candidly to you.

But I also need to remember the second paradigm of synergy: "I See *You*." That means I have profound respect for you. I value your ideas, your experience, your perspective, and your feelings.

Therefore, I practice the third paradigm of synergy: "I Seek You Out." I am fascinated—not threatened—by the gap between us. Nothing defuses the negative energy of a conflict faster than to say, "You see things differently. I need to listen to you." And mean it.

If you practice these paradigms, you'll inevitably arrive at a 3rd Alternative that makes the conflict irrelevant: "Let's look for something better than either of us has thought of." Everybody wins, everybody is energized. Often you won't even remember what the fight was about.

Hubris: The Great Barrier to Synergy

The synergy mentality short-circuits conflict in the workplace, and the resulting spark of genius can be dazzling. But synergy does not come cheap, and the forces working against it are formidable. The toughest barrier to synergy is *pride*. It's the great insulator that prevents the creative blending of human energies. There is a whole continuum of pride, from the familiar "NIH Syndrome" ("If it's Not Invented Here, it can't be worth anything") all the way to the hubris that leads to the downfall of people, organizations, and nations.

The ancient Greeks taught that *hubris*, or extreme arrogance, was the worst of crimes. In those days, a soldier who boasted of his own strength and humiliated his enemies was guilty of hubris. So was a king who abused his subjects for his personal gain. The Greeks believed that hubris would bring on *nemesis*, or inevitable ruin. Hubris, they said, always leads to tragedy in the end—and they were right. Today we've seen the collapse of some of our most trusted institutions because of hubris at the highest levels. In the financial debacle of 2008, many key leaders were guilty of everything from blind overconfidence to outright fraud.

The main symptom of hubris is a lack of conflict. If no one dares to challenge you, if you receive little input from others, if you find yourself talking more than listening, if you're too busy to deal with those who disagree, then you're heading for a fall. An example is the former head of the Royal Bank of Scotland. According to reports, this man "brooked no criticism. . . . Every morning his immediate circle took part in a meeting where on occasions executives could be reprimanded seriously." He referred to his unfriendly acquisitions as "mercy killings." The *Times* of London called his leadership "hubristic." Thus he was isolated from the truth about the oncoming banking crisis, for which his aggressively risky business dealings were said to be partly responsible. In 2007 his bank was worth £75 billion; by 2009 it was worth £4.5 billion and had suffered "the biggest loss in British banking history."[1]

Looking at another example, it's probable that the anti-synergy mind-set at Enron brought that company down. Observers see in Enron the classic model of a hubristic culture: "This was a company that purposely shut down alternative and conflicting views of reality to protect the status quo. In the name of preserving success and being in hard-nosed pursuit of greatness, an inflexible, intolerant culture developed in which new ideas were ignored, concerns were dismissed, and critical thinking got you fired."[2]

The "GET"

Of course, you don't have to be a top corporate leader to suffer from the kind of hubris that prevents synergy. Anyone can be guilty. Most of the un-

---

1 Patrick Hosking, "Hubris to Nemesis: How Sir Fred Goodwin Became the 'World's Worst Banker,'" *Times* (London), January 20, 2009, http://business.timesonline.co.uk/tol/business/economics/articl e5549510.ece.

2 Sydney Finkelstein, *Why Smart Executives Fail* (New York: Penguin, 2004), 268.

The "GET"	
G	G is for GAIN, my personal gain, what I've earned, what is due to me.
E	E is for EMOTION, my feelings, my insecurities, my fears, my identity.
T	T is for TERRITORY, my turf, my headcount, my budget, my project, my expertise.

productive wrangling that goes on in the workplace is due to hubris at some level. Greg Neal, one of the top sales executives in the global pharmaceutical industry and a sharp observer, has broken down this plague of pride into three elements he calls "the GET" (illustrated in the chart above). These are natural human instincts we all share, and too often they keep us from going for the 3rd Alternative. We worry about losing the fight. We worry about our identity ("Am I a loser?"). We worry about our territory ("Who's going to get credit?"). Neal says, "The GET will get you when you're trying to go for synergy." Ironically, if we can go on to synergy together, there is more gain, more security, and more influence for everyone. But it's hard to see past the GET.

A classic workplace conflict is the eternal feud between the sales and marketing departments. It's "universal and persistent," some say, just "part of the natural order of things." *Business Week* observes that "marketers routinely dismiss sales people as greedy and egotistical. And sales people, well, they're a little more blunt. They think marketers are fluffy and dumb."[1] And yet sales and marketing have essentially the same mission: to understand, reach, and satisfy customers. Companies try hard to bring the two functions together through shared information systems and processes. But as *Business Week* says, "The real problem is one of culture and personalities and attitudes." Benson Shapiro, a professor of business at Harvard, generalizes this way: "The field force is made up of more independent, free-spirited people who idealize a 'fighter pilot' mentality. Marketing is more 'buttoned down' and idealizes

---

1 Christopher Kenton, "When Sales Meets Marketing," *Business Week*, February 19, 2004, http://www.businessweek.com/smallbiz/content/feb2004/sb20040219_0464.htm.

a more sophisticated, centralized approach." And they look down on each other.[1]

That was the problem Greg Neal faced as an executive of a large pharmaceutical company. "We had a powerful marketing organization and a very effective and conscientious sales force. But there was a large gap between them—everything from basic communication to the power struggle over ownership of the brand. Marketing thought their research enabled them to be experts on the customer, while sales lived with the customer day and night." The gap was actually causing his company to lose market share.

Neal was assigned to close this gap. Company leaders asked him to create a new department "to pull it together." He hired his integration team, got a vision, and got excited about it. Soon he learned how big and complicated the gap really was. "We were very siloed. The cardiovascular marketing team didn't talk to the respiratory or the neurology or the osteoporosis group." He also learned how unwelcome he was. "I ran headlong into the GET—it was very emotional, very territorial. I would just drop on their doorstep, go through some pretty nice PowerPoint slides, and there was just silence. It was not the silence of appreciation."

After a few months of little progress, Neal slowly realized that he had started wrong. The people he worked with were not emotionally ready for synergy. "What should have happened? The executives over sales should've gotten with their counterparts on the marketing side. They could have gone out and talked with the regions, elicited their views on the problem. 'What could we do to tighten up this gap, make your job easier, communicate better?' Get opinions from everyone. Instead of doing that, they imposed a solution: my integration team."

But it wasn't too late to do it right. He stopped giving presentations and started listening. "We needed buy-in across the field, as far down as the opportunity and the patience of the organization would go. The idea was to give them a voice in the process and see what bubbles up. We spent enormous amounts of time getting buy-in." He devoted nine months to this "trial by fire."

A crucial product launch was coming up in the respiratory field. Neal's

1 Benson P. Shapiro, "Want a Happy Customer? Coordinate Sales and Marketing," *Harvard Business School Working Knowledge*, October 28, 2002. http://hbswk.hbs.edu/item/3154 .html.

company had never been in this market before, and it had to go well. A previous launch in the lipid market had gone poorly because of the "Great Gap" between sales and marketing. National marketing plans had been executed very unevenly across the sales regions. "We'd had pockets of extraordinary execution, other pockets of moderate success, others of low success"—a real frustration for the marketing people.

In preparing the new launch plan, Neal's integration team carefully listened to every sales region. "Their input was there. The synergies were there. We decided together what success would look like—call activity measures, resource utilization, market-share numbers. We were more prepared than ever before, more unified, and I crossed my fingers that we would have a good launch."

It was the most successful product launch in the history of the firm—and in a market they had never participated in before. Up against companies with decades of experience, they gobbled market share. "We exceeded our objective by 30 percent. Variances between regions were much smaller than before. Product adoption rate was much greater than historically." Today the company's portfolio of respiratory products is worth hundreds of millions of dollars.

Greg Neal's success came because he dived headlong into the GET, the defensive mind-set that straitjacketed a silo-bound company. He charged into the firm's numerous fiefdoms with respect and empathy and the constant question, "What can we do together to make your job easier?" As a 3rd Alternative thinker, he went in without any preconceived solution in mind, just a determination to overcome the GET and make synergy happen.[1]

When It Gets Personal

Today's workplace is intensely challenging. We are pressed to do more with less, compete globally, and meet ever-rising expectations against shrinking deadlines. In a fast-moving environment, friction develops, and sometimes it gets personal. Shunning, sulking, sarcasm, shouting matches—occasionally even violence—can blow up in such a supercharged atmosphere.

Dozens of books and websites will tell you how to "resolve" a personal-

---

1 Interview with Greg Neal, October 7, 2010.

ity conflict at work (it's a common problem). They all say pretty much the same thing. If you're a manager, try separating the foes or mediating between them or sending them to a class. If you're involved in the conflict, remain calm, separate the issue from the person, withdraw from the situation. None of this is bad advice. But it isn't transformational. It's transactional. It's about transacting your way through an issue, when the real problem is the relationship.

If you have the synergy mentality, you're looking to *transform* the relationship. You know your own worth, and you see deeply into the worth of the other person. Find a private place and sit down with her and say, "You see things differently. I need to listen to you." And then listen.

You might have to listen to some outrageous things. You might feel your own face reddening as the other person vents at you. But let it come. Don't give in to the temptation to defend yourself—your chance will come later. You're there to understand, not to fight.

You'll likely discover that the issue is not the issue. Whatever has touched off the conflict is probably only the surface of a deeply submerged problem with the GET. The employee's identity, emotional security, or territory is at stake. It can be really difficult to empty your mind and move into the other person's mind, to understand what it's like to be that person—and this may be the greatest test of your ability to synergize.

Some or all of what you hear might be rubbish. On the other hand, you might learn a few things about yourself. You might have your eyes opened. You'll undoubtedly grasp more clearly a perspective that wasn't visible to you before. None of this can hurt you or impinge on your own self-worth—not if you're a truly synergistic person—and it might help you by broadening your own views.

A friend of mine, a successful business consultant, tells this story:

I'd been in the consulting business for several years and was getting pretty good at it. One of my colleagues (I'll call him Sid) was an older man, short, balding, liked to wear outdoorsy clothes while the rest of us were buttoned down.

I figured he resented my rise in the company because in meetings he would snicker at the things I said. Although he didn't come right out and say it, his comments implied that I was young and naïve and "had a lot to learn." But from the accounts I heard of his work, some of his clients weren't too happy with him.

Well, one day I'd had it with Sid. I blew up at him and called him a dried-up, desiccated old man who had lost his touch. The next day I got a curt letter from him refuting what I had said. I tried to laugh it off. For nearly two years, Sid and I avoided each other.

Then one day we were assigned to travel to Washington, D.C., and work together for a client. I was uncomfortable, but he and I were the only ones with the expertise to do this particular job. I sat down next to him for a four-hour airplane ride. He gave me a cold stare. Not knowing how to handle this, I just said to him, "We haven't talked for a long time, Sid. Tell me about yourself." And gradually, he started to talk.

Several hours later, my whole perspective was altered—not just about Sid himself, but about the entire consulting business. Over the years, he had become a student of "root-cause analysis," the science of finding and correcting the root causes of business problems. He had enormous knowledge of this area and expressed his frustration that none of his colleagues took it as seriously as he did.

When, years before, he had indicated I had a lot to learn, he was right. I did have a lot to learn. For the next three days, while tutoring our client, he also tutored me in a field I had known little about and radically changed my ideas about how to do my work.

Each evening after work we would jog around the hotel, and Sid opened up to me about the disappointments he had faced in our company, how his specialized knowledge wasn't valued. He explained why some clients were turned off by him—he had an annoying habit of telling them the truth. He also told me how much my outburst had hurt him, and I grieved over it.

I also learned about his life, about a tough childhood and a bewildering divorce. I learned how hard he had worked to become an educated person, not just about business but also about art and literature. I learned about the discipline he applied to everything he did, including golf and skiing and fly-fishing.

My three days in Washington just listening to Sid—that was a turning point for me. My own consulting practice was transformed by the insights I gained into problem solving, and I became hugely more effective at my work. Of course, I didn't adopt everything Sid taught me; I thought he was too brusque with clients. But even that was sort of endearing. Most important, I gained a cherished friend and adviser whose influence on my life has been profound.

The formidable walls between Sid and my friend came down because one of them was willing to sit back and listen to the other one's story. It took days, but the return on that investment was a transformed business practice and an enduring friendship. In later years, they together engineered creative solutions for all kinds of tricky client problems.

When we feel unjustly dealt with, it's very easy to become preoccupied with the injustice. Often we deny any responsibility for the conflict: it's all the other person's fault. It can eat away at us, making us more defensive and resentful, and the cycle of conflict intensifies until our work starts to suffer.

We can take a different path. We can choose to really listen to the needs and concerns of the person we are in conflict with. If we really seek to understand, without hypocrisy and without guile, we will be stunned at the pure knowledge and understanding that flows from another human being, as my friend experienced with Sid. He didn't even find it necessary to talk in order to empathize. In fact, sometimes words just get in the way.

Now, there are people who won't accept empathy from others. They can become emotionally or even physically abusive, and of course no one should tolerate abuse. But most personality conflicts at work don't rise to that level. Usually walls go up over perceived slights, territorial issues, personality clashes—all the elements of the GET.

In the latest books on managing conflict in the workplace, you will see hundreds of references to mediation, negotiation, and compromise—but not a single reference to synergy. Those books are all about the transactional approach, the superficial techniques for getting through a conflict and restoring equilibrium. But they say little about the transforming of relationships.

The danger of the transactional approach to conflict is that the emotional damage remains. People can settle, shake hands, and get back to work, but if there's no structural change to the relationship, submerged feelings continue to rankle.

The transactional approach to conflict is all about "me": "How do I get what I want with the least possible damage?" The transformational approach to conflict is all about "we": "How do we create something amazing together?"

You can do this by yourself. If you're in an argument, stop arguing and start listening. If you feel the overwhelming need to be "right," postpone that for a while and just listen. And if you're caught in a 2-Alternative trap, ask the other person, "Are you willing to look for an alternative that's better than either one of us has thought of before?"

Beyond Win-Win: Synergy in Sales and Negotiations

The traditional salesperson is gradually disappearing. There are many reasons why. One major factor is the internet, which does away with the intermediary in many billions of transactions that used to be done face to face.[1] However, salespeople are fading away even in the business-to-business world, where personal contact between seller and buyer has always been the norm. I believe the main reason is that the old notion of a "seller" is becoming obsolete.

Why? Because selling as a profession has never really moved beyond the 2-Alternative "us against them" mentality. Of course, there are many fine exceptions, but the classic motive behind professional sales is "the numbers": revenue trumps everything else. Please don't misunderstand me. Profits are essential, and if there is no margin, there's no mission either. But if a salesperson's heart is set on the numbers and not on serving the client, he will ultimately fail at both. The principle is clear and unshakable: The key to life is not accumulation but contribution—not building up material goods but service to others.

The most primitive kind of selling or negotiation is haggling, the zero-sum game of win-lose or lose-win. It consists of each side trying to get the advantage of the other. These salespeople brag about being "hunters" and "going for the kill." Then there are the many different varieties of "consultative selling," in which salespeople try to create a win-win outcome that satisfies both sides. Win-win selling is a definite improvement over haggling.

I believe the win-win mentality is fundamental not just to business, but to all of life's relationships. It's the ticket to entry into any human being's heart. Without a win-win mentality there is no trust, no confidence, no

---

1 See James Ledbetter, "The Death of a Salesman: Of Lots of Them, Actually," *Slate,* September 21, 2010.

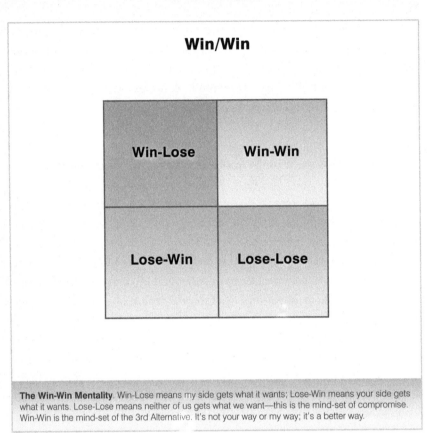

The Win-Win Mentality. Win-Lose means my side gets what it wants; Lose-Win means your side gets what it wants. Lose-Lose means neither of us gets what we want—this is the mind-set of compromise. Win-Win is the mind-set of the 3rd Alternative. It's not your way or my way; it's a better way.

moving forward together. I believe most business people understand that, and it's been gratifying to me over the years to see how the concept of win-win thinking has spread around the globe. I've tried to do my part in making that happen.[1]

Still, one reason sales as a profession has declined is that win-win thinking is not as widespread or as deep as it should be. Professor Horacio Falcao believes that the win-lose paradigm is still the "default setting" for most: "Win-win many times is considered soft and that's a big misconception. Win-win can come across as naïve because some people might misidentify it or wrongly identify it as 'soft.' However, win-win is supposed to be positive, not naïve, and that's a very important distinction."[2]

---

1 See *The 7 Habits of Highly Effective People,* Habit 4: Think Win-Win.
2 Falcao, "Negotiating to Win," *INSEAD Knowledge*, April 16, 2010. http://knowledge .insead.edu/strategy-value-negotiation-100419.cfm?vid =404.

At the same time, win-win thinking is not the end but the beginning of any productive relationship. Likewise, in the world of business, win-win thinking is the beginning, not the end, of synergy. A win-win deal is not necessarily the best deal. Win-win means that both parties have not lost anything, are satisfied, and feel good about the outcome, and there's nothing wrong with that. But synergistic minds can do much better. There is no limit to the value they can create together.

In the old haggling days, people bought cars from dealers they rarely trusted and just hoped they wouldn't get cheated. The stereotype of the low-life car dealer was an old joke. In time, most car dealers became far more sophisticated and transparent and genuinely tried to give customers good deals.

Then there's that rare synergist who is constantly seeking 3rd Alternatives to provide value to his customers. For most people who own cars, losing money on them is inescapable. The value of an automobile drops steeply until, after a few years, the owner's investment dries up. This is the great frustration of car ownership. Realizing this, one car dealer I know has found amazing ways to help his clients preserve the investment they make with him. Every year, most of them buy new cars from him for just a few hundred dollars over cost. He then helps them sell the car during the next model year for roughly the price they paid for it. As a result, his clients always drive a new car and lose little or no money on the transaction—year after year! He does research to make sure he offers clients only cars with the highest resale values. Although he makes only a small profit on each vehicle, his high volume of sales makes him wildly successful. "I'd rather sell a hundred and fifty cars a month at five hundred dollars than twenty-five at eighteen hundred dollars," he says. Because all his cars are new and rarely need repair, he has no service department and thus no overhead except for a small show lot. And he has an utterly loyal clientele.

This car dealer's 3rd Alternative for doing business eliminates the need for a time-consuming sales and negotiation process. He simply doesn't have to do those things. He has to turn business away because he's so popular. In his determination to save his customers from losing money, he saves himself tremendous amounts of time and stress, and the business just flows to him.

Buyers used to have to do business with salespeople. Only through them could buyers get the products, services, or information they wanted. Quite often buyers resented salespeople and their mind games. Today buyers can get much of what they want from the internet, so even a win-win–minded salesperson is unnecessary. Still, the one thing you cannot get from the internet is *synergy*, the help that comes from a creative human being like this car dealer—a person who genuinely has your interests at heart.

My friend Mahan Khalsa, a true proficient in the world of negotiation, says, "Selling means doing something *to* somebody rather than *for* or *with* somebody. Sales has become a fear-based relationship. Customers fear they will be 'sold' a bill of goods, and salespeople fear failure." No one likes to be "sold."

I suggest that this concept of sales is dying. It should be replaced with the concept of synergistic partnership. In our company, we have "client partners" whose job is to find synergy with our customers, to help them create 3rd Alternatives that provide competitive advantage. Their task is to help our clients succeed.

Mahan says, "You *must* help your client succeed. That's a big switch in thinking." Synergistic partnership is a paradigm shift for most of us. It's no longer enough to get the customers to buy. You have to reduce their costs, increase their revenues, leverage their capital, help them build their productive quality and customer loyalty, or boost their performance. You help them achieve their own great purposes.

Becoming a 3rd Alternative Negotiator

Seeing Myself

To move to a 3rd Alternative mind-set, we must first see ourselves differently. We are no longer product pushers (hagglers). We no longer ring up the client and say, "I've got a new and improved whatsit—want to take a look?" Instead we are synergists. We're constantly looking for new ways to help clients succeed at the job they're trying to do.

You often hear that it's important to negotiate from a position of strength. Usually, that means to be in some power position in relation to the other party. To me, it means something quite different. Regardless of my power relation to the other party, I negotiate from a position of strength only when I have integrity, honesty, and a win-win mentality on my side. One who negotiates using power as a club to beat up on the other party might score a temporary victory, but that person or company is not worthy of the trust of

3rd Alternative Thinking

I Synergize With You

I Seek You Out

I See Myself

I See You

the marketplace. To be a 3rd Alternative negotiator, I must first see myself as a win-win person. I will not accept anything less than a win for you and a win for me. I don't want either of us to lose anything.

My son David was for a time sales director for our company. One day a major corporation approached us about doing business with us. The members of David's sales team were incredibly excited—this was one of the biggest companies in the world, and they were offering us tremendous revenues to buy our services.

On looking closely at the terms of the deal, however, David realized it was so deeply discounted that our firm would realize no profit at all. He didn't want to do the deal, but the sales team pressured him to take it. "Think of having them as a client! This is just a loss leader—they'll give us more and more business and surely we'll get better terms down the road."

Long ago, David was inculcated in the win-win mentality—it was not a good deal if the client won at our expense, regardless of the volume of business and the vague promise of something better in the future. So he went to the prospect's headquarters and tried unsuccessfully getting to a 3rd Alternative with them.

"Everybody knows the game," David says. "They are a big company. The role of their negotiators is to hammer vendors into submission, and they're used to having their way. They want to go back to their bosses and say, 'Look what I did for you.' But we were not going to play that game. If it's not a win-win, it's no deal."

In the end, we never knew whether the prospect was impressed with our firmness or just really wanted our services, but they finally met our terms. It was a win for both of us, and we have a good and creative relationship.

The foundation of synergistic negotiation is the win-win mentality, and it starts with me. But that mentality is just the beginning. I have to be willing to go on to create something with you that will surprise us both.

Some years ago, we wanted to research the reasons companies fail to execute successfully their most important goals. So we figured we would do a survey. We called up the best survey companies in the business and asked for bids. They very politely accommodated us with bids, which scared us. We did what salespeople call a classic "flinch." "What?" we screamed. We never dreamed doing a survey would cost so much.

Then we found Pete. He represented a very prominent survey company. Instead of giving us a bid, he asked us a simple question: "Why do you want to do this survey? What are you trying to do?" We talked through our project. We explained to him that we had been in business for many years teaching individuals how to become more effective, and many of these individuals now wanted us to help their organizations become more effective. We talked about our need for information, about the frustrations of our clients, and about our vision for helping them.

Pete listened to all this. It turned out he had a dozen suggestions for us, none of which involved big outlays of money. Some of his suggestions would bring no revenue to him at all, such as introductions to people we could interview on the subject. He explained how we could save money on a survey by crunching our own data. He talked freely about the issues his own company had with executing strategy.

Pete was doing many of the things that professional negotiators tell you not to do. He was making concessions, leaving money on the table by showing us how to do survey work ourselves instead of with his firm. His suggestions were something for nothing. He was totally transparent about his costs and margins, showing his hand. It was a long time before Pete gave us a bid to do anything.

Was Pete being naïve and unproductive? In my opinion, not at all. Because Pete was fascinated with the problem—not just with making a sale— he became a trusted partner in our project. He suggested new and ingenious ways of getting at the problem. He connected us with people who could train us on the latest science of survey design. He helped reframe in our minds the concept of research: why do it, how to do it, what are its limitations. And our money started to flow to him. Ultimately, we did commission a major survey from Pete's firm, but that was only the first one. When we ourselves became a survey provider, he and his associates provided invaluable expert help in designing our products. Over the years we have worked with Pete, he has done us countless services, and we think of him as a key resource.

Over time, partners like Pete become more valuable. They see themselves as synergists, not product pushers. But because most professional salespeople fail to go on to synergy, their value is declining. Buyers have become impatient with sellers who can't synergize, whether they are win-win–minded or not.

Seeing You

Going for a 3rd Alternative negotiation requires you to *see* the other party as a person, not as a side in a war or game in the hunt. It's too easy to slip into the "us against them" mentality. Professor Grande Lum warns, "It's important not to demonize the people we perceive to be difficult negotiators. . . . Maybe they don't trust your organization. Maybe someone has cheated them in past negotiations. Maybe they simply don't know another way to negotiate. In the end, we are all advocates of our own self-interests and each of us believes what we are doing will produce the best outcome." [1]

The old stereotypical salespeople created heroic stories of how they fought and fought a hard battle against a ruthless enemy and prevailed in the end. It made them feel and look better to themselves. But it was a delusion. This 2-Alternative thinking ("It's us against them") prevented them from really

---

1 Grande Lum, *The Negotiation Fieldbook: Simple Strategies to Help Negotiate Everything* (New York: McGraw-Hill Professional, 2004), 90.

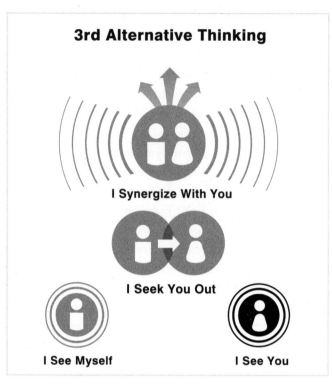

3rd Alternative Thinking

I Synergize With You

I Seek You Out

I See Myself

I See You

seeing the prospect as a person. As a result, they would treat the prospect as an adversary. Conventional sales and negotiation training is replete with tricks and techniques for getting the upper hand in that kind of contest. There's the "door-in-the-face" technique of delivering a huge bid early and then backing off as the negotiation proceeds. There's the "foot-in-the-door" technique of getting a small concession and then gradually increasing the size of the concessions from the other side. There's the "lowball," where the initial price looks great, but little things get added at the last minute to drive up the price. This is akin to the "nibble," where the prospect invests a lot of time in the deal and then gets hit just before closing with a new requirement. The reasoning goes that clients won't balk at paying new last-minute costs because of the effort they've already put forth.

Subjected to this kind of game, buyers have come up with their own defensive techniques. As Mahan Khalsa says, "Dysfunctional buying practices have arisen to combat dysfunctional selling practices."[1] There's the "krunch,"

1 Mahan Khalsa, *Let's Get Real or Let's Not Play* (Salt Lake City: White Water Press, 1999), 5.

where the buyer gradually wears down the seller's price by saying things like "We're almost there. . . . You're getting close . . . getting closer. . . ." Then there's the "flinch": "What can you be thinking? Are you crazy? I can't imagine anybody paying that price." Buyers can use the "nibble" just as well as sellers can. And naturally, sellers have come up with countermoves—there's the "reverse flinch," and I assume there's a "triple-reverse flinch" as well.

Beyond this crude choreography, more sophisticated negotiators use higher methods. They analyze the pressures on the other side, their risk tolerance, the psychology of deadlines, the length of time between concessions. They calculate to give smaller and smaller concessions, tying a string to each. The rules: Be opaque, never talk straight, answer questions in a roundabout way. Make the other side work; it increases their stake in the deal.

Every single one of these conventional methods undermines trust. Everybody's trying to give back a little of what they get, and we wonder why the sales process is so difficult, so frustrating, and takes so long. But that's not the worst of it.

You can always lie. A friend of mine recently told me about an intense seminar on negotiation he had attended. He said they did a role play in which each side was given a limited amount of information about the other side. Their task was to use that information to make a deal, and the team who made the best deal would get a prize. My friend's team was beaten, and afterward he asked the leader of the winning team how they had gained the advantage. "We lied," he said. "We told you our base cost was higher than it really was."

So my friend complained to the seminar leader. "They won by lying," he said. The seminar leader, a mature businesswoman who had been teaching negotiation skills for decades, turned to him and replied, "Where there is no truth, there are no lies."

I would add that where there is no truth, there is no hope of synergy. These deceptive games are becoming more and more useless in the age of the internet, when we can effortlessly get comparative information about costs, quality, and service. The "flinch," the "krunch," and so forth are relics of a bygone time when it took real work to verify information. Today, if you tell me your price is the best I can get—well, you'd better be right because I can check your claim on my smartphone as I stand there. I can find out all about your firm, your competition, your product, your service levels, and even about you personally. It's all there, and you can't hide it.

The era of the devious negotiation game is over. No one has the patience for it anymore. Those who try to play you simply reveal their disrespect for you. Those who say that all of life is that kind of negotiation game live in a scarcity mind-set. If I'm going to be a 3rd Alternative thinker, I must have the mind-set of abundance—that together we can come up with infinite exciting alternatives we haven't even thought of yet. I must see you as a human being whose trust and respect I value, not as a mark in a confidence game.

By simply talking straight and listening for understanding, you often bypass the need for negotiation. My son David tells this story:

> My daughter Madeleine applied to a prominent creative-writing program across the country, but was turned down because the course was full. My immediate 3rd Alternative reaction: "No, it's not full." I rang up the woman in charge and talked to her a little about Madeleine and the kind of person she was and how she was really hoping to get in. I said, "Tell me more about the situation. I just want to understand, I'm not trying to be pushy or manipulative in any way." So I just listened, and in the process built a relationship with the woman. Twenty minutes after the call ended, she sent my daughter an acceptance.

The rule today is Talking Stick communication. I deal with you by listening for understanding. I talk straight and remain utterly transparent.

Seeking You Out

Going for a 3rd Alternative negotiation requires the paradigm "I Seek You Out." That means it requires deep empathy.

Almost all sales training deals with listening skills. Most of the time, however, the focus is on listening for "buying signals," not for understanding. One major best-selling book on the art of negotiation mentions listening only once, and then only as a "concession" to the buyer that "costs you nothing." That kind of listening requires no empathy at all.

If you prize the relationship you have with the other party in a negotiation, you'll listen to him actively, reflectively, and empathically. You won't listen superficially, just waiting for a chance to pounce. You'll show empathy because that's the kind of *person* you are, not just because it's in your best interest.

If you're striving to be a synergistic partner rather than just a seller, em-

3rd Alternative Thinking

I Synergize With You

I Seek You Out

I See Myself   I See You

pathic listening will put you in the place of your clients. You'll see the world from their perspective, puzzle with them over their uncertainties, feel their pain, share their vision. I know it's hard for you as a sales representative to let go mentally of your product or solution; but if you're wise you'll move out of your own mental space and into theirs. As Mahan Khalsa advises, "Look at the entire conversation as a discovery of the unknown. . . . Get clear on the fact that you are not finding the solution for the client. You are both engaged in a process of mutual discovery."[1] This is a powerful insight: it's about mutual *discovery* of solutions, not about *providing* solutions. No solution you have in your bag of goods will exactly fit the customer. But together you can construct a creative solution that *will* fit.

If you're listening empathically, you'll sense your clients' frustrations. You'll hear expressions like "It's killing us," "We're bleeding," "What's stopping us is . . ." You'll catch their vision: "If only we could . . . ," "Our ultimate goal is . . . ," "I can see a day when . . ." Your task as a synergist is to

---

1 Khalsa, *Let's Get Real*, 29.

focus on and feel the weight of those moments. Reflect and restate those expressions of frustration and hope. Eventually, you will ask them to turn those soft expressions into hard measures. Like a physician, you'll want to know how much they're bleeding. You'll want to know in terms of numbers what their vision will mean to them—how much more revenue, how big an increase in share, exactly how achieving their goals will benefit them. Khalsa observes of his clients, "Often they haven't been through the intellectual or emotional rigor to figure out what the real consequence of their problem or opportunity is. Getting to the heart of the matter provides added value to the client."[1] Once you know what's in their hearts and what contribution you can make, you can price your services accordingly. You might find that the value of your services far outstrips your price list. You might ask for a percentage of the gain. "Burn your fixed price list," says Khalsa.

The listening salesperson is, of course, the opposite of the stereotypical talking salesperson. Most sales professionals talk too much, which accounts for problems like misalignment with the customer and overselling. And even when they seem to be listening, they're talking—inside their heads.

Jim Usry, a veteran sales executive in the pharmaceutical industry, says that years ago the relationship between drug sellers and physicians evolved into one-way communication. "We would give the same message repeatedly regardless of whether the customer was interested." "The strategy of drug companies in those days was called 'reach and frequency'—more reps calling more often on more doctors. We got to the point where as many as eight representatives from one company would be calling on one doctor with a single product, a single message, and the same drug samples." In the United States alone, the number of pharma sales representatives calling on physicians reached 95,000. "It was unsustainable, inefficient—insane."

Usry knows that doctors resent this bombardment. "The poor doctor had increasing demands on his or her time. Managed-care organizations, patients, office staff, and paperwork all needed access. Add pharmaceutical representatives to the mix and something had to give." Doctors began to revolt "If they bring something new, I'll listen. But I don't have time to listen to the same old story; I have patients to see."[2] Dr. Jordan Asher, prominent physician and health-care executive in the southern United States, represents the

---

1 Khalsa, *Let's Get Real*, 97.
2 Interview with Jim Usry, Nashville, TN, August 3, 2010.

view of many doctors: "Pharma is no different from a fast-food company. They're publicly traded, their goal is to make money for their stockholders; the only difference is they happen to be in the drug business. Their whole premise is different from ours. They'll say whatever they can to make a sale."[1]

"That's the dysfunctional relationship," says Usry. "Nobody asks, 'Where does the patient fit in here?'" The walls between the two worlds were—and still remain—incredibly high. Constantly accused of trying to buy influence with physicians through fellowships, grants, speaking fees, and even lunches, pharma companies have been backing away from even this kind of contact.

But some more synergistic thinkers have broken through, finding 3rd Alternatives by actually listening to each other. An example is Jim Fuqua, a highly experienced, top representative of one of the major American drug companies. "We'd told and sold pharma products forever," he says, "but we needed to reinvent ourselves to enhance not only our commercial success, but also our relationships with our customers. We had done a poor job of showing our value; instead, we just looked like a great way to make a ton of money. So we spent a lot of time to rework our model."

Synergizing with You

Listening is the basis of a strong workplace relationship. Once I've developed the habit of empathy, I can move on to synergy.

Ironically, drug companies were building walls between themselves and their customers through the "reach and frequency" model of selling. The more they knocked on the gates, the more the customers resisted. Some hospitals actually banned drug salespeople from the premises. But when people like Jim Fuqua and his associates started listening to doctors instead of talking at them, the synergies began to emerge. By using Talking Stick communication with doctors, Fuqua and his associates learned what they would really value from the pharma companies instead of what they were getting.

"It was science. That's what they valued. They wanted to know about the scientific issues around the appropriate use of our products." This understanding gave birth to a 3rd Alternative approach to the customer, a unique new health-science group made up of twenty-four top-tier company representatives who met with the most influential physicians in the country. Fuqua led the team: "Their job was to understand the concerns of top

---

1 Interview with Jordan Asher, October 15, 2010.

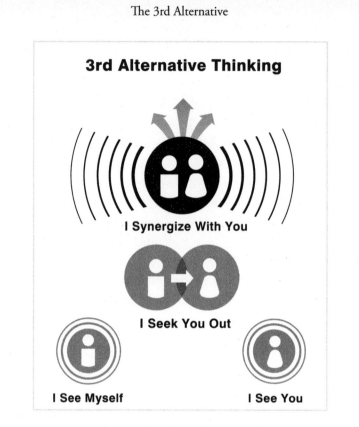

3rd Alternative Thinking

I Synergize With You

I Seek You Out

I See Myself   I See You

thought leaders and make sure they had the best information about the science with no promotional veil at all."

There was resistance within the company. Some sales leaders called the health science group a waste of effort: "What are they selling? Where's the revenue?" But Fuqua defended the approach: "We knew that was the most effective way to work with the doctors—to provide them something they needed rather than to advertise a product. They don't need more samples or more brochures or more tchotchkes. We knew that if you got to the very top thought leaders, they would affect their networks of physicians and sales would grow."

As they listened, they learned more about other issues that deeply worried doctors. "Patient compliance is a big problem. The doctors tell their patients what they need to do, but they won't do it," Usry says. "They want to eat too much, smoke too much, don't want to exercise. 'Just gimme a pill that makes it better.'" The firm began focusing on how to improve patient compliance. "Take one disease—diabetes, for example. It costs a lot, the burden of illness is huge. If you could get patients to comply, that burden would go down. Now we were talking about a common interest in making sure the patient complies with the treatment regimen. Well, I'm a pharma person, I want my product taken as prescribed, so I benefit; the doctor is satisfied, and the patient does better. The whole medical system benefits because it costs much less."

It turns out that some of the skills of great sales professionals can also be useful to doctors in encouraging their patients to cooperate. Doctors can "sell" the treatment. They can probe for reasons why the patient isn't complying and then listen empathically, get to the underlying causes. ("You don't have time to exercise? It sounds like time is a problem. If I could show you an exercise program that isn't time-consuming, would you be willing to try that?") They can follow up more carefully, as a salesperson would. And so another 3rd Alternative is born: train doctors in the art of sales.

Another issue that deeply concerns major health-care providers is disparity in care. "A perfect example is the American Southeast," says Fuqua. The hard measures are troubling. "In Alabama, you have about the right number of physicians per capita, but they're all in the same four towns. There's nobody in west Alabama, where we see huge problems with obesity and cardio disease, like 75 percent prevalence. Right where the problem is worst, we have no health care." So Fuqua and his networks began to focus on reducing these disparities. "We had products for these conditions, so we worked at identifying some strategic opportunities with people who were trying to move better health care into those areas. You don't do it by having a bunch of reps calling on doctors; there's nobody to call on. What you have to do is step back, spend time listening to the medical association and the state health officers and the university, and see how a corporation our size can help them." [1]

In transforming themselves from "drug commercials with legs" to valuable resources in resolving key health-care problems, Usry and Fuqua and others like them are discovering 3rd Alternatives that work for patients, doctors, and their own firms—and enjoying a lot of excitement and satisfaction in the process.

If I have the typical negotiation mind-set, I see only 2 Alternatives: I win or you win; for me, all of life is made up of concessions and gains. It's a zero-sum view of the world. By contrast, if I have a 3rd Alternative mind-

---

1 Interview with Jim Fuqua, October 18, 2010.

set, I will never see the end of ways you and I could create value. Zero-sum transactions end in compromise, win-lose, or lose-win. By contrast, 3rd Alternatives transform the world. People change, they become more open in their hearts and minds, they listen and learn, they see things in fresh, new, more expansive ways. It's the transformation of people that is the miracle of the 3rd Alternative.

The goal of synergistic partnership, as the Harvard scholars Deepak Malhotra and Max Bazerman put it, is "not simply to help you reach agreements that both parties *consider* to be 'win-win'; [the] goal is to help you maximize value."[1] Everyone in business is looking for "the great discriminator," the one thing that will make them stand out in the marketplace. I would suggest that the greatest of all discriminators—the thing that will make you more distinctive than anything else—is to learn to synergize.

Synergy Versus Traditional Negotiation

If you work from the paradigm of synergy, you're ready to find 3rd Alternatives routinely in the process of negotiation. The four steps for getting to a 3rd Alternative contrast starkly with the phases of traditional negotiation.

Whether you're on the buying or the selling side, traditional negotiation usually starts with asking for more than you think you can get. The euphemism for this is "Aim high." The buyer wants to get as much value for as little as possible, and the seller wants to get the highest price. Everyone understands that the opening move is just a way to find out how crazy the other party is. There is usually a good deal of flinching going on.

We, however, are synergists. For us, that step is a childish game and a waste of time. Instead we start by asking the 3rd Alternative Question: "Are we all willing to go for a deal that is better than anyone has thought of yet?" In some situations, we might have to earn the right to ask that question by establishing trust with the other parties. But if we have built a good reputation, we have nothing to lose by asking.

In traditional negotiation, the next step after the opening move is to justify that move. No one wants to concede too much too fast, so they rationalize their positions, bringing out the facts and figures and amazing stories to show why they have "aimed high." But if the other parties are willing to

---

1 Deepak Malhotra and Max H. Bazerman, *Negotiation Genius: How to Overcome Obstacles and Achieve Brilliant Results* (New York: Random House, 2008), 64.

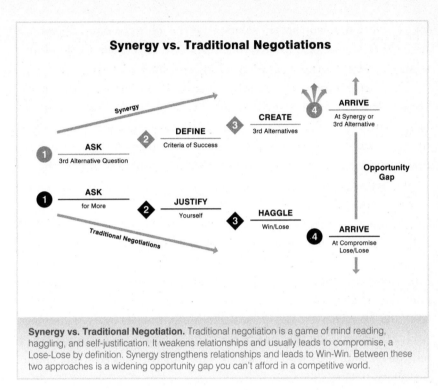

Synergy vs. Traditional Negotiation. Traditional negotiation is a game of mind reading, haggling, and self-justification. It weakens relationships and usually leads to compromise, a Lose-Lose by definition. Synergy strengthens relationships and leads to Win-Win. Between these two approaches is a widening opportunity gap you can't afford in a competitive world.

go for a 3rd Alternative, we get together and define the criteria of success, the job to be done. What would be a win-win outcome for all of us? Now we have moved into a kind of partnership to create that outcome.

The traditional negotiator has sweated over making a case and is now ready for the next step. The euphemism for this step is "Discover the limits," but it's actually just haggling. Both sides are trying to get as much out of the deal for as little as they possibly can, to see how far they can push each other before somebody walks away. For us synergists, haggling is unnecessary. By this time, all parties are deeply engaged in creating models for a solution—candidate 3rd Alternatives. This is exciting, creative, energetic work, partly because no one knows how it will turn out.

The last step in the wearying traditional process is to finally settle on a compromise, a "best and final offer," in the parlance, that all can sign off on. Although they shake hands and move on more or less satisfied, nobody is delighted with the outcome. After all, everybody loses something in a compromise. Meanwhile, we synergists arrive at a 3rd Alternative. It's invigorating, a beautiful, unanticipated solution for the job to be done. Everybody wins—there's more in it for everyone than we thought, our relationship is stronger, and we can go on creating a future together.

The difference between these two approaches is a vast opportunity gap that keeps widening with time; you can't afford to be on the downside of this gap in a competitive world. While traditional negotiators squander their energies trying to read minds and manipulate others only to end up with a compromise anyway, 3rd Alternative thinkers invest their energy in transforming the relationship with future opportunities in mind.

The Innovative Power of Synergy

The most extensive research project ever done on successful companies pinpoints innovative power as a key to the formula for sustained business success. The Evergreen Project marshaled scholars from Harvard, Columbia, MIT, Dartmouth, the Wharton School, and many other universities over a ten-year period. Their task: to identify what differentiates great and enduring companies from the mediocrities.

Not surprisingly, they found that great companies innovate in big ways, and they are not shy about it: "Their eye is on the main chance, an altogether new product idea or technological breakthrough that has potential to transform their industry. . . . For most companies satisfied with nothing less than double-digit increases in growth and earnings, modest improvements do not suffice. Their focus is more on the blockbuster innovation, the idea that will set competitors back on their heels." [1]

Where does "the altogether new" idea or breakthrough come from? Experts on innovation will tell you that it comes from synergy. My good friend Professor Clayton Christensen, perhaps the world's top thinker on the subject, says that the blockbuster idea is always disruptive. [2] It tends to appear "on the edges," where there is a rich interplay of diverse viewpoints and odd

---

1 William F. Joyce, Nitin Nohria, and Bruce Roberson, *What Really Works* (New York: HarperCollins, 2003), 219–20.
2 See his books *The Innovator's Dilemma* (Cambridge: Harvard Business Press, 1997) and *The Innovator's Solution* (Cambridge: Harvard Business Press, 2003).

connections. It does *not* come from the mainstream, homogeneous thinking that goes on in most corporate offices.

This is a paradox. We know that great companies can be highly innovative, but we also know that high innovation comes from quirky, unanticipated disruptions in the marketplace. So how do those successful organizations, by definition part of the relatively inertial "corporate world," get hold of great innovation?

By seeking it out! They understand how synergy works and they actively cultivate it. Many of them are constantly nurturing 3rd Alternatives. By contrast, mediocre companies deeply distrust new thinking. They hate disruption. They live in a 2-Alternative universe where it's "us against them." They blame outside forces for their lack of progress and see disruptive technologies as threats. The creativity expert Edward de Bono describes this peculiar psychology: "The organisations that are in deep trouble and desperately need new ideas are the last to seek them. Such organisations have convinced themselves that there is nothing wrong with their thinking but the 'world around' is giving them a hard time—so there is no point in better thinking. . . . I once had a very well known corporation tell me that they were in such serious trouble that they had no time for creativity!! Maybe it was that sort of attitude which had gotten them into such trouble."[1]

Meanwhile, 3rd Alternative thinkers love disruption. They welcome the diverse, the different, the rich new insights that come from outside, while maintaining the existing business successfully. They develop a split personality that nurtures both the present and the future.

The culture of a 3rd Alternative organization is different from the culture of uncreative companies. Scientists point to "emergent forces" in an ant colony that can help it thrive in the most inhospitable places, such as under a concrete foundation or in a crack in the pavement. What they call "emergence" is the subtle properties of the individual ants coming together and solving the problem of survival. I like to compare a 3rd Alternative culture to a coral reef. If you go snorkeling in the Caribbean or off Australia, you'll see these ornate structures rich with fish, ferns, mollusks, and sea plants of all kinds and colors. The surface of the reef looks alive, waving with the

---

1 Edward de Bono, "Creativity Only for the Successful?" November 12, 2001. http://www.edwdebono.com/msg09i.htm.

current like a garden in the wind, while the deeper parts of the reef turn into limestone. Biologists tell us that new coral species arise in the "edge zones," where there is greater biodiversity, more interaction with what they call "centers of high species richness."[1] The same is true of organizations. Those that value differences, that seek out hotspots of diverse thinking, will thrive, while those that adopt the defensive mind-set will become calcified and die off. The best place to find synergy is "at the edges," where people with divergent strengths and viewpoints cluster.

3rd Alternative Teams

True innovation depends on synergy, and synergy requires diversity. Two people who see things in exactly the same way cannot synergize. In their case, one plus one equals two. But two people who see things differently *can* synergize, and for them, one plus one can equal three or ten or a thousand. Therefore, innovative companies deliberately organize themselves into teams of people with widely divergent strengths. A complementary team is one whose strengths are made productive and weaknesses made irrelevant; the team members complement, or complete, each other. Only such a team is capable of creating 3rd Alternatives.

I work with a complementary team. The strengths of my team members compensate for my weaknesses. Modern technology is one of my weaknesses, but my associates make this weakness irrelevant because they are superb at it.

There are no limits to the size or configuration of a complementary team; it can contain two people or the whole world. But such a team must respect rather than repel differences and be devoid of hubris and territorialism, the great enemies of synergy.

Converging Divergence

Complementary teams turn out divergent insights. They reproduce the environment of a coral reef, where fertile connections can be made and synergies develop. As the writer Steven Johnson says, "Allow the hunches to connect

1 Ann F. Budd and John M. Pandolfi, "Evolutionary Novelty Is Concentrated at the Edge of Coral Species Distributions," *Science*, June 10, 2010, 1558.

with other people's hunches. You have half of an idea, someone else has the other half, and if you are in the right environment, they turn into something larger than the sum of their parts." [1]

An amazing complementary team is the Intellectual Ventures group founded by Nathan Myhrvold, former chief technology officer for Microsoft. He brings together people with amazingly divergent backgrounds to solve important problems "for fun and profit," as he says. One of those problems is how to get vaccines to people in developing countries and save millions of lives.

Vaccines must be kept cold at all times or they spoil and become useless. Even a few minutes of exposure to warm temperatures can destroy a whole shipment of vaccine; then lives are lost and millions of dollars wasted. This is easy to avoid in developed countries with refrigeration and stable power supplies, but it is a big problem in developing countries. To solve the problem, Myhrvold brought together at his laboratory in Washington a very unusual team: experts in vending machines, coffee dispensers, and automatic weapons. Their invention looks like a large Thermos bottle; inside is another bottle where the vaccines are kept, and between the bottles is a reservoir of cold liquid nitrogen. For the vaccine to stay cold, the bottle can't be opened, so a trigger ejects a vial of vaccine like a vending machine ejects a can of soda. To maintain the seal and keep warm air out, the dispenser works like the bullet magazine of an AK-47 assault rifle. This low-cost contraption can keep vaccine cold for six months with no power source at all—and save millions of people from debilitating disease.

Meanwhile, the 2-Alternative thinking grinds along. Politicians, business people, economists, and engineers argue over how to provide stable electric power and refrigeration to developing countries. They fight over socialism versus capitalism, corporations versus populists, renewable energy versus fossil fuels. These territorial fights might be engaging, but while the powerful debate, the powerless sicken and die for lack of viable vaccines. Myhrvold says, "A better vaccine container may be a band-aid to the real problem of poverty and under development, but it can make a huge difference to millions of children, alleviating the disease burden for entire generations that would otherwise fall sick while waiting for the wheels of progress to develop

---

1 "Steven Johnson, "Where Good Ideas Come From," *TED.com*, July 2010, http://www .ted.com/talks/steven_johnson_where_good_ideas_come_from.html.

their society."[1] Myhrvold's 3rd Alternative is the product of a complementary team synergizing around a compelling problem. If you can imagine a room with people connecting soda machines, coffee pots, and AK-47s, you have a picture of Nathan Myhrvold's Magic Theater. No one person, not even the brilliant team leader, could come up with the solution alone.

I love this observation by the novelist Amy Tan: "Creativity is synergy plus what matters."[2] It surely applies to the team at Intellectual Ventures.

Teaming Without Frontiers

One of the great things about our high-tech century is that complementary teams know no boundaries. Groups can synergize in ways undreamed of only a few years ago. We can talk and meet and think with anyone anywhere anytime we want. The only walls standing in our way are cultural walls, and some great organizations are working hard to raze those walls as well.

A wonderful example is LEGO, the Danish toymaker that is often called the most trusted company in the world. LEGO counts its millions of customers as an active part of a complementary team.

How would you react if customers secretly began hacking into your company's computers? Call the police, right? When this happened to LEGO, they reacted with dismay, just as anyone would. But then they asked themselves, "Why would customers do this?" And being the LEGO company, they became fascinated with the question and tried Talking Stick communication with the culprits.

When they talked to the hackers, they found they were LEGO fans who wanted to build their own creations. The hackers had broken in so they could go around the company's inventory system and order individual parts that normally came packaged with other parts. Tormod Askildsen, LEGO's director of community development, remembers this:

> *Our lawyers were ready to go after these consumers and say, "You can't do that." But we also realized that there was a lot of talent and a lot of very great skills out there in the community. Yes, they are tinkering with our product, but they are improving it. So what happened was that*

1 Nathan Myhrvold, "On Delivering Vaccines," *Seedmagazine.com*, December 30, 2010, http://seedmagazine.com/content/article/on_delivering_vaccines/.
2 Tan, "Creativity," Ted.com.

we basically let consumers hack this, and that is the amazing thing. If you trust your consumers, then they may do something that is actually a benefit. The LEGO brand is not owned by us. It's owned by the consumers. We own the trademark, yes, but the brand lives in the minds of the consumers.[1]

So LEGO developed software that would allow fans to create new LEGO designs and to encourage them to share their designs with other customers. The response has been hundreds of thousands of ideas for new products that the LEGO firm never has to develop. "This is the platform for LEGO in the twenty-first century," says Askildsen. "This is how we can be relevant. We can really make a product line that will be completely designed by consumers and put it on the shelf."

In the minds of 2-Alternative thinkers, LEGO had no choice but to shut down what was clearly illegal tampering with their internal systems or suffer the consequences. Two-dimensional, legalistic thinking would have killed this huge business opportunity in a heartbeat. But 3rd Alternative thinking won the day as LEGO discovered an entirely new way to do business: have the customers design their products while they provide the raw materials. This pure synergy would have been impossible if LEGO lacked a 3rd Alternative culture. The traditional corporate mind-set does what it can to stop this sort of thing. But, as the British journalist Charles Leadbeater says, "Intelligent organizations will move into new models, mixing 'closed' and 'open' in tricky ways." He describes an intelligent organization he encountered in China:

> *In one of the 2500 skyscrapers built in Shanghai in the last 10 years, I met with the leader of Shanda Games Ltd., which has 250 million subscribers. He employs only 500 people. He doesn't service them; he gives them a platform, rules, tools, and then orchestrates the action. But actually the content is created by the users themselves. It creates a stickiness between users and the company.*
>
> *If you're a games company and you've got a million players, you only need one percent to be co-developers and you've got a development workforce of 10,000 people.*

---

1 *The World's Most Trusted Company,* FranklinCovey video, 2008.

Like LEGO and Shanda, great organizations avidly look for synergies in the hotspots of innovative thinking among their own customers. The whole world is their Magic Theater. Leadbeater goes on to ask these provocative questions: "What if one percent of all students were co-developers of education? What if one percent of the patients were co-developers of hospital services? Turn users into producers, consumers into designers?"[1]

Merging into a 3rd Alternative

Companies merge for many reasons: economies of scale, access to new markets, diversification, and so forth. I believe that forming a synergistic, complementary team is by far the most important reason to merge with or acquire another company. It's a priceless opportunity to create a 3rd Alternative company, to make the whole greater than the sum of its parts.

However, few mergers actually achieve synergy. A landmark study by KPMG showed that "83 percent of corporate mergers and acquisitions fail to enhance shareholder value."[2] More often than not—60 percent of the time—most so-called megadeals actually destroy shareholder value.[3] "The false promise of strategic synergies," says Jeffrey Rayport, the originator of viral marketing, "has created a trail of tears on Wall Street."[4]

Why is this so? Because too often mergers are motivated not by synergy but by hubris. Another major study found "CEO hubris positively associated with" the vast majority of mergers, "as reflected by media praise and compensation"—in other words, status and money for the top leaders.[5] A classic example is the historic swelling of Saatchi & Saatchi, the legendary advertising company that in the 1980s tried to become "the world's leading professional services firm." This goal drove them to merge with scores of "businesses for which they possessed neither competence nor passion. . . . As

---

1 "Charles Leadbeater on Innovation," TED.com, July 2007, http://www.ted.com/talks/charles_leadbeater_on_innovation.html.

2 D.R. King et al., "Meta-analyses of Post-acquisition Performance: Indications of Un-identified Moderators," *Strategic Management Journal*, February 2004, abstract; "KPMG Identifies Six Key Factors," Riskworld.com, November 29, 1999, http://www.riskworld.com/pressrel/1999/PR99a214.htm.

3 Anand Sanwal, "M & A's Losing Hand," *Business Finance*, November 18, 2008.

4 Jeffrey F. Rayport, "Idea Fest," *Fast Company*, December 31, 2002, http://www.fastcompany.com/magazine/66/ideafest.html?page=0%2C5.

5 Patrick A. Gaughan, *Mergers, Acquisitions, and Corporate Restructurings* (New York: Wiley, 2007), 159.

Maurice [Saatchi] used to say, 'It's not enough to succeed, others must fail.' " But their merger fever led to the collapse of a once great company. Maurice Saatchi himself later confessed, "Hubris? That would be about right, yes." [1]

When mergers happen, leaders talk about the synergies to be gained; too often, though, it's just talk—a cover for thinly veiled hubris. That's why so many business people are allergic to the very word "synergy." All the excitement about synergy seems disingenuous when everyone knows a merger can make executive leaders "truly, titanically, stupefyingly rich," especially when most merged companies underperform "while executives benefit from these large, one-time payouts." [2] Mergers truly succeed only when they produce synergy, and synergy can't happen when employees from two different cultures are demoralized and their jobs are threatened. Ultimately, they are the ones who must create the 3rd Alternative business that arises out of two businesses. The same KPMG study I cited earlier identified synergy as the first and hardest criterion to meet in deciding whether to merge. We should merge only when we can create a complementary team, when we can clearly see that our strengths are your opportunities and your strengths are our opportunities.

"Synergy is real," Dr. Peter Corning assures us. "Its effects are measurable or quantifiable: e.g., economies of scale, increased efficiencies, reduced costs, higher yields." [3] As Jeffrey Rayport points out, "Synergy is a transformation strategy for business. It's synergy that can create entirely new businesses and industries." [4]

And so it does. Over a century ago, Henry Royce and the Honorable Charles Rolls met for the first time in the lobby of the Midland Hotel in Manchester, England. You cannot imagine two more different men. The grizzled, bearded Royce, the son of a miller, was a seasoned mechanic with a reputation for perfectionism in building steam cranes for the British Army. At six foot five, Rolls towered over Royce in status as well as height. Only twenty-seven, Rolls was the son of a baron, a privileged dandy and the first English university student to own his own car. In Edwardian England, a

---

1 Sydney Finkelstein, *Why Smart Executives Fail* (New York: Penguin, 2004), 92, 94.

2 Gretchen Morgenson, "No Wonder CEOs Love Those Mergers," *The New York Times,* July 18, 2004.

3 Peter A. Corning, "The Synergism Hypothesis,"1998, http://www.complexsystems.org/ publications/synhypo.html.

4 "The New Business Conversation Starts Here," *Fast Company,* December 31, 2002, http:// www.fastcompany.com/magazine/66/ideafest.html?page=0%2C5.

huge social gulf yawned between these two. But they both loved cars. In those days, the infant automobile was little more than an expensive—and highly unreliable—curiosity. For three years Royce had been fiddling in his shop with a French car and was sure he could make a better one. His philosophy was "Strive for perfection in everything you do. Take the best that exists and make it better. When it does not exist, design it."

The resulting handmade car impressed Rolls, who had started a new kind of business: an automobile showroom in the fashionable West End of London. He too was dissatisfied with the French cars on his show floor. So the rich young promoter and the hardened old mechanic decided to launch the Rolls-Royce motorcar company.

This was a 3rd Alternative company, a marriage of high-quality craftsmanship and flashy business sense. While Royce went to work to build the best-engineered car on the planet, Rolls inspired a silver body design and a publicity campaign that would bring them all the business of the wealthy British upper class. In 1907 the first Silver Ghost, so called for its shine and its silent engine, drove out of the factory.

Rolls took a huge risk and invited the press to accompany a cross-country endurance trial for the new car. The reporters were stunned by its performance. "The motor beneath the bonnet might be a silent sewing machine," one wrote. Day after day, over miles of English countryside, they waited for it to break down, but it never did. Finally, at nearly 15,000 miles, they called off the test and pronounced the Silver Ghost "the best car in the world." The reputation of Rolls-Royce was made. It continues today as the premium marque in the auto industry.

Rolls-Royce, which has survived the rise and fall of more than two hundred other British car companies, still makes the Ghost. In February 2011 it introduced the first luxury electric car, the 102EX, which charges itself wirelessly. Insured at $57 million, the original 1907 Silver Ghost is the most valuable car on earth.

The merger of Rolls's showy dealership and Royce's grimy crane works was a new thing, a 3rd Alternative business. The two men grew to love and respect each other. When Rolls died in an airplane crash, Royce broke down emotionally and could never again face going to the factory. But their legacy persisted. It was a merger based on personal affection, deep respect for complementary strengths, and a shared vision of excellence.

No merger can truly succeed without these elements. No synergy can be expected. A merger is not just a matter of combining assets. When you propose a merger, you're treading on sacred ground—on the livelihood, the identity, and the dreams of many people. Talking Stick communication is essential. If you respect those people, if you see them as more than just job descriptions and seek to understand their strengths, you will discover more treasure than you thought was there. You will discover synergies you did not imagine.

3rd Alternative Skills

A complementary team does best in an environment where synergy can happen. Carl Rogers understood this: "I have found that if I can help bring about a climate marked by genuineness, prizing, and understanding, then exciting things happen. Persons and groups in such a climate move away from rigidity and toward flexibility . . . away from being predictable toward an unpredictable creativity."[1]

So how do you bring about a climate like that? Finding a 3rd Alternative requires asking the question "Are we willing to look for a solution that's better than anyone has thought of before?" If the answer is yes, then we become creators, not simply perpetuators of old ideas. But it takes more than just a resolve to be creative. De Bono says, "As an exhortation creativity is almost useless. When specific techniques and skills are applied it becomes possible to generate new ideas in any field." These specific techniques and skills are found in the Magic Theater. Remember that the principle governing the Magic Theater is abundance, not scarcity. Thinking should thrive, bloom, and burgeon. If the Magic Theater doesn't look like a jungle of ideas when you've finished, you haven't been synergizing. Any practice that provides that kind of abundance can lead to the discovery of 3rd Alternatives.

Prototyping and Countertyping
Let me focus with you on two key practices of the Magic Theater:

- Make models. Draw pictures on whiteboards, sketch diagrams, build mockups, write rough drafts. Show what you think instead

---

1 Rogers, *A Way of Being*, 43.

of telling it; play it out so everyone can see what you have in mind. This practice is called "prototyping."

- Turn ideas on their heads. Reverse the conventional wisdom, no matter how upside-down it sounds. This practice is called "countertyping."

A *prototype* is a model built to test an idea. It can be anything from a simple sketch on a whiteboard to a fully working sample of a product. Electronic engineers build "breadboards" and software engineers build "wireframes" to simulate a final product. A writer might construct a detailed outline with sketchy graphs and charts long before writing any text and then ask others to review it. A business owner might experiment with a different store design just to prove a concept.

The advantage of prototyping with a complementary team is that you get a strong sense of all the issues very early instead of too late. *Rapid* prototyping is working quickly through a number of prototypes so that everyone

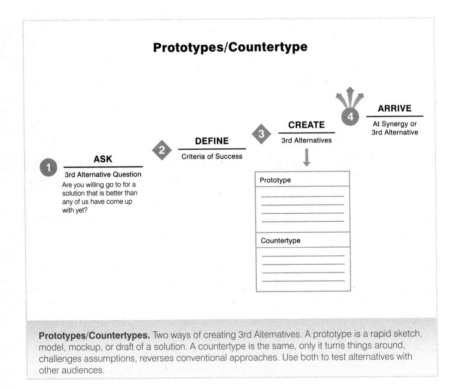

Prototypes/Countertypes. Two ways of creating 3rd Alternatives. A prototype is a rapid sketch, model, mockup, or draft of a solution. A countertype is the same, only it turns things around, challenges assumptions, reverses conventional approaches. Use both to test alternatives with other audiences.

feels heard and understood before the debate starts. It requires Talking Stick communication. As you explain your prototype, my job is to listen to your reasoning, get the picture as you see it, and grasp the insights you bring to the issue. When it's my turn to show the team my prototype, you do the same for me.

You can see why it's essential to have a diverse group of thinkers. My prototype reflects my worldview, my slice of truth. If I'm wise, I'll want to see many other prototypes that reflect other slices of truth. Only then will we together arrive at robust solutions that account for all the issues out there. For example, computer programmers often create a rapid prototype of a program and convene a diverse group of stakeholders to review it quickly and raise issues with it. A customer might find it hard to use; another engineer might catch a glitch; a marketer might question the applicability of the software. It's best to discover these issues early.

A *countertype* is a model that overturns expectations. Often countertypes are the most creative solutions of all; by turning an assumption on its head, we often see totally new ways to solve a problem. The purpose of a countertype is to provoke, to challenge, to see what it sets off in the minds of the team.

The simplest countertype turns around the usual way of doing things. For example, a countertype car rental agency might bring the car to you instead of waiting for you to pick it up. A countertype power company might pay you to generate excess electricity at home instead of charging you more and more because of their decreasing generating capacity. Or you might get tired of surfing in the sun and sea, take your board into the mountains, and surf the snow, as in snowboarding.

I love Edward de Bono's engaging countertypes. He suggests, for example, that kids could form "positive gangs," getting the same satisfaction from belonging to the usual negative gangs but by benefiting society. Here's his countertype for dealing with falling home prices:

> *When the property market is falling buyers tend to wait until it falls further. Why buy now when you can get a lower price in a few months' time? So the market falls further because some people need to sell and lower their price.*
>
> *We could create a new type of contract. You sell at today's price but contract with the buyer that in a year (or two years) if the house price*

index has fallen by a further twelve per cent then you refund that twelve per cent to the buyer. There is now no point in waiting. So the market stops falling and you may not have to refund anything.[1]

Countertypical ideas are booming in the twenty-first-century economy. For example, Nike now buys shoes instead of just selling them. They grind up old shoes and recycle the rubber for track surfaces, the fabric to pad basketball courts, and the foam to give spring to tennis court surfaces. Walkers, a potato-crisp maker in the U.K., has eliminated the use of water in cleaning potatoes. The potatoes clean themselves in a process that draws their natural moisture out. Countertypes rule.

Countertyping averts "groupthink," that fatal syndrome of teams whose members think too much alike. The more everyone shares the same outlook, the more you need countertypes as antidotes to weak, unexamined ideas that might be adopted just to achieve consensus. In a famous example of countertyping, George Romney, who took over as head of the struggling American Motors Company (AMC) in the 1950s, looked around and saw that American cars were getting bigger every year—and burning through more fuel. He broke the groupthink of U.S. car makers who all assumed their customers wanted to drive giant "gas-guzzling dinosaurs" and countertyped them with the idea of the "compact car." His company produced the little Rambler, which broke sales records in 1958. This countertype showed the industry that many of their customers just wanted to get from one place to another and didn't care how big their cars were. All the companies started making their own compact cars, and by 1977 most cars made in America had shrunk to the size of the Rambler or even smaller.

Every member of a team should freely propose countertypes. This role is more than a devil's advocate who challenges ideas and raises objections. A countertypist reverses the thinking of the group, turns a prototype around, and suggests the opposite: "Hey, let's buy shoes instead of just selling them" or "Hey, with cars, maybe *little* is the new *big*."

Prototyping and countertyping are rapid, efficient ways for complemen-

1 Edward de Bono, "Positive Gangs," March 2, 2009, http://sixthinkinghats.blogspot .com/2009/03/edward-de-bonos-weekly-message-positive.html. "Property Market," November 4, 2008, http://www.makinginnovationhappen.blogspot.com.

tary teams to arrive at a 3rd Alternative. The goal is the exciting solution that transcends all of our prototypes and solves the problem in a miraculous fashion. We might end up preventing malaria with a mosquito-zapping laser gun. If we want to keep vaccines cold, we might end up with a double-lined Dewar flask that shoots out vials like an AK-47—a wild thing we never foresaw—and we'll be delighted with it!

Blending Prototypes

A 3rd Alternative often arises out of combining elements of many prototypes. As you go through the prototyping process, you'll see in other people's models great ideas you never thought of. For example, in the 1990s many consumer-electronics companies were racing to get to market with an optical disc that could play digital video. They all remembered the costly war between the VHS and Betamax videotape formats; for nearly ten years, the industry angered consumers as it dithered (in classic 2-Alternative fashion) over which standard to support. Fearing another such tug of war, industry leaders got together and formed a complementary team called the Technical Working Group, or "TWIG," to come up with one standard format for digital video. Chaired by Alan Bell of IBM's laboratories, the TWIG reviewed numerous concepts. Fiercely competitive engineers from companies like Toshiba, Sony, Phillips, Apple, and IBM had the chance to play their prototypes and learn from each other. Eventually the TWIG favored Toshiba's two-sided superdensity disc with its enormous 10-gigabyte capacity. But they were also impressed with a concept from Sony and Phillips called "EF modulation," which cut back on the skipping and sticking problem caused by dust, scratches, or fingerprints.

The final product was released by a consortium of companies in 1996. Called the "digital versatile disc," or DVD, it combined the best features of many prototypes and was a far better solution than any one of the companies could have created on its own. The DVD became wildly popular; in the peak year of 2007, 1.7 billion DVDs were shipped for revenues of $24 billion.[1]

The most robust solution usually comes from bringing together as many minds as possible as early as possible. The prototyping process enables that.

---

1 See Jim H. Taylor et al. *DVD Demystified* (New York: McGraw-Hill Professional, 2006).

Finding Prototypes in Nature

In coral reefs, rain forests, deserts—everywhere you look, you will see that the natural world produces miracles of synergy. Instructive examples are infinite, as the writer William Powers beautifully describes:

> *While human industrial processes can produce Kevlar, it takes a temperature of thousands of degrees to do it, and the fiber is pulled through sulfuric acid. In contrast, a spider makes its silk—which per gram is several times stronger than steel—at room temperature in water. Humans manufacture ceramics with similarly high temperatures, but the abalone makes its shell in seawater by laying down a small layer of protein and precipitating the calcium out of the seawater around it. The abalone shell is self-healing because cracks within it actually strengthen the ends of the cracks so they don't get bigger, unlike, say, an auto windshield.*[1]

If I were a manufacturer of Kevlar vests, I might want to hire an arachnologist, an expert on spiders. If I were a builder, I might want to bring on a marine biologist. Imagine a protective vest made from spider's silk, or a window that repairs itself like an abalone shell. Teeming with possibilities, nature is just waiting for us to make connections.

For example, one day in 1941 a Swiss electrical engineer named George de Mestral came home from a hunting vacation with his dog. Both he and the dog were covered with burrs. As he picked the irritating burrs from the dog's fur, he wondered why they were so sticky. Putting a burr under a microscope, he saw tiny hooks attached to the dog's hair and suddenly realized he was looking at a natural fastener that could take the place of buttons and zippers. The result of de Mestral's walk in the woods was the invention of Velcro. Years later, when Velcro was a hugely successful product, de Mestral joked with the manufacturers, "If any of your employees ask for a two-week holiday to go hunting, say yes."

Ivy Ross was made head of product design at Mattel in Los Angeles after the toy-making company had suffered some bad years. Many felt Mattel had lost its creativity. As Ross thought about ways to inspire a new spirit of inventiveness at Mattel, she came across an article about the platypus of

---

1 William Powers, *Twelve by Twelve* (Novato, CA: New World Library, 2010), 74–75.

Australia. One of the most unusual animals in the natural world, the platy-pus looks like a beaver but with the bill and webbed feet of a duck. It has the venom of a reptile and lays eggs like a bird. Ross decided to build a product-development team modeled after a platypus, with people from many back-grounds and functions. She brought together in her Magic Theater an actor from Disney, people from accounting and packaging, a psychologist, a brain scientist, a researcher in music, and architects. She sent them to play-grounds to just watch kids play. Then the "platypi," as they were called, got busy. Within a month they had thirty-three prototypes for new toys on the wall. After a few more weeks they had produced Ello, an ingenious build-ing set that led to an entirely new segment of toys for girls. The Platypus complementary team became a legend at Mattel and spawned many more teams like it. Ivy Ross describes what happens when she organizes a Platypus team:

> When we first start, everyone wants to know about the deadlines. Every-one wants to know about the stages in the process. I tell them the net net is that in 12 weeks we have to have developed a new opportunity for Mattel that doesn't yet exist and that we need to deliver the business plan, the products, the packaging, the whole bit. How do we get there? I don't know yet. It's an adventure. Then my job is to let things grow organically. It takes time to self organize. "Oh oh, we're eight weeks into this thing and we still don't have a product." I tell them to relax, don't panic, that chaos is part of the process. I tell them to go to La Brea tarpits, to go to the zoo, to come back with a fresh perspective. And then suddenly it happens. . . .
>
> There's the "aha." Someone gets on a roll, and the idea builds, and people start looking at each other. Suddenly, they know that they have something brilliant. And it's not just one person. Everyone feels it. When it happens, even if it's late in the game, people are so excited that they do what it takes to pull it together. Everyone works as hard as they can to make this idea work, because they are invested in it. We're really col-laborating and building ideas together as opposed to the old model where everyone works in silos and is competitive with one another. This is true collaboration.[1]

---

1 David Womack, "An Interview with Ivy Ross," *Business Week*, July 19, 2005.

Of course, what Ross is describing is the synergy process. She brings together a team with the diverse strengths of the platypus. The result is an explosion of creativity.

Provoking Prototypes

Asking provocative questions can unlock the imagination and spur new alternatives: "What if we had to solve this problem using only our current products?" or "What if we had to solve this problem with no resources?" or "What if we had unlimited resources?" For example, Barry Nalebuff, a Yale Business School strategist, builds conceptual prototypes by asking the question "What would Croesus do?" In Greek myth, Croesus was a king with unfathomable wealth. Nalebuff says that asking this question might lead to inventive yet manageable solutions. Suppose you want to be able to watch any movie you want anytime you want. If you were a multibillionaire, how would you solve the problem? Here's Nalebuff's answer:

> In his day Howard Hughes had a Croesus-like flair for spending money to find solutions to problems. Imagine that it's 1966 and that you're Hughes. You sometimes have a hankering to watch old Humphrey Bogart films. Unfortunately, the video recorder has yet to be invented. What do you do?
>
> Hughes bought a Las Vegas television station and used it as his private VCR. Whenever he wanted, he'd call up the station's general manager and tell him what movie to put on that night. We understand that the station played a lot of Casablanca and The Maltese Falcon.[1]

Asking the Croesus question, you don't start with a practical solution—you start with the best possible solution you can imagine. You could buy your own TV station. From there you could lower your sights and move toward the more practical prototype of a machine or an online service that would provide you with the same result.

Countertyping Business Models

Every company wants to be a 3rd Alternative company—or they *should* want to. Scores of studies reveal that there is something singular about every successful company. None of them is a "me too" outfit that looks like a dozen

---

1 Barry Nalebuff and Ian Ayres, "Why Not?," *Forbes.com,* October 27, 2003.

other companies. They stand out because they've found a strong synergy with their customers and their employees. When you read the customer and employee loyalty literature, you see that that these great companies have found a countertypical formula for gaining extraordinary levels of faith and trust.

Consciously or unconsciously, 3rd Alternative companies go through a countertyping phase in which they diverge from the norm. Often their business models go against what on the surface looks like common sense. They often reverse the conventional wisdom in captivating ways.

Think of Disney, which spends lavishly on finding, teaching, and developing just the right people to staff their world-class theme parks. Who else focuses on employees as Disney does? Think of Costco, a one-stop shop that carries a fraction of the products other supermarkets carry, but whose customers flock to it like children on a treasure hunt. Think of Singapore Airlines, where even coach passengers enjoy unparalleled personal service: footrests, a personal telephone, and a flow of champagne. Meals come at the customer's request, hot from the galley, as in a gourmet restaurant. Singapore does all this and makes money at a time when most airlines have utterly abandoned customer service and lose money anyway.[1]

Each of these 3rd Alternative companies has a countertype business model. Each does things no other company would think of doing. What they all have in common is that they are prepared to fly in the face of convention to truly serve and care for their customers as human beings rather than as bookings or units. As Singapore Airlines' CEO Chew Choon Seng says, "At the end of the day, this is still a people-intensive industry. From the moment you speak to a sales agent, to boarding the plane, to picking up baggage, it is people."[2] Every day they ask themselves this variant of the 3rd Alternative question: "What can we do for our people today that's better than anyone ever thought of before?"

One of my good friends, a consultant who works in Canada, was leading a seminar on synergy near Toronto. About forty business people attended— manufacturers, shopkeepers, lawyers, government workers, accountants, nurses. They were of all ages and ethnic groups, and well over half were

---

1 See Pervez K. Achmed et al., *Learning through Knowledge Management* (Maryland Heights, MO: Butterworth-Heinemann, 2002), 283.

2 Siva Govindasamy, "Interview: Singapore CEO Chew Choon Seng," *FlightGlobal*, January 21, 2010, http://www.flightglobal.com/articles/2010/01/21/337362/interview -singapore-ceo-chew-choon-seng.html.

women. At one point in the seminar, my friend asked if anyone in the room would volunteer to be the guinea pig for an experiment in synergy.

A nicely dressed, soft-spoken man in the front row raised his hand. We'll call him Rinaldo. My friend asked him what his situation was.

"I own a large hardware store," he began. You could hear a faint Latin accent in his voice. "I've worked for many years to build it up, and I have a wonderful clientele. It's been a good business, and I'd like to see it grow. But I think it's all over.

"You see, two big-box retail home centers are going to be built in my town. Not one, but two! I'm situated halfway between them. They are huge and powerful. I surely won't be able to compete with them on price, and I'm afraid my customers won't have much choice but to leave me."

My friend gulped and turned to the seminar group, which had become very quiet. You could tell that everybody felt sympathy for this man.

"All right," my friend said. "We've got to save Rinaldo. We're going to do some countertyping. What can Rinaldo do to keep his customers? What can we come up with that no one has ever thought of before?" And the group went to work. They took markers and chart paper and feverishly drew countertypes, new business models that would turn the world on its head and make Rinaldo's retail store thrive. It was loud and chaotic—a delightful kind of chaos that you see when people are excited.

When my friend called time, it was obvious that people couldn't wait to share their ideas. And the ideas flew. There were hundreds of suggestions, such as:

- Why wait for customers to come to you? Go to them! Put a truck on the road full of product and carry it to building sites.
- You have seasoned staff members. Turn your store into a learning center where people can get real advice on construction projects from real experts.
- Start a just-in-time service. If a customer calls or texts and needs a tool, deliver it!
- If I want one nail, sell me one nail so I don't have to buy a whole package of them.

The most fruitful set of suggestions came from the women in the room. Many of them talked about how home centers and hardware stores intimidated them, and how much they would like a store that catered to their needs and interests. Rinaldo should hire women, develop classes for women, find out which products women needed most for home projects. "Countertype! How about a hardware store for women?" one of them called out.

My friend said it was the most productive countertyping session he had ever seen. The many professions and perspectives in the room served up a rich mix of ideas, and Rinaldo blushed with pleasure as he sat down. "Now I have hope," he said. In the following months, he totally reconceived his business model as a countertype to the big-box home centers. Where the home centers sold generic product and their untrained staff offered blank looks, Rinaldo served up amazing expertise and personal attention, with a special outreach to women customers. Whatever the big retailers did, Rinaldo countered it.

On one side of town was Big Box A and on the other side of town was Big Box B. They fought it out for market share in a classic 2-Alternative showdown, although there wasn't much difference between them. Meanwhile Rinaldo, the 3rd Alternative, sat in the middle, happily distinguishing himself from both and delighting his growing clientele with his exceptional blend of service and skill.

These 3rd Alternative organizations are marked by a deep respect and empathy for the people who work for them and the people who do business with them. They are always asking themselves the countertype question: "What can I do that reverses the conventional, that turns things upside down, not only to distinguish myself in the marketplace, but also to provide radically exceptional value to my neighbors?"

What would you think of a restaurant where the customers decide what they will pay for a meal? By any measure, Panera Bread is a success. With thousands of café-style bakeries covering forty American states, Panera has a mission to "put a loaf of bread under every arm." It ranks highest in the United States in customer loyalty among casual restaurants. And now Panera wants to give back.

"Panera Cares is a new kind of café . . . a community café of shared responsibility." The company has opened several of these countertype restaurants where customers pay what they feel like paying. The goal, says Panera's chairman, Ron Shaich, "is to ensure that everyone who needs a meal gets one. People are encouraged to take what they need and donate their fair share. There are no prices or cash registers, only suggested donation levels and donation bins." Some customers donate more than others, some give a lot, and some give little. Some volunteer to work for their food. Shaich has found that about a third of the customers leave more than the suggested donation. The cafés cover their costs and are self-sufficient.[1]

I believe that Panera's countertype cafés will pay the company back many times the investment it is making. Panera is gaining the goodwill of good people. It is transforming neighborhoods where people sometimes need a place of refuge from life's storms. It is giving people a chance to help themselves and each other. Panera is teaching us that there is more than one way to profit in business.

Finding Countertypes in the Developing World

The ingenuity of emerging countries is turning the world upside down. Nimble, low-cost, low-energy technologies from the developing world are strikingly innovative and might dramatically change the global economy.

On a visit to Mongolia, my friend Clayton Christensen was walking through a market and came across some inexpensive solar-powered television sets. They worked fine, and the price was low. He wondered if that kind of product might just disrupt the big, heavy investments and infrastructure of the traditional electrical power industry. "Those TVs are closer to doing the job people want done. People don't want giant power grids; they want working television sets."

Nearly half the homes in India have no electricity. Without electrical power, millions lack employment and educational opportunities. Furthermore, the power shortage actually harms the environment; millions of cooking fires pollute the atmosphere. Big debates go on year after year over how to get electricity to the people. Corporations battle environmentalists, cities battle the rural interests, politicians battle each other. As in the rest of the world, 2-Alternative thinking can stymie any meaningful progress.

Meanwhile, a young engineer and 3rd Alternative thinker from Bangalore named Harish Hande asked himself the countertype question: how to generate electricity for people at virtually no cost and save the environment

1 "Panera Bread Foundation Opens Third Panera Cares Community Café in Portland, OR," *Marketwire,* January 16, 2011; Bruce Horovitz, "Non-Profit Panera Café," *USA Today,* May 18, 2010; "Panera's Pick-What-You-Pay Café Holds Its Own," Reuters, July 28, 2010, http://blogs.reuters.com/shop-talk/2010/07/28/paneras-pick-what-you-pay -cafe-holds-its-own/.

at the same time? What about something better than anybody has thought of before?

Today Hande has found a way to bring to his fellow Indians power that is totally clean and costs virtually nothing. His company, Selco India, has installed 115,000 low-priced solar power systems. His customers, whether poor day-wage workers or small businesses, pay a few hundred dollars for a 40-watt system that can light a small home. Few of them have much money, so Hande arranges credit for them. As a result, children can do their home-work under bright, clean light instead of kerosene lamplight. Small textile shops plagued by power outages can now keep their sewing machines run-ning throughout the day. Families can cook their food on electric stoves instead of smoky cooking fires. A young taxi driver can charge extra batteries for his three-wheeled taxi and double his income. Street lighting provides security to remote villages.

Harish Hande's 3rd Alternative has transformed the lives of thousands of families in southern India. The same is happening in China, where a company called Chi Sage has developed a reversible heat pump that cools or warms a home using any water source, including wells or nearby streams or lakes, at little cost and with no impact on the environment.[1]

These and other environmentally neutral, low-cost innovations could easily disrupt the economics of more developed countries, thinks Professor Vijay Govindarajan of Dartmouth: "We may be at the cusp of a new era in which breakthrough innovations happen first in developing countries. . . . The icing on the globalization cake is that such innovations are scalable not only across other emerging markets, but more importantly, they can be scaled up for the developed world."[2]

We live in a time when 3rd Alternative thinkers are connecting around the globe. Connections are now common among, say, a solar engineer in India and a promoter in America and a manufacturing team in China. Busi-ness synergies unlike anything in history are bubbling up everywhere. But it takes a paradigm shift to join this revolution. We have to be comfortable with a world where countertypes can blow up overnight and knock down

---

1 See "What American Entrepreneurs Can Learn from Their Foreign Counterparts," *MIT Entrepreneurship Review,* December 6, 2010.
2 Vijay Govindarajan, "Reverse Innovation at Davos," *HBR Blogs,* February 4, 2011, http:// blogs.hbr.org/govindarajan/2011/02/reverse-innovation-at-davos.html#.

every convention. We can't just acknowledge 3rd Alternative thinking and play at it—we have to get *good* at it.

The Age of Synergy

In a sense, businesses no longer exist. The old boundary between inside and outside has crumbled as the distinction between customer and employee evaporates. *All* are customers. A tide of technology has worn down the old barriers of time and distance. The Industrial Age model of the corporate fortress has eroded away in an age of transparency and fluid change. We are no longer units on an organizational chart. We connect as human beings or we do not connect at all.

I believe, however, that many people are still caught inside the remaining walls of the Industrial Age prison. Here are some of the comments from our Serious Challenge survey:

- "Every day I feel I give the job more effort but I get so little in return."
- "I am searching for more meaning in the work I do. Without meaning, doing a job is difficult and quickly leads to burnout and depression."
- "Sometimes I can't find where I go [*sic*], and what is the purpose of my work."
- "I enjoy my job, but I don't love it, it doesn't 'feed' my soul. At this point in my professional career, I have spent so many years working that I don't even know what I would do if I were not doing exactly what I'm doing today."
- "It's a problem, the mismatch between my values and the values of the financial sector I work in."
- "Feeling a lack of purpose makes me feel like I am not making a difference in the world."
- "The owners micro-manage every aspect of the business."
- "People often try to overcome a conflict by confrontation, unknowingly exacerbating the problem."
- "Organisational conflict increases drop-outs and fails to maintain consistency."

- "Some management workers refuse to accept blame and always take credit for what's not theirs. Passing along more work to others instead of doing it themselves."

Note the feelings of aimlessness, isolation, and injustice. People who don't feel they are part of something great, some synergistic effort that's bigger than themselves, fill up with self-doubt. Now the only walls left are within us. These are cultural, mental walls: "I'm alone here. I have no purpose, no sense of belonging. I don't share these values. How did I end up spending my life in this prison?" The interpersonal walls trap us within our tiny territories and a mind-set of blame and defensiveness: "If you are different, you are a threat. If you don't see things my way, you will when I'm done with you."

How liberating it is to leave that caged-in 2-Alternative thinking behind, that hubristic obsession with self. How archaic it seems in an age of global synergy.

Have you ever worked on a truly synergistic team? When you knew that you couldn't afford to lose a single member? When you could shine as an individual and yet feel the deep connection with each other, as if you were one person? When every day you grew closer and your combined capacities grew stronger? When you amazed yourselves with the 3rd Alternative results you were producing? When it was fun and exciting just to be alive and to be together? I have experienced it many times, and I feel for those who never have. To me, the bond of love with my friends who work with me far surpasses in strength the weak grasp of personal gain or position.

"Neither power nor money has sustainable impact upon happiness—the happiness of individuals, partnerships, relationships or organizations," says my friend Colin Hall, the legendary South African business leader. People are engaged and happy at work "only when synergy abounds and the whole is greater than the sum of its parts." [1]

---

1 Colin Hall, "Mergers and Acquisitions," *Learning to Lead,* November 2004, http://www .ltl.co.za/public-library/mergers-and-acquisitions.

TEACH TO LEARN

The best way to learn from this book is to teach it to someone else. Everybody knows that the teacher learns far more than the student. So find someone—a co-worker, a friend, a family member—and teach him or her the insights you've gained. Ask the provocative questions here or come up with your own.

- Why are "fight" and "flight" the two dominating paradigms of leadership in most organizations? What happens when a leader wants to fight? When a leader wants to flee?
- Describe 3rd Alternative leadership. In what ways is it different from "fight or flight"? What are the benefits of 3rd Alternative leadership?
- How can the paradigms of synergy help you resolve a conflict at work?
- How does hubris keep a leader or an organization from getting to synergy?
- What are the dangers of a transactional approach to conflict? What are the benefits of a transformational approach?
- Describe the differences between traditional negotiation and 3rd Alternative negotiation. What are the paradigms of a 3rd Alternative negotiator? How do you get to a synergistic partnership with other parties in a negotiation?
- What does it mean to say "Synergy begins at the edges"? How would you capitalize on that insight?
- Describe a synergistic or complementary team. How does it differ from ordinary teams? Why is diversity so important to such a team? What can we learn from the LEGO story about the mindset of a synergistic team?
- Explain how the prototyping and countertyping processes work. Why are these processes so useful for a synergistic team? What can we learn from Rinaldo's story or the other stories in the chapter about those processes?

- I believe that Panera's countertype cafés will pay the company back many times the investment it is making. Do you agree? Why is the Panera café a good example of a countertype?
- Have you ever worked on a truly synergistic team? What did it feel like? What could you do to help transform your own work group into such a team?

TRY IT

Do you have an important problem or opportunity at work? A difficult decision to make? Start prototyping 3rd Alternatives. Invite others to contribute. Use the "4 Steps to Synergy" tool.

4 STEPS TO SYNERGY

1 **Ask the 3rd Alternative Question:**

"Are you willing to go for a solution that is better than any of us have come up with yet?" If yes, go on to step 2.

2 **Define Criteria of Success**

List in this space the characteristics of a solution that would delight everyone. What does success look like? What is the real job to be done? What would be a "win-win" for all concerned?

3 **Create 3rd Alternatives**

In this space (or other spaces) create models, draw pictures, borrow ideas, turn your thinking upside down. Work quickly and creatively. Suspend all judgment until that exciting moment when you know you've arrived at synergy.

4 **Arrive at Synergy**

Describe here your 3rd Alternative and, if you want, how you intend to put it into practice.

USER GUIDE TO THE 4 STEPS TO SYNERGY TOOL

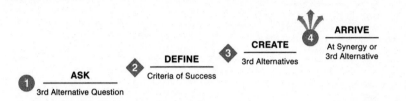

> **The 4 Steps to Synergy.** This process helps you put the synergy principle to work. (1) Show willingness to find a 3rd Alternative. (2) Define what success looks like to everyone. (3) Experiment with solutions until you (4) arrive at synergy. Listen empathically to others throughout the process.

How to Get to Synergy

① Ask the 3rd Alternative Question

In a conflict or creative situation, this question helps everyone move past firm positions or preconceived ideas toward developing a third position.

② Define Criteria of Success	③ Create 3rd Alternative
List characteristics or write a paragraph describing what a successful outcome would look like to everyone. Answer these questions as you go: • Is everyone involved in setting the criteria? Are we getting as many ideas from as many people as possible? • What outcomes do we really want? What is the real job to be done? • What outcomes would be "wins" for everyone? • Are we looking past our entrenched demands to something better?	Follow these guidelines: • Play at it. It's not "for real." Everybody knows it's a game. • Avoid closure, premature agreement, or consensus. • Avoid judging others' ideas—or your own. • Make models. Draw pictures on whiteboards, sketch diagrams, build mockups, write rough drafts. • Turn ideas on their heads. Reverse the conventional wisdom. • Work fast. Set a time limit to keep energy and ideas flowing rapidly. • Breed lots of ideas. You can't predict which offhand insight might lead to a 3rd Alternative.

((④)) Arrive at Synergy

You recognize the 3rd Alternative by the sense of excitement and inspiration in the room. The old conflict is abandoned. The new alternative meets the criteria of success. Caution: Avoid mistaking compromise for synergy. Compromise breeds satisfaction but not delight. Compromise means everyone loses something; synergy means everyone wins.

The 3rd Alternative at Home

4

The 3rd Alternative at Home

Where there is joy, there is creation.
—The Upanishads

The family can be the ultimate expression of synergy. There is a miracle in the transformational, intimate connection that can happen in marriage. And every child who comes into the world is a 3rd Alternative. The newborn is the greatest synergistic marvel of all.

My grandfather Stephen L Richards taught me to analyze any problem at any level—local, national, international; political, educational, organizational—from the standpoint of the family. If it works in the home, it will work anywhere. Families in debt are not so different from nations in debt. Trust and fidelity work the same in business as they do at home: it takes years to build up, seconds to destroy. The problems of society start at home, and so do the solutions.

As a husband, father, and grandfather, I am so thrilled with my family. They are my greatest blessing and my greatest joy. To lose the respect and intimate connection I enjoy with even one of my family members would be my greatest tragedy and my greatest sorrow.

People have universal needs. They need to feel safe, appreciated, respected, encouraged, and loved; these needs can find their sweetest fulfillment in the bonds between son and mother, daughter and father, husband and wife. So it's tragic when the family fails to fulfill these needs.

Our survey respondents report these serious challenges in their lives:

- "We are growing apart. We have different opinions as to what is important in life."
- "Open communication never is easy with the ones most close to oneself."
- "My wife doesn't share the happiness I get with every step ahead I walk."
- "I am a single Mom and it has always been a struggle to provide a well-balanced and satisfying lifestyle for my family."
- "I've been married for 31 years and have two children in college. I am going through horrible empty-nest syndrome. It's affecting my marriage and home life. I miss being a Mom and being needed . . . end of story."
- "Family is very important to me—when that goes wrong it tips everything else out of balance."

Family conflicts are the most heartbreaking of all of life's toughest problems. This is a great irony: at home we can experience the most sublime synergies or the deepest distress. I believe that no success in life can compensate for failure at home.

No loss is as profound and painful as the loss of a family member. Most parents know the sickening sensation of losing track of a child even momentarily, when, in a marketplace or a crowd, our child disappears for a minute or two and we hold our breath for an eternity, searching in a frenzy until the little one shows up again.

For some, that intense pain can last forever. Zainab Salbi, founder of Women for Women International, tells of a night in Baghdad when she was a child and awoke in terror to the sound of a missile descending closer and closer toward her. It exploded nearby, and she prayed in shaken gratitude that her family had been spared. Later she felt ashamed of her prayer, for the bomb had destroyed the house of a neighboring family. The father and little boy, a friend of her brother, were killed, while the mother survived. "His mother showed up the next week at my brother's classroom and begged six- and seven-year-old kids to share with her any picture they may have of her son, for she had lost everything."[1]

Yet every day in our culture people throw away almost casually that most precious of all of life's gifts: their family. Wives and husbands who once had a passion for each other grow cold toward each other. The United States has the highest divorce rate in the world, at 40 to 50 percent of all first marriages. Russia is second, with the nations of northern Europe close behind. Even in countries with low actual rates (usually because of cultural disapproval of divorce), "emotional separation" is far too prevalent.

Divorce affects more than a million children annually in the United States alone. The data show that children of divorce are more likely to suffer from discipline problems, psychological disturbances, lower academic achievement, and poorer health.[2]

Treasuring the Differences

In many cases, divorce stems from real betrayal—physical abuse or infidelity—but too often it's the result of a debilitating spiral of 2-Alternative thinking.

A woman might say: "My husband spends too much time watching sports, playing video games, and golfing, and then comes home and thinks I should take care of the kids and the house, not realizing that I've been working all day too. He's so much like his lazy father. He has stopped doing the little things that won me over in the first place, like small acts of kindness or asking how my day went, and all he wants is sex. And then he wonders why I've checked out of the marriage."

A man might say: "My wife just wants me for my money and doesn't appreciate how hard I work. She's so busy with the kids that she has no more time for me. Our home is disorganized and messy while my wife is off at her book club. Plus, I can't seem to do anything right. My wife is cold and distant and doesn't greet me with the same zest she once did when I come

---

1 Zainab Salbi, "Women, Wartime, and the Dream of Peace," *TED.com,* July 2010.
2 Alison Clarke-Stewart and Cornelia Brentano, *Divorce: Causes and Consequences* (New Haven, CT: Yale University Press, 2007), 108.

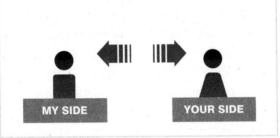

home; in fact, she doesn't even notice if I come home. I wish her mother would just leave us alone. My wife doesn't look as good as she used to and doesn't take care of herself anymore, and the women at the office are looking better all the time."

With this mind-set—or rather, this *heart-set*—love turns into profound disrespect. Some marriages morph into spiteful Great Debates. Family members become all good or all bad, and it's "my side against yours." Psychologists refer to this phenomenon as "splitting." The marriage therapist Mark Sichel observes, "In families with borderline dynamics, splitting allows for frequent and deadly divide-and-conquer games. . . . Children often become embroiled in competitive stances between 'good child' and 'bad child.'"[1] So the home becomes a battlefield instead of the safe and loving refuge that all children need and deserve.

Some families are afflicted by less overt, more nuanced forms of emotional abuse, such as low-level squabbling, nitpicking, and backbiting in a sort of perverse competition to see who can make whom the most miserable: "If you loved me you'd clean that garage." "I work hard all day, and what thanks do I get?" "They're your children too, you know." The walls go up gradually, almost unnoticeably, until cold silence reigns. "If you want to destroy something in this life," says the Turkish novelist Elif Shafak, "all you need to do is to surround it with thick walls. It will dry up inside."[2]

One family attorney with years of experience speaks of a case in which a wife came to her office demanding a divorce. "I can't take it anymore," she

---

1 Mark Sichel, *Healing from Family Rifts* (New York: McGraw-Hill Professional, 2004), 83.
2 Elif Shafak, "The Politics of Fiction," TED.com, July 16, 2010, http://www.ted.com/talks/elif_shafak_the_politics_of_fict ion.html.

said. The woman's husband was an excellent provider and community leader, but he contradicted everything she said and reversed everything she did. If she hung a picture on a wall, he would move it. If she wanted to eat out, he demanded they eat in. If she said something to a friend, he would make sure the friend knew she was wrong. The tipping point came when she invited her parents to dinner. At the table, the sun was shining through a window onto her father's face, so she closed the blind. Her husband promptly got up and flicked it open again. For years, she had lived with this infuriating man but could stand it no longer. He had diminished her world until she burst from an attack of emotional claustrophobia. This kind of emotional abuse, this assertion of power and control, can be nearly as bad as physical abuse.

Often marriages like this one end for good reasons, but far more often they end because wives and husbands become discouraged over their differences. This husband was an extreme case of intolerance of differences, but to some degree the same syndrome afflicts all miserable marriages. "Incompatibility" is cited most often as the reason for divorce. The word can cover a range of problems—financial, emotional, social, sexual—but it comes down to resentment of differences rather than valuing differences: "We've never seen eye to eye." "I can't understand how she thinks." "He's totally irrational." Over time, despair sets in and divorce looks like the only hope.

By contrast, great marriages arise only when the partners treasure their differences. For them, the cultures, quirks, talents, strengths, reflexes, and instincts each partner brings to the marriage become sources of delight and creativity. His impatience makes him terrible at bookkeeping, but his spontaneity makes him fun. Her reserve sometimes frustrates him, but her aristocratic manner awes and charms him. And because they cherish each other so much, they blend joyfulness and dignity.

When two people marry, they have the opportunity to create a 3rd Alternative, a unique family culture that never existed before and will never exist again. Beyond their inborn individual traits, each partner represents a wholly formed social culture, a set of beliefs, norms, values, traditions, even language. One comes from a family culture where relationships are deep but a bit distant, where conflicts are suppressed or quietly handled in private. Another comes from a family culture where relationships are loud and loving, where conflicts boil up like little volcanoes and then subside and are forgotten. Now a new culture is born. Synergy lies in the relation between these two preexisting cultures. It can be a positive synergy or a negative synergy, depending on the mind-set of the partners. If they see differences as threatening, there will be a big problem. On the other hand, if they delight in the differences, in learning about one another and exploring what's new and exotic about each other, they will flourish. Someone once said, "Marrying my wife was like moving to a foreign country. Getting used to the strange customs was interesting at first. She felt the same way, but now we know the discoveries will never end. It's the greatest adventure of all."

A friend of mine was a retired schoolteacher. When he died, his wife said, "I spent forty-five years criticizing him for forgetting to take out the garbage or clean his own dishes. Now I wish I could see his smile when I come home at night. I wish I could hear his crazy whistling in the garden. I'd love to have one more day with him to tell him how much I admired his skill as a teacher, not just of his thousands of students, but also of our daughters. He was truly a gifted man." Too often we see the true value of something only after we've lost it.

A caution: When I say "Value the differences," I do *not* mean putting

3rd Alternative Thinking

I Synergize With You

I Seek You Out

I See Myself   I See You

up with anything illegal or repugnant. No one should simply tolerate addictions to alcohol, drugs, or pornography, or stay in an emotionally or physically abusive relationship without the help of competent authorities. I believe you should courageously confront abusive behaviors straight on and without delay.

Still, in the absence of illicit behavior, marital conflict usually happens because two cultures collide in a clash of values, beliefs, and expectations. People don't marry in order to fight or cause each other pain, but half of all marriages collapse because they fail to create a thriving 3rd Alternative that transcends both cultures.

A friend told me recently about his sister and her husband. They had started life together clearly in love and devoted to each other. They moved to a distant city and it became their paradise. Two girls and a little boy joined the family, and everything seemed idyllic. But, as it turns out, the husband had inherited a bit of a sarcastic streak from his mother, and the wife had grown up in a home where it was okay to hit each other. As a result, she was a "slapper." Steadily, their lives fell into a constant round of cutting remarks and slaps in the face. The transformation was so gradual they didn't realize what was happening, until a day came when the family disintegrated. A cold, hard divorce ensued, leaving three anguished little children behind.

In contrast to this destructive cycle of negative synergy, the most successful families are imbued with positive synergy. They produce not only 3rd Alternatives to conflict, but also a 3rd Alternative spirit. Synergy is the ultimate expression of a beautiful family culture, one that's creative and fun, filled with deep respect for every person and the infinite variety of each person.[1]

A 3rd Alternative Family

How do I build a 3rd Alternative marriage and family? How do I get beyond a stale or conflicted relationship to the miraculous, transformational intimacy that deep down I really want?

---

1 I am indebted to Kathleen McConkie Collinwood, a deeply experienced family lawyer and mediator, for helping me with data and understanding about these points.

I See Myself

Of course, it starts with me. As my friend Brent Barlow, a family counselor, says, "If you want to improve your marriage, look in the mirror." If I think the problem is with my partner or my child, that's the problem. By that statement, I don't mean to say that I am necessarily to blame for the conflict (although I might be). I mean that the deeper root of the problem is my view of myself. The poet Rumi said, "People of the world don't look at themselves, and so they blame one another." If I see myself as the helpless victim of an irrational, insensitive, or irritating family member, I deny a simple human truth: that I am free to choose my response to any stimulus. No one can *make* me feel or do anything without my consent. What happens to me might be beyond my influence, but I decide what to think, feel, or do about it.

Too many people fail to grasp that basic principle. These are the predictable complaints: "He makes me so mad." "She drives me up the wall." "I hate it when he does that." "It's not my fault she's impossible to live with." Although others might victimize me, ultimately the role of victim is a role I choose whether or not to play. If I'm mentally trapped in a "me-good, partner-bad" paradigm, I have fallen under the sway of 2-Alternative thinking. Dr. Steven Stosny speaks from deep experience treating injured marriages: "The problem with victim-identity is that it keeps you perpetually reactive to your resentful, angry or abusive partner, instead of proactive." If see myself as a victim, I will do nothing but moan helplessly about the injustice of it all. I will disbelieve in the 3rd Alternative.

On the other hand, if I see myself as I really am, capable of independent judgment and choice, I will choose my own response. I can choose to answer an unkind remark with a kind remark. I can choose to smile instead of taking offense. If faced with a cranky spouse who's had a hard day, I can choose to be considerate and caring instead of complaining about my own hard day in a dreary race to see which of us ends up more miserable.

I believe this fundamental insight would save most troubled families. I can choose to break the cycle of resentment. I bring more than my culture to the marriage—I bring *myself*. I am not merely "my side" in a conflict—I am always looking for a 3rd Alternative.

At bottom, most family conflicts are identity conflicts. If my self-worth is threatened, I respond by attacking the self-worth of others; this response is a way of compensating for my own deep vulnerabilities. In cases of emotional and physical abuse, most abusers have a fragile sense of self. Family members become aggressive when they feel "disregarded, unimportant, accused, guilty, devalued or disrespected, rejected, powerless, inadequate or unlovable."

Stosny describes how these family storms suddenly erupt. A wife will say, "It's cold in here." Suddenly irritated, the husband will retort, "How can you say that? It's 70 degrees!" He interprets her saying she feels cold as an attack on his character and competence as a husband: "If she's cold it must be my fault. I've failed to make her happy and protect her from discomfort." To protect himself, he devalues her feelings: she couldn't possibly be cold. "Now they both feel devalued by the other, even though no one is trying to devalue anybody."[1] Things get worse from there as they continue to beat each other up emotionally: "Well, *I'm* cold! Something must be wrong with you if you're not!" "There's nothing wrong with me! You're the one who's crazy!" And so it goes.

This cruel cycle is caused by what I have called "the real identity theft." His authentic identity as a unique, inherently valuable, powerful individual has been stolen from him. As with so many of us, he is wired to believe that his value as a human being comes from other people's estimation of him. This conditioning might be the result of a family culture of comparison: "Why can't you be smart like your brother/athletic like your sister/hardworking like your cousin Leo?" Or it might be the result of our competitive society that force-fits us into perverse and predetermined stereotypes: "You're just the dumb suburban husband on a hundred TV shows, the typical bungler who hasn't got the sense to keep himself warm." He sees only a distorted reflection of himself in the social mirror. So he becomes hypersensitive even to insults that are imaginary, and those around him, as we say, learn to walk on eggshells.

It's an appropriate metaphor: because he has a hollow identity, his self-regard is as fragile as an eggshell. He is dependent on others for his sense of self-worth. As a result, both marriage partners remain enslaved to negative synergies that destroy rather than build the relationship. In Edward Albee's *Who's Afraid of Virginia Woolf?*, an intense psychological drama about a disintegrating marriage, the wife cruelly sums up her husband's lack of a true

---

1 Hara Estroff Marano, "The Key to End Domestic Violence," *Psychology Today*, February 18, 2003.

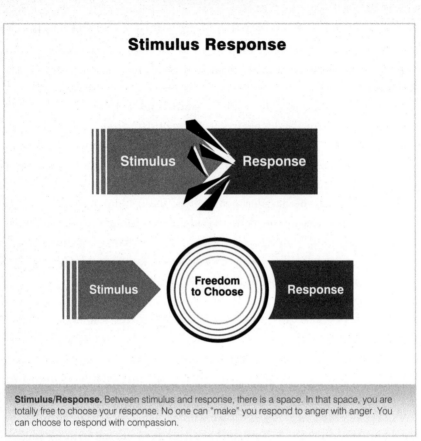

Stimulus Response

Stimulus/Response. Between stimulus and response, there is a space. In that space, you are totally free to choose your response. No one can "make" you respond to anger with anger. You can choose to respond with compassion.

identity of his own: "I sat there and I watched you, and *you* weren't *there*. . . . I swear, if you existed, I'd divorce you."[1]

Recapturing a lost identity isn't easy, but it's possible. And it can happen in an instant. When I've taught people that they are independent human beings with absolute freedom to choose, sometimes they shoot up from their chairs at this sudden insight. "All this time I've been thinking it's my husband who's making me miserable," a woman might say. "But no one can make me miserable but myself!" A man might stand up and say, "I'm choosing not to be angry and embarrassed any longer!" Other people might hurt you—perhaps even on purpose—but as Eleanor Roosevelt said, "No one can make you feel inferior without your consent." Between the stimulus and

---

1 Edward Albee, *Who's Afraid of Virginia Woolf?* (New York: Simon & Schuster, 2003), 17, 159.

the response there is a space, and within that space is *you,* perfectly free to decide how you will respond. In that space you will at last see *yourself.* There you will also find your deepest values. If you pause in that space thought-fully, you will connect once again with your conscience, your love for your family, and the principles of life. And you will decide accordingly.

Unfortunately, most people just aren't aware of that mental space. Be-cause they don't understand their own freedom, they react in one of two ways: they express their anger or they repress it in the mistaken belief that if they ignore a problem, it will go away. Everyone knows the signs of re-pression: tight lips, the silent treatment, the nervous walking on eggshells. Neither expression nor repression of anger is helpful. Trapped between these 2 Alternatives, what can you do?

There is a 3rd Alternative: you can choose to transcend those feelings. To be offended is a choice you make. It's not done to you; you do it to yourself. You have within that space of decision the power to choose *not* to be of-fended. Others can't shame you; you can only shame yourself. You cannot control the behavior of others, but you can control your own response to it. Experts agree: "The far healthier alternative to holding in your emotions or letting them spew out is transforming them. . . . The capacity to stay true to your deepest values—and thereby transform most of your fear and shame— lies entirely within you."[1] "There is a much better alternative to both 'hold-ing it in' and 'getting it out.' Transform it. Replace resentment, anger, and abusive impulses with compassion."[2]

I've said you can switch your mind-set from slavery to freedom in an instant. But it takes effort to move permanently into that new mind-set. The old mental wiring that makes you react thoughtlessly will keep buzzing away until you rewire your brain. It requires deliberate, conscious, repeated practice to pause thoughtfully in the space between stimulus and response and choose compassion.

Steven Stosny has specialized in helping perpetrators of domestic vio-lence to transform their impulses. First, he introduces them to the space between stimulus and response. He connects them to their core values in that space: "You want to be loved, right?" Of course. Then he gets them to

1 Patricia Love and Steven Stosny, *How to Improve Your Marriage Without Talking About It* (New York: Broadway Books, 2007), n.p.

2 Steven Stosny, *You Don't Have to Take It Anymore* (New York: Simon & Schuster, 2005), 63.

The 3rd Alternative

think logically within that space. "In the history of humankind has anyone ever felt more loveable by hurting someone they love?" he asks. His patients come to understand that the only way to feel better about themselves is to choose compassion instead of aggression.

Next, Stosny helps them break the cycle of abuse through intense drill and practice. Over about a month, patients go through 750 different exercises designed to rewire the brain for compassion. Each time they encounter a conflict situation, they envision the outcome they really want and then respond with kindness. Eventually, they overcome the learned reflexes of the past and build new "mental muscles" so that compassion becomes a habit.

Now when the wife says "I'm cold," the husband responds rationally. It's no longer about him—it's just the sensation she's feeling. He now has the reflex to help her instead of attacking her. As he repeatedly shows consideration, her trust and appreciation for him grow and the relationship is transformed. They are now into positive synergy.

Another positive response is humor. "How can you be *cold* when you're so *hot*?" the husband jokes and then warms her in his arms. Humor is always a 3rd Alternative because it's a surprise, an unexpected twist that makes you laugh. You'll often hear people laugh with delight when they discover a 3rd Alternative that really works. "That's pretty good," they'll say. Experts tell us that humor is the easiest way to transform tension; the "threat reaction" relaxes and disappears.[1]

We don't have to go through a month-long rehab session to break our cycles of conflict, but we do have to switch mind-sets and practice at it. Ultimately, says Stosny, "anger is not a power problem; it's a self-value problem."[2] It's not a question of who can get the upper hand in a relationship, which would be a meaningless contest anyway. It's about my identity. In the space between provocation and anger, I decide who I am and the kind of person I want to be.

I'm familiar with a couple who lost their child in an automobile accident when the wife was driving. For a long time, the wife's grief and guilt feelings were so intense that the husband felt isolated from her. Although he suffered the loss deeply, as men often do he repressed his emotions and dealt with them by working harder. She interpreted his reaction as heartless. While they continued to live in the same flat, they resented each other and grew very far apart. This misunderstanding went about as deep as it's possible to go.

Things began to change one evening when, after a long silence in their lives, the husband happened to walk past the bedroom door and saw his wife sitting on the bed upright and motionless. Seeing once again in his mind the girl he had married and how much she meant to him, he couldn't bear her sadness. Utterly at a loss how to comfort her, all he could do was sit down by her. She twisted slightly away from him, but he didn't move, and for an hour or so they just sat wordlessly together. Eventually she murmured, "Time to turn in," and they both went to sleep. This scene was repeated each evening. Without having to say anything, husband and wife began to feel a spirit of empathy growing between them, and one night she reached for his hand.

Today, many years later, they are as close as a couple can be. The transition point was the night the husband, stirred by compassion, decided not to

---

1 See David Rock, "Your Brain at Work," Google Tech Talks, November 12, 2009, http://www.youtube.com/watch?v=XeJSXfXep4M.

2 Maria Colenso, "Rage: Q&A with Dr. Steven Stosny," *Discovery Health*, n.d., http://health.discovery.com/tv/psych-week/articles/rage-q-a-sto sny.html.

respond in kind when his wife turned her back on him. The faintest gesture toward a 3rd Alternative to *my* grief and *your* grief—our *shared* grief—put this marriage on a better road. Intriguingly, they now talk about what they learned from each other through their ordeal. He found that burying his sorrow not only baffled and angered his wife, but also made him chronically depressed. He needed to acknowledge and express it. And she learned from him that getting back to work helped her to contribute and feel a part of society again. Their differences in grieving became gifts they gave each other, and they emerged a stronger family.

The choices you make in the space between stimulus and response make all the difference to the relationship between you and your spouse or partner, your parents, children, and friends.

We make life-changing decisions within that space. Many parents have a two-way internal switch; they can go from seeming self-controlled to purple-faced and screaming in an instant, thus teaching their children fear and insecurity. My own philosophy is a 3rd Alternative: have some fun with the discipline. Like all kids, mine hated work and complained like crazy when asked to do chores or something difficult. Instead of snapping back at them, I always gave them a "Two-Minute Moaning Time" in which they could whine and grumble all they wanted. When it was over, we'd get back to work.

On vacation once, my wife and I decided to take our children on a hike to a lovely mountain lake. It would be a chore to get there because it was a long, steep climb and a hot summer day. This is my daughter Cynthia's memory of it:

> We thought we were going to die on this hike up to Coffin Lake. My parents wanted us to see this beautiful place and exert ourselves for it. All we wanted to do was lie on the beach, so we attacked [Dad] for his dumb idea. "This is so stupid, we have nothing good to eat, just these stupid sandwiches, it's too hot, I'm sweating." A lot of dads would have shouted, "Shut up and stop whining!" Instead, my dad announced, "Two-Minute Moaning Time!" And we vented. "Okay, Moaning Time is over," and on we went. He just let us get it out, and somehow it kind of worked. We said all the mean things we wanted to, he just smiled through it, and it worked! It changed our outlook. When we got to Coffin Lake, it was beautiful and we did appreciate it more for making all that effort.

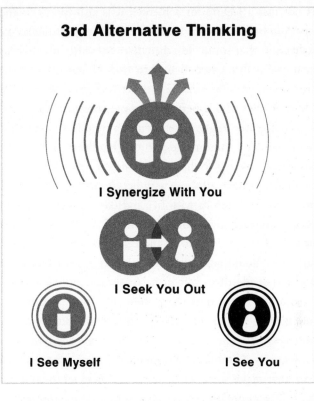

3rd Alternative Thinking

I Synergize With You

I Seek You Out

I See Myself   I See You

In the end, if I want to have a happy marriage, I must be the kind of person who generates positive synergy. If I want to have a more pleasant, cooperative teenager, I must be a more understanding, empathic, consistent, loving parent. As I design my own identity, I also determine the destiny of my family.

I See You

To say "I see you" means saying "I acknowledge your unique individuality." It's often hard to do that in a family setting. Naturally, I enter marriage or parenthood with my ideas of what I want it to be like. I have expectations of family members. But it's a great mistake to *impose* my ideas and expectations on them. If I love them, I will see them first as individuals and then seek to understand their differences. To reduce loved ones to my idea of what they should be is to turn them into things. And people are not things. Dostoevsky said, "To love someone means to see him as God intended him," not as *I* intend him.

Love is not just a feeling for someone; it is also the willingness to see her as a person in her own right. In the words of Iris Murdoch, "Love is the difficult realization that someone other than oneself is real." This certainly means that we value differences—not just tolerate but *celebrate* differences. To celebrate is to rejoice in the differences between us, to leverage the unique gifts of each. A mother who hyperventilates over the amount of time her son spends on the computer might instead make a friend of her son by learning about video games and joining the party. A hardheaded, practical brother who sees his artistic sister as foolish might find creative ideas for his business by going to an avant-garde art show with her. A father who hates his daughter's earphones might listen in with her and come to understand what the music she loves can teach him about her world. If we celebrate others' values, they are more likely to respond to us and celebrate what we value as well.

Of course, we should guard family members against harmful or wasteful behavior and guide them out of it. In some families, those behaviors get out of hand. No one is under any obligation to respect or even tolerate illegal or offensive behavior: I'm not going to empathize with child abuse or drug trafficking. But that doesn't mean that every difference is a menace. Far too many family members make enemies of each other by rejecting the very qualities that make them who they are. Where a husband or wife sees differences as threatening, the energy they could use in complementing one another's strengths and weaknesses becomes malignant. Where parents or siblings don't value each other's differences, the negative synergies can become very damaging.

The great psychiatrist Stella Chess lived to be ninety-three years old, which was a blessing because she lived long enough to conduct an unparalleled forty-year study of a group of people she observed from babyhood to adulthood. Beginning in 1956, she followed the lives of 238 newborns from different backgrounds to see how their parents, with their different approaches to child rearing, would affect the development of the children. After the first decade of the experiment, she published a book with the provocative title *Your Child Is a Person,* arguing that children are not little robots just waiting to be programmed by their parents.

Chess saw that every child is unique, and noted that where parents appreciate that uniqueness, children thrive. Her studies verify what a successful parent once said to me about raising children: "Treat them all the same by treating them differently," respecting their differences. Chess also found that

some children and their parents are a "poor fit," meaning that their tempera-
ments, goals, and values don't match.

This was the case with "Norman," one of her study children. When the
little boy started school, his parents came to see her with a real concern.
Norman had begun life as a cheerful, friendly child; but in the playroom
he would quickly drop one activity after another. Chess diagnosed a short
attention span, but the problem was not severe. She told his parents he
was distractible but could learn well in "short spurts." "Nothing doing!" the
father grumbled. "What I call his behavior is irresponsibility and a lack of
character and will power. He has to shape up and that's that."

Chess wrote, "All we could do was watch, feeling helpless and disheart-
ened. Year by year Norman's symptoms grew worse, and his academic standard
slipped. His father, a hard-driving, very persistent and successful professional
man, became increasingly hypercritical and derogatory." Convinced his son
was irresponsible and headed for failure in life, the father "provided the seeds
of a self-fulfilling prophecy." By age twenty-two, Norman was "essentially
nonfunctional, slept most of the day, and talked about grandiose plans for
a career as a musician." When Chess closed the study after forty years, she
wrote that Norman's had "truly been an inexorably tragic life course."[1]

Today we know that children with mild attention problems like Norman's can thrive with strong parental support. Indeed their energy and curiosity can bring huge value to a team of people who are more thoughtful or
passive. Inside the Magic Theater, where creativity is at a premium, Norman
would be a great asset. If his father had valued Norman's quick, inventive
mind, Norman might have flourished and his father learned about the power
of spontaneity. In turn, Norman might have responded better to his father's
coaching about focusing himself and concentrating on a task. Instead Norman's condition grew worse. Although scientists believe brain chemistry can
cause attention-deficit disorder, they know that "family dysfunction" can
contribute to it.[2]

I know of a woman with three nearly grown children. The older son is an
aimless drug addict; the daughter is obsessed with her weight to the point of
anorexia; the younger son, buried in an underworld of escapist video games,

1 Stella Chess and Alexander Thomas, *Goodness of Fit: Clinical Applications from Infancy
   through Adult Life* (London: Psychology Press, 1999), 8, 100–108.
2 See Eric J. Mash, *Child Psychopathology* (New York: Guilford Press, 2003), 77.

is failing in school. Each of these children was born bright and healthy and gifted. But their mother, a farmer's daughter, blustered and bullied them from childhood over what she perceived as faults in their character. She rags them constantly about their laziness. "I was up at five every morning to haul hay and milk cows," she growls. "What's the matter with these kids?" She plays manipulative games, such as withholding food or locking them out if they're late coming home. She demands they conform to her image of a good kid, constantly threatening to kick them out if they don't. In other words, she wants them to be *her*. Now that they are about to leave her, I doubt they will look back.

I also know of a father who is a classically trained musician. Although not a wealthy man, he lives in a refined world. He reared his daughter in an atmosphere of symphonic music, good books, and lots of conversation about ideas. The daughter, however, likes fishing and rock music. How does he get along with her? "I can't think of anything more boring than fishing," he says, "but I can't think of anything more interesting than my daughter." So he goes with her. He comes home smelly, sunburned, scratching mosquito bites, and laughing alongside her at their shared jokes. She mixes rock music for him to listen to. The recordings make him wince but also open his mind to new beats and musical ideas. And he was secretly delighted one day to overhear his daughter telling a friend how much she loved classical music too. "You've never heard of Sibelius?" she said to the friend. "No, he's a composer, not a rock band." This rare little family culture is not split but united by differences.

Every child is a 3rd Alternative with his or her own gifts. When children are labeled by their parents or compared negatively to another, it immediately diminishes their feelings of self-worth and they begin to "own" their label. I have heard parents say in the presence of their children, "Peter is our lazy one" or "Kim can't sing" or "This is our smart child." As you look at the child as the parent is describing him or her, you can almost see the child *becoming* that label. Rather than comparing or labeling my children, my wife and I tried very deliberately to value them for their unique personalities and characteristics. This I believe has made them comfortable and confident in their uniqueness. A lot of sibling rivalry can be avoided when a parent refuses to compare children or to take sides between them. Each one is equally precious to me.

When my grandson Covey was living abroad for a few years, he wrote his parents (my daughter Maria is his mother) a letter explaining that he was doing a self-inventory and he wanted them to list his strengths and weaknesses. He reasoned that since they had raised him and most likely knew him best, their insights would help him discover areas in which he could improve. They wrote back to him, but only acknowledged his strengths. "If there are weaknesses," his mother wrote, "they are between you and God. He will make known to you how you can become the person you were meant to be." Personally, I'm a believer that people are fully aware of their weaknesses, but not so much their strengths. Jonathan Swift believed this too: "It is in men as it is in soils, where sometimes there is a vein of gold which the owner knows not of."[1] When they are defined according to their *potential* and not some narrow characteristic, that treatment inspires children rather than turning them into stereotypes on a shelf.

I'm impressed with the tender wisdom of the great cellist Pablo Casals, who gave countless children music lessons over his long life:

> *What do we teach our children? We teach them that two and two make four, and that Paris is the capital of France. When will we also teach them what they are?*
>
> *We should say to each of them: Do you know what you are? You are a marvel. You are unique. In all the years that have passed, there has never been another child like you. Your legs, your arms, your clever fingers, the way you move.*
>
> *You may become a Shakespeare, a Michelangelo, a Beethoven. You have the capacity for anything. Yes, you are a marvel. And when you grow up, can you then harm another who is, like you, a marvel?*
>
> *You must work, we must all work, to make the world worthy of its children.*[2]

"We're not at all alike." "We're too different." "We have nothing in common." So often these complaints lie behind the infamous "incompatibility" divorce. Alienated parents and children talk about each other the same way. Yet divergent interests, singular gifts, quirky personalities—these make life

---

1 Jonathan Swift, "A Treatise on Good Manners and Good Breeding," in *The English Essayists*, ed. Robert Cochrane (Edinburgh: W.P. Nimmo, 1887), Google e-book, 196.
2 Pablo Casals, *Joys and Sorrows* (New York: Simon & Schuster, 1974), 295.

and love intriguing and compelling. What's missing in these relationships is the mind-set my musician friend has: to really *see* the loved one as a treasure like no other and her differences as gifts.

The true opposite of "incompatible" is "compassionate." Both words are rooted in the concept of "feeling together." As Steven Stosny says, compassion "sensitizes you to the individuality and vulnerability of your loved ones. It makes you see that your wife is a different person from you, with a separate set of experiences, a different temperament, different vulnerabilities, and in some respects, different values."[1]

Too many wives and husbands want to worship images of themselves in each other. Too many parents want clones of themselves instead of children. Cloning their kids gives parents social mileage and a false sense of security. When you have children who think like you, act like you, speak like you, and even groom like you, your identity feels validated.

But sameness is not oneness, and uniformity is not unity. The family is the ideal complementary team, where unity is achieved by people who have different talents and who are united in love for each other and deeply appreciate their contrasting roles, perceptions, and capacities.

This is the best advice I can give my married children: Don't try to make your spouse better: try to make him or her happy. We have a tendency to want our spouses to be more like us, as if our way were the better way. As I learned myself in my own marriage, that never works, and it disregards the unique gifts they bring to the marriage. Instead of trying to make them over into your own image, appreciate their differences, run with them, and put your efforts into trying to make them happy.

I Seek You Out

"Family quarrels are bitter things," said F. Scott Fitzgerald, "like splits in the skin that won't heal." The way to heal divisions in your own family is to seek out your loved ones and practice Talking Stick communication with them. Although quarrels involve more than one person, it takes only one person to start the healing process. It's the absolute prerequisite to 3rd Alternative solutions to problems.

It works like this. I go up to you and say, "You've got the Talking Stick." That means I can't say anything except to restate your position. I can ask a

---

1 Stosny, *You Don't Have to Take It Anymore*, 208.

3rd Alternative Thinking

I Synergize With You

I Seek You Out

I See Myself   I See You

question to make sure I understand your point, but I can't make my own point, I can't agree, and I can't disagree. All I can do is communicate your point back to you until you feel understood. Then you pass the Talking Stick to me. Now it's my turn, and you are quiet and you listen with empathy until I feel understood. Then I pass it back to you.

Talking Stick communication transforms defensive, negative energy into creative, positive energy. Here's why: when you really listen to others in depth until they feel understood, you are communicating how much they mean to you. You are affirming them. It is so therapeutic, so healing, that they cannot fight you, and they gradually become more and more open.

Talking Stick communication takes time, but I guarantee it will save endless time and stress in your family life. People who have been stubbornly divided for years open up to each other. Deep animosities dissolve in tears as family members embrace one another again.

Unfortunately, Talking Stick communication is rare.

I once heard a man refer to his wife as a "contradiction machine." She's

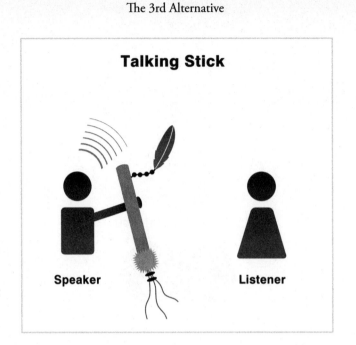

Talking Stick

Speaker   Listener

impatient, he said, and it doesn't matter what anyone says, she will say the opposite: "My daughter will say nobody likes her. My wife will say, 'That's ridiculous, everybody likes you.'" This pattern might seem innocuous, but it stifles communication: the child learns that her feelings are "ridiculous" and that no one is interested in hearing her out. The girl will say, "I'm not going to school anymore." Her mother will respond, "Are you out of your mind? You most certainly are going to school." This response cuts off the daughter's psychological air, and eventually she will lash out and start her own counteroffensive.

If, like this mother, you are formulating your answers while your daughter is talking, you are not listening to her. Can she really be free and open with you if you reflexively counter everything she says? If she can't face school, will you ever begin to grasp the real hurt she feels or understand why there is such pain?

Well-intentioned parents often feel that their job is to fix their children's problems. It's instinctive. This mother simply denies that the problem exists—that's one strategy. More sensitive parents respond with advice. When their child says, "I've got a problem," they say, "Well, here's something you should consider." But a parent's *real* job is to raise children who can come up with their own 3rd Alternatives. When your child says, "I've got a problem," that's your signal that he or she is probably caught in a

2-Alternative situation. Her boyfriend is pressuring her. He's not making the grade at school. The other kids are caught up in drugs. The wise parent responds this way: "Tell me more." "You're really struggling with this." "You're not sure what to think."

There are several problems with just handing out advice, no matter how good it is. You take away a growth opportunity for the child, for her to talk through—and think through with you—all her complex feelings about the problem. You short-circuit her resourcefulness and initiative. You rob her of the chance to come up with her own 3rd Alternative. You make her more dependent on you, and dependence breeds helplessness and resentment.

You could say, "Stay away from those dopeheads. I don't want you involved with them." Good advice, but will it calm the turmoil she feels if you reduce the issue to such a simple answer? These are her friends, people she has ties to and affection for. Can she just turn her back on them? Should she try to help them? Or should she cut them off? Before dealing out advice, you can listen empathically to all of this in the realization that she will work out most of her *own* answers. And together you might come up with a 3rd Alternative that will keep her safe and help her friends as well. The great child psychologist Haim Ginott wrote:

> *The beginning of wisdom is listening. Listening that is empathic enables parents to hear the feelings that the words try to convey, to hear what children are feeling and experiencing. . . . Parents need an open mind and an open heart, which will help them to listen to all kinds of truths, be they pleasant or unpleasant. But many parents are afraid of listening because they may not like what they hear.*[1]

You may want to solve your children's problems for them, and they may want you to. But if you do, you deprive yourself and your children of the chance to work together toward synergy. When parents see their children's problems as opportunities to build the relationship instead of as negative, burdensome irritations to be quickly dealt with, it totally changes the nature of parent-child interactions. Parents become more willing to, even excited about deeply understanding and helping their children. When a child comes to you with a problem, instead of thinking, "Oh, no! I don't have time for

1 Haim Ginott, *Between Parent and Child* (New York: Random House Digital, 2009), n.p.

this!," your paradigm is "Here is a great opportunity for me to really help my child and to invest in our relationship." Strong bonds of love and trust are created as children sense the value parents give to their problems and to them as individuals. I'm grateful now that, although there were many lapses, I tried to seek out my own growing children and understand their problems. My efforts, such as they were, have paid many dividends. This is what my daughter Jenny recalls:

> *Growing up, I never felt I had cause to rebel because my parents always made me feel understood. They truly listened to me. I saw with my friends that even a simple thing like a curfew could cause so many problems because the parents said, "This is the rule, no discussion." And it stopped there. But my parents would discuss it with me, ask my opinion, and listen to me about it. I didn't feel defensive. Any urge to fight back was dissipated by the feeling of being understood. Now, with my own children, if I just take the time to really listen, to understand, the kids are much more willing to listen to me.*
>
> *Once when I was a teenager, the family was going to Sundance resort for a weekend trip. I didn't want to go because I had something going on with my friends. My dad said, "No, we're all off to Sundance tonight, and that's my decision." Like teens do, I got really mad, retreated to my bed, and swore I would never forgive him. He hadn't listened to me one bit and didn't care how I felt. Then a few seconds later there was a knock on the door. It was Dad. He said, "I'm sorry I didn't listen to you. Tell me why you want to stay home." After listening to me, he said, "I completely understand," and we figured out a way for me to stay home and even bring my friends to Sundance later in the weekend.*
>
> *Apologizing and listening really can fix the problem if it's sincere. I'm fortunate because I've felt listened to my whole life. Honestly, I never got into slamming doors and getting mad at my parents while they shouted "My way or the highway." Because I felt validated, I was very open to what they had to say.*
>
> *Now as a parent I try to remind myself, "Don't come in with your answers. Just stop and listen to what they have to say."*

If you end up caught in a quarrel with a loved one, you can choose the compassionate, empathic response. One expert says, "If you step on a family member's toes, or if a family member, in the heat of the moment, says some-thing to anger or upset you, treat it as a miscommunication—an invitation to find out more about why you are at cross-purposes."[1] I like this approach. You have the power to decide whether to be offended or to understand the story your loved one is telling herself. A moment of tension can lead to a stronger bond rather than a break between you if you use it as an opening to synergy.

There might be a flare-up between you and your daughter. When you say, "I want you to give up those dopehead friends of yours," she may respond, "No, I won't. They're my friends, they're the only ones who care about me." All your instincts tell you to fight back: "If they want you to do drugs, they are not your friends. And they most certainly are not the only ones who care about you. *I* care about you a lot more than they do!" But if you're a wise parent, you will back off from dispensing advice and dictating solutions. You will recognize that she just took an unfair shot at your own identity as a loving parent, and you will feel hurt. But if you're a 3rd Alternative thinker, you'll grasp at this chance to go for something better than either of you has thought of before. First, you'll invite her to tell you her story, and you will listen with real empathy. Calm down and say, "Okay, help me to understand what's going on here." It's a neutral invitation.

She replies, "All you care about is yourself. You just don't want a dope-head daughter. It'll make you look bad."

Ouch. This, of course, is totally unfair to you. But please remember, you are not interested in fairness—you are interested in your daughter's welfare. Put yourself in her mind and let go temporarily of your own hurts and anxieties. It's her story you're concerned about right now, not yours. You say, "This has been hard for you."

After a while she replies. "I just feel like I'm all alone. You have your work. Everybody at school has something. I don't have anything. Ria and Matt are the only ones I can talk to."

A thousand responses crowd your brain: "You're not alone, little girl. I'm always here for you. You're far more important to me than my work. And you have a lot going for you. You're smart, you're pretty, you have talent. Ria and Matt are such a bad influence." And so on, ad infinitum. But you say none of it. You don't have the Talking Stick right now. Instead you reflect her thinking, not yours: "So you really depend on Ria and Matt."

---

1 Sichel, *Healing from Family Rifts,* 166.

"I try to fit in," she says. "I've tried to make friends, but nobody wants me around except them. And they're good to me. They love me. We talk all the time now. I know they're making real trouble for themselves with the drugs and all."

You say, "You're very worried about them."

She says, "They offered me some last night. They kept talking about how cool it was, how it makes you feel. But I've seen them when they come down off the high. It's pretty awful to watch."

You say, "It must be hard to see your friends suffer."

She says, "Yeah, I can't imagine doing that to myself."

And so it goes. As an empathic listener, you've discovered deeply important things about your daughter. You've found out about her loneliness, her struggle to be accepted, her devotion to some young people who have taken her in and who are struggling themselves. You've also found that she's conflicted about the drugs; she knows the risks and recognizes that her friends are in crisis. You've learned that what you *thought* was the problem *isn't*. She's not headed for addiction. She is not in rebellion against you. Despite her cutting comments, which were a defensive move on her part, this isn't really about you at all.

Consider what's happening in your daughter's heart and mind. Your willingness to listen makes it possible for her to share these tender insights. Gradually, you are becoming her friend instead of being walled off as an enemy in an "us against you" story. The story has changed. You're now "one of us."

Notice that you haven't agreed or disagreed with anything she says. You haven't condoned her friends' use of drugs or their action in offering them to your daughter. You haven't bought in to her image of herself as unwanted and unloved. You have simply listened so that you can understand the story. At this point, your job is to see what she sees and feel what she feels, to say, "You see things differently. I need to listen to you."

Now you are preparing to move on to the 3rd Alternative. By definition, you don't know what it will be. There's always a risk in going for the 3rd Alternative; you have no guarantee that you'll arrive at something better. You don't know where you and your daughter will end up in this journey of feelings. But if you fail to listen empathically, I guarantee you will throw up thick walls between yourself and your daughter, walls of misunderstanding and pain. Breaking through those walls can be tough indeed.

By contrast, the more you listen to her story, the lower the emotional barriers between yourself and your daughter. "Stories take us beyond those walls," says Elif Shafak. Where walls are made of hard stone, "stories are flowing water" that erode the walls.[1] Like a stream, the story finds its own course and it may take you to an unexpected destination. The more you follow the current of the story, the better your prospects for getting to the 3rd Alternative.

In our fix-it, cut-to-the-chase, problem-solving culture, we lose a great deal of perspective because we have no patience for each other's stories, the complex story of struggle, suffering, loss and triumph that is unique to each of us. We think we already know it all. Experts say, "One of the greatest difficulties in building relationships is that we cannot always see clearly or completely within the heart, mind, and experience of another person. This is especially problematic in marriage where, based on years (or sometimes just months) of experience, we think we know our partners completely."[2] As a result, we dismiss, avoid, and close our ears to each other's stories. Instead of listening to each other, we isolate ourselves and our children from conflict. The result is an "empathy deficit."

Some cultures do better. For millennia the Xhosa people of South Africa have resolved conflicts by encouraging everyone to tell their stories in an open meeting called a *xotla*. The purpose of the *xotla*, which can go on for days, is to allow everyone a chance to be heard "until the parties have literally exhausted their negative feelings." War is unknown among them.[3] Similarly, the aboriginal cultures of Canada use stories to defuse tension and teach children how to resolve conflicts. When there's a quarrel, the family or the community will meet in a "talking circle" so that empathy can flow. One participant in a First Nations family workshop explains how this works:

> *We don't usually think of using "time out" with a child who is not doing what we want him to do. To many of us here, isolating a child from his community seems to be the opposite of what we want him to learn. Maybe the child needs to be brought in even closer within the circle of his*

---

1 Elif Shafak, "The Politics of Fiction," July 16, 2010, TED.com.

2 H. Wallace Goddard and James P. Marshall, *The Marriage Garden: Cultivating Your Relationship So It Grows and Flourishes* (New York: Wiley, 2010), 80.

3 See William L. Ury, "Conflict Resolution among the Bushmen: Lessons in Dispute Systems Design," *Negotiation Journal*, October 1995, 379–89.

community and to hear talk from his friends about what they are trying to accomplish. Then he might see how he is needed to help the group.

As they hear stories of how others resolved their problems, children learn empathy, along with "the moral values and behavioral expectations of the community." Better than direct instruction or correction, stories can "speak to the spirit of the child."[1]

My son Sean shared with me how seeking out his son transformed their relationship.

In college, I achieved a lifelong dream of becoming a college-football quarterback. After leading my team for two years, my dreams were cut short when I tore my knee ligaments. Years later, now married and working, you can imagine how thrilled I was to have my first child be a boy. How fun it would be to train him to be a great quarterback! So I coached him and trained him from first to eighth grade, season after season, and he became an outstanding quarterback. As you can imagine, I was so proud and would say as I watched him play, "Yep, that's my boy."

Then one day in the summer between his eighth- and ninth-grade years, Michael Sean told me he didn't want to play football the following year. I was shocked. "Are you crazy? Do you know how good you are? Do you know how much time I've spent training you?" He responded simply that he didn't want to play. The idea was very threatening to me and shook me to my core. Obviously, a lot of my emotional security depended on his becoming a great football player. For days I kept trying to persuade him but didn't make much progress.

Ironically, at that time, in my job as a product developer, I was designing a seminar on how to be a better listener. It hit me one day that I had yet to really listen to my son. I think I was afraid that he really might not play. As I prepared myself to really listen, I had to come face to face with my motives. Was I trying to raise a football player or a son? Was I

1 Jessica Ball and Onowa McIvor, "Learning About Teaching as if Communities Mattered," paper presented at World Indigenous People's Conference on Education, Hamilton, NZ, November 27, 2005, 6, http://www.ecdip.org/docs/pdf/WIPCE%20FNPP%20Learning%20Points.pdf.

doing this for him or for myself? As I thought it through, it became clear to me that I needed to raise a son; and that in the great scheme of things, football didn't really matter much.

Soon I had my chance. "So Michael Sean, you don't feel like playing football next year."

"Nope," he replied.

I was quiet.

"I didn't really like it much last year," he said.

"So last year didn't go too well for you?"

"Not at all."

I simply nodded, acknowledging the statement.

"I hated it last year, Dad. I got thrashed on the field. I mean, take a look at me. I'm half the size of everyone else."

"You got beaten up last year, huh?" By this time Michael Sean could tell that I really cared and had no other agenda except wanting to understand him. So he really opened up.

"Yeah, I mean, everyone is so much bigger than me. I haven't got my growth yet, Dad, and I haven't grown this summer. You were big when you were young, so you wouldn't understand."

"You don't think I would understand."

And so it continued. As I listened, I learned many new things about my son. He felt small. He felt insecure and vulnerable. We had just moved to a new area and he didn't know many people. He got beaten up the year before. He felt pressure to measure up to my expectations of him.

After a few minutes while I genuinely tried to understand him, he asked, "So, Dad, what do you think I should do?"

I said, "Hey, I'm good either way. Seriously. If you want to play, great. If not, great. You decide. I'll support you either way."

Only a few days later he came to me and said, "Dad, I want to play football next year." I was happy to hear that, but it wasn't a big deal to me. I would have been just fine the other way. The good news was that my son and I got closer that day and have remained close since. I discovered that when it comes to relationships, fast is slow and slow is fast. Spending thirty minutes really trying to understand put an issue to rest that might have gone on for months or caused a lot of friction between us. Truly, empathy is the fastest form of communication.

Deep understanding of the other person's story inevitably inspires compassion. When we truly see through the tears, when we finally feel what's in the heart of a loved one, we are transformed. Our paradigms change radically. An impudent teenager becomes a lonely, struggling young girl or boy. A silent, morose husband becomes a man who's always had to wrestle with inner inadequacy, depression, and heartbreak. We see into the heart of an aged and cranky parent who hurts over long-gone opportunities and despairs over her diminishing life. The heart of each one is tender, and when we touch that tenderness, we are in a sacred place.

In the story "The Last Judgment" by the Czech writer Karel Čapek, the soul of a brutal murderer is brought to the judgment bar of heaven. Three bored judges try his case. They call a witness to testify, "an extraordinary gentleman, stately, bearded, and clothed in a blue robe strewn with golden stars." It turns out this is the only witness needed because he is "the Omniscient God." The defendant is warned not to interrupt the witness because "He knows everything, so there's no use denying anything." The witness verifies that the defendant committed atrocities, but tells more. As a child, he loved his mother dearly, but was unable to show it. At six, he lost his only toy, a precious colored-glass marble, and he cried. At seven, he stole a rose so he could give it to a little girl, who grew up and rejected him to marry a rich man. Homeless as a youngster, he had shared his food with other vagrants. "He was generous and often helpful. He was kind to women, gentle with animals, and kept his word."

Nevertheless, as expected, the judges condemn the defendant to everlasting punishment. At one point the defendant asks God, "Why don't You Yourself do the judging?" God replies, "Because I know everything. If the judges knew everything, absolutely everything, they couldn't judge, either: they would understand everything, and their hearts would ache. . . . I know everything about you. Everything. And that's why I cannot judge you."[1]

To me, this story illustrates that the more I understand about you, the more tender I feel toward you and the less inclined I am to rule on your worth as a human being. The less I understand, the more likely I am to see you as a "thing" to be judged, manipulated, and dismissed.

---

1 Karel Čapek, "The Final Judgment," in *Tales from Two Pockets*, trans. Norma Comrada (North Haven, CT: Catbird Press, 1994), 155–59.

Starting with yourself, you can create a family culture of empathy just by inviting others—your children, your aged parents, your partner—to tell you their stories, especially in a troubled situation. Exercise your empathy muscles. Ask them about conflicts they've faced, misunderstandings they've encountered. Listen to their tales of struggle. As you develop an empathic bond with others, you will find that they respond in kind. Empathy is contagious.

My brother John, who has deep experience counseling and training families, told me this story about a family that looked ideal on the surface but suffered intensely from an empathy deficit:

> *This was a family of productive people, smart parents, great kids. The parents asked us to visit with them because all hell was breaking loose with their teenagers.*
>
> *So we began by inviting the parents into another room and then sat down just with the kids. At first, they were unwilling to talk, but these were bright, articulate people. Soon they opened up and told us their parents simply didn't listen to them. There was no respect or empathy. Talking Stick communication is not just listening. It's also showing deep respect. So here we were empathizing with them. They had been told what to do all their lives, but had never had an expression of their own free will. They had started to bury alive deep resentments. They had never been listened to, never been allowed to synergize, to flower.*
>
> *We listened to them all day. Then we invited the parents in and gave all of them an exercise. "Put down on a piece of paper any word that comes to you around the word* friends.*"*
>
> *Then we compared the lists. Not one word was the same. It was night and day. When the mother realized the point of this exercise, she at last understood. She took a ruler from a drawer and gave it to her children. "From now on, if you've got something to say, you pick up that ruler. That means 'I want to talk and I've got something to say.'" Then the mom listened. The culture changed.*
>
> *Every Sunday afternoon, they said, we're going to take a bike ride, just to get acquainted. Just to get to know each other.*[1]

1 Interview with John Covey, February 18, 2011.

The Islamic sages tell us that "knowledge that takes you not beyond yourself is far worse than ignorance."[1] The more willing I am to know your heart, the more power you and I have to move together beyond our divisions to a third place that is far better than where we are now.

I Synergize With You

The family itself is a 3rd Alternative. It begins as a literal marriage of two unique human beings and two cultures. If governed by the paradigms of respect and empathy for self and partner, the result is a third culture, a new and infinitely fruitful relationship where we can find our deepest joys and our most profound satisfactions.

We create a 3rd Alternative family by deliberately adopting the mind-set of synergy: not my way, not your way, but *our* way—a higher and better way. We train ourselves to adopt this mind-set by persistently going for the 3rd Alternative in all our important interactions. How to raise children, manage money, balance careers, make religious choices, promote intimacy—these are important issues and need to be handled with synergy.

Too often these issues are handled not only without synergy, but also without respect or empathy, as in these exchanges:

- "I don't understand why we're always in debt. We make plenty of money." "Oh, get off my back."
- "I wish you weren't so hard on the kids." "How will they ever learn if they don't get disciplined?"
- "You're never home." "I work myself to the bone to provide for this family, and all you do is complain."

Most of our conflicts don't involve such tough issues. Say we're on vacation and I want to lie on the beach while you want to play golf. This sort of thing doesn't usually need synergy; we can do both, split up for the afternoon, or choose one. It's no big deal.

Years ago, when my son Josh was about thirteen, I took him to play golf on a Saturday afternoon. I intended to play nine holes with him and then return home to listen to an important radio broadcast. I didn't realize that he expected we would play all eighteen holes, and he was very sad when

---

1 Shafak, "Politics of Fiction," TED.com.

3rd Alternative Thinking

I Synergize With You

I Seek You Out

I See Myself   I See You

I told him we'd have to quit and go home. He loved to play golf, and we had precious little time together as it was. Suddenly I had a real dilemma on my hands—to disappoint my son and miss spending time with him, or miss a broadcast that was important to my work. But there's always a 3rd Alternative: I had a small radio in my car, and I plugged in an earphone and did both. Josh and I had a great time together and I got the gist of the broadcast.

We can find 3rd Alternatives like this all day. Small conflicts just need a little creativity and the instinct to go for a 3rd Alternative. Still, if we're chronically in conflict over much bigger issues, a small skirmish can blow up into a battle. In such a case, the issue is not the beach versus golf, it's the nature of our relationship. Do we choose to live in positive or negative synergy?

If you want to move into positive synergy, I can't overemphasize the importance of the paradigms "I See Myself," "I See You," and "I Seek You Out." Unless I have a respectful and empathic character, I can't even think of going for a 3rd Alternative with you. Otherwise, attempts at synergy are just mind games. Synergy comes from the inside out, and if I start playing games with you, you'll know it.

Although empathy is essential, it is not enough by itself to resolve really tough challenges. As the philosopher J.D. Trout says, "Empathy is a place to start. Unfortunately, many are paralyzed before the finish."[1] In itself, empathy can be transforming, but unless we go for the 3rd Alternative, the problem remains. Family contention just exhausts some people. Others simply don't believe a 3rd Alternative is possible. They may deeply understand why their wives or husbands or children or parents behave as they do and even empathize with them, but they've given up hope that anything can ever change. Still others believe in synergy, and believe that other families can achieve it, but don't believe they have the skills or aptitude to do it in their own homes. They doubt themselves.

Couples can live together for decades in such a state of "emotional divorce," battling again and again over the same issues because neither has the courage to ask the other, "Are you willing to go for something better than we have?"

But if we do, we can enter into what some experts call the "Third Space." Rather than dragging you over to my view or abdicating to your view, we look for a new place that incorporates the best of both of our insights. In the Third Space, we "make a fundamental shift from dualistic, exclusive perceptions of reality and adopt a mind-set that integrates the complementary aspects of diverse values, behaviors, and beliefs into a new whole." In simpler terms, we stop thinking in terms of "my way versus your way" and start thinking in terms of "our way," a way that takes advantage of what's special about us. In the Third Space, "where we are is where we've never been."[2]

As we've seen with the empathic exchange between a parent and daughter about drugs, the story doesn't end there. As the daughter talks, they gradually move together into a Third Space, a Magic Theater where alternatives can be played out. Recall that the daughter has just revealed how awful it is to watch her friends' agonizing drug binges.

You say, "It must be hard to see your friends suffer."

---

1 J.D. Trout, *The Empathy Gap: Building Bridges to the Good Life and the Good Society* (New York: Penguin, 2009), n.p.
2 Isaura Barrera, Robert M. Corso, and Dianne Macpherson, *Skilled Dialogue: Strategies for Responding to Cultural Diversity in Early Childhood* (Baltimore: P.H. Brookes, 2003), n.p.

She replies, "I think it scares them, but they don't know how to stop. There's nobody for them to talk to. They can't talk to their parents . . . not the way I can."

Now you're thinking to yourself, "That's better. Empathy has its benefits." But she still has the Talking Stick, so you say, "It would mean a lot if Ria and Matt could get some help."

She continues thinking aloud. "Their parents would kill them if they knew. The teachers at school go on and on about drugs, but nobody listens anymore. And the guidance counselors are all right, but they're so busy. Who could they talk to?"

"What do you think?" you ask.

So far all you have done is reflect her own inner turmoil, and now she's easing herself into the Magic Theater—with your help. Many alternatives are now possible, and none of them involves your daughter getting into drugs. Instead, it sounds like she's made her own choice and wants to find some way to help her friends escape.

Some years ago a young man named Gerardo González faced the same issues. His parents had taken him to Florida from Cuba as a boy, and he had grown up in a workaday refugee culture where college was nowhere on the horizon. While working in a shop, he enrolled with a friend in a community college course and became fascinated with the intellectual life. He read great books and got into debates. "My worldview was being completely transformed through education and I simply could not get enough of it!" he later said.[1]

Gerardo wanted more, and soon his dream was realized when he was admitted to the University of Florida. But once there, he found himself surrounded by a nightmare he never expected: the other students, his friends and classmates, would get wildly drunk on the weekends. Auto accidents, alcohol poisoning, assaults—all the frightening consequences haunted him. Of course, the university campaigned against binge drinking and the police fought it, but nothing seemed to work. Unwilling to abandon his friends or join them in their self-destructive behavior, Gerardo started thinking about a 3rd Alternative.

---

1 Gerardo M. González, "The Challenge of Latino Education: A Personal Story," Indiana University, October 23, 2008, 9, http://education.indiana.edu/LinkClick.aspx?fileticket =8JJOYwMZ3wc; pc3D&tabid=6282.

Realizing that young people his age would be more likely to listen to each other than to the authorities, he helped gather a group of students together to educate their friends and support them in stopping the binges. The group called themselves BACCHUS—Boosting Alcohol Consciousness Concerning the Health of University Students. It was a stunning success, and soon chapters spread to other universities affected by the plague of excessive drinking. Decades later, the BACCHUS Network is "the largest active student organization in higher education today." Gerardo and his friends set in motion an entirely new approach to helping young people avoid risky behaviors, what is now called the "peer education" or "peer support" movement. In its many forms, peer education has become a standard tool for most schools in the battle against drug and alcohol abuse.[1] It is a powerful 3rd Alternative to suppression on one hand and neglect on the other—and it works, perhaps better than any other approach out there.[2] Incidentally, today Dr. Gerardo M. González is a college professor and dean of education in one of America's great universities.

I can imagine our parent-daughter partnership coming up with something like involvement in a peer-support program as a way to help her friends. For the daughter, it would have to be a genuine 3rd Alternative that avoids both "de-friending" them and joining them in their destructive activities. There might be many other viable 3rd Alternatives to this false dilemma. They might not work out, but the very process of going through synergy achieves so much. The bond between parent and child will become stronger with mutual respect and empathy. In the Magic Theater, their relationship is transformed as they work together on creative solutions for a real problem. Consider the parent's other options: to dictate, advise, plead, lecture, bribe, lock the child in her room, give her the silent treatment, "kick butts and take names." Would any of those be as transformative?

---

1 "The BACCHUS Network Organizational History," http://www.bacchusgamma.org/history.asp.
2 See Judith A. Tindall et al., *Peer Programs: An In-Depth Look* (Oxford: Taylor & Francis, 2008), 55.

Family Crisis and the 3rd Alternative

It may be in crisis moments like this that synergy is most needed. The toughest problems we face can be transformed into our most satisfying opportunities for growing the family relationship. The birth of a child, loss of a job, substance abuse, a debilitating accident or illness—life-changing episodes like these can wreck or renew a family, depending on the mind-set. I'm not talking about having a positive attitude. I'm talking about adopting a paradigm of creation rather than destruction.

For example, a layoff can add financial stress to a new identity crisis; it's a blow to self-worth to be suddenly unwanted. Domestic violence increases as unemployment rates go up. Unemployed people at home most of the day get depressed, and "drugs and alcohol provide the fuel for an already explosive situation."[1] These volatile synergies can destroy a family.

But if you adopt the paradigm of creation, you will *see yourself* and realize that *you have more talent, intelligence, capability, and creativity to offer than your old job required or even allowed you to offer*. Losing that job gives you the chance to contribute the best you have to give. If you *see others*, you will begin to understand their needs and how you can use your ingenuity to meet them. If you *seek them out* and listen empathically to them, you will soon discover how you can create a much better life for them—and they will pay you for it. There is no shortage of work in the world—just a shortage of 3rd Alternative thinking.

I know of an older man who lost his job at a particularly bad time, as his wife had developed a chronic illness. With no income, their situation quickly turned bleak. But he had worked in the furniture business and had noticed over the years that many window-shoppers would come into the store and leave without buying. He made an appointment with the owner of a large retail furniture chain and said, "About four thousand people leave your stores every day without making a purchase. Based on your average sale, how much money is walking out the door?" The owner calculated it in the millions per year. "If I could get only 20 percent of those people to buy, what would that mean to you?" The owner got the message and hired this man on the spot. Now he had to figure out how to make good on

---

1 Alan Schwartz, "Recession and Marriage, What Is the Impact?," *MentalHealth.net*, January 14, 2010, http://www.mentalhelp.net/poc/view_doc.php?type=doc&id=35065& cn=51.

his promise. Here's where his wife came in. She had a solid background in business management, although she was unable to hold a conventional job. Through 3rd Alternative thinking, they engineered together a number of creative ideas that brought in more business than promised.

The family is a portfolio of strengths. When financial trouble looms, your family can be your most valuable synergistic resource. For thousands of years, families have pulled together to succeed. In our specialized age, that might be more difficult. But consider this case of a husband and wife who both lost their jobs. The wife was a tax accountant, the husband a seller of convenience foods. They had three tall teenage sons to provide for. Instead of standing in unemployment lines or sinking into despair, they decided as a family to create something together. The sons were nimble and strong, the wife understood finances, and the husband was a natural salesman. They lived in an area with a lot of new housing developments, so they started a fencing business. The husband sold, the wife managed the business, and the sons installed the fences. It was a great success.

Of course, you don't have to go into business with your family. Still, although families should not hesitate to get the outside help they need in tough times, the challenges they face together can be tremendous opportunities to strengthen family bonds, build capacity, and create a new future for themselves. For too many, the first alternative is to wear themselves out searching for another insecure job, a pigeonhole to fit themselves into. A second alternative, again for too many, is to give up and settle into permanent victimhood. The promise of the 3rd Alternative is to design your own job, something you love to do and that would answer a real need in the world, and then go market it. Think of the resiliency of a family that is blessed with such a 3rd Alternative mind-set.

Another major challenge is the birth of a child. Everything about the marriage—communication, finances, priorities, intimacy—changes with this seismic shift in relationships. The number of household tasks goes up sixfold. Parents have drastically less time for themselves and not much for one another.[1] Sadly, a new baby can lead to emotional separation and divorce.

But a child is a miracle, a wonderful 3rd Alternative that transforms us.

---

1 Beth A. LePoire, *Family Communication: Nurturing and Control in a Changing World* (Thousand Oaks, CA: SAGE Publications, 2005), 116.

A child can strengthen marriage bonds if even one partner is willing to adopt a new mind-set of seeking 3rd Alternatives. Many women are torn between their roles as mother and wife and worker. A 3rd Alternative is to plan creative ways to fulfill your important roles without getting overwhelmed. You can ask yourself, "What's the most important thing I could do this week in my role as a wife?" You might plan just two hours alone with your husband; for a man who's feeling a little displaced, those two hours will pay dividends far beyond your investment of time and make up for times when you just can't be with him. As a father, you might do the same with your child: What is the value of an hour or so alone with your baby? It might be priceless to your wife, to your child, and to you. In that private time, you become a *dad*. One of my sons is fond of saying, "There's a big difference between being a father and being a dad."

For many single parents, life can be one tough dilemma after another. You're often stuck between your roles as mom and worker. Your child gets sick on a day you can't stay home from work. Your child's school declares a snow day and no sitter is available. You want to see your child's school play, but your boss needs you just then. Fortunately, many workplaces are flexible these days, but you can't go on missing work. What do you do?

If you're a single parent, 3rd Alternative thinking can save you. You know these conflicts will happen, so you work out *in advance* 3rd Alternatives to missing the play or missing work. Set up a meeting with your boss and explain the role conflict you face. Listen empathically to your supervisor: How does he or she feel about the situation? There may be acceptance and willingness to work with you. If not, don't become defensive. The more you listen, the more likely the boss will be to listen to you.

Then get into a Magic Theater mode. Come with solutions, not just the problem. Can someone cover for you in an emergency? Can you bring your child to work? Beyond these obvious ideas, you might get very creative and use the opportunity to redefine your role at work. What problems in the business can you solve if you're allowed to work at home? You might even be more profitable that way, as you'll consume less overhead for the employer. One young single mom got an entry-level job at a bank. The inflexible hours became a real problem for her, so she proposed something new. She had noticed that the bank had many foreclosed properties to manage. She offered to clean and maintain those homes for less money than the bank was paying a professional service to do it. They liked the idea, and she could do the work on her own schedule and even take her child with her (this is called a "win-win"). Eventually she made this 3rd Alternative into a business of her own, hiring others to do the work, and she did quite well financially!

You don't need to *have* a crisis to be *in* crisis. Families are fragile, and the forces tearing at them are persistent and powerful. Unless we value the differences among us, those differences can break us apart.

I know of a family where stark differences could have been a disintegrating force. As a young man, the husband excelled in sports, starring on every team in town. The quality of his play was legendary. He was also gifted at math and had a head for business. But he married a woman with little interest in any of those things. She loved dance, the theater, the artistic life. He was solid working class; her parents were well off. He was tall, robust, and earthy; she was petite, dramatic, elegant. You can't imagine a less compatible pair.

But you probably *can* imagine a life of real conflict. As their interests didn't coincide, you would expect them to become more and more estranged with time, the wife going to the opera by herself while the husband stayed home glued to TV sports. But it didn't happen that way. This was a truly 3rd Alternative family. These two people were wise enough to *celebrate* their differences.

The wife got their children involved in a local community theater. It was barely limping along, giving shows in an old restaurant space in a dingy strip mall. Thousands of dollars in debt, the theater was always on the edge of shutting down. The wife lured her husband to see their excited kids in a little play, and it softened his heart; clearly, his wife and kids loved this dilapidated place. As he looked around, he could see so many things that needed to be done. He enjoyed working with his hands, so he volunteered to help build sets. With his business brain, he got involved in fund-raising, and soon found himself a trustee of the theater and then general manager.

The dad never performed himself, but the more he watched his children and neighbors light up the stage every night, the more fascinated he became with every aspect of the theater. His wife became the creative director. Soon the couple were recruiting friends to do costumes or scenery, play music, and get up on the stage. For the husband, quality was the watchword; everyone involved soon found that he was as much a perfectionist about the theater as he had been on the playing fields as a youth.

The young family grew up with the theater. Each of their children added a strength to the company. One son was a terrific actor, another learned to dance like a pro. A teenage daughter who was planning to be a veterinarian changed her mind when she showed an unusual talent for analyzing the business. She ran the numbers and demonstrated how to ramp up season ticket sales and save money on operations. She became a true professional at stagecraft and theater management.

Excitement over the little theater grew. Eventually, it was clear they were outgrowing the tiny mall location and plans were made for a beautiful new facility. With his business skills, the husband helped pilot a major community effort to raise money. After fifteen years of working together, this little family celebrated along with the whole town the opening of a magnificent theater—a permanent monument to their dedication and synergy as a family.

United by their differences, the members of this family illustrate what I mean by a 3rd Alternative culture at home. Everyone counts, everyone contributes, no one is left out. This melding of the two cultures of husband and wife into an unprecedented third culture clearly adds up to more than the sum of the parts.

If It Doesn't Work Out

The reality is, many families choose to split. So what do you do when your efforts to create and build together don't work out?

Divorce does not necessarily mean the end of synergy in a family. People divorce for many reasons, but they need not be enemies in a 2-Alternative universe of recrimination. By adopting a mind-set of respect and empathy, an ex-spouse can transform the lives of the children and the nature of the ongoing relationship. It takes only one to break the cycle of resentment, even if the other spouse doesn't respond. Remember, we can choose not to let others offend us.

One day my friend Larry Boyle, who is a federal judge, had the chance to observe another judge well known for achieving 3rd Alternatives in the most bitter of all legal proceedings: the fight over who gets the children in a divorce. Even highly publicized murder cases can be less volatile than a child custody case in a family court. That day, the destiny of a seven-year-old girl and a five-year-old boy would be decided. "The parents sat at separate tables, neither looking at the other. While the lawyers talked, the wife gently wiped her eyes with a wadded-up tissue and the husband stared straight ahead, his arms folded." Then the judge entered and took her seat.

The wife's attorney began, announcing that he would present evidence that the husband spent most of his time fishing and hunting with his buddies, bowling, and staying out late. The husband's attorney would show that the wife was having an affair with a co-worker. Both wanted exclusive custody of the children.

Taking her reading glasses off, the judge paused and then spoke quietly:

Today I will hear evidence for several hours. Then I will decide whom to believe. I could conclude the father is a partying bum. On the other hand, I could find that the mother is having an illicit affair. Then I will make a decision, and that is the risk you take by having me decide something that you as parents should decide, not based on your own selfish interests, but for the good of the kids.

You know, I don't love your children. I care for their welfare, but I don't love them as you do. But I will make a decision that will affect the lives of those two little children. It may well be the wrong decision.

I suggest that you two parents grow up and put the kids' interests ahead of yours. I'm going to recess this trial for thirty minutes. During that time, both of you go with your attorneys and talk about what really is best for those children. Make plans for their future. If you are able to put your pride and ego aside, you should be able to do what is best for them.

If you don't do this, you will put their future in my hands, the hands of a complete stranger who doesn't even know them. I'll see you in thirty minutes.

Several weeks later, Larry learned what happened. The husband and wife met for hours that morning, at times with their attorneys, but mostly in private, listening to one another and apologizing. They faced the reality of what they had done in declaring war on each other. The husband wasn't really a carouser, and the wife wasn't really having an affair; these were the gross, infantile accusations of people with an attack mind-set. Discouraged, she had spent some time talking with her supervisor about her problems, but no more than that. And he was immature, but not a bad father.

Though they had grown apart and chose not to get back together, once they began focusing on the children, they decided to remain joint parents. The husband agreed that his wife was better equipped to be the custodial parent, and the wife agreed that he could take the kids any time. They would remain as much of a family as they could be.[1]

"I had seen a true peacemaker in action," Larry Boyle says. Instead of listening to a day's worth of childish accusations and trying to make a decision based on the worst kind of 2-Alternative thinking, that family-court judge was the catalyst for a 3rd Alternative. The judge knew that her job was not to give the parents a forum for their feud, but to create for a little girl and boy the best future possible. Fortunately, the parents realized that was their job too.

Of course, divorced men and women don't need the catalyst of a courtroom to choose a synergistic relationship instead of a destructive one. It's *their* choice. They don't need to remain the victims of each other. The laws of synergy are as true for them as for anyone: respect for self and spouse, empathy for one another, and a determination to go for the 3rd Alternative on every issue they confront, whether it's about the family, the property, or their relationship.

When the ex-spouse doesn't respond, it takes great courage and strength of will to adopt a 3rd Alternative mind-set. But it's possible, and the inner peace that results is priceless.

I was teaching at a professional gathering a while ago when I experienced something remarkable. As I spoke about some of the principles of being responsible for your own life, a gentleman from the audience stood up on his chair and said the following (I'm paraphrasing): "Last week my wife left me. It was totally unexpected. I have felt a mixture of hurt, anger, betrayal, and embarrassment. But listening to this today I have decided to not be angry anymore. I am going to choose to be happy and not be hurt or embarrassed any longer."

I was so taken by this man's sense of humility and courage and his desire to be the creative force of his life rather than being victim to his circumstances or his relationship with his wife. I'm sure he was in a lot of turmoil and feeling that the world had crashed down on him. But he gained the self-

---

1 Larry M. Boyle, "A Peacemaker in Family Court," unpublished ms. in author's possession, published with permission.

awareness that he could still choose his response to his devastating personal challenges. He saw that he could act and not feel acted upon.

I commended him for his decision and affirmed that he could choose to let the anger go, to forgive and create a new life. This is so hard to do in painful situations like his. The audience applauded him. I applauded him. I had never seen anything like it. I don't know what will happen to him and his wife. But I do know that if he will grasp the paradigm of creation and begin to see himself as the creative force of his own life with the choices he makes, he will find meaning and fulfillment in his life. He will eventually find peace of mind.

"The family is society's first and most important institution—the seedbed of commitment, love, character, and social as well as personal responsibility."[1] I wholly agree with this statement of the Commission on Families chartered by the president of the United States. In no other part of life is synergy so needed and at the same time so misunderstood.

A woman I'm familiar with pauses for a moment when she comes home from work. Before entering the house, she takes a minute to think about her family. She visualizes the kind of world she wants to create with them. Then she opens the door and makes it happen.

---

1 *Families First: Final Report of the National Commission on America's Urban Families,* Washington, D.C., January 1993.

TEACH TO LEARN

The best way to learn from this book is to teach it to someone else. Everybody knows that the teacher learns far more than the student. So find someone—a co-worker, a friend, a family member—and teach him or her the insights you've gained. Ask the provocative questions here or come up with your own.

- How does 2-Alternative thinking contribute to the current high rate of divorce?
- What's the best definition of "incompatibility"? Why is compassion the opposite of incompatibility?
- "Successful families are imbued with positive synergy." Why is synergy crucial to a successful family?
- "At bottom, most family conflicts are identity conflicts." Why do family members often quarrel bitterly over what might look trivial to outsiders? How does "the real identity theft" undermine families?
- Why celebrate the differences among your family members? How is this done?
- What are the steps for transforming anger and resentment into synergy?
- How can you tell if a family member is caught up in a 2-Alternative problem? How can you help him or her move on to a 3rd Alternative?
- What is the value of treating an offensive remark or action as an invitation to empathic listening?
- What are the advantages of empathy in a situation of family conflict?
- What steps might you take to create a family culture of empathy?
- What kinds of challenges in your home life could you meet with 3rd Alternative thinking?
- What tributes would you give to your own family members who practice synergy?

TRY IT

Are you involved in a conflict at home or with a friend? Do you need creative solutions to a challenge with your family? Start prototyping 3rd Alternatives. Invite others to contribute. Use the "4 Steps to Synergy" tool.

4 STEPS TO SYNERGY

1 Ask the 3rd Alternative Question:

"Are you willing to go for a solution that is better than any of us have come up with yet?" If yes, go on to step 2.

2 Define Criteria of Success

List in this space the characteristics of a solution that would delight everyone. What does success look like? What is the real job to be done? What would be a "win-win" for all concerned?

```
┌─────────────────────────────────────────────────────────┐
│                                                           │
│                                                           │
│                                                           │
│                                                           │
│                                                           │
│                                                           │
└─────────────────────────────────────────────────────────┘
```

3 Create 3rd Alternatives

In this space (or other spaces) create models, draw pictures, borrow ideas, turn your thinking upside down. Work quickly and creatively. Suspend all judgment until that exciting moment when you know you've arrived at synergy.

```
┌─────────────────────────────────────────────────────────┐
│                                                           │
│                                                           │
│                                                           │
│                                                           │
│                                                           │
│                                                           │
│                                                           │
│                                                           │
│                                                           │
└─────────────────────────────────────────────────────────┘
```

4 Arrive at Synergy

Describe here your 3rd Alternative and, if you want, how you intend to put it into practice.

```
┌─────────────────────────────────────────────────────────┐
│                                                           │
│                                                           │
│                                                           │
│                                                           │
│                                                           │
└─────────────────────────────────────────────────────────┘
```

USER GUIDE TO THE 4 STEPS TO SYNERGY TOOL

The 4 Steps to Synergy. This process helps you put the synergy principle to work. (1) Show willingness to find a 3rd Alternative. (2) Define what success looks like to everyone. (3) Experiment with solutions until you (4) arrive at Synergy. Listen empathically to others throughout the process.

How to Get to Synergy

1 Ask the 3rd Alternative Question

In a conflict or creative situation, this question helps everyone move past firm positions or preconceived ideas toward developing a third position.

2 Define Criteria of Success	3 Create 3rd Alternative
List characteristics or write a paragraph describing what a successful outcome would look like to everyone. Answer these questions as you go: • Is everyone involved in setting the criteria? Are we getting as many ideas from as many people as possible? • What outcomes do we really want? What is the real job to be done? • What outcomes would be "wins" for everyone? • Are we looking past our entrenched demands to something better?	Follow these guidelines: • Play at it. It's not "for real." Everybody knows it's a game. • Avoid closure, premature agreement, or consensus. • Avoid judging others' ideas—or your own. • Make models. Draw pictures on whiteboards, sketch diagrams, build mockups, write rough drafts. • Turn ideas on their heads. Reverse the conventional wisdom. • Work fast. Set a time limit to keep energy and ideas flowing rapidly. • Breed lots of ideas. You can't predict which offhand insight might lead to a 3rd Alternative.

(4) Arrive at Synergy

You recognize the 3rd Alternative by the sense of excitement and inspiration in the room. The old conflict is abandoned. The new alternative meets the criteria of success. Caution: Avoid mistaking compromise for synergy. Compromise breeds satisfaction but not delight. Compromise means everyone loses something; synergy means everyone wins.

The 3rd Alternative at School

5

The 3rd Alternative at School

Free the child's potential, and you will transform him into the world.
—*Maria Montessori*

In every nation I visit, I look into the eyes of the children and see the same sparks of light and the same smiles. Anybody who bothers to look can sense the limitless promise in each unique face. Anything less than the achievement of that promise is a devastating loss to society.

We trust much of the achievement of that promise to our schools. Across the globe, there are parents and teachers who struggle together, sometimes against great obstacles, to give their children the best chance they can. Most people agree that educating children is not only the answer to persistent poverty of all kinds—physical, mental, spiritual—but also the key to our very future on this planet.

For me, this issue is both global and personal. I've seen satellite views of Earth at night strung with a web of lights. I know those lights represent countless families and children dreaming about their possibilities, and I wonder how many of them will be fulfilled or frustrated. I also have many grandchildren of my own, and their joy in the future is deeply important to me.

Most people share my concerns. In our Serious Challenge survey, we asked respondents on every continent to name the biggest challenge their country faces. Along with "resolving unemployment," "providing a good education" was ranked topmost. When asked why, respondents offered these answers:

- "Education is the basic building block towards finding the answer to all the other difficulties that we face."
- "A good education is the foundation upon which we can build for a better, more innovative future. The world is advancing faster than we are and the amount of money put toward education is severely lacking compared to other formidable nations."
- "Through education the other problems could be solved. Our education system is not working. The teachers are lazy, corrupt, and not prepared."
- "We need an educational model that truly empowers and provides opportunities for students."
- "Good education is the base for everything. Educated people have their own mindset and don't fall for wrong messiahs or promises. If we get education right, everything else follows—automagically!" (Although it's probably a typo, I love this word!)
- "Many children in poor and emerging countries like ours have very little education, especially girls. Education can solve many of the other problems of the world."
- "Good education is the basis for prosperity/employment/economic growth."
- "Poor education has gotten us where we are today. I taught in our public schools for 10 years. We need to change our structure before it's too late."
- "Education is most important. All other efforts will be more successful after that."

Clearly, one of our biggest challenges is how best to help children learn and fulfill the promise of the future. In China and India, education excels in major cities but lags badly in the hinterland. Education in Finland and South Korea is of very high quality due to a supportive and homogeneous culture. In Canada, Britain, and America, however, the headlines are disturbing:

- Toronto: "Johnny Can't Read, and He's in College"
- London: "British School Leavers Can't Read or Write and Have an Attitude Problem"
- Washington: "82% of U.S. Schools Failing"[1]

Every nation faces different challenges, but the same question confronts the whole world: Is it possible to provide every child an excellent, or even a decent, education?

The Great Debate

This question has spurred a great debate with many shades of difference, but it generally breaks down to two sides. On one side are those who believe that lagging achievement is due to a lack of equity: poverty, racism, dysfunctional families, and political unwillingness to give all schools adequate resources. These voices tend to come from the educational establishment. On the other side are those who believe that the educational establishment is itself the problem, that it is hidebound, mediocre, failing to keep pace with a changing world. These tend to belong to the business community.

Business leaders can't understand why educators won't listen to them. Frustrated with what looks like a swamp of mediocrity, they contend that schools can't succeed unless they adopt the "traits that have long made the American private sector an engine of global prosperity—its dynamism, creativity, and relentless focus on efficiency and results." To their eyes, the educational establishment is a floundering dinosaur that lacks the incentives of the marketplace to thrive. Schools, they say, need competition that will force innovation and quality improvements. Many advocates of the "separation of school and state" say the entire system should be sold off and privatized.

What business leaders think they hear from educators annoys them: "Pay us more or your kids will suffer. Your stinginess is the reason educational

---

1 "Johnny Can't Read, and He's in College," *Globe and Mail* (Toronto), September 26, 2005; Andrew Hough, "Tesco Director: British School Leavers 'Can't Read or Write and Have Attitude Problems,'" *Telegraph* (London), March 10, 2010; Nick Anderson, "Most Schools Could Face Failing Label Under No Child Left Behind, Duncan Says," *Washington Post*, March 9, 2011, http://www.washingtonpost.com/local/education/duncan-most -schools-could-face-failing-label/2011/03/09/AB7L2hP_story.html.

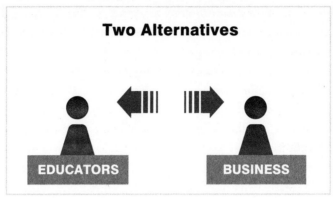

Two Alternatives

EDUCATORS　　BUSINESS

results are slipping. You obviously don't value your children or you'd fund us properly. Just leave us alone to work our short hours and take our months-long vacations and mind your own business." Many business people resent the educational establishment as a money pit that yields less and less return.

Of course, educators have an entirely different paradigm. They hold that business differs fundamentally from education, so business leaders have no business in the schools. Teaching should be exempt from the taint of the profit motive; it's a calling, not a job. A privatized system will quickly lead to gross inequities, wherein rich families can afford the best schools and poor families get the crumbs. A huge "achievement gap" separates struggling minorities from more privileged children. Private schools can take who they want when they want, but public schools are duty bound to take whoever walks in the door. A new arrival might have a learning disorder or speak only a foreign language. He might come from a dysfunctional home or even from jail. Regardless, the public schools have a moral responsibility to nurture him. "Unlike corporations, we don't have the option of laying off low performers to make the end-of-year bottom line look better."

What teachers think they hear from business leaders alarms them: "We want you to train our employees at public expense to produce a widget, drive a truck, or run a spreadsheet—and you can't even do that right. We're interested only in mass-produced worker units that do what they're told. Beyond that, all these 'interchangeable units' need to learn is how to read and do a little math. Grandiose buildings, arts education, feel-good curriculum—it's all expensive, unnecessary fluff." No wonder so many educators see business as oppressive and soulless.

In the words of the U.S. Chamber of Commerce:

Put bluntly, we believe our education system needs to be reinvented. After decades of political inaction and ineffective reforms, our schools consistently produce students unready for the rigors of the modern workplace. The lack of preparedness is staggering. Roughly one in three eighth graders is proficient in reading. Most high schools graduate little more than two-thirds of their students on time.[1]

Business people fume over these results, while educators feel overwhelmed, persecuted, and starved for resources. So the fingers point in both directions.

Of course, neither view is fair to the other. Neither side is listening to the other. Both sides reveal their 2-Alternative thinking. They caricature each other as enemies, and they set up just another false dilemma, an "us or them" choice. What slivers of truth show through their arguments don't change that at all.

Our children and youth are caught in this clash of cultures, and they manage as best they can. Many despair, quite a few have a great experience in school, but most muddle through and exit the system with passable skills. Although there are islands of brilliance, no one believes that the public education system consistently enables every child to fulfill his or her potential.

Industrial Age Education

In my view, both sides in this great debate share responsibility for the often dehumanizing effect of the education establishment. A century ago, growing industries demanded that public schools produce a "product" useful to them, as we see in this article from 1927: "A dispassionate study of the product of the educational system forces the conclusion that the product is falling far short of what modern business is demanding."[2] In response, too many schools became factories and children became "products" instead of people.

There always have been, ever will be, inspiring men and women who are teachers in the highest and most noble sense of the word—believing in and committed to unlocking the potential of those they guide. To them

---

1 U.S. Chamber of Commerce, *Leaders and Laggards: A State-by-State Report Card on Educational Innovation*, November 9, 2009.
2 "The School Executive," *American Educational Digest* 47 (1927): 205.

we owe our deepest gratitude. However, many in the teaching profession uncomfortably acquiesced to the Industrial Age mind-set and now help perpetuate it. The industrial model is evident in the overreliance on test results to the neglect of the whole child. Ironically, even though the public schools have in many ways adopted the factory model and mind-set of business, the business community is more dissatisfied than ever; their complaints haven't changed since 1927.

This Industrial Age thinking about children as commodities is the root of our educational challenge.

In the Industrial Age, people were treated like things, necessary but interchangeable. You could churn through "worker units" and simply replace them when they burned out. If all you want is a warm body to do a job, you don't really care about a mind, a heart, or a spirit. A controlling Industrial Age model of education suppresses the release of human potential, and it simply will not work in a Knowledge Age economy.

I know of a woman who has spent much of her adult life in prison. An alcoholic and drug addict, she was at one time a promising college student, the daughter of a high educational official. She has struggled nobly for many years to overcome her debilitating problems. One day she confided that prison was very much like school: the same classes, scheduling, regimentation, and constant queuing up. What most reminded her of school was the ever-present surveillance, the knowledge that someone was watching her at all times.

In 1785 the philosopher Jeremy Bentham proposed a new kind of prison called a "panopticon," an ingenious building that would allow guards to watch all prisoners at the same time. A modern philosopher, Michel Foucault, saw the panopticon as the symbol of the modern "surveillance society," in which we live under constant observation. Take one look at a schoolroom or a "cubicle farm" in one of our large corporations and you see what Foucault meant: both schools and businesses resemble the panopticon. He argues that as surveillance increases, respect for our individuality decreases. Reward and punishment is based on how well we shut up and follow instructions rather than how we volunteer our unique gifts to make a contribution. When we orient people to be *led* instead of *leading*, society and opportunity suffer.

The prisonlike mind-set of the Industrial Age takes hold of us during our school years but influences the whole of our lives and our society. It can create in us a fundamental misinterpretation of life: that we are like passive worker ants in a vast colony. Too many of us exist as children to be told what to do, as adults to fit into a job slot, and as senior citizens to retire to pointless leisure. We are trained into a subtle victimhood. If we don't fit in at school, we are ciphers or nonpersons. If we lose a job, we lose our identity. Eventually we can become conditioned to dependence: if we can, we find someone to take care of us, or to point fingers at if we can't.

Parents have their own struggles within the framework of Industrial Age education; some are boosters, some opt out, some soldier on within the system. On one hand, we see children whose lives are so overprogrammed that they never learn to decide for themselves how to live. Their parents push them to achieve without helping them discern between winning in a competition and making a meaningful contribution in life. On the other hand, we see children suffering from PADD, parental attention-deficit disorder, who just don't care because their parents don't care. So they drop out. In the end, this group accounts for about a third of all students. The Great Middle hangs on, hoping for the best. Few parents are astute enough to see that their children are being prepared for a life of dependence.

As long as education means training children how to be dependent, how to be good followers, we will never begin to tap into the promise that each child brings to the world. And while the great debaters go on hacking at the leaves of the ailing tree of education, fighting over the best way to keep the industrial model alive, the cancerous root keeps growing unnoticed.

The Job to Be Done

When I met with the president of the United States a few years ago, he asked me what I thought was our top educational challenge. I said something like this: "Creating partnerships among teachers, parents, and the community *to unlock the potential of all children to lead their own lives instead of being led.*"

This would be a transformational change in education, not a transactional change. In the mode of all 2-Alternative thinkers, the great debaters wrangle endlessly over the transactional question of how best to "turn out the product": Through endless restructuring of the public system or through market efficiencies? Through a technical or a humanistic curriculum? Through online training or the traditional classroom? Through more or less testing?

The point, however, is not to "turn out a product" at all. Children are not raw materials to be packaged into products for the marketplace. Each child brings distinctive gifts into the world and the power to choose how to use those gifts. The job of education is to help each child to succeed at maximizing that potential.

My good friend Professor Clayton Christensen of Harvard Business School, a lifelong teacher, believes that schools have been doing the wrong job for too long. He likes to think about students as if they were independent contractors hiring a school to do a certain job for them. What is that job?

> It matters a lot to understand what job people hire schools to do for them. Why are students not motivated? Dropout rates, absenteeism in suburban as well as urban schools, students sitting there with defiant or bored looks on their faces—you know the signs. What job do they want done?
>
> Students and their teachers want to feel successful every day! That's the job they want done. Now, they could hire a school to do that, or they could hire a gang to do that. Or they could hire a car to cruise around in and look successful. What the schools are competing against are all the other ways a young person can feel successful.
>
> Our schools are designed to make most students feel like failures. Once you understand that, you can start thinking of a very different way to help students feel successful.[1]

If school doesn't do the job of helping young people feel successful every day, they will find other providers of success. And if forced to comply, they will do what any unhappy customer does: submit resentfully or figure out how to game the system. They will substitute some other form of success, perhaps the familiar teenage refrain "It doesn't matter, I don't care, it makes no difference," phrases that desperately snatch at the last tatter of a shredded identity, the last defense against failure.

---

1 Sue Dathe-Douglass, "Interview with Clayton Christensen," *FranklinCovey Facilitator Academy,* March 2011.

3rd Alternative Education

The 3rd Alternative in education is to learn to become a leader.

Let me quickly say that I don't define a "leader" as one of the few who end up in big leadership positions. We are too used to thinking of leaders as people with titles like CEO or president. This view of leadership is an artifact of the Industrial Age, and we are long past that kind of hierarchical thinking. I'm talking about the ability to lead your own life, to be a leader among your friends, to be a leader in your own family—to be the active, creative force of your own world.

True leaders define and achieve enduring success by developing character and competence and taking principled action; they don't wait for others to define it for them. Because they see themselves as uniquely gifted, they compete against no one but themselves. In economic terms, they are the only providers of what they provide, so they can auction their talents to the highest bidder. These leaders create their own future. With time and circumstances, they might fall short of a goal, but they never actually *fail*.

For a child educated to be this kind of leader, success comes from the inside out, not from the outside in. From the outside comes only a lesser, secondary sort of success, rewards like good grades and academic notoriety in the short term and big money or an impressive title later on. People fight over these scarcer successes. But from the inside comes primary success, feeling good about yourself, discovering what you're good at, the rewards of respect for others and self, deep satisfaction from making a unique and creative contribution, of honest, upright service. These richer rewards are available to anyone. No one competes for them, though naturally they often bring secondary success with them.

Some children find their own way to this 3rd Alternative because they naturally possess that kind of primary inner strength. Ory Okolloh, an attorney and an executive at Google, has journeyed from a troubled background in Kenya through Harvard Law School to help lead political reform in Africa. She explains how she determined to break out of the mental prison of an educational paradigm in her culture:

> *My parents could never save because they supported siblings, cousins, their parents. Things were always dicey. In Kenya we have an entrance exam before going to high school . . . my dream school. I missed the cut-off by one point. I was so disappointed.*
>
> *My father said, "Let's go try and talk to the headmistress. It's just one point. Maybe they'll let you in if there're slots still there." We went to the school and because we were nobodies and because we didn't have privilege and because my father didn't have the right last name, he was treated like dirt. I sat and listened to the headmistress talk to him, saying, "Who do you think you are? You must be joking if you think you can get a slot."*
>
> *I had gone to school with other girls, kids of politicians who had done much, much worse than I did, and they had slots there. And there's nothing worse than seeing your parent being humiliated in front of you. We left and I swore to myself, "I'm never, never going to have to beg for anything in my life." They called me two weeks later and they said, "Oh, you can come now," and I told them to stuff it.*[1]

---

1 See "Ory Okolloh on Becoming an Activist," *TED.com,* June 2007, http://www.ted.com/index.php/talks/ory_okolloh_on_becoming_an_activist.html.

Okolloh could have submitted to the system. Instead, she took charge of it and made it work for her. She is a leader in the primary sense because she refuses to allow success to be defined for her by a scarcity-minded society. To help others escape prisons of the mind around the world, she became a pioneer of the crowd-sourced newsgathering so essential to the democracy movement in the emerging nations of Africa and the Mideast. She funnels information on strife zones to social networks and the media so that injured and brutalized people can get help quickly.

To my mind, by far the most important purpose of education is to create Ory Okollohs, leaders with the character to transform the world around them. And it doesn't matter how big that world is, whether a single family, a neighborhood, a town, a nation, or the entire globe.

Mike Fritz, the principal of Joseph Welsh Elementary School in Red Deer, Alberta, Canada, told me about one of his kids who learned to become the leader of his own life. Having adopted *The Leader in Me* leadership model at his school (described below), Mike had been teaching his students that they were the leaders of their own lives, empowering them with leadership roles in the school, adopting a common leadership language, holding leadership events, and more. Every couple of years, Mike's superintendent would ask each of the principals in his district to make a presentation to the board of education and senior administrators on what they were doing in their schools. Mike had usually done this with other staff members. But now that he was running a leadership school, he decided to ask the students to do it.

Several volunteered, including Riley, a third-grade student who is on the autism spectrum. Riley had just learned about the 8th Habit: Find Your Voice, and told Mike that this was how he wanted to find his voice. The staff wholeheartedly supported the children in doing the presentation and were proud that Riley wished to be part of it.

So the big day came, and Mike, Riley, and the other kids arrived at the superintendent's office for their presentation. For his part, Riley had prepared a large poster of a brain with blue, red, and black spots. As he held up the poster, he explained that he was autistic and that his brain was different from other people's brains. Red signified anger, black frustration, and blue calm. Riley pointed out that there were many others like him in the district, and that the district needed to be aware of them and their special needs. At the end, Riley received a standing ovation, and many of the board members were in tears.

The next day at school, Mike found it interesting that Riley showed up wearing a collared shirt and a tie. In fact, for the next several weeks Riley wore a tie to school every day. At last, Mike ran into Riley's mother and curiously asked, "What's up with Riley? He's been wearing a tie every day for weeks." His mother said, "Before he came to this school he used to wake up and say, 'I don't want to go to school today, Mom. I'm stupid and I don't want to feel stupid.' But since coming here, he has blossomed. He is told every day that he is a leader and that he is talented. After giving that presentation to the superintendent Riley was so proud of himself that he came home and told me. 'Mom, from now on I'm going to wear a tie, because important people wear ties!'"

At the writing of this book, it's been over a year and Riley still volunteers for many leadership tasks, plans on going to college, and still wears a tie every few days.

The primary purpose of education—to make a leader of Riley—is being accomplished in his life.[1] Of course, education has secondary purposes as well, like shaping a thinking, informed citizenry and passing on skills we need for a prosperous economy. I particularly like a goal suggested by Clayton Christensen: "Nurture the understanding that people see things differently—and that those differences merit respect rather than persecution."[2] But helping each child become a leader is the inspiring and powerful primary purpose of education. It is primary because the success of the secondary purposes depends on it. We all know of highly skilled people who lack character, and they can truly be destructive.

I once had a talented, handsome business associate with several university degrees. He also had a beautiful family. At one time a college professor and director of humanities education for an entire American state, he went into business for himself and with his quick mind made a fortune for his company. But the secondary successes were not based on primary success. Hubris and alcohol can be a ruinous combination; in this case, neither the marriage nor the business survived it.

_____

1 To see a touching video about Riley, go to http://www.The3rdAlternative.com.
2 Clayton M. Christensen et al., *Disrupting Class: How Disruptive Innovation Will Change the Way the World Learns* (New York: McGraw-Hill Professional, 2010), n.p.

As my friend's tragic experience illustrates, along with the mind, the heart and the spirit of each child must be educated if primary success is the goal. Deep down, we all know this. Most parents do. And if it's going to be done, likeminded people must do it.

"Se Puede"

A perennial whine in the great education debate is that a dysfunctional society can't expect to have excellent schools. Of course, many schools barely survive in troubled neighborhoods filled with crime and disease. For other schools, things look good on the outside, but the students inside struggle; many become addicted to drugs, computer and video games, and other means of escaping the banality of our society. All of these excuses are true— but they are still excuses.

Excellent schools can and do rise up in even the most grim conditions. One who has seen it is a remarkable 3rd Alternative thinker named Wendy Kopp, founder of Teach for America, an organization that recruits some of the brightest college students to teach in disadvantaged schools for a limited time. What she has learned surprised her: "We do not have to fix society or even families in order to fix education. It works the other way around. . . . Low-income parents leap at educational opportunities that can break the cycle of poverty. Teaching successfully in challenging schools is totally an act of leadership by people passionately invested."[1]

Richard Esparza is such a passionately invested leader. When Esparza became principal of Granger High School in Yakima Valley, Washington, the situation was not hopeful. Most students were children of agricultural workers with no education themselves. The students had little hope of rising out of poverty. The statistics were bleak:

- Only 20 percent met state reading standards.
- Only 11 percent met state writing standards.
- Only 4 percent met state math standards.

1 Cited in George F. Will, " 'Teach for America' Transforming Education," *Washington Post*, February 26, 2011.

Esparza came from the same background, but he knew he was not what others said of him and young people like him, that they were "as dumb as a box of rocks" and incapable of learning. He proved it to himself by graduating from college and returning as a teacher with a mission: to make sure other kids could see themselves for what they really were. The new principal saw his role as being a transformer of expectations. His criteria of success were clear and measurable: "I expect all students to succeed and I believe that they can, and I expect the faculty to believe the same thing. My goal is to eliminate the bell curve—there's no reason for it. All our students are capable."

Of course, the barriers to his goal were formidable. For two years, he says, it was "nothing but fighting." Nine out of ten students were members of minority groups. Not only the parents and students believed they were hopeless—so did the teachers. Gangs flourished, graffiti covered the walls, police officers escorted visitors to basketball games. Clearly, Esparza had to help students change their minds about what constitutes success. He had to help each one find the leader within himself or herself.

But he did not know how to go about it, and there were no models out there to guide him. How do you turn a bottom-performing high school into an excellent high school? "If I'd had a framework to follow," Esparza says, things would have gone more smoothly. Forced to improvise, he turned Granger High School into a Magic Theater of inquiry and experimentation.

His first trick was to make the graffiti disappear. Symbols of gang power, the tagging had to go. In addition to asking the custodians to paint over any graffiti within twenty-four hours, he carried his own cans of spray paint in his car and used them constantly. After about two years of this, the artists got discouraged and the school stayed clean. At the same time, he strictly banned all gang clothing and signs.

In any school, a key to success is parental support and involvement. But at Granger High only 10 percent of parents even bothered to show up for teacher conferences. "If they won't come to us," Esparza announced, "we will go to them." He organized teachers to visit each student's family to talk candidly with them about their child's progress. The goal was to persuade families to be part of the school and to participate in teacher conferences.

Some of the teachers didn't want to do these home visits, so Esparza gave them this speech: "You are a great teacher. We have a difference in philosophy. I'd be happy to write you a recommendation for a job with another school." And he lost some. (I'm reminded of Japanese schoolteachers who ride their bicycles up and down the streets to visit their students in their homes. Sometimes they work until late at night to do this, but they merge the power of the school with the power of the home. It's an excellent model.)

A few years of this effort paid off at Granger High School. Eventually 100 percent of parents were attending conferences. The conferences are run not by the teachers but by the students themselves, who review their learning progress, graduation requirements, grades, reading levels, and post–high school plans. The goal of the conferences is to make sure everyone—students, parents, teachers—is on the same page with the same information. "People often ask me how our high school can get 100 percent of parents to attend the conferences," says Esparza. "The answer: one parent at a time."[1]

Esparza also believed in "personalizing" education to ensure that every single student had an individual success plan and a mentor. The idea was that each student would account *every day* to an advisor-teacher for his or her personal progress. But a given teacher couldn't meet personally with 150 students a day, so they divided the student body into groups of twenty, assigning a teacher as advisor to each group. The teacher met with them four days a week to review individual progress. Again, one teacher said he didn't want to do this, that he was "not a social worker," so Esparza gave him "the speech."

The advisory groups turned out to be transformative, according to Esparza's successor, Paul Chartrand:

> *Every student had a voice and an adult who looked after them. The students always knew they had somebody they could go to, somebody they could trust. Somebody who would see and greet them and give them a friendly hello. . . . Personalization is the key. Each of those students knows that they are going to be held accountable. When they stop showing up, the advisors call home or even go to their homes and find out what's going on and how we can help.*[2]

1 "A Second Set of Parents: Advisory Groups and Student Achievement at Granger High," LearningFirst.org, February 2008, http://www.learningfirst.org/second-set-parents -advisory-groups-and-s tudent-achievement-granger-high.

2 Claus von Zastrow, "Taking Things Personally: Principal Paul Chartrand Speaks about His School's Turnaround," LearningFirst.org, August 31, 2009, http://www.learningfirst .org/visionaries/PaulChartrand.

Esparza used every device he could think of to motivate students. Although he knows money is not the only motivator of excellence, he kept a suitcase stuffed with phony cash, $420,000 in photocopied twenties, roughly the amount a student will lose in earnings over his working life if he does not graduate from high school. In frequent "honor-roll assemblies," Esparza would place the symbolic cash in front of the podium next to a hand-drawn poster of the "Three Roads of Life": the high-achievement road for those with high grades, the middle, and the low. He confronted the students with reality: "Your education is your one chance, unless you know someone who owns a yacht club." Then he gave each honor-roll student a certificate and a T-shirt with the phrase "No grades, no glory" and excused them to get ice cream in the cafeteria.[1]

One tough problem was absenteeism; Granger students were used to cutting classes. Esparza brainstormed a scoreboard that he put up in the school's main hall showing the amount of time each absent student "owed" the school. For credit, students had to "pay back" this time with a tutor before or after school. Over two years, absenteeism dropped by a third.

Most of all, Esparza was determined to ensure the academic success of every single student, so he established a brash "no-failing rule." Advisors descended on struggling students, mentoring them every day in weak areas. Students were encouraged to take and retake tests and quizzes until they got a C or better. No one was allowed to just slide toward failure.

When Richard Esparza took over at Granger High, graduation rates hovered around 30 percent. After five years, that number rose to 90 percent. Student reading scores tripled from 20 percent to 60 percent of the state standard. Math and writing achievement went up at a similar rate. Students who entered Granger unable to read left ready for college. One student named Pedro started ninth grade at Granger High reading below the fifth-grade level. But he says, "The school kept pushing me. In my senior year I took Advanced Placement history and earned the dean's scholarship at Central Washington University." Pedro's story is common now.

Wendy Kopp's lesson that parents in poverty will "leap" to break the cycle for their children turned out to be true. To this day, 100 percent of parents attend student-teacher conferences at Granger High. And Principal Chartrand says that he has stacks of applications from surrounding commu-

---

1 Linda Shaw, "WASL Is Inspiration, Frustration," *Seattle Times*, May 8, 2006.

nities, from parents who are mostly low-income and undereducated themselves, pleading for a chance for their children to study at Granger. Another interesting side effect of the transformation of Granger High School was a significant drop in the crime rate as everyone began taking more pride in the surrounding community.

Although Esparza is proud of what was achieved, he was never satisfied. "To me, making it is 100 percent of our kids making it. I know it will take a little more time, however. I'm an idealist at heart . . . but a realist in mind." The license plate on his car reads *Se Puede*—"It *can* be done."[1]

Richard Esparza is an astounding example of a 3rd Alternative educator. He could have become just another time-serving bureaucrat, sitting in his office in a state of denial, pointing the finger of blame at society, at the parents, at the teachers' union, or at the legislature for his failure to make a difference. Or he could have quit and joined the chorus of critics who say the whole system should be junked.

Instead he deliberately chose a 3rd Alternative. He chose to change the story where *he* was, without waiting for the great socioeconomic-political debate over education to resolve itself. He chose to see each student as a distinctive gift to the world instead of just another failure statistic. He erased the gangs' distorted picture of success and substituted a new picture of primary success: the rewards of hard work, persistence, and achievement. He brought hope to hopeless families. The results speak for themselves, as nine of ten Granger students graduate and go on to college or trade school.

Although Esparza understood as well as anyone the shortcomings of the educational system, he proved that the system itself is not the problem with education. The problem is a mind-set that says, "I can't do this. It's too hard. The system/the union/the community/the world is against me. There's never enough money or resources. No one will cooperate. Nobody cares anyway." This reactive, hopeless paradigm becomes a self-fulfilling prophecy.

Nevertheless Esparza and his team showed a cynical world that great achievements are possible from *within* the system. No system we can devise will work if our paradigms are wrong. The real question is whether or not we

---

1 Interview with Richard Esparza, November 20, 2007; Karin Chenoweth, "Granger High School: Se Puede (It Can Be Done)," in *The Power to Change: High Schools That Help All Students Achieve* (Washington, DC: The Education Trust, November 2005), 17–23.

have the paradigm of synergy, the spirit that asks of us "Are we willing to try for something better than anyone ever thought possible? *Se puede!*"

"The Leader in Me"

In 1999 the A.B. Combs Elementary School in Raleigh, North Carolina, was struggling as a magnet school within the Wake County public system. (A magnet school draws students from outside normal school-district boundaries to focus on some particular theme or skill set.) The school had capacity for more than eight hundred students, yet only three hundred and fifty had enrolled. Combs had the lowest test scores in the district, with only two-thirds passing end-of-year tests at grade level or above. Teacher morale was low. The school lacked a common mission and vision. The facility was dirty. Parents were dissatisfied. In addition, the socioeconomic conditions of the school were challenging. Twenty-nine different languages were spoken in the school, and more than 50 percent of the students were on free and reduced lunch. Principal Muriel Summers faced an enormous challenge.

That year Summers attended one of my presentations in Washington, D.C. I was teaching *The 7 Habits of Highly Effective People*, a set of universal, timeless, self-evident principles common to every enduring, prospering society, organization, family, and individual. During a break in my presentation, she came up to me, introduced herself, looked me straight in the eye, and asked, "Dr. Covey, do you think these habits can be taught to young children?" I answered, "How young?" She said, "Five years old." I thought about it briefly, and said, "I don't know why not. Let me know if you ever try them out in your school."

Frankly, she didn't think much about it again for a while. Then the bad news hit: the district office called her in to tell her that Combs School's magnet program would be closed. Summers pleaded for more time and another chance. "The superintendent sat back in one of those leather chairs that only superintendents seem to get. He relented and told me to come back in a week with a proposal to attract more students." She cried all the way home, but when she met with her staff, they realized that this threat could actually become a great opportunity. "We decided to send up a proposal to make a school like no other in the U.S.A.—the ideal school—and we had one week."

Summers quickly met with everyone who held a stake in the school—

the children, their parents, teachers, community and business leaders—and asked them a version of the 3rd Alternative Question: "If you could create the ideal school, what would it look like?" With no preconceptions, she was essentially asking, "What could we come up with that's better than anyone ever thought of before?"

It was a week of rapid prototyping. The time pressure might have helped because ideas gushed rapidly from all directions. The children wanted teachers "who love us, who know who we are, who are nice to us, forgive us when we make mistakes, know our hopes and dreams." Teachers idealized respectful children committed to making a difference in their lives, eager to learn and kind to each other. Parents valued responsibility, problem solving, goal setting, and self-direction.

The input of business leaders was a little unexpected. Where they might have said they wanted concrete job skills, they actually asked for "honesty and integrity, teamwork and interpersonal skills, strong work ethic." Technology skills were way down the list.

Interestingly, nobody mentioned excellent basic skills or higher test scores, which Summers was committed to improving anyway. But what struck her was a theme that kept surfacing in all the discussions: *leadership*. All stakeholders set great store by the characteristics of effective leaders, such as self-direction, responsibility, problem-solving skills, teamwork, integrity. Underneath it all she heard a cry to make a difference, to bring back hope and promise to the children. It was a cry for leadership. "That's it!" she said. "We will use leadership as our theme."

Summers later recalled, "We searched the Internet and found nobody who was making leadership a foundation for a school. We would be unique. The next Monday at three o'clock I stood before the school board and announced that we would like to become the first elementary school in the nation focused on leadership. I will never forget the expression on the superintendent's face. He quickly reminded me I would receive neither additional money nor human resources, but gave us 'his blessing' to go forth and make a difference."

The newly energized A.B. Combs Elementary adopted a mission: "To develop global leaders one child at a time." Muriel Summers knew this was a big mission and it would not be achieved casually. It wouldn't be enough to stop class and talk about leadership for a few minutes each month; the mission would have to permeate everything.

It was one thing to have a mission, and another thing to know what to

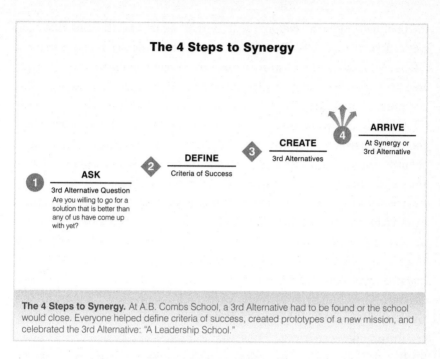

The 4 Steps to Synergy. At A.B. Combs School, a 3rd Alternative had to be found or the school would close. Everyone helped define criteria of success, created prototypes of a new mission, and celebrated the 3rd Alternative: "A Leadership School."

do every day to fulfill the mission. Summers and her team read and studied everything they could find on leadership. They became fascinated with the quality-management literature and decided to adopt a "continuous improvement" approach to measure each student's progress. Each student would set measurable learning goals and track them in the spirit of "Six Sigma," an accountability process used by businesses trying to improve the quality of their operations.

But what about the attributes of leadership, traits such as initiative, vision, decision making, problem solving, building relationships—all so crucial to an effective leader? The teachers needed a framework of some kind for instilling these attributes into the students' lives. Then Summers remembered my presentation on the 7 Habits, and she saw in it the foundational framework for inspiring children to internalize the qualities of effective leaders. "We now embed the 7 Habits into every curriculum area," she says. The approach is "inside out," with the teachers and administrators learning and living by the habits first and then integrating them into their teaching every day. There is no new curriculum. Teachers creatively weave the principles of effectiveness into every subject: reading, math, art, history, science, and social studies. From the moment they walk into the school each day until the final bell rings, the children soak in their adult leaders' belief that they are leaders of their own lives, have irreplaceable talents, and can make a difference. Each student learns the mantra, "There's a leader in me." They are taught the disciplines of a leader—that leaders take initiative, set goals, and put priorities first ("Homework, then play"). They learn about win-win ("Everybody can win—don't choose to lose!"). Every day they learn more about empathy ("Listen first, then talk") and about synergy ("Don't fight about it, think of a better way"). They learn to "sharpen the saw"—to balance work and play, exercise and study, friends and family.

The school continually reinforces these leadership qualities. It's a permanent Magic Theater of ideas for doing so. If you visited Combs, you'd see posters about the 7 Habits on the walls and hallway signs reading "Proactive Place," "Win-Win Way," and "Synergy Street." You'd hear the children singing songs about them. You'd watch the children act out role plays about leaders. You'd find Talking Sticks everywhere. You'd see pictures of great leaders and hear their stories told. The children interview different community leaders, including the governor, about what it takes to be a leader.

If a teacher models leadership, students quickly absorb the example. When a student with a rough reputation enrolled at Combs, he met his teachers by yelling at them, "Get the #*@! out of my face!" The teachers responded calmly: "We don't use that kind of language here, we use a different kind of language, but we're happy you're here nonetheless." The teachers told that boy every day that they loved him, and he continued to curse. But soon he was telling them that he loved them back. His life changed. He earned a place on the honor roll. Watchful students were impressed that the teachers chose to respond with kindness and patience, and they too warmed up to their troubled classmate.

The children also learn how to look the part of a leader: how to shake hands, how to lead a meeting, how to stand and deliver. Their ticket into the classroom is greeting their teacher and student peers; the ticket out is to show their gratitude and thanks to the teacher. The children thank the teachers for returning their papers. They say "Yes, Ma'am" and "No, Ma'am." Relationship-building behavior is taught as part of the "win-win" mentality.

"If this is a leadership school, shouldn't the students be running the school?" Summers asked herself. With this in mind, she developed numerous leadership roles throughout the school. At A.B. Combs you can be a leader of music, art, or science; an audio-visual leader; a classroom-greeter leader; a snack-monitor leader; a playground leader; and on and on. Kids apply for these positions and take them very seriously. The roles are constantly rotating, and every child has the opportunity to be a leader of some kind. As much as possible, Summers allows the children to operate the school. Thus, they lead assemblies, give morning announcements, and serve as escorts when visitors come to the school. When I asked if we could film the great things going on in her school, Summers said, "Of course, and I will assign you to work with our audio-visual student leaders." [1]

Maybe the most gratifying result is the spreading mind-set of synergy among such young children. They know they can choose their response. They know how to transcend conflict. They know how to get together to find a better way, as illustrated in this story told by Gayle Gonzalez and Eric Johnson, parents of three students at Combs:

> *A new boy came to our daughter's classroom with significant anger issues. The way the teacher handled this student was inspiring. The teacher visited honestly with the children one afternoon when the boy was not in class. She said, "The recent blowups in our classroom are not working for us." She involved them in the solution. The children understood that much of the problem was this new student. On their own, they formed a support team. They said they could help this new boy even better than the teacher. This young man responded well and started making great academic progress for the first time in life. When he later moved away the students in the class cried. They had learned to love him.*

These children are 3rd Alternative thinkers. Instead of fighting the bully or shunning him, they invented their own 3rd Alternative for solving the problem so that everyone could win. Clearly, the students at Combs know what primary success is.

Now, what about the academic results?

Within the first year, Combs Elementary's academic scores went from among the lowest in the district to 97 percent at or above grade level. Discipline referrals dropped immediately. There was a strong sense of teacher engagement and collaboration. Parent surveys showed 100 percent were

---

1 To see this compelling video about the transformation of A.B. Combs School, go to The3rdAlternative.com.

satisfied. As the children learned how to lead their own lives and take responsibility for themselves, it became second nature to them to perform at their best. The averages have varied over the years, but the overall picture is extremely positive.

A vital question at Combs (and in education as a whole) is how to help every student excel. Schools of thought differ. Some say the notion of excellence is culturally elitist; others believe that unless students are held to a high standard of excellence (whatever that is), mediocrity reigns. Again, both sides have a point.

But Combs has a 3rd Alternative, which Muriel Summers calls "a huge paradigm shift." Instead of focusing on the performance standard itself, they focus on teaching the leadership principles that produce high performance. Academic excellence is, frankly, a secondary goal, a byproduct of their emphasis on primary success. The principle is "Teach the paradigm, and the behavior follows," and it works beautifully. She recalls how the staff initially thought it would be wonderful to get 90 percent of the students scoring at or above grade level. "Then," she says, "we got to 95 percent. There was a pivotal point when we said that was no longer acceptable, not until we are at 100 percent."

As word spread about the remarkable turnaround of A.B. Combs, other educators were eager to learn more. Hundreds from around the world now come to the school's Leadership Days twice a year to learn how to implement the same approach in their schools. One of the visitors, Jeff Janssen of the Championship Coaches Network, made this report:

> *I immediately knew the school was special when I walked in the front door and a young kindergarten student approached me unprompted, looked me in the eye, gave me a firm handshake, and said in a welcoming and clear voice, "Good morning sir. My name is Michael. We are so happy to have you here at our school." This warm, sincere, and professional greeting was then followed by similar ones from other students of all ages as I walked toward the office.*[1]

From the threat of closure because of underenrollment, Combs is now overenrolled. The school increased from 350 students to 860 and typically

---

1 Jeff Janssen, "Leadership Lessons from the Nation's Best Principal," *Championship Coaches Network*, http://www.championshipcoachesnetwork.com/public/404.cfm.

has a waiting list of more than five hundred children. Housing prices in the area have skyrocketed, and some parents will drive an hour to bring their children to school. Muriel gets hundreds of applications for every teacher job that opens up. (By the way, the fifth graders in the school are involved in interviewing new teacher candidates.) This little "school of leadership" has been recognized across the United States, winning

- National Blue Ribbon School of Excellence
- National Magnet School of Excellence, 2006
- North Carolina Governor's Entrepreneurial Award and School of Excellence
- National Title "Best of the Best"
- #1 National Magnet School of America
- National School of Character, 2003

Most important are the lives transformed at A.B. Combs. Here is just a sampling of the tributes:

- Nathan Baker, disabled student: "You learn to focus on the best things you can do. Don't blame others."
- Liliana, student: "Last year at the end of the year I went to see the guidance counselor to tell her I've been sexually abused for three years. But I can choose. If I continue to live with this, I am choosing not to tell. I want my life to be better and I need your help."
- John Rapple Jr., cadet, West Point Military Academy: "I'm probably sitting at West Point today because I was a student at Combs."
- Pam Allman, teacher: "My husband, a policeman, was shot between the eyes. Because of the things I've learned at Combs, we were able to get through the hardest time of our lives."
- Preenegoe Shanker, student from India: "The things I learned at Combs are what helped me gain confidence for the rest of my life. I learned to focus on my Circle of Influence rather than my Circle of Concern."

Long after all this started at Combs Elementary, Muriel Summers contacted me, as she had promised, to tell me what was going on. I was astonished. I knew this story had to be told, so I prepared a book called *The Leader in Me*, which describes in detail what happened at A.B. Combs and at many other schools that have followed the model. The whole idea of the book is to see children as leaders rather than little receptacles for education.

While visiting A.B. Combs one day, my son Sean was challenged by Summers: "I get calls every day from principals everywhere wanting to implement this leadership model. I don't have the time or know-how to take this to the world. I'm trying to run a school, for crying out loud. It is your moral imperative to do something about this!" Sean took Summers's charge seriously, studied the model, codified it, and put it into a process that any school could implement. Since the release of the book and the process, *Leader in Me* schools have sprouted everywhere: Guatemala, Japan, the Philippines, Australia, Indonesia, Singapore, Thailand, India, Brazil, the UK, and throughout the United States. As I write, there are more than five hundred of them. The results are transformational. Students are increasing in confidence. Teachers are more engaged. Test scores are improving. Positive reports keep pouring in. Parents are clamoring for more schools. After reading the book, a professor at Columbia University packed up his family and left New York for North Carolina so his children could go to Combs.

I've been amazed by the transformational results of these *Leader in Me* schools and have been led to wonder why this leadership model works so well when so many other reform initiatives don't. I see four reasons. First, it starts with a different paradigm. Instead of seeing children through the lens of a normal distribution curve—some kids are smart and some less smart—it sees that every child is capable, every child is a leader. This paradigm changes everything.

Second, it works from the inside out. As Muriel will attest, she first had to get her own teachers on the same page and improve the climate among her staff before she could make it come alive with the students. They couldn't expect changes in their students until they had changed themselves. As the great educator Roland S. Barth puts it, "The nature of the relationships among the adults who inhabit a school has more to do with its quality and character, and with the accomplishments of its pupils, than any other factor."[1] This model, you see, is just as much about the adults as it is the children. It's inside out. First teachers, then students, and then parents.

---

1 Roland S. Barth, "Sandboxes and Honeybees," in Louis B. Barnes et al., *Teaching and the Case Method* (Cambridge, MA: Harvard Business Press, 1994), 151.

Third, it uses a common language. When everyone—teachers, students, and parents—begins using the same language, you get a compound-interest effect that is truly amazing. The 7 Habits create that common language. For example, what a difference it makes when everyone knows what it means to "put first things first" or to "seek first to understand" or to "be proactive." *Leader in Me* schools often find their students using the language among themselves and with their parents: "I need to put first things first and do my homework before I play"; "I should have thought win-win"; or "Dad, you're being reactive."

Finally, the implementation is ubiquitous, meaning everywhere and all the time. Instead of "teaching leadership every Tuesday at one p.m.," Muriel and her team use an integrated approach and make leadership training part of everything they do. So the model impacts everything—the traditions, events, organization, culture, instructional methodologies, and curriculum of the school. But as teachers will tell you, "It's not doing one more thing; it's doing what you're already doing in a better way." [1]

While the great education debaters continue to point fingers at each other, loudly calling for this or that structural reform, blaming each other for everything from their child's stuffy nose to the breakdown of civilization, people like Muriel Summers and Richard Esparza are quietly transforming the lives of children by bringing out "the leader in me." They represent a true 3rd Alternative to the bluster on both sides of the Great Debate. They don't point fingers at anyone; instead they enlist the input and involvement of the whole community. Local business leaders will do anything to help. Parents dive in with vigor. Teachers benefit as much as the students do. These synergistic people have progressed so far beyond the 2-Alternative debate that it seems primitive by comparison.

Not long ago I was invited to speak on education to a large audience at a university in Pennsylvania. I was met there by several young students from A.B. Combs Elementary School. Before going to the podium myself, I invited them to speak about their school and what they had learned. There they stood in front of more than a thousand people, scholars and professors and administrators. They blew the audience away with their courage and confidence, with their message about finding the leader within themselves—

---

1 If you are interested in learning more about *The Leader in Me* process and how to implement it in a school near you, please go to www.TheLeaderInMe.org.

it was just an amazing experience. At that moment, the Great Debate seemed so hollow and so far away.

I don't oppose restructuring the educational system, nor do I stand with those who want to toss the whole system into the fire. However, I would be delighted to see the debating end and the collaborating begin around doing the real job of education: to unleash the leader in every young person, to release the infinite potential of each one to transform their own lives, the lives of their families, and the world.

All children are like stars in their potential. Scientists tell us that buried in each atom is approximately 35 billion times its weight in energy. Inside a star, the atoms fuse and release this tremendous power as light and warmth. Likewise, a child has infinite latent capacity for remaking the future, and it doesn't matter what the arena might be. It is just as important to educate a mother as it is a Nobel Prize winner, for the contributions of both will reverberate forever. The truly great educators will abandon the Industrial Age of control over the human spirit and help bring in a new age of liberation.

The University as Trim Tab

Universities and colleges too are undergoing an identity crisis I've been talking about, asking, "What is the purpose of a university?" Some say it's to prepare people for the job market. They see current universities as ivory towers of effete intellectuals who do young people no favor by wasting their time for four years on irrelevancies and then pushing them out the door with "degrees to nowhere." They insist that the real job to be done is vocational training, thus the huge boom in for-profit universities that focus on job skills.

This narrow mind-set has influenced most college teachers. William Damon, a professor of education, says that if you visit a typical university classroom and ask the professor why a student should take the class, "you will hear a host of narrow, instrumental goals, such as doing well in the course, getting good grades, and avoiding failure, or perhaps—if the students are lucky—the value of learning a specific skill for its own sake." [1]

---

1 Susannah Tully, "Helping Students Find a Sense of Purpose," *Chronicle of Higher Education,* March 13, 2009.

No wonder the focus on secondary success infects the minds of most college students today. The distinguished professor of education Arthur Levine reports that students see college as just another consumable on the market: "I asked some students in this new breed what relationship they wanted with their colleges. They told me that it should be like the relationship with a utility company, supermarket, or bank—their emphasis was on convenience, service, quality, and affordability."

A corporate entrepreneur told Levine, "You know, you're in an industry which is worth hundreds of billions of dollars, and you have a reputation for low productivity, high cost, bad management and no use of technology. You're going to be the next health care: a poorly managed nonprofit industry which was overtaken by the profit-making sector."[1] (Of course, the rise of for-profit higher education has not exactly solved the problems of cost and access any better than for-profit health care has done.) This trend alarms many in higher education. Those who see the university as the sanctuary of scholarship don't like it at all. This complaint is typical:

In barely a generation, the familiar ethic of scholarship, baldly put, that the central mission of universities is to advance and transmit knowledge, has been largely ousted by the just-in-time, immediate-gratification values of the marketplace. Gone is any commitment to maintaining a community of scholars, an intellectual city on a hill.[2]

An echo of the ancient "town versus gown" conflict, today's tension between the marketplace and scholarship is another unfortunate false dilemma. Though their slices of truth are thin, both sides make excellent points, and both have much to offer one another if they can get past 2-Alternative thinking. Ironically, when they do work in synergy together, miracles happen—otherwise, we wouldn't have the sophisticated, high-tech civilization we enjoy today, with its countless accomplishments in the arts and sciences.

At the same time, I believe neither side in this debate has grasped the real job to be done. One side sees the job as all business. It's about making money first, last, and at all costs. All of our accumulated wisdom tells us that this pursuit is spiritually empty—or worse. The global financial disaster of 2008,

1 Arthur E. Levine, "The Soul of a New University," *New York Times*, March 13, 2000.
2 David L. Kirp, "The New University," *The Nation*, April 17, 2000.

far more damaging to the livelihood of millions than any terror attacks we've experienced, was the consequence of this kind of thinking and this kind of education. In the words of historian Robert Butche:

> *The reasons for the world-wide catastrophe are largely known: When large numbers of people and organizations game the system, it fails under the weight of deceit, theft, fraud and greed.*
>
> *How our MBAs are educated, the ways in which they learn to approach problems, how they think about issues, and single issue management, have created a socially and ethically crippled management class. The heart of the MBA conundrum is not bad people or bad intentions, but bad outcomes foretold by win at any price values, short-term goals, and an enveloping profit at any cost mentality.[1]*

However, what the other side of the debate offers isn't necessarily better. The academy long ago divorced itself from its ideals, and it's a little late to assert them now. It's too much about tenure tracks and the politics of self-promotion, and the students get in the way of all that. Someone once said that the definition of a university is a school that has lost interest in its students. As one thoughtful observer puts it, today's university is a place

---

1 Robert Butche, "The MBA Mentality: Enabler of Catastrophe," *Newsroom Magazine,* April 8, 2009, http://newsroom-magazine.com/2009/business-finance/mba-thinking -enabler-of-castastrophe/.

of "private spiritual malaise with many faculty experiencing a loss of both the idealism and the sense of community." It's a world of "mounting disappointment and frustration driven into isolated pursuits and fragmented lives."[1]

On both sides, too much emphasis on secondary success distorts the real purpose of higher education. Of course, everyone should learn how to earn a living, but the true mission of the university is to enable people to make the great contributions they are capable of. Incidentally, when people focus on primary success, the secondary rewards often flow to them automatically.

As a college professor and administrator for nearly thirty years, I struggled with these pressures. I'm well aware of the gradual evolution of the university into a "diploma mill" centered on career preparation. At home, I tried to raise my children with the philosophy that you go to college primarily to learn how to learn and only secondarily to get a job. All nine of them have college degrees in such varied subjects as history, English, international relations, political science, and American studies. Six of the nine have graduate degrees. I'm so grateful that each one has valued a university education. Above all, it has given them the ability to *think about what they think*, which is crucial to going for the 3rd Alternatives in life.

In my view, that's the transformative role of the university: to create 3rd Alternatives. New knowledge is born in 3rd Alternatives. The advancement of knowledge, as Thomas Kuhn said, "depends on a process of revolutionary change. Some revolutions are large, like those associated with the names of Copernicus, Newton, or Darwin." Some are less far-reaching. But all revolutions in knowledge require "putting on a different kind of thinking cap," a mind-set of synergy.

So the real "job to be done" in higher education is the same as in lower education: to develop leaders who make the distinctive contribution only they can make.

Some time ago the administrators of a large university in Canada invited me to consult with them about their future direction. They didn't know which way to navigate. They were undergoing the kind of identity crisis I've described here: "What is our purpose? Are we in business to package

---

1 John Saltmarsh and Edward Zlotkowski, *Higher Education and Democracy: Essays on Service-Learning and Civic Engagement* (Philadelphia: Temple University Press, 2011), 21.

skilled workers for the marketplace? Or should we dedicate ourselves to pure knowledge and keep ourselves magnificently isolated from the 'real world'?"

I suggested a 3rd Alternative by describing to them how the pilot of a great ship controls its course. Fixed on the big rudder of every ship is a tiny second rudder called a trim tab. As the trim tab swings to one side, it creates a vacuum in the water and the big rudder slips easily into that vacuum. By manipulating the trim tab, which is minute compared to the bulk of the ship, a pilot can effortlessly steer, say, an oil tanker weighing a half million tons across an ocean.

So I invited those leaders who were searching for a new purpose to envision the university as a trim tab for making revolutionary change in their community and across Canada. I invited them to renew their mission to become something larger than themselves, larger than their turf, larger even than their own institution.

Now, to help this group come to a 3rd Alternative was an incredibly challenging process. They were mired in politics and contention, with turfism, infighting, interdepartmental resistance, all looking out for themselves and

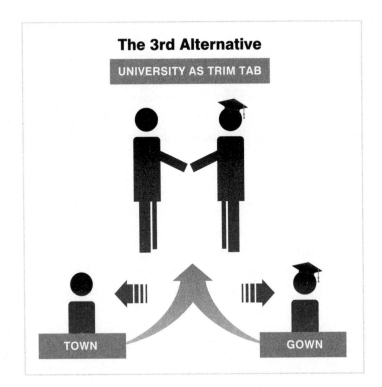

protecting their own territory. Their goals were wildly contradictory. There was so much professional jealousy among them I wasn't sure they would make it. But they wanted strong guidance from me, so I tried to give it: I insisted on deeply involving people all through the institution, on holding up the Talking Stick and really understanding each other's perspectives. Gradually, as they got outside of themselves, outside their departments and disciplines and politics, their mission as a trim tab began to take shape. When they really bought into that idea of leaving a significant legacy, the littleness of their souls shrank away and the magnanimity of soul flowered. Today they are a great university with a clear, superordinate purpose, mentoring and influencing colleges and universities throughout the country into following their lead.

A university becomes a trim tab by fully engaging with the "real world," by serving the community and in the process helping students become trim tabs themselves. As an abundant source of 3rd Alternatives, a university can transform the world around it. And some are now doing just that, as you will see.

Let's Rise and Do It Ourselves!

Stenden University of Leeuwarden in the Netherlands is a trim-tab university. Instead of wringing their hands over their identity, the people of Stenden, teachers and students alike, combine career preparation with scholarship and service. In fact, it's hard to tell where one domain ends and another begins. Former Chairman of the Board Robert Veenstra says, "I wanted a leadership-focused university. Leadership is for me the way to bring out the best in people. What we need is leaders who are all about being trim tabbers. It always comes back to me, 'Be a trim tab.' We need people who dare to stand up and who want to take action for good."

For Veenstra, this is the true work of the university: to unleash the leader in each person. With eleven thousand students in the Netherlands and various campuses in South Asia, Stenden explicitly calls itself a "Leadership University" and defines leaders as people who "act according to universal principles, take responsibility, value differences in people, synergize, and develop themselves."

How does this mission translate into reality? In 2003 the university set up a campus on the coast of South Africa in the beautiful beach town of Port Alfred. The new institution would train people to work in the hospitality industry: hotels, restaurants, and tourism. Because of its climate and incredible coastline, Port Alfred is a holiday destination and home to many well-off retirees. But next door is a completely different world: NeMaTo, the Nelson Mandela Township, still plagued with high unemployment, illiteracy, and crime. The small shops barely survive. Most tragically, street children swarm the streets with no place to go and nothing to do but beg and "huff" petrol and smoke marijuana.

Robert Veenstra and his associates knew this place was perfect for the 3rd Alternative university he had in mind. The new campus was to be called the Educational Institute for Service Studies (EISS); this name had a double meaning: students would be trained in the service industry in the classroom and at the same time provide service to the needy community. There was to be no boundary between class work and field work. Fittingly, the first president of EISS was Raymond Mhlaba, a hero of the apartheid resistance movement and one of Nelson Mandela's fellow prisoners on Robben Island. Although he served only briefly before his death, Mhlaba understood the challenges facing NeMaTo better than anyone.

Like all 3rd Alternative experiments, EISS "started as a big adventure," in Veenstra's words. "The people involved did not know what the outcome of the initiative would be. They only knew they wanted to bring higher education and community development to one of the poorest regions of South Africa, and they saw a great potential in building a bridge for youngsters to a better life." They wanted the students to learn not only a service *job* but also a service *mind-set*.

Miraculous synergies came about as the people of EISS and NeMaTo came together to serve one another. As baking was part of the curriculum, the university founded a bakery in NeMaTo not only to teach baking to students but also to provide jobs for the townspeople and help them develop a spirit of self-support. The bakery's slogan was "Progress Is Our Lifestyle!" Other projects included kitchen gardens, a multipurpose activity center, an AIDS prevention program, and tutoring at the Enkuthazweni School for the Disabled, all staffed by students.

Students also learned alongside small-business owners involved in EISS's "Let's Rise and Do It Ourselves" project for entrepreneurs. Students tutored the owners in business planning, bookkeeping, and marketing, and the owners hired the students to work in their stores. This synergy benefited everyone:

the owners learned new skills, and the students solidified their mastery of the content. A young woman named Joyce had tried to hire herself out to do sewing, but didn't know how to attract customers. EISS students taught her budgeting and basic marketing, transforming her little business. Simphiwe Hlangane had a woodworking shop but knew little about business. He was so kindhearted that he charged only what the customer could pay and even gave away his services. His EISS partners taught him accounting, marketing, and business acumen.

In addition to these institutional helps, EISS organized students to help improve the lives of NeMaTo's many street children, like Xolani and Noncini. Xolani, thirteen, hadn't been to school since the second grade. His mother spent her days at the town dump, where she lived on cheap alcohol; his grandmother was too old to care for him. Xolani wanted to go to school, but as he had lost the tip of his index finger, he decided he couldn't write and was too embarrassed to try. Noncini, a teenager, lived on and off with her grandmother but spent most days hanging around the dump. She tried to go to school but soon became discouraged and ran back to the dump. One horrible day, she got high from sniffing petrol and was gang-raped by a group of boys.

Stories like these are too common in NeMaTo. But EISS "adopted" Xolani and Noncini and many others like them. Students made behavior contracts with them. Xolani agreed to leave the dump and go to the Activity Center every day, where he was enrolled in a special program for young children abusing drugs. At first, his behavior contract was short and simple: "I will not drink alcohol this weekend." Eventually EISS interns started tutoring Xolani's mother in parenting skills and trained Xolani in grooming and hygiene. They monitored his school attendance very closely. Likewise, Noncini got help with her schooling and dealing with her sexual trauma. Her grandmother became key to her healing; with training, they once again became a family. With students taking the lead, EISS rescued children who would otherwise be lost forever to drugs and discouragement.

Greatly extending its reach, the college now sponsors Students in Free Enterprise, a friendly competition involving forty-two thousand students to lift up their struggling communities across more than forty emerging countries. They do things like building a computer center in a remote village and repairing and supplying a school for farmers. These are not extracurricular projects; they are core to the curriculum. In helping small businesses and farmers become more self-reliant, in rescuing children from the living death of addiction, in cultivating within themselves the values of compassion and service, these young people exert an enormous trim-tab effect wherever they go.

EISS (now known as Stenden South Africa) enables students to learn service skills and a service ethic at the same time. Academics are enriched by daily application as the wall between classroom and community comes down. Both mind and heart are educated. Students find out what it means to make a contribution. Robert Veenstra admits that Stenden is unusual in the world of higher education, and he has his skeptics: "I meet resistance all the time. People just don't know if this community work and leadership work is a good idea, or they don't want to do it," he says.[1]

As for me, I think it's the educational model of the future. It will be a shame if universities continue to isolate themselves from the lives of their students and the communities they could be serving. It will be a tragedy if the college experience for most students is reduced to sitting in front of a computer screen, interacting with no one, and taking multiple-choice tests. By contrast, Stenden is an authentic 3rd Alternative, a better way than a purely academic college or a preprogrammed trade school toward its high aim to form people into leaders.

Stenden's innovative method for achieving this aim is known as engagement learning or service learning. Dr. Ernest Boyer, the former U.S. commissioner of education, was a far-seeing leader and an early champion of this kind of synergy between college and the community. He wrote:

> *The scholarship of engagement means connecting the rich resources of the university to our most pressing social, civic, and ethical problems, to our children, to our schools, to our teachers, and to our cities. . . . At a deeper level what's needed is not just more programs, but a larger purpose, a larger sense of mission, a larger clarity of direction in the nation's life.*[2]

1 Information about Stenden South Africa comes from a series of interviews in 2007 with Dr. Robert Veenstra.
2 Cited in Saltmarsh and Zlotkowski, *Higher Education and Democracy*, 22.

That larger purpose is now motivating other colleges to help students learn through service. Every discipline can get involved. For example, in one university, accounting students adopt a homeless shelter in a large American city and conduct workshops for the residents on banking and budgeting skills. Unless they learn to save, they have little hope of getting into their own homes. As part of the training, a local bank sets up savings accounts requiring a first deposit of only a dollar. Coaching people in their need has a profound impact on the students. One wrote, "The people here have honestly taught me more than I ever thought possible. The realities I have been exposed to over the last few weeks have affected my emotions like few things around the university." In a classic role reversal, while he was teaching them, his homeless clients taught him empathy and the value of each human being. This is what I mean by synergistic learning.

In one major law school, students get the opportunity to work for free with low-income clients in a community law center. Some represented an immigrant Mexican baker named Rafael who had been unjustly fired. In addition to working with his case, the law center called on other students in finance and auditing to help him open his own bakery. These students helped him prepare a business plan and obtain a small loan. Language students volunteered to interpret for him. Even alumni got involved in supervising the legal and business contracts. Soon he didn't even need his old job back; he was ready to stand on his own. For him, the legal issue was moot, and that's what a good 3rd Alternative does to legal issues. Genuine synergy across disciplines knocked down walls in all directions.[1]

This kind of synergy leads us to redefine what we mean by education. Too often it has meant dispensing information into empty minds, then asking for it back on a test. This is called the "vending machine" model (the teacher drops coins into the machine and out pops a candy bar) and is another artifact of the Industrial Age. This model is very limited compared to the model of synergistic education where everyone—teachers, students, and the community—contributes knowledge and the results are 3rd Alternatives that transform our understanding and bring us fruitful new para-

1 Curtis L. Deberg, Lynn M. Pringle, and Edward Zlotkowski, "Service-Learning: The Trim-Tab of Undergraduate Accounting Education Reform," n.d., www.csuchico.edu/sife/deberg/CHANGE4A.DOC.

digms. An outstanding example is the work of the University of Victoria
with the First Nations of Canada.

Two Sides of an Eagle Feather

In Canada there are more than six hundred bands of Indians known today as
the First Nations. Many First Nations people want to join the mainstream,
to get schooling and good jobs, but they also want to hold on to their own
ancient ways. For years, the authorities tried to educate them to Western
ways and guide them out of their native cultures. But post–high school education has had a dismal record among the First Nations. Teachers reported
that students simply would not participate in class; they would stare at the
floor and speak so little and so quietly they could not be heard. Only a
very few ever graduated with anything like a college degree. They have been
stereotyped as primitive or backward, unable to cope with the complex demands of modern civilization.

This dilemma helps explain the so-called achievement gap in our schools
that we hear so much about. Minority students chronically fall behind on
skills tests, yet they are as capable of learning as anyone. But imagine how you
would respond if aliens took over your town, forced you into their schools,
and tested you on your mastery of their cultural wisdom and knowledge.
Imagine further that these aliens consider only their own culture worthwhile
and your culture to be valueless. Is it just possible that a lack of empathy
might partially account for the achievement gap?

Caught in this cultural clash but unwilling to give up, the tribal council-
ors of Meadow Lake, Saskatchewan, approached Professors Jessica Ball and
Alan Pence of the University of Victoria to help them develop courses in
childhood development for the young families among their nine tribes. They
were deeply worried about unemployment and exploding drug and alcohol
abuse among the youth of the First Nations and wanted to help parents develop new patterns for raising children.

Because the experience of the First Nations with the Canadian educational system was not promising, Ball and Pence, both child-development
experts, decided to listen to the people first instead of just dispensing a solution. They brought together tribal elders, parents, and other community
members to hear their concerns. These people at last had an opportunity
to use their voices, some for the first time. All sides shared their perspec-

tives, including the professors, and by this route they arrived together at a new curriculum unlike any other for a college degree in child and youth care. It was a 3rd Alternative curriculum that combined the wisdom of *both* the indigenous "words of the Elders" and the Euro-American "words of the West."[1] The students learned Cree and Diné caregiving traditions and practices alongside the mainstream science. When they found that their own traditions were respected, the students began to speak up with new confidence. Furthermore, the curriculum was not set in concrete; insights from the students became part of the course. One teacher called it a "lived curriculum." Because of their respect for the flood of ideas from the First Nations culture, the instructors agreed not to "preordain exactly where the journey of generating curriculum will lead."[2]

In this setting, the instructors learn as much as the students. For example, a textbook remedy for a temper tantrum is to isolate the child, to give him "time out" to calm down. The Cree do the opposite; they bring the child into a family circle and let him "talk out" his frustrations. Without rejecting either idea, the class explores these possibilities and considers them respectfully.

At first, this experience disoriented teachers who were used to "controlling the syllabus." To put decision making in the hands of the students and the community is a countertype for most people in education. One instructor said, "I felt like I was sitting backwards in my desk." But they soon recognized that "all families have strengths and that much of the most valid and useful knowledge about the rearing of children can be found in the community itself—across generations, in networks, and in ethnic and cultural traditions."[3]

These university instructors caught a new paradigm of teaching in which their students become their colleagues. It opposes the scarcity mind-set that

---

1 Alan R. Pence, "It Takes a Village . . . and New Roads to Get There," in *Developmental Health and the Wealth of Nations*, ed. D.P. Keating and C. Hertzman (New York: Guilford, 1999), 326.

2 Jessica Ball, "A Generative Curriculum Model of Child and Youth Care Training through First Nations–University Partnerships," *Native Social Work Journal* 4, no. 1 (2003): 95.

3 Alan Pence and Jessica Ball, "Two Sides of an Eagle's Feather: Co-Constructing ECCD Training Curricula in University Partnerships with Canadian First Nations Communities," n.d., 9–10, http://web.uvic.ca/fnpp/fnpp6.pdf.

claims only some people have worthwhile knowledge and raises up the abundance mind-set that says everyone brings something valuable to contribute. It is empathy in the classroom, and empathy always returns huge dividends of greatly enlarged understanding for everyone. The great teacher Carl Rogers knew this: "The attitude of standing in the students' shoes, of viewing the world through their eyes, is almost unheard of in the classroom. But when the teacher responds in a way that makes the students feel *understood*—not judged or evaluated—this has a tremendous impact." [1]

The synergies of the Meadow Lake experiment bore impressive fruit. A 20 percent graduation rate soared to 78 percent. Instead of suffering the usual brain drain of college graduates, the community retained 95 percent of them, as the students felt much more connected to their own ancestral values. Four of five parents reported that their parenting skills had increased dramatically. [2] The trim-tab effect on the community was noticeable, as young families raised children with more confidence and self-respect. An elder of the Flying Dust First Nation speaks gratefully:

> *We see on the news all these stories of disasters and problems, suicides and gas sniffing among our youth, financial mismanagement, alcoholism and violence in our communities. You start to think: Isn't there anything good about us? But we know that there is a lot of wisdom from experience and a lot of love in First Nations. We need programs that bring out the love and build on the strengths of our people.*

A tribal councilor says, "Everybody walks a lot taller because of this program." Commenting on the synergistic mix of traditional and mainstream knowledge, another elder compared the program to "the two sides of an eagle feather . . . both are needed to fly." [3]

What we see in these examples is definitely a higher form of higher education, a 3rd Alternative to the self-focused careerism and intellectual isolation of the university, both of which are extremely limiting. Students at places like Stenden South Africa and Meadow Lake learn to lead not only

---

1 Carl Rogers, *A Way of Being* (New York: Houghton Mifflin, 1995), 273.
2 "First Nations Partnership Program," http://www.fnpp.org/home.htm.
3 Ball, "A Generative Curriculum," 93–94; Pence and Ball, "Two Sides of an Eagle's Feather," 12.

with their minds but also with their hearts and hands. As the great Catholic educator Peter Hans Kolvenbach has said, "When the heart is touched by direct experience, the mind may be challenged to change. Personal involvement with innocent suffering, with the injustice others suffer, is the catalyst [for] intellectual inquiry and moral reflection."[1]

On a plaque at the entrance to the university where I taught is written the motto, "The World Is Our Campus." I used to think as I passed it on the way to work, "That's a nice sentiment." Now, however, I think it has to become a solid reality for all of higher education. We have an opportunity to revolutionize teaching and instill in our youth the importance of service to the world around them as the key to successful leadership. Through service learning, they can become servant leaders who value primary over secondary success. We can be a trim tab for the next generation of leaders, and they in turn can be a trim tab for positive change in the world.

1 Peter Hans Kolvenbach, "The Service of Faith and the Promotion of Justice in American Jesuit Higher Education," *Company Magazine*, October 6, 2000, http://www.company magazine.org/v184/asiseeit.htm.

TEACH TO LEARN

The best way to learn from this book is to teach it to someone else. Everybody knows that the teacher learns far more than the student. So find someone—a co-worker, a friend, a family member—and teach him or her the insights you've gained. Ask the provocative questions here or come up with your own.

- What is the 2-Alternative thinking behind the Great Debate over education? What are the dangers of following either side in this debate?
- In what ways are our schools still caught in an Industrial Age mind-set?
- Why is the root of our educational challenge the view of children as commodities?
- The 3rd Alternative in education is to become a leader. Not everyone can be the president of the nation or CEO of the company. In what ways can everyone become a leader?
- We all want children to succeed, but we should get clear on what "success" means. What is the difference between primary and secondary success? Why does primary success often lead to secondary success? In what ways are you caught up in the pursuit of the secondary successes at the expense of the primary successes?
- How did Richard Esparza and Muriel Summers manage to transform their schools from within the system and without any additional resources?
- Muriel Summers's mission at A.B. Combs Elementary School is to help each student develop "the leader in me." What does she mean by that mission statement?
- The purpose of the university is to be a trim tab. What is a trim tab? In what ways can a school or a college or a university become a trim tab for the surrounding community? How could you personally become a trim tab within your Circle of Influence?

- In what ways was the Meadow Lake experiment an example of productive synergy? What were the "two sides of the eagle feather"?
- If you are in school now, how can 3rd Alternative thinking help you meet your challenges as a student?
- If you have children in school, what kinds of challenges in their schooling can you meet with 3rd Alternative thinking?
- Consider the question the Canadian university administrators asked and apply it to yourself: "What is my purpose? Am I just a set of skills packaged for the marketplace? What contributions should I make in my most important life roles?"

TRY IT

Choose an educational problem or opportunity in your family, school, or community and start prototyping 3rd Alternatives. Invite others to contribute. Use the "4 Steps to Synergy" Tool.

4 STEPS TO SYNERGY

① Ask the 3rd Alternative Question:

"Are you willing to go for a solution that is better than any of us have come up with yet?" If yes, go on to step 2.

② Define Criteria of Success

List in this space the characteristics of a solution that would delight everyone. What does success look like? What is the real job to be done? What would be a "win-win" for all concerned?

③ Create 3rd Alternatives

In this space (or other spaces) create models, draw pictures, borrow ideas, turn your thinking upside down. Work quickly and creatively. Suspend all judgment until that exciting moment when you know you've arrived at synergy.

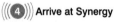 **Arrive at Synergy**

Describe here your 3rd Alternative and, if you want, how you intend to put it into practice.

USER GUIDE TO THE 4 STEPS TO SYNERGY TOOL

The 4 Steps to Synergy. This process helps you put the synergy principle to work. (1) Show willingness to find a 3rd Alternative. (2) Define what success looks like to everyone. (3) Experiment with solutions until you (4) arrive at Synergy. Listen empathically to others throughout the process.

How to Get to Synergy

1 Ask the 3rd Alternative Question

In a conflict or creative situation, this question helps everyone move past firm positions or preconceived ideas toward developing a third position.

2 Define Criteria of Success

List characteristics or write a paragraph describing what a successful outcome would look like to everyone. Answer these questions as you go:

• Is everyone involved in setting the criteria? Are we getting as many ideas from as many people as possible?

• What outcomes do we really want? What is the real job to be done?

• What outcomes would be "wins" for everyone?

• Are we looking past our entrenched demands to something better?

3 Create 3rd Alternative

Follow these guidelines:

• Play at it. It's not "for real." Everybody knows it's a game.

• Avoid closure, premature agreement, or consensus.

• Avoid judging others' ideas—or your own.

• Make models. Draw pictures on whiteboards, sketch diagrams, build mockups, write rough drafts.

• Turn ideas on their heads. Reverse the conventional wisdom.

• Work fast. Set a time limit to keep energy and ideas flowing rapidly.

• Breed lots of ideas. You can't predict which offhand insight might lead to a 3rd Alternative.

4 Arrive at Synergy

You recognize the 3rd Alternative by the sense of excitement and inspiration in the room. The old conflict is abandoned. The new alternative meets the criteria of success. Caution: Avoid mistaking compromise for synergy. Compromise breeds satisfaction but not delight. Compromise means everyone loses something; synergy means everyone wins.

The 3rd Alternative and the Law

6

The 3rd Alternative and the Law

Stephen R. Covey and Larry M. Boyle

A successful lawsuit is the one worn by a policeman.
—*Robert Frost*

I n the little English village of Breedon-on-the-Hill, the annual pantomime brought all the townspeople together for a night of silly songs and
fancy-dress theatricals. It took weeks to prepare, and everybody loved
watching their neighbors make fools of themselves. The tradition was to
hold the panto in the school hall, built decades before largely through dona-
tions from the village.

But the tradition abruptly ended when a new headmistress took over
the school, invoked new safety codes, and suggested staging the panto elsewhere. The town balked, and she raised the fee for the use of the hall to

---

Larry M. Boyle has served as a justice of the Idaho Supreme Court, as chief U.S. magistrate
judge, and as a state district judge. A deeply experienced and highly regarded jurist who
excels in the art and skill of peacemaking, he sees his work with lawyers and their clients
not as a battlefield but as a "peace tent on the battlefield," where arguing turns into listening
for understanding. Judge Boyle and I are working together on a forthcoming book about
synergy and the law titled *Blessed Are the Peacemakers*.

£800, which made everyone gasp. Nobody could pay that kind of money. So they demanded the local council give them free access to the hall, but the council barred them, and for the first time in half a century, no panto was held in Breedon.

Soon the quarrel went to court. The villagers protested the fee and the new Criminal Records Bureau checks that had to be done on anyone who entered the school buildings. Years before, they had paid £3,000 toward the construction of the hall and felt entitled to use it free of charge outside school hours without being investigated like criminals.

School officials argued that the expense of maintaining the hall had shot up and that they couldn't afford to host the panto any longer; the request was "unreasonable and unworkable." They couldn't bear up under the "massive exercise in form-filling" required on every single villager who came into the hall.

After seven years and £6.7 million in fees, the lawsuit worked its way through the High Court of England, where the Lord Chief Justice finally decided it—against the people of Breedon. He also ordered them to pay the crushing costs. The headmistress and the vicar of the parish have long since resigned over the tension. Old friends no longer speak. Relationships between town and council are irretrievably broken. And the village pantomime, where foolishness was once a source of fun, is gone for good.[1]

This story is so typical that most of us shrug it off. The case of Breedon-on-the-Hill is just another skirmish in the wasteful, destructive war we wage on each other through our courts. The adversarial justice system is the formalization of 2-Alternative thinking.

Our courts are crammed with lawsuits ranging from the frivolous and inane to those destined to shape an entire nation. Even the countless cases with merit are so costly in money and broken relationships that in the end neither party really wins. Abraham Lincoln always advised, "Discourage litigation. . . . The nominal winner is often a real loser in fees, expenses, and waste of time."

The stories are endless. When a young volunteer with Teach for America

---

1 See Robert Hardman, "A Very Uncivil War," *Daily Mail Online,* June 21, 2010, http:// www.dailymail.co.uk/news/article-1288182/A-uncivil-war-How-spat-village-hall-divided -community-turned-neighbours-sworn-enemies.html#ixzz1HlBZYBdj; "Breedon-on-the -Hill Villagers Lose Hall Court Appeal," *BBC News,* January 18, 2011, http://news.bbc .co.uk/local/leicester/hi/people_and_places; shnewsid_9365000/9365108.stm.

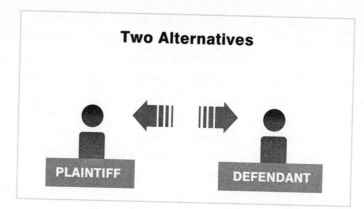

Two Alternatives

PLAINTIFF   DEFENDANT

ejected a misbehaving twelve-year-old from class, the parents sued the school for $20 million. In another case, a man sued his dry cleaner for $67 million for losing his pants. No one knows how much money is awarded in judgments each year—the number would be astronomical—but in the United States alone, billable hours for attorneys add up to $71 billion. There are now more than a million lawyers in the United States, a half million in Brazil, and 150,000 in Britain.

The Incomparable Role of Peacemaker

We deeply honor and respect those who enter into the noble practice of law. Theirs is the *supreme* opportunity to bring relief, creative solutions, peace, and healing to individuals in a world overridden with strife, contention, and intractable problems. The New Testament teaches, "Blessed are the peacemakers, for they shall be called the children of God." If there ever was a time when we need peacemakers, it is today, and lawyers are uniquely positioned to take that role. "As a peacemaker, a lawyer has a superior opportunity," said Lincoln.

A key purpose of this chapter is to help those who deal with lawyers as well as those who practice law to understand this great opportunity. To the practitioners, Larry says this:

At the outset, I must acknowledge a bias and make a disclosure; I like lawyers and have enjoyed working with them for more than forty years. In the years preceding my service in the state and federal judiciaries, my partners and I had a successful and rewarding private practice representing clients ranging from individuals to Fortune 500 companies. I understand the demands placed on lawyers and the great pressures they experience in their professional lives. Over many years I have gained great respect for lawyers and the legal profession. The vast majority of lawyers are honest, competent, and decent men and women providing quality service to clients in a timely manner and at a fair price. There is much of a positive nature to the legal profession. However, there are serious issues with the legal process that affect the health and happiness of all involved. This chapter will address some of those issues openly and frankly.

We're both convinced that most attorneys enter the practice of law with the highest of ideals, with a love of justice and the rule of law, with a desire to earn a good living and provide a good life of opportunity for themselves and their families, and with a sincere desire to serve humanity. Many succeed at creating a practice anchored in these ideals and enjoy remarkable careers bringing relief and creative solutions to countless beneficiaries. However, as young attorneys get sucked into the whirlwind of "the firm," the "partner track," and the adversarial battle with the other side, many become disconnected from these ideals. They compartmentalize their work life from private life and are often left feeling emotionally, mentally, and spiritually empty.[1]

In the end, many lawyers feel far from peacemakers. Patrick J. Schiltz, a former law professor and dean, now a federal court judge in Minnesota, warns law-school graduates: "I have good news and bad news. The bad news is that the profession that you are about to enter is one of the most unhappy and unhealthy on the face of the earth—and, in the view of many, one of the most unethical. The good news is that you can join this profession and still be happy, healthy, and ethical."

According to Schiltz, lawyers seem to be among the most depressed people in America. One study cited found elevated rates of anxiety, hostility, and paranoia among law students and lawyers.

---

1 See "In the Interests of Justice: Reforming the Legal Profession," *Stanford Law Review* 54 (June 2002): 6.

Schiltz also notes that lawyers appear to be prodigious drinkers, citing a study that a third of lawyers in one state suffer from problem drinking or drug abuse. In addition, studies suggest that divorce rates may be higher for lawyers than for other professionals, and that lawyers reportedly think about suicide more often than nonlawyers.

Schiltz cites a study of California lawyers by the RAND Institute for Civil Justice, which found that "only half say if they had to do it over, they would become lawyers." Also, 40 percent of North Carolina lawyers reported they would not encourage their children or other qualified persons to enter the legal profession.

Adds Schiltz, "People who are this unhealthy—people who suffer from depression, anxiety, alcoholism, drug abuse, divorce, and suicide to this extent—are almost by definition unhappy. It should not be surprising, then, that lawyers are indeed unhappy, nor should it be surprising that the source of their unhappiness seems to be the one thing that they have in common: their work as lawyers."[1]

What is there about the practice of law that produces such quiet misery for so many? We believe it's the result of the largely inherited adversarial mind-set, which is 2-Alternative thinking codified and institutionalized. Add to the system a strong-minded client who is making the decisions, and the pressure on the lawyer can be heavy.

The adversarial system in law has an ancient and distinguished history. Most nations, particularly in Europe and the Americas, use some variant of it. No doubt it began in the days of trial by combat, but today it's an elaborate system in which the duties and rights of plaintiffs and defendants are carefully spelled out. When properly used, this system serves justice well, but as we have said, 3rd Alternative thinkers are always looking for ways to transcend justice and fairness and go on to synergy. As Schiltz points out, "[Lawyers] are playing a game. And money is how the score is kept in that game."[2]

1 Patrick J. Schiltz, "On Being a Happy, Healthy, and Ethical Member of an Unhappy, Unhealthy, and Unethical Profession," 52 Vand. L. Rev. (1999).
2 Schiltz, 905.

The distinguished former justice Sandra Day O'Connor of the U.S. Supreme Court expresses alarm over the trend to use the law as a means for escalating conflict instead of resolving it:

It has been said that a nation's laws are an expression of its people's highest ideals. Regrettably, the conduct of lawyers in the United States has sometimes been an expression of the lowest . . . of a professional environment in which hostility, selfishness, and a win-at-all-costs mentality are prevalent. One lawyer who recently stopped practicing explained his decision to leave the profession in these bleak terms: "I was tired of the deceit. I was tired of the chicanery. But most of all, I was tired of the misery my job caused other people."

We speak of our dealings with other lawyers as war—and too often we act accordingly. Consider the language that lawyers use to describe their everyday experiences: "I attacked *every weak point of their argument."*

"Her criticisms were right on target.*"*

"I demolished *his position."*

"If we use that strategy, she'll wipe us out.*"*

"I shot down *each of their contentions."*

Lawyers are dissatisfied with their careers not simply because of the long hours and hard work. . . . Rather, many lawyers question whether, at the end of the day, they have contributed anything worthwhile to society.[1]

The all-too-often endpoint of 2-Alternative thinking is the courtroom. The great paradox is that the courts could be the best venue we have for 3rd Alternatives, and lawyers the greatest practitioners of synergy. The adversarial system encourages people to think in terms of "win or lose," "my way

---

1 Sandra Day O'Connor, *The Majesty of the Law* (New York: Random House Digital, 2004), 226–29.

or your way." But the pathway to peace—in the heart, and not just between individuals, but in the world—is *our* way, a 3rd Alternative.

A 3rd Alternative Law Practice?

Is it possible that the practice of law—even if the client is powerful and demanding—could be transformed by 3rd Alternative thinking? Yes, and to a degree it's already happening. One positive sign is the explosive growth of "alternative dispute resolution" (ADR) in many jurisdictions, government agencies, and corporations, in which people meet with a mediator or an arbitrator instead of going to court. As the prominent professional mediator Peter Adler says, "Mediation is now fully married to the law and hardwired into the judicial system."

ADR can be a wonderful way to ease the strains and stresses of going to court. Contrasted with a lawsuit, an ADR approach to resolving conflict can

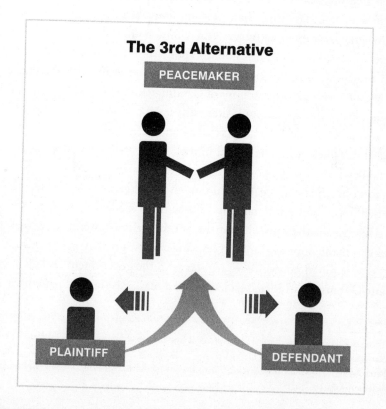

produce much better, faster, and cheaper results with far less wear and tear on the parties. Among ADR approaches, mediation is the most like synergy. Mediators are usually more interested in how to solve the problem than in who wins or who loses. They also work hard to maintain the relationship between disputants. A skillful mediator can turn a bitter divorce into a workable arrangement whereby parties can get on with their lives and cooperate on child custody, property sharing, and so forth. How we admire and applaud the efforts and immeasurable positive impact of mediators!

An early proponent of ADR, attorney and mediator Thomas Boyle said of mediation, "Like a peace tent on the battlefield, it unites the parties in the common goal of settlement."[1]

But without the three paradigms of 3rd Alternative thinking, ADR too often ends up as litigation in disguise; by itself, ADR has little power against entrenched paradigms of disrespect and defensiveness. ADR is in the business of achieving fair, just, and equitable solutions, but not necessarily going on to synergy. Reflecting on the limitations of ADR, Adler says, "Too often the shared values and techniques that seemingly link us together turn out to be surface yearnings rather than real common ground."[2]

Synergy is all about getting to "real common ground" and requires a fundamental paradigm shift. It's about escaping from the mind-sets of competition and compromise and embracing the mind-set of the 3rd Alternative.

We are inspired by the actions of Gandhi, who mentally broke out of the limitations of the 1st and 2nd Alternatives. A London-trained lawyer, Gandhi was well versed in the adversarial system. After joining a South African legal firm, you'll recall, he found himself continually abused as an Indian working within a white power structure. He was thrown off a train for daring to sit in a first-class coach even though he held a first-class ticket. Hotels refused to put him up, restaurants refused to serve him.

He was not the only victim; the South African state of Transvaal was home to many oppressed minorities. Angered by a new Asiatic Registration Act that required nonwhites to register with the government and be fingerprinted, Transvaal's Indian residents held a mass meeting on September 11,

---

1 Thomas D. Boyle, "Mediation and the Legal System: New Tricks for an Old Dog," *Federal Bar Journal* 58 (October 1991): 514.
2 Peter Adler, "The End of Mediation," http://www.mediate.com/articles/adlerTheEnd.cfm. Accessed July 19, 2010.

1906, to decide on a response. The crowd debated whether to submit or fight back. A respected voice in the crowd, Gandhi had wrestled in his heart with how to respond. As angry as anyone would be at being mistreated, he understood very well that violence would be answered with violence. At the same time, he could not live under tyranny. Somehow he found his answer, a 3rd Alternative, in the synergy of two overriding principles: justice and the Hindu tradition of *ahimsa,* doing no harm to any living creature.

In a speech to the crowd, Gandhi proposed his 3rd Alternative: nonviolent resistance. He would not give up human rights and dignity by complying with the unjust law; this would be a violation of principle. But he would not use force to resist and urged others to accept arrest without violence.

The Indians faced violence with nonviolence. More than ten thousand went to jail peaceably rather than give up their rights, and this massive show of quiet protest drew the attention of a stunned world. Eventually, Gandhi himself went to jail and spent his time there making a pair of sandals as a gift for the president of Transvaal, Jan Christiaan Smuts. This act demonstrated the true uniqueness of Gandhi's 3rd Alternative. He did not merely resist injustice; he sought to make a friend of his adversary. Although Smuts imprisoned him three times, Gandhi never despaired of changing the president's heart, and he eventually succeeded. The "Black Act," as it was called, was eventually repealed. Many years later, Smuts attended Gandhi's birthday celebration and said, "I am not worthy to stand in the shoes of so great a man."

Back in his homeland, Gandhi advocated the liberation of India from British rule. He felt that separation would be as good for the British as for the Indians. "If the British withdraw," he wrote, "they become eased of a tremendous burden, if they would calmly consider the meaning of the enslavement of a whole people."[1] He insisted on treating the British as beloved friends even when faced with mistreatment and imprisonment, and advised others to do the same. "My brothers," he said to his countrymen, "we've come a long way with the British. When they leave, we want them to leave as friends. If we really want to change things, there are better ways than attacking trains or killing someone with a sword. I want to change their minds, not kill them."

The vast nonviolent resistance movement that led to India's independence is legendary. The remarkable thing is that Gandhi, the leader, never

---

1 Mohandas K. Gandhi, "My Appeal to the British," *Harijan,* May 24, 1942.

held any office or formal authority of any kind. A trained lawyer, he had chosen to take the role of a peacemaker rather than the role of an adversary. It was solely through the force of this 3rd Alternative mind-set that he brought about the liberation of hundreds of millions of people. When the British left in 1947, they did so in peace and friendship.

This is a powerful secret of the 3rd Alternative mind-set: it's about turning foes into friends. Gandhi never lost faith that "even the most hardened human heart is capable of conversion—of being moved by an opponent's genuine gestures of love."[1] With these gestures, this diminutive Indian lawyer changed the world.

Of course, the first change was in Gandhi's own mind and heart. "As human beings, our greatness lies not so much in being able to remake the world," he said, "as in being able to remake ourselves."

Along with Abraham Lincoln, one of the other great influences on American law was Thurgood Marshall. He was known for his absolute integrity and honor. In addition, he was a 3rd Alternative thinker. He had every reason to take offense and return barb for barb, insult for insult. Instead he took the high road, knowing his goal was equality, not to skirmish and quarrel. In response to critical comments made to him by his African American colleagues because he had lunch with opposing counsel, a segregationist, Marshall simply replied, "We're both lawyers, we're both civil. It's very important to have a civil relationship with your opponent."

When finalizing the briefs for the landmark case *Brown v. Board of Education* for submission to the U.S. Supreme Court, it was said, "Marshall edited the briefs several times himself to remove little 'snide' remarks about the opposing white lawyers arguing for segregation. It was typical of Marshall to keep the fight on the most professional level."

Marshall succeeded through his 3rd Alternative to contentious attacks on one hand or surrender to the status quo on the other. With history as a measuring stick, his thinking and approach led to monumental new legal protections for minorities in the United States.[2]

Lawyers who see themselves as peacemakers first, as gifted communicators and learned creators of concord instead of discord, view each case as an

---

1 Uma Majmudar, *Gandhi's Pilgrimage of Faith* (Albany, NY: SUNY Press, 2005), 144–45.
2 Juan Williams, *Thurgood Marshall: An American Revolutionary* (New York: Three Rivers Press, 1998), 213, 215.

opportunity to arrive at a 3rd Alternative, a far greater and more satisfying challenge than trying to tear down the opposition.

Litigants willing to see themselves and their opponents as flawed human beings still worthy of respect can move toward a deeper understanding of each other. They can face the reality that no issue is either black or white, that we all have our slices of truth, and that their indignation might be blinding them to mounting disaster for everyone involved—including themselves.

The Law and the Talking Stick

A lawsuit can become a "search and destroy" form of warfare: the goal is to search out weaknesses and destroy the opposition. By contrast, the first requirement of a peacemaker is empathy—a determination to seek out and truly understand the opposition. Larry tells the following story.

I remember in one mediation, the lawyers for both sides told me, "These parties are so far apart that we really don't see that we can narrow the gap." In my forty years in the law, I had never seen jaws as tight or faces as serious. The only thing tighter than their jaws were their purse strings.

It was a tragically familiar story: two business associates, once friends with a great relationship, now stubborn enemies demanding staggering damages from each other. I wondered how much business had been lost, how many opportunities bypassed, how much money wasted as these two squandered their time and energy on fighting one another.

I had rarely seen a closer case with so little advantage to either party, as both sides were backed by a host of facts and arguments. But one thing was clear to me: neither really understood the other's position. Both sides were so focused on telling their version of the facts that they were blind to the argument of the other side. At one point I turned to the lawyers and asked, "Do both of you understand the other side's position?"

"Yes," one answered confidently.

But the other lawyer paused and said, "I know what they've argued, but I really don't understand the basis of their position." That's when I figuratively gave them the Talking Stick.

My next requirement was a twist they had never before experienced. I

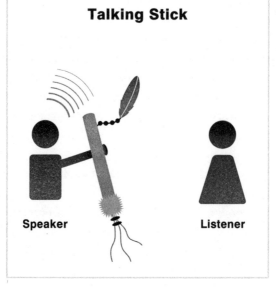

Talking Stick

Speaker   Listener

explained that the attorneys would be given an opportunity to speak, but before they could make comments in support of their own position, they would have to state the other's position to his satisfaction. In essence, they would be making the case for their opponents.

It took the defendant's attorney three tries before he stated the plaintiff's position to the satisfaction of the plaintiff. Then it was the plaintiff's turn; it took his counsel two tries.

Then a very interesting thing happened. The defendant no longer had his arms folded over his chest, and his stern, serious expression was gone. He looked at the plaintiff and said, "Brad, is that your position?"

"Yes, pretty close."

"I thought you . . ."

And the attorneys sat back and watched their clients open a dialogue that had been closed for the two years since one sued the other. Eventually, they came to a settlement that was attractive and beneficial to both of them. What's more important, their mutual respect, which had all but evaporated, returned.

I knew that if this case had gone to trial, one side would win it all and the other would walk away with empty hands and heavy costs to pay. That's how the system works. Both would spend a fortune in the process, which factored in meant the winner would also be a big loser. But instead of fighting each other to the bitter end, the two sides arrived at a peaceful, voluntary settlement they had never envisioned before. It happened because the Talking Stick spirit opened up the route to reconciliation.

I cannot tell you how revolutionary empathic communication in court proceedings can be. Although our Western justice system is adversarial, that doesn't mean we need to use it in an adversarial spirit. There is no reason why a mind-set of empathy and synergy can't replace the mind-set of "search and destroy."

Many justice systems rely on empathy rather than the adversarial mind-set. Many nations resolve disputes without that win-lose mentality. In Japan the goal of the *chotei* courts is not retribution but the restoration of "peace and tranquility," which makes Japan perhaps the least litigious society on Earth.

The Jews, with their ancient tradition of respect for law, also put a high value on compassion and reconciliation. The rabbinical courts are not about "winning the case." For Jewish lawyers and judges, the biblical figure of Aaron, brother of the lawgiver Moses, is the example to follow. As high priest and judge of Israel, Aaron "loved peace and pursued peace and made peace between people," putting human relations at the center of the law. The great Jewish scholar Rabbi Nathan describes how Aaron carried out his role:

> *Two people had quarreled with one another. Aaron went and sat with one of them. He said to him: My son, look what your friend has done, his heart is distraught and he has torn his clothes [out of sorrow over the quarrel], and he is saying: Woe is to me, how will I raise up my head and look at my friend? I am embarrassed in his presence, because I am the one who wronged him. And he [Aaron] sits with him until he removes the jealousy from his heart.*
>
> *And Aaron then goes and sits with the other party and says to him: My son, see what your friend has done, his heart is distraught and he has torn his clothes and he is saying: Woe is to me, how will I raise up my head and look at my friend? I am embarrassed in his presence, because I am the one who wronged him. And he [Aaron] sits with him until he removes the jealousy from his heart. And when the two opponents met, they embraced and kissed one another.*[1]

---

1 From "Avot de Rabbi Nathan," in "Mediation," *Jewish Virtual Library,* http://www.jewish virtuallibrary.org/jsource/judaica/ejud_0002_f0012_0_11960.html.

Tradition says that Aaron would run after the people in a dispute before it ever came to the court. He would never talk about the issue itself—it was all about emptying the wounded heart and maintaining the relationship. "What is going on?" he would ask. "What is making you angry? You've both had the same experience; you've both been disrespected." Fighting couples would listen to him and each other and then name their children after him. For the great high priest Aaron, the end product was not a legal decision in which one side prevails and the other loses, but rather a peaceful 3rd Alternative and a stronger relationship.[1]

While the adversarial mind-set is "winner take all," the mind-set of the Jewish court is traditionally to help everyone win in a dispute. When an Israeli worker used his company-provided gun to kill a man, the victim's family sued the employer on the grounds that the company should have known about their employee's disturbed mental state and foreseen how he would use the weapon. The case went to the Supreme Court of Israel, where Justice Menachem Elon decided in favor of the company. But when he addressed the winner he said, "Here are a widow and orphans. You should do what you can for them even though you are not required in law. . . . It is the practice of every Jewish court to compel the wealthy to perform their obligation where it is right and proper." In other words, the court said to the company, "The law is on your side; but beyond that, you need to do what is right and good."[2] The win-win solution is the ideal Jewish lawyers and judges aspire to, and that's why even non-Jews around the world often resort to Jewish courts to help resolve conflicts.

Islamic law also values reconciliation above retribution. A key tool of Islamic law is the *sulh*, a council that hears delegations from both sides of a dispute. First, the delegations ask for a truce, which dignifies the victim's family. Then they talk; the *sulh* is communication-driven, a place to come together and listen to each other. The council asks, "What do you think of what he is saying? How would you answer him?" If agreement evolves, they all go home, satisfied with the outcome. The process works better than a formal court trial, where a decision usually doesn't end the issue; there's an old

---

1 Interview with Rabbi Marc Gopin, Hebrew University of Jerusalem, January 11, 2011.
2 The principle is known as *lifnimmishurat ha-din*, "beyond the letter of the law." See "Damages" and "Law and Morality," *Jewish Virtual Library*, http://www.jewishvirtual library.org/jsource/judaica/ejud_0002_0012_0_11960.html.

Muslim saying that "half the people are the judge's enemies." By contrast, the *sulh* is more practical, less costly, and ends in agreement.[1]

With the adversarial mind-set, there are really no winners. Just as no country is better off after a prolonged war, precious few lawsuits ever leave the litigants better off. Both sides often end up beaten, emotionally defeated, and in worse financial shape. In court, you turn over your fate to an independent forum with no emotional interest in you. During a trial, things can change dramatically, in an instant. A witness can be unpersuasive. Exhibits can be excluded from evidence. When that happens, there can be unanticipated results. Bad things can happen when parties fail to find 3rd Alternative solutions. Larry's son Brian Boyle is a skilled and successful lawyer. He describes the effect of conflict and litigation on the clients:

More than even the financial strain of going to court is the emotional and psychological strain. Participants become obsessed with the case and it keeps them from being productive in other areas of their lives. They find that legal time is second only to geological time in speed. What happens is people lose sleep over it. By the time they end up in a lawyer's office, they're often so emotional and angry, all they want is vindication.

In divorce cases, for example, you get a woman or man with a lot of pain. The financial issues are often fifth priority. What the wife really wants is for the judge to tell her husband he's as big a jerk as she thinks he is, and the same on the other side. It reduces you, distracts you from every other aspect of your life.

The rise of mediation will hopefully move the legal system more toward synergy. Now mandatory in many areas, mediation is far less costly and bruising than court trials, but mediation cannot lead to 3rd Alternatives until the adversarial mind-set is replaced with empathy.

Another remarkable peacemaker, Judge William Sheffield, has been called "the mediator of last resort" in the state of California. When no one else can break an impasse, Sheffield is called in. His first "impasse breaker,"

---

1 Interview with Qadi Achmed Natour, president of the High Shari'a Court of Appeals in Jaffa and professor of law, Haifa University, at Hebrew University of Jerusalem, January 4, 2011.

as he terms it, is empathic listening. Where some mediators fly in, spend a morning on a case, present a proposal, and then fly out in time for dinner, Sheffield takes off his coat and gets to know each party intimately. He wants them to talk until everyone feels completely understood. "You can't do this sort of thing in ten minutes," he says. "They have to know that you understand them before they'll trust you." If no settlement is forthcoming, he's willing to wait for it, unlike many mediators.

His goal is to persuade the parties to get real. "If you don't settle and the case is heard in court, what are your odds?" Typically, each side of a legal dispute comes into it with the mind-set "I'm going to cream you." His job is to disabuse them of that. "I have frequently said, 'You'd better call that condo dealer on Maui and tell them to pull the deal because it's not going to come from this case.'"

What is Sheffield's second "impasse breaker"? *More* empathic listening.

If there's no progress, then I get to know the parties even better. I had a stubborn client, a plaintiff in a wheelchair who raised tomatoes on land he leased from the city. He claimed the city wouldn't properly accommodate his disability, and neither party would settle. After a while, I went out to his field and sat down, started eating tomatoes with him, and we tasted all the varieties he grew. He told me all about his life and his struggles, about his time on the Wheelchair Olympic team. We got very close. The more he felt understood, the closer we bonded, and the easier it was for him to feel that he was not being ignored. That's all-important. So often they say, "What I want is a hundred thousand dollars and an apology," but more often what they really want is to feel important, to feel understood and not minimized.

You have to give them the time to really vent and feel like you really get it. Then you can settle the case and avoid a year or two more of expensive litigation. Devote just one day to listening and you can often put to bed a dispute that's been going on for years.[1]

No one, lawyer or litigant, has to approach a dispute with an adversarial mind-set. The cost is too great and the benefit doubtful. We can choose to see the dispute as a misunderstanding and approach it in a spirit of empathy

---

1 Interview with William Sheffield, October 21, 2010.

and synergy. And we don't need the permission of the court to do that. Stephen offers an example.

One day I received a phone call from the president of a company asking me if I would help him resolve a very costly high-stakes lawsuit. I knew this executive well. Over the years we had talked about the 3rd Alternative mind-set and I felt he understood it. He was extremely capable, but when it came time to actually apply what we had discussed, he was not confident. The lawsuit he was involved in was a major threat to him and his business, and he wanted me to mediate. But I told him, "You don't really need me. You can do this yourself."

So he rang up his opponent in the lawsuit, who was also a company president, and asked if they could meet to discuss the situation. The other president did not want to meet, but my friend explained what he was trying to do and why. "Listen," he said. "I'm not going to bring my attorney. You can bring yours, and if your attorney counsels you not to say anything, then don't say anything."

On that basis, the other president agreed to meet. Later he described to me what happened at that meeting.

The man showed up with his attorney, and they all sat down at a conference table. My friend pulled out a writing pad and said, "First, I want to see if I understand your position in this suit."

Hesitantly, the other man started to talk. He laid out the problem from his perspective, which had something to do with a dispute over product ownership.

My friend just listened and made notes. At last he said, "Let me see if I've got it." He then restated as fully and completely as he could what the president had said and asked, "Is that your position?"

The man looked over the notes and said, "Yes, yes, that's it, but there are two points you're not clear about."

The man's lawyer interrupted. "You know, I don't think we need to go into all the details here."

Surprisingly, the man turned to his lawyer and said, "Jeffrey, I know I asked you to be here, but why don't we just try this." The lawyer sensed the momentum toward a 3rd Alternative. So the other president carefully described his remaining two points.

My friend wrote them down, restated them, and then asked, "Is that a complete and fair understanding of your position?"

"Yes, it is."

"Is there anything else I need to understand?

"No, that covers it."

"Good," said my friend. "Now would you be willing to listen to me the way I've listened to you?"

There was a pause, but then the man said, "Fire away."

And a two-way dialogue began. Out of their new understanding came humility. Walls came down. They began to believe that a 3rd Alternative was possible.

Several hours later, these two men emerged from that meeting with that 3rd Alternative, a solution to their problem that saved the relationship, avoided the costs of litigation, and laid the foundation for better ways of working together in the future. The whole situation changed.[1]

Synergy and the Law

A common response to getting hurt is to get even: "They can't do this to me. Who do they think they are? I'll sue!" We all have an interest in justice and fairness, and when someone has injured us, we rightly expect him to make it good. That's why we have lawyers and judges and courts.

But remember that if we have a synergy mind-set, we are not satisfied with fairness—we are looking for something better than just what's fair. We want stronger, not weaker relationships. We're less interested in retribution than in reconciliation. We are searching for a solution that's superior to just getting even, a solution that leaves everyone involved much better off than before.

Additionally, we synergists are not very interested in compromise. It's a well-worn legal tool, but compromise means all parties have to give up something; why should we do that before we've explored 3rd Alternatives? Compromise can also be morally hazardous because it often means backing away from principles we cherish. We're impressed by this insight from the great Nigerian writer Chinua Achebe: "One of the truest tests of integrity is its blunt refusal to be compromised."

---

1 To see a video reenactment of this transformational story, go to The3rdAlternative.com.

When we run into a conflict, we don't want "an eye for an eye," nor do we want to settle for some stopgap compromise. We hope we are more imaginative than that. Stephen offers the following example.

After years of working and saving, a friend of mine finally finished building his dream house. He'd hired the best contractor in town to carry out his vision, and with its high cathedral ceilings and painstakingly carved moldings and woodwork, it was a work of art. Then the painter came to add the last touch.

When my friend walked into the house that night after the painter left, he nearly collapsed. The paint job was ruinous. Every wall, every room, every molding was defaced with smeared, uneven paint. Smudges covered doors and tiles. Paint dribbled down the arched windows, some of which were custom made and artworks in themselves. It looked as if a child had taken a can of spray paint to the house.

My friend punched two numbers into his phone—his contractor's and his lawyer's. Fortunately, the contractor got there first. He was a wiry, energetic man with a reputation for integrity and quality; otherwise my friend would not have hired him. When the contractor saw the work, his jaw fell open and he immediately phoned the painter and asked him to come back to the house.

What happened next astounded my friend. It was late in the evening, and my friend expected that the contractor, who had had a long, tiring day, would chew out the painter, fire him, and demand his money back plus damages. Instead he met the painter at the door and shook hands with him.

The painter was a young man, barely out of his teens, who grinned and asked the contractor nervously how he liked the work. The contractor put his arm around him and walked him coolly through the house, pointing at this and that problem, and then all three sat down to talk. The contractor asked a few questions, and it became clear that in his bid the painter had really overstated his qualifications to do the work. Although he'd done a few smaller jobs before, this was the first house he had ever painted.

The contractor didn't stop there. He asked the young man about his family, where he had gone to school, what his life had been like. My friend wondered why any of this was relevant, but soon they learned that he had struggled in school and dropped out, gotten married very young, and had a wife and baby to support. Obviously he was trying to make a living the only way he could think of.

When they stood up, the contractor apologized to my friend for not checking out the painter more thoroughly before hiring him, and then asked the boy to bring his painting equipment back into the house. Calmly he said, "I'm going to teach you how to do this kind of job right."

Doubtful about this, my friend shrugged and left to go to bed. Over the next few days, he dropped in to see how things were going. The contractor was there with the painter. They were talking and laughing as they cleaned windows, scrubbed smudges away, sanded and repainted walls. At last, under the contractor's supervision, the end product was truly beautiful. In the months that followed, the young man apprenticed to the contractor and became more and more capable until he could do work exactly as the older man specified. He became the contractor's painter of choice and had more jobs than he could handle.

With his 3rd Alternative paradigm, this small-town general contractor proved that synergy-minded people are full of surprises. Instead of firing the painter in a huff—or worse, ruining him with demands for damages—he chose to help the young man build a life and in the process become a valuable asset to his own business. He was truly a builder, and in more than one sense.

When the lawyer showed up, she assured my friend he had handled things well. There would be no lawsuit, no court fight, no demolition of a vulnerable young family. No 1st Alternative wrestling the 2nd Alternative. No demands for fairness or justice or equity.

This kind of synergy and peacemaking is possible throughout the whole legal system; however it will require a seismic Paradigm Shift. Some have already made that shift. Some cultures build into their justice systems the prospect of a 3rd Alternative. In the Jewish *zabla* courts, for example, each party chooses a judge, and then a third independent judge is seated specifically to look for a 3rd Alternative. But nobody needs to change the Western system of jurisprudence; what needs to change is the *mind-set behind it*. When the mind-set changes, the practices change. Larry describes the process.

At the request of my federal-court colleagues, I conduct judicially supervised mediations in their cases. In our federal district, we regularly conduct settlement conferences for each other. I try to introduce Talking Stick sessions in conferences and in chambers whenever possible. Moving opposing parties from hostility to empathy and understanding is a methodical process.

Once everyone in a dispute feels heard, I ask the parties to list their criteria of success—and failure. I draw a vertical line on a sheet of paper, and say, "If you were to be satisfied, the left column would be a list of reasons why the jury might find for you," and "If you were to be disappointed, the right column might be a list of reasons why the jury might find against you." Without using the actual terminology, I ask the parties to draft prototypes of a 3rd Alternative. At the top of a page, I write the three words: "Plan for settlement," and leave the parties to write their plans in private. Sometimes it takes three or four drafts. In most cases where I have used this technique, they settle, because the parties and their attorneys have analyzed in depth the pros and cons and then been creative about a reasonable plan to settle. I used this 3rd Alternative process to resolve one of the most complicated court cases I've ever faced: the Blackbird Mine case.

The old Blackbird Mine in the mountains of Idaho was America's only source of cobalt, a metal of great strategic importance during the cold war. Miners worked furiously through the 1950s and 1960s. Finally abandoned in the 1970s, the mining operations left behind a terrible stream of acid and metallic poison that was devastating to the land, water, and wildlife of the beautiful Salmon River wilderness. Then, like a series of tipping dominoes, the state, private environmental groups, and a dozen federal agencies sued the mine owners and each other to force cleanup. A blizzard of claims and counterclaims flew.

By the time it came to me for mediation, the case had languished in court for more than a decade. At stake were cleanup costs of more than $60 million, for which no one would take responsibility. Prior attempts to settle the case failed because the parties were so divided. Files had grown to thousands of pages with scores of motions awaiting decisions. The trial would take months, featuring hundreds of exhibits and dozens of expert witnesses, after which there would be years of appeals. The whole mess was in judicial gridlock.

Faced with this complicated case, my colleague advised me not to worry about resolving it: "That isn't possible. I'm hoping you can just settle some of the peripheral issues so the trial will be manageable." I decided to try for a 3rd Alternative approach.

After meeting with all parties in a packed courtroom—even the jury box was full—I decided to shut down the courtroom, installed each interest group in a conference room, and invited the lead lawyers to my private chambers. "Each of you understands the facts of the case and knows the strengths and weaknesses of your positions," I told everyone. "I will have someone from my staff come get each of you in two hours so you can report to me your group's plan to settle this case."

Surprised at this request, the lawyers went to their rooms and started sketching their proposals on easel pads. I made the rounds of these meetings, not because I wanted to see the plans but because I was looking for someone: a leader, a person with a 3rd Alternative mind-set. I found him in John Copeland Nagle, who later became associate dean of research at the Notre Dame School of Law. This distinguished attorney and professor of law has literally written the book on American environmental law.[1] But more important to me, Nagle seemed unthreatening, highly capable without being aloof, and an instinctive leader. I asked him to be my liaison to the parties as they worked out their plans, but I was really counting on his natural leadership ability to produce a solution. He'd come back to me and say, "Here's position A," and we'd synergize and come up with a better solution than A. As the teams wove together their own solution, they began to take ownership of it, as I knew they would. People are never as committed to an imposed solution as to a 3rd Alternative they produce themselves.

In the weeks and months that followed, I had the parties and their counsel return for two more meetings. Each time they got closer to complete resolution, not just narrowing issues, all because of the 3rd Alternative thinking that permeated the atmosphere of their work together.

There would be no dramatic trial, no packed courtroom, no breathless media drama, because within a few months the decade-long debacle was all over. The parties shared responsibility and went to work to repair the damage. The Blackbird Mine is a success story. It was a quick agreement—the first major environmental settlement to focus primarily on achieving a quick and efficient restoration. The cleanup went forward, one of the biggest in history before the *Exxon Valdez* disaster, and soon the salmon could return to the streams once polluted by the Blackbird Mine.

Without the settlement, a federal judge would have presided over the

---

1 See J.B. Ruhl, John Copeland Nagle, and James Salzman, *The Practice and Policy of Environmental Law* (New York: Foundation Press, 2008).

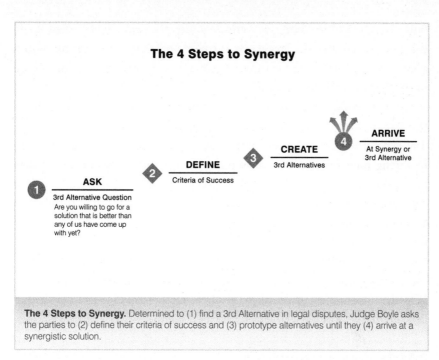

The 4 Steps to Synergy. Determined to (1) find a 3rd Alternative in legal disputes, Judge Boyle asks the parties to (2) define their criteria of success and (3) prototype alternatives until they (4) arrive at a synergistic solution.

case in that same courtroom for another year or more, hearing motions, settling procedural and legal issues, watching fingers point, and listening to eloquent arguments about the villainy of the other side. Millions of dollars in costs and fees could have been spent. The trial judge would have labored long and hard guiding the case through trial, and once a decision was made, the process would have started over again in the court of appeals while the pollution remained. I chose to do everything possible to prevent that, setting in motion the power of the principles and process of creating 3rd Alternatives. The power of the result did not come from me—it resided in the process and in the unleashed creative genius within these brilliant attorneys.

For a 3rd Alternative thinker, the goal is not retribution but renewal. That's easy to say until it becomes personal. But what if someone hurts us—*really* hurts us? What about offenses that are truly ruinous? What about the incompetent or negligent or malicious ones who cause serious injury? Shouldn't they be accountable? Shouldn't they pay a price for what they do?

Of course they should. We have every right to protect our society from people who are vicious or engaged in criminal activity. But in the U.S. courts only about one in five filings is a criminal case; the rest are civil lawsuits.[1] It is in the civil area of the law, where disputes and conflicts most commonly arise betwen people, that the timeless principle of the 3rd Alternative can be most effective and beneficial.

In such cases, the question for a synergistic thinker is "What job do we really want done? What outcome are we truly after?" Every case is different. The general contractor, faced with a bungling painter who was less than truthful, had every reason to take him to court, ruin him, and make sure he never worked again. The people of Idaho and the U.S. government had every reason to sue the operators of the Blackbird Mine for the damage they caused. But what about the government that pressured them so hard to produce cobalt as fast as they could? What about the environmental regulators who were supposed to prevent the damage but apparently looked the other way? What about the people of Idaho themselves, who were quite happy with the money the mine brought to their state? In each of these cases, the 3rd Alternative was unquestionably the best alternative, as it always is.

Consider the 3rd Alternative approach the people of South Africa took to begin resolving the searing racial conflict in that country. Centuries of segregation, oppression, and abuse theoretically came to an end with Nelson Mandela's election as president in 1994 and the abolition of apartheid. But these great symbolic events did not by any means heal all of the festering emotional injuries of the apartheid years, when people were herded into ghettoes, abused, imprisoned without trial, and even "disappeared" by the regime.

A great legal storm threatened. Some who were newly in power wanted Nuremberg Trials of those responsible, following the example of the famous Nazi war-crimes trials. Others proposed a general amnesty, letting bygones be bygones.

For thinking South Africans, neither alternative was acceptable. "We could very well have had justice," says Archbishop Desmond Tutu, "retributive justice, and had a South Africa lying in ashes." The Nuremberg Trial approach would likely have meant civil war. "But the victims cannot simply forgive and forget. . . . General amnesty was really amnesia," Tutu said, finding that option equally undesirable. "None of us possess a kind of fiat by which we can say 'Let bygones be bygones.' . . . The past, far from disappearing or lying

1 "2010 Year-End Report on the Federal Judiciary," http://www.supremecourt.gov/public info/year-end/2010year-endreport.pdf.

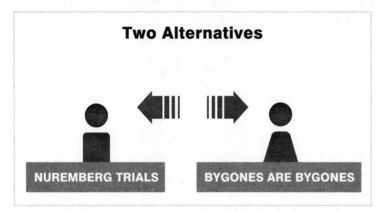

down and being quiet, has an embarrassing and persistent way of returning and haunting us unless it has in fact been dealt with adequately."

To get past this 2-Alternative thinking, wiser South African leaders asked themselves what outcome they really wanted, what kind of a nation they envisioned for the future. After much soul searching, they opted for what Archbishop Tutu called "a third way . . . amnesty to individuals in exchange for a full disclosure relating to the crime for which amnesty was being sought." In other words, if perpetrators would publicly disclose the whole truth about their crimes, they would not be prosecuted.

So a new institution was created: the Truth and Reconciliation Commission (TRC). Those seeking amnesty for their crimes appear before this commission and tell their stories. Their victims get to listen and tell their stories as well. Then, when all parties feel that everyone's truth has been told and heard, the commission grants amnesty.

The TRC probably seems very strange to non-Africans, but it is deeply rooted in the African tradition of *Ubuntu*. According to Archbishop Tutu, "This third way of amnesty was consistent with a central feature of the African Weltanschauung—what we know in our languages as *Ubuntu*." Recall that *Ubuntu* means that I can't be truly human unless I fully see and value your humanity as well. I can't demonize you, which means to literally see you as an inhuman demon, and still remain human myself.[1]

Of course, the TRC is widely criticized. Where is justice if people don't have to pay for their crimes? What kind of 3rd Alternative is this?

---

1 Desmond Tutu, *No Future Without Forgiveness* (New York: Doubleday, 1999), 19, 23, 28, 30–31.

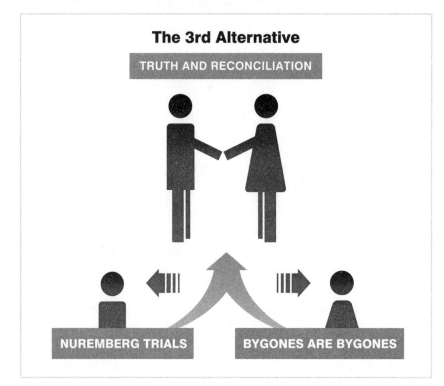

The 3rd Alternative

TRUTH AND RECONCILIATION

NUREMBERG TRIALS   **BYGONES ARE BYGONES**

In our view, the TRC does meet the standards of a 3rd Alternative. It's ingenious. It is beyond compromise. But most of all, it works for the people. As Marc Gopin points out, "They just want to be heard—not necessarily to see their opponents hung. Everyone has to be heard, and the TRC is a legal process for enabling people to be heard. The law isn't flouted, but the law takes account of their suffering."[1] Interestingly, those who were hurt most by apartheid, the Xhosa and other peoples, are most satisfied with the outcomes of the TRC process. A major study found that "acceptance of the results of the TRC was much greater among South Africans of African descent than it was amongst those of European descent. . . . The Xhosa were far more likely to accept that the TRC uncovered the truth and brought about reconciliation."[2]

---

1 Gopin Interview.
2 Douglas H.M. Carver, "The Xhosa and the Truth and Reconciliation Commission: African Ways," n.d., 17, http://tlj.unm.edu/archives/vol8/8TLJ34-CARVER.pdf. Accessed January 21, 2011.

Archbishop Tutu answers the critics of the TRC this way:

Justice fails to be done only if the concept we entertain of justice is retributive justice, whose chief goal is to be punitive. . . . There is another kind of justice, restorative justice. . . . In the spirit of Ubuntu the central concern is the healing of breaches, the redressing of imbalances, the restoration of broken relationships, a seeking to rehabilitate both the victim and the perpetrator, who should be given the opportunity to be reintegrated into the community he has injured by his offense. . . . Justice, restorative justice, is being served when efforts are being made to work for healing, for forgiving, and for reconciliation.[1]

When a people so abused can reconcile themselves with those who committed such grave offenses against them, we are certainly invited by conscience to reflect more deeply on the tendency we have to drag each other into court on the slightest provocation.

Extending the Hand of Peace

The eminent attorney John W. Davis, who ran for president of the United States in 1924, spoke of the law as the profession of peacemaking: "True, we build no bridges. We raise no towers. We construct no engines. We paint no pictures. . . . There is little of all that we do which the eye of man can see. But we smooth out difficulties; we relieve stress; we correct mistakes; we take up other men's burdens and by our efforts we make possible the peaceful life of men in a peaceful state."[2]

In their heart of hearts, many practicing attorneys will be drawn philosophically to the prospects of living the life of a peacemaker. But the nagging question remains: "Can I make a living at this?" Our experience and conviction is that they can be the most successful attorneys in the world—successful financially (word simply gets around that someone is a straight shooter and quickly and creatively solves problems), successful in meaning-

---

1 Tutu, *No Future*, 54–55.
2 John W. Davis, "Address at the 75th Anniversary Proceedings of the Association of the Bar of the City of New York," March 16, 1946.

ful relationships with colleagues and clients, successful in great service and contribution, successful in health and happiness, successful in the home, successful in life. For true primary success is always sustainable and encompasses the whole of life.

As for the rest of us, members of the most litigious society in history, we ought to be looking for the 3rd Alternative in every conflict instead of filing lawsuits, if only for our own good. There is absolutely no reason the people of Breedon-on-the-Hill could not have sat down over a cup of tea and figured out how to break their impasse. They could have listened, really listened, to understand one another's concerns. They could have gone on to synergize any number of 3rd Alternatives: Perform service for the school in lieu of the fee? Volunteer someone to handle the security checks? Turn the panto into a joint town-school learning experience for the students, who could have painted scenery, played music, or built props? They could have chosen positive rather than negative synergy. They could have come out a stronger, better community; instead they chose to impoverish themselves and lay waste to cherished friendships and traditions.

If you get involved in a serious dispute, you have the same power of choice. You can choose positive or negative synergy, but choose you must. If you refuse the 3rd Alternative, you may well be choosing tragedy in its place. You might find yourself in court, which can be like riding a runaway train with a wreck at the end of the line. We are not suggesting you should not use the legal system—some situations absolutely require it—but to see it as a court of last, not first, resort. Once you get there, you lose control of the means to resolve the dispute—unless you find a 3rd Alternative at last.

You might be asking, "How can I choose positive synergy when others are attacking me?" Although you can't control the paradigms of others, you can be synergistic within yourself, even in the midst of a very adversarial environment. You can choose not to be offended. You can seek out your adversary and listen with empathy; you will enlarge your own perspective, and you might find that empathy alone defuses the conflict. You can persistently ask the 3rd Alternative Question: "Would you be willing to look for a better alternative than what either of us has ever thought of before?"

We've known many people who were angry at each other and went to court to defend their positions, which just exacerbated the problem as they made their way through the legal process. And we have asked them the 3rd Alternative Question. The results in almost every case have been astounding. Problems they had legally and psychologically wrangled over for months or years have been settled in a matter of a few hours or days. The release of creative energy was incredible.

Beyond this, we have learned that we strengthen our own self-respect when we rise above the "getting even" side of our nature and go for a 3rd Alternative instead. Perhaps it's counterintuitive, but our peace of mind depends on extending the hand of peace to others. As the Reverend Martin Luther King Jr., said, "That old law about an eye for an eye leaves everybody blind. The time is always right to do the right thing."

The shift from a 2-Alternative mind-set to 3rd Alternative thinking can be made one person, one lawyer, and one court at a time. When should that process begin? The words of John F. Kennedy illustrate our view that it should be now: "We must think and act not only for the moment but for our time. I am reminded of the great French Marshal Lyautey who once asked his gardener to plant a tree. The gardener objected that the tree was slow-growing and would not reach maturity for a hundred years. The marshal replied, 'In that case, there is no time to lose; plant it this afternoon!' "[1]

---

1 Quoted in Brian Thomsen, *The Dream That Will Not Die: Inspiring Words of John, Robert, and Edward Kennedy*, (New York: Macmillan, 2010), 78.

TEACH TO LEARN

- How do you explain the trend in today's legal system of escalating conflicts instead of resolving them? What are the consequences of this trend for lawyers and their clients?
- Abraham Lincoln said, "As a peacemaker, a lawyer has a superior opportunity." What is that opportunity? Why don't more lawyers take advantage of that opportunity?
- Is it possible that the practice of law could be transformed by 3rd Alternative thinking? In what ways would the practice of law be transformed?
- What was the great change in Gandhi's mind and heart that transformed him into a peacemaker? What was the fruit of that change in his life and the lives of others?
- Describe the synergy process used by Judge Boyle in arriving at 3rd Alternative solutions. How is this process a countertype to the usual legal proceeding?
- In the story of the company president who was trying to cope with a disastrous lawsuit, what steps did he take to resolve the conflict? Was his approach realistic? Why or why not?
- What relationship do you have right now where there is a wall that needs to be torn down?
- How is the story of the contractor and the painter an example of positive synergy that could have turned negative?
- What were the two unthinkable alternatives South African leaders faced when the apartheid system collapsed? What is your opinion of the 3rd Alternative they came up with? What do you believe are the advantages and disadvantages of that 3rd Alternative?
- How can you choose positive synergy when others are attacking you?

TRY IT

Are you involved in a dispute that might have legal implications? Start prototyping 3rd Alternatives. Invite others to contribute. Use the "4 Steps to Synergy" tool.

4 STEPS TO SYNERGY

1 **Ask the 3rd Alternative Question:**

"Are you willing to go for a solution that is better than any of us have come up with yet?" If yes, go on to step 2.

2 **Define Criteria of Success**

List in this space the characteristics of a solution that would delight everyone. What does success look like? What is the real job to be done? What would be a "win-win" for all concerned?

3 **Create 3rd Alternatives**

In this space (or other spaces) create models, draw pictures, borrow ideas, turn your thinking upside down. Work quickly and creatively. Suspend all judgment until that exciting moment when you know you've arrived at synergy.

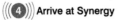 **Arrive at Synergy**

Describe here your 3rd Alternative and, if you want, how you intend to put it into practice.

USER GUIDE TO THE 4 STEPS TO SYNERGY TOOL

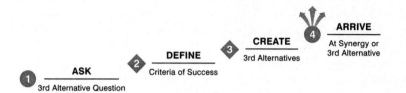

ARRIVE
At Synergy or
3rd Alternative

CREATE
3rd Alternatives

DEFINE
Criteria of Success

ASK
3rd Alternative Question

The 4 Steps to Synergy. This process helps you put the synergy principle to work. (1) Show willingness to find a 3rd Alternative. (2) Define what success looks like to everyone. (3) Experiment with solutions until you (4) arrive at synergy. Listen empathically to others throughout the process.

How to Get to Synergy

1 Ask the 3rd Alternative Question

In a conflict or creative situation, this question helps everyone move past firm positions or preconceived ideas toward developing a third position.

2 Define Criteria of Success

List characteristics or write a paragraph describing what a successful outcome would look like to everyone. Answer these questions as you go:

• Is everyone involved in setting the criteria? Are we getting as many ideas from as many people as possible?
• What outcomes do we really want? What is the real job to be done?
• What outcomes would be "wins" for everyone?
• Are we looking past our entrenched demands to something better?

3 Create 3rd Alternative

Follow these guidelines:

• Play at it. It's not "for real." Everybody knows it's a game.
• Avoid closure, premature agreement, or consensus.
• Avoid judging others' ideas—or your own.
• Make models. Draw pictures on whiteboards, sketch diagrams, build mockups, write rough drafts.
• Turn ideas on their heads. Reverse the conventional wisdom.
• Work fast. Set a time limit to keep energy and ideas flowing rapidly.
• Breed lots of ideas. You can't predict which offhand insight might lead to a 3rd Alternative.

((4)) Arrive at Synergy

You recognize the 3rd Alternative by the sense of excitement and inspiration in the room. The old conflict is abandoned. The new alternative meets the criteria of success. Caution: Avoid mistaking compromise for synergy. Compromise breeds satisfaction but not delight. Compromise means everyone loses something; synergy means everyone wins.

The 3rd Alternative in Society

7

The 3rd Alternative in Society

In many cases, the solution lies in coming to the realization that there actually is an absence of choice, that one is in fact not being presented with any real alternatives. If real change is to occur, one will have to step outside the framework itself and find a third alternative.

—*Paul Watzlawick*

The tough challenges that face our society are as old as society itself: crime, disease, poverty, war, and the spiritual and environmental pollution that breeds them. Our progress against these ancient ills is encouraging but uneven.

As individuals, we might dismiss the problems of society as far above our pay grade. There's not much we can do about them, we think to ourselves, but they still affect us—and deeply. We might not be aware *how* deeply. Science now believes that the pain of others, no matter how remote they are from us, can literally hurt us. "Social pain activates the same pain regions of the brain as physical pain! The brain is deeply social. We have massive amounts of social circuitry." [1] For our own well-being, we can't afford to tuck down our heads and ignore the suffering of this round world. To paraphrase

---

1 David Rock, "Your Brain at Work," November 12, 2009, http://www.youtube.com/watch?v=XeJSXfXep4M.

Charles Dickens, "Mankind is my business. The common welfare is my business; charity, mercy, forbearance, and benevolence, are all my business."[1]

Also, you can learn more about how to apply 3rd Alternative thinking to your own problems by seeing it applied to social problems. Rabbi Marc Gopin, who has worked for peace in the most troubled spots in the world, believes the only difference between social conflict and personal conflict is one of scale:

> *I have discovered a fundamental similarity between the intractable feuds among rival nations that cause so much strife in the world and the destructive personal and family struggles that affect us so deeply as individuals. While the scale and the stakes are obviously very different, the underlying process, the drama is the same.*[2]

Although we might think of our most difficult problems as private, they are usually both personal and global at the same time.

Next to the scourge of war, respondents to our Serious Challenges survey chose "eliminating poverty and unemployment" and "managing the environment—land, water, air" as the most important social challenges we face. They are also concerned about crime and health care. Here are samples of what they had to say:

- Asian middle manager: "The majority of our population lives in poverty classes. There is a lack of employment, poor education, infrastructure facilities are hardly available, huge debt, poor governance, and corruption is rampant."
- North American business executive: "Poverty is so often the catalyst that leads to the anger, hate, greed and jealousy behind wars, terror and unemployment—solving the poverty problem has got to be the point of greatest leverage."
- Latin American financial manager: "It's very important to eliminate poverty in the world. Sometimes hunger makes you do ugly things in order to survive."

---

1 Charles Dickens, *The Annotated Christmas Carol* (New York: Norton, 2004), 13.
2 Marc Gopin, *Healing the Heart of Conflict* (Emmaus, PA: Rodale, 2004), xiii–xiv.

- European IT manager: "Poverty has no place in a world with such riches."
- Asian businessperson: "It looks like people don't care for each other anymore. The society is getting harder. It's all about me, me, me, and the rest will be forgotten."
- South Asian business manager: "Corruption is [a] way of life here. It has been the most serious bottleneck for the country to unleash its full potential."
- European businessperson: "Our natural resources are finite. There is a limit to them, and we are being overly greedy. There won't be anything left for future generations, and for a country that rests on the identity of being a beautiful landscape—it won't continue that way for long."
- North American lawyer: "If we don't have our health, nothing else matters."
- European manager: "To prevent child pornography on the Internet. . . . This is actually the most serious problem Europe is facing."
- Southeast Asian middle manager: "Globally, no healthy environment, no life at all. Because we poison the environment there will not be tomorrow for the planet."

Everyone wants to eliminate violence, hunger, disease, homelessness, and pollution. Everyone wants their children to inherit a peaceful, prosperous, and healthy world. The job to be done is clear enough, but our society is hopelessly divided on how to do that job. Two fundamentally opposed philosophies vie for votes around the world: the philosophy of the Left and the philosophy of the Right. Most developed nations swing uncertainly back and forth between these two wings, like a bird uneasy about which direction to fly. And the division is not shrinking but growing.

The Great Divide

Many thoughtful people are alarmed, in the words of Alan Greenspan, about "a general schism in this society which is becoming ever more destructive."

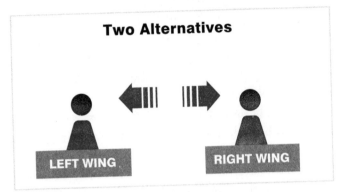

The rhetoric, as these actual examples show, grows more toxic by the day. From the right wing, we hear this:

- Liberals! Can't live with 'em, can't shoot 'em.
- Like spoiled, angry children, they rebel against the normal responsibilities of adulthood and demand that a parental government meet their needs from cradle to grave. Liberalism is a mental illness.
- Liberals are charitable all right—charitable with other people's money!
- Liberalism is entirely destructive, taxing and regulating us out of business and buying votes from lazy, good-for-nothing welfare cheats.

And from the left wing, we hear this:

- Conservatives are people too—mean, selfish, greedy people.
- Wherever there's a greedy boss growing filthy rich by shamelessly exploiting his employees, you'll find a gaggle of conservatives worshipping him and his godlike, free-market genius.
- Conservatives want us to remain sick, stressed, and helplessly hopeless, just so their big investments in Big Drugs and Big Insurance can continue making an obscene killing.
- Conservatives are socially irresponsible, bigoted, staggeringly hypocritical, sad excuses for humanity.

Meanwhile, as they shout abuse at each other and the decibel levels rise, the social problems they're arguing about continue to worsen. Crime and corruption run wild, the cost of health care soars, unemployment festers, pollution darkens the skies. The vast middle, unsure what to believe and not very hopeful, leans one way or the other every few years, thinking that just maybe this time will be different. But the ideologues seem more focused on getting and keeping power than on facing the tough challenges. Their primary goal is to create an image that sells well in the marketplace, even though it's superficial and lacking in substance, in order to get votes. So the ideologies they use to whip up passions come across as cynical.

Of course, most people enter politics with a true desire to make a difference, and they do much good. But too many make an art of demonizing their opponents in order to stay on top. Anybody (just about) can see through the rhetorical tricks they use to reduce complicated issues to simple-minded "us versus them" sound bites.

Still, once we get past the silliness, there really is a fundamental philosophical difference between the two sides.

A basic principle of the Right is individual liberty. They emphasize personal responsibility and distrust any measure that limits the individual's freedom of action. So they are suspicious of social action and even of the idea of "society" itself, trusting that the free market will automatically eliminate social ills. Margaret Thatcher, the respected Conservative leader of Britain, put it this way:

> *Too many people have been given to understand that if they have a problem, it's the government's job to cope with it. "I have a problem, I'll get a grant." "I'm homeless, the government must house me." They're casting their problem on society. There is no such thing as society. There are individual men and women, and there are families.*

By contrast, a basic principle of the Left is social responsibility. They emphasize working together as a community to alleviate social ills and share the burdens of life. They suspect the motives of conservatives who are usually economically better off and seem to them more interested in guarding their privileges than in defending liberty. Hillary Clinton, the American secretary of state, is a prominent liberal:

> *We must stop thinking of the individual and start thinking about what is best for society. . . . We are all part of one family. To raise a happy, healthy, hopeful child it takes all of us. Yes, it takes a village.*

These are provocative statements, and howls of protest from the opposing wings greeted both these women when they made them. Like you, no doubt, I can find much to admire in them both and much to agree with in both conservative and liberal philosophies. I've spent most of my teaching life reminding people that they are powerful individuals, endowed with resourcefulness and initiative and capable of great contributions. At the same time, I worry about the unfettered ego, the pursuit of individual goals with little regard for the welfare of society.

Although I agree at times with one more than the other, my view is that both wings have flawed paradigms. The liberal ideal of community action carries the seed of dependence; when others step in to take care of you, you become disempowered, you stop growing as an individual, and your potential to contribute is diminished. On the other hand, the conservative ideal of individualism carries the seed of independence, which in itself is valuable. But independence is not supreme. People don't get to synergy by themselves; working together, they accomplish far more than they can independent of each other.

The 3rd Alternative to the two wings is *interdependence*. Interdependent people are fully self-reliant *and* fully responsible to each other at the same time. Where conservatives and liberals push one set of values at the expense of the other, 3rd Alternative thinkers seek an interdependent route to resolving social ills. Where some shout pointlessly at each other in the gridlock of 2-Alternative thinking, others are moving toward synergy.

The Emperor of Interdependence

When Emperor Ashoka of India attacked and destroyed the peaceful land of Kalinga more than two thousand years ago, he found himself in the midst of the bloodshed and rubble, horrified at what he had done. To his credit, he spent the rest of his life trying to atone for it. He renounced his greed for lands to conquer and dedicated himself to the eradication of violence and poverty, both economic and spiritual. He issued hundreds of edicts carved on stone from one end of the empire to the other, urging his people toward peace and generosity, pleading with them to be respectful, dutiful, and pure.

Ashoka gave up his royal trappings and spent the remaining twenty-eight years of his reign traveling the empire from Persia to Thailand, meeting with the people, learning about their problems, and doing his best to teach them self-reliance and compassion for one another. It's said that the Golden Age of Ashoka was the most prosperous and peaceful time in the history of that land. H.G. Wells said of him, "Amidst the tens of thousands of monarchs that crowd the columns of history, their majesties and graciousnesses and serenities and royal highnesses and the like, the name of Ashoka shines, and shines almost alone, a star."[1] Ashoka may have been the first great monarch in history to try to solve the problems of society instead of making them worse through greed and cruelty. He strove to teach—and to live by—the *dharma*, the duty to love oneself and others.

Ashoka's ideal of *dharma* is close to what I mean by interdependence. Two major aspects of *dharma* are self-discipline and compassion, which are fundamental to the interdependent mind-set. If you have the self-discipline of *dharma*, you become a solution, not a problem. You see yourself as infi-

---

1 H.G. Wells, *The Outline of History,* vol. 1 (New York: Barnes & Noble Publishing, 2004), 394.

nitely capable, with the initiative and the inner resources to give to society, not to take from it. If you have the compassion of *dharma*, you see into the hearts of others, and their ills become yours and their happiness becomes yours. This was the great Emperor Ashoka's creed engraved in pillars all over India:

> *What I desire for my own children—and I desire their welfare and hap-piness both in this world and the next—that I desire for all men. You do not understand to what extent I desire this; and if some of you do under-stand, you do not understand the full extent of my desire.*

On these principles, this remarkable man transformed himself from the worst kind of bipolar thinker, attacking and massacring anyone who op-posed him, into the embodiment of synergy. He became an energetic social innovator alongside his people, devising roads and roadhouses, universities, irrigation systems, temples, and a new thing called a hospital. He banned violent punishments for crimes. He never went to war again because he resolved conflicts in the spirit of *dharma*. He was the first to institute laws for the protection of minorities and promoted tolerance for all religions. He even envisioned a kind of synergistic religion that, he said, would encom-pass the truths of all faiths. There is some evidence that he sent embassies to the kings of the Greeks and the Persians, inviting them to join him in this brotherhood of man.

"One who does good first does something hard to do," Ashoka said. It takes his kind of heroism to escape the arena of 2-Alternative "us versus them" thinking and seek radical change. For one thing, you have no constituency for a 3rd Alternative because everyone is playing the liberal-conservative tug-of-war. For another thing, both teams in this game have misplaced faith in big forces that don't merit their faith—the one, government, the other, the marketplace—and both are about as reliable as the weather. But you can't wait for large, unpredictable, impersonal forces to swing your way. As a synergist, you are in the game to change it, not to play it. You believe that in synergy with other resourceful, intelligent people, you can start creating a new future undreamed of by the ideologues with all their weary rhetoric.

The key to a healthy society is to align the social will, the value system, with the principles of synergy. That's why I'm not really interested in the liberal-conservative debate. I'm much more interested in the real job to be done: to discover through the miraculous power of synergy 3rd Alternatives, innovations that will actually help cure the ills we confront as a society. In this chapter, we will meet remarkable people who are doing that job now. They are eliminating crime, healing the whole person, reversing environmental desolation. They are solving the chronic crisis in health care. They are instilling pride and self-reliance in the poor.

We are not kings, but within our Circles of Influence, we also have the power to do good first. When Ashoka began his trek through his vast empire, it was in the spirit of synergy. He would squarely confront injustice, poverty, sickness, and spiritual darkness. He would counsel with his people. He probably had no clear idea what to do. But wherever he went, he left behind solutions to these problems that no one had conceived of before, which is why historians call his reign "one of the brightest interludes in the troubled history of mankind."[1] More than twenty centuries later, another great synergist named Mohandas Gandhi would again create a new future for India, and centered on the flag of the new India would be the *dharma* wheel, the symbol of the Emperor Ashoka.

The Renaissance of the City

The intersection of Broadway and Forty-Second Street in New York City claims to be the center of the world, and with good reason. Victory parades, giant electronic signs displaying the latest news, massive throngs on New Year's Eve—Times Square is the pulsing heart of the greatest American city. The hub of the entertainment district a century ago, the neighborhood was once crowded with famous old Broadway theaters. The beautiful Hotel Astor presided over the scene, a gemlike granite fortress. The "Great White Way" drew its audience from all over the world.

But by the 1970s, in the words of Professor Lynne Sagalyn, the nature of "entertainment" in the once great theater district degenerated into an "intense scene of social depravity" teeming with "misfits, sexual deviants, alcoholics, druggies, runaways, panhandlers, pimps . . . a boulevard of filth instead of a Great White Way."[2] Most of the old theaters were shuttered;

---

1 Wells, *The Outline of History*, 163.
2 Lynne B. Sagalyn, *Times Square Roulette* (Cambridge, MA: MIT Press, 2003), 6, 7.

those that stayed open featured pornography around the clock. Urban decay, a spreading national problem, corrupted the city right at its heart. "The worst block in town" became the symbol of a financially and morally bankrupt metropolis dying from the inside out. Many worried that this most dangerous sinkhole of a hard city would draw a whole civilization into itself.

Now things have changed—radically. Times Square, once a symbol of our worst social ills, shines again as a very different symbol. Today it represents what wonderful people can achieve together through the power of synergy. The story of the "spiritual and physical renaissance of Times Square," as one author terms it, teaches us how we can transform our society if we are determined to break the cycle of 2-Alternative thinking and go on to the 3rd Alternative.

Although many people can rightfully take pride in their contributions to the renewal of Times Square, the impetus came from a 3rd Alternative thinker hardly anyone has ever heard of, an unassuming community activist named Herb Sturz. An idealistic boy from New Jersey, Sturz set out to be a writer but ended up in the middle of numerous social causes as he grew up. He loved the Boy Scouts, and once out of college he got a job writing for their magazine, *Boys' Life*, where he suggested in a letter to the presidential candidate John F. Kennedy that he set up a national youth service corps.

Still a young journalist in the early 1960s, Sturz learned that the New York City jails kept hundreds of "juvenile delinquents" languishing for months because they were too poor to pay bail. As he read the U.S. Constitution, excessive bail was not to be required of anyone, and he started a campaign to help these boys. He soon found himself caught between two ideologies: the "get tough" people who saw his effort as "bleeding-heart liberalism" and idealists with fervor but no time or money to contribute.

So Sturz quietly moved forward, experimenting with prototypes for a system to help teenage offenders exercise their rights. He recruited students from New York's law schools as advisers. They collected data on the boys and used what were then newfangled computer punch cards to process profiles for each one. They submitted to judges forty-point reports showing that few of the defendants were true flight risks. He demonstrated to opponents how the Manhattan Bail Project would save the taxpayers far more than it cost. It was a great success.

The Bail Project was just the beginning for Herb Sturz. Over a long career of finding 3rd Alternatives to help drug addicts, unemployed youth, and children in afterschool programs, he demonstrated a kind of genius in defining what the real job was and then building innovative systems to get it done. His great strength was always to see the 3rd Alternative in a bipolar world. According to his biographer, Sturz "recoiled at the facile and reflexive pat responses" of the liberal-conservative mind-sets, "decentralize, regulate; spend more, spend less," preferring instead to solve social problems with a workable strategy. Of antigovernment conservatives he said, "Some people start with the position that government doesn't work because they don't want it to work." But he also believed that government alone cannot effect real social change.

In 1979 Sturz joined the government for the first time as a deputy New York City mayor. By then, Times Square was a truly frightening place, and the oldest joke in town was "Something needs to be done." So he actually *defined* the job to be done: "We want to bring fantasy back to Times Square and replace the grim reality." [1]

"An Intractable Mess"

When the city unveiled its plan for reconstructing the Square, many people were shocked at the blueprints. The district would be torn down to make way for four new skyscrapers, which were "monolithic and monotonous . . . too big, bulky, bland, staid, stolid, lifeless, and alien to Times Square . . . great gray ghosts of buildings . . . turning Times Square into the bottom of a well." [2] At the same time, this prototype had the effect that a good prototype should have: it galvanized action.

Property owners immediately slapped the city with dozens of lawsuits. The seedy businesses in danger of condemnation protested. They were making good money—why should they be forced out of business? From another corner, environmentalists and city activists objected to the scheme: it would turn Times Square into just another faceless business district. Sturz didn't like it either; he wanted something that would keep "Times Square's light and energy a reality."

Key dissenters in this multisided squabble, the family of Seymour Durst owned much of the property surrounding Times Square. The Dursts ob-

---

1 Sam Roberts, *A Kind of Genius: Herb Sturz and Society's Toughest Problems* (New York: Perseus, 2009), 5, 246.
2 Sagalyn, *Times Square Roulette,* 174.

jected on principle to government subsidies for private development. Seymour Durst so despised government spending that he had erected on a Sixth Avenue building he owned a huge electronic clock that ticked off increases in the U.S. national debt by the second. New York City was offering millions in public dollars to help developers willing to invest in the area, and while many property owners held out for the best deal they could get, the Dursts refused on principle to participate at all.

Into this intractable mess stepped Rebecca Robertson, an experienced city planner. Herb Sturz recruited her, and the city made her head of the redevelopment project. She knew that Times Square had become "the armpit of New York."[1] But she also relished the fascinating synergistic challenge: How to bring together dozens of wrangling city leaders and their constituencies to create a new heart for the New York of the future?

Robertson threw out the city's plan and asked all concerned, in essence, "Who's willing to step up and build something better than what anybody has thought of before?" This question is the absolute prerequisite to the 3rd Alternative.

She convened a citywide discussion, a Magic Theater session all about what New York's magical new theater district should be like. Divergent voices were welcome, including environmentalists, historians, artists, as well as city planners and private developers, from prominent developer Carl Weisbrod to Jean-Claude Baker, owner of the exotic Chez Josephine Restaurant on Forty-Second Street; from the formidable Durst family to Cora Cahan, a theater impresario determined to bring children's theater to Forty-Second Street.

Eventually, agreement on a vision surfaced among these diverse views, a set of criteria everyone could share. "What makes a great city great is its mythology," Robertson said. For Times Square, that mythology drew from "naughty, gaudy, bawdy, sporty 42nd Street" and grand Broadway theaters and colossal old movies like *Broadway Melody* and *The Ziegfeld Follies*. "I did not want to end the chaos and populism of that street," she insisted. "A clean street that was free from crime, definitely—but I felt that the mythology of

---

1 Pranay Gupte, "Her 'To Die For' Projects Include Times Square and the Seventh Regiment Armory," *New York Sun*, March 9, 2006, http://www.nysun.com/new-york/her-to-die-for-projects-includetimes-square/28837/. Accessed June 30, 2010.

the area was in its chaos, clangor."[1] For Robertson, "Aesthetics should have the number one priority. . . . People come to Times Square to see things." The idea was to preserve the natural "cacophony, excitement and democracy of the sidewalk, where everyone had equal access. . . . It should be a zoo . . . but a well-maintained zoo, instead of a depressed, unemployed and crack-smoking kind of zoo."[2]

Robertson's vision brought new energy to the project. A different paradigm, a 3rd Alternative, began to take shape in people's minds. They came to realize, as the author James Traub says, that "42nd Street was not simply a case of urban pathology, but a great mecca of entertainment in serious disrepair."[3] The criteria of success were clear and widely shared. It was time to move to the prototyping stage.

In place of the four proposed buildings, a new prototype emerged that capitalized on the entertainment history of the Square. The original plan was "not a very salable image to the entertainment companies because it said to everybody litigation, delay, and office towers." The new prototype would "market the image to groups like Disney and Viacom." It was "all about great pedestrian traffic, the best tourist market in New York . . . 20 million tourists a year, 39 Broadway houses with 7.5 million theater goers . . . 200,000 commuters a day."[4] The most innovative feature of the prototype: developers on Times Square would get a big tax break if they would also restore a theater in the buildings they built. The first theater was the New Victory, "restored to its original turn-of-the-19th-century glory." Then Ford Motor Company bankrolled the restoration of the Lyric and Apollo theaters into a new performing arts center.[5] And perhaps most important, Disney agreed to renew the most famous of Broadway theaters, the New Amsterdam, for live shows based on popular Disney movies.

1 Gupte, "Her 'To Die For' Projects."
2 Sagalyn, *Times Square Roulette*, 302.
3 James Traub, *The Devil's Playground* (New York: Random House Digital, 2004), 162.
4 Sagalyn, *Times Square Roulette*, 302.
5 Robin Pogrebin, "From Naughty and Bawdy to Stars Reborn," *The New York Times*, December 11, 2000, http://www.nytimes.com/2000/12/11/theater/naughty-bawdy-stars -reborn-once-seedy-theaters-now-restored-lead-development.html?ref=peter_schneider. Accessed Jun. 30, 2010.

The Square Reborn

Still the Durst organization held out, refusing to take part in any govern-
ment-subsidized project. But Douglas Durst, manager of the company,
began to think past ideology. At one time Robertson's "arch-antagonist,"
Durst had gained an intimate knowledge of the project through the lawsuits
he filed. Soon he realized that the city's proffered tax breaks would enable
development that would pay the city back many times, so he dropped his
objections and proposed to build on his property a revolutionary new kind
of office tower: 4 Times Square. He says of Rebecca Robertson, "We litigated
against her for a good many years, and it was a difficult time. But now working with her, it's terrific." [1]

Today the new Times Square buzzes with excitement and energy. It's
pedestrian gridlock every day. Gigantic digital signboards light up the night.
Sparkling restored theaters feature the best live shows anywhere. Instead of
the fifty thousand people who hung around New Year's Eve in 1980, now a
million show up to watch the ball drop, with its five hundred crystal lights
and rotating pyramid mirrors, marking the exact moment the new year begins. You can even buy a model of Times Square made out of LEGOs. Rebecca Robertson says, "It's reborn, it feels like a place where you want to
be. It's to die for!"

Let's reflect on the synergy process and the lessons we can learn from the
renaissance of Times Square.

Much of the success of the Times Square redevelopment project was
due to the calm persistence of Herb Sturz in transcending the complicated
quarrels. "It never would have gotten off the ground without his leadership
and zeal," the mayor said. [2] His openness to 3rd Alternatives was contagious.
To their credit, city government leaders were able to get past their massive
scheme to turn the Square into a business center, which frankly required
discarding much invested effort. Rebecca Robertson and Douglas Durst had
fought each other so long that it took considerable emotional strength for
them to look together for a better solution than either had conceived of.
Fortunately, both were willing to put aside their biases and bruised feelings
long enough to get excited by a new vision neither had started with. [3]

---

1 Roberts, *A Kind of Genius,* 250.
2 Roberts, *A Kind of Genius,* 252.
3 Sagalyn, *Times Square Roulette,* 433.

Sharing the criteria of success helped all parties in the renewal of Times Square to express their deepest desires and vision for the future. Some of those criteria:

- The new Times Square must carry forward the theatrical mythology of the old Times Square, a hub of urban entertainment with its "gaudiness and bawdiness." Thus the restoration of some thirty-nine theaters, starting with Cora Cahan's groundbreaking children's theater at the Victory.
- The pulsing media heart of the city must be renewed. Thus the jumbo video displays flashing news and advertising day and night, and the production home of ABC News at Times Square Studios. Here is the headquarters of MTV and of Condé-Nast, the glittery publisher of *Vogue, The New Yorker, GQ,* and *Vanity Fair.*
- Access must be open and free to accommodate millions of visitors. Thus the vibrant new subway station and pedestrian park.
- Although located in a business district, the architecture must be edgy and avant-garde, while still to be taken seriously.

Visitors to the new Times Square can testify that these hopes were more than realized.

A 3rd Alternative Building

When Douglas Durst planned to build at 4 Times Square, he faced a lot of consternation in the community about his proposed forty-eight-story skyscraper. Would it be just another faceless New York megabox? Would it ruin the raffish ambience of Times Square?

A powerful real-estate magnate, Durst could have closed his ears to these concerns. But he didn't. The architects he hired, Fox and Fowle, were well-known for creative, environmentally friendly design. Listening carefully to the many stakeholders in Times Square, the designers accumulated their own challenging set of success criteria. The new tower had to synergize around what looked like conflicting cultural demands: the needs of the business community versus the iconic expectations of the entertainment hub of America. To succeed, the building would have to accomplish the following:

- Present a "refined personality" to fit in with the business district of Midtown Manhattan and Bryant Park.[1]
- Reflect the flash and sizzle of Times Square with its buoyant theaters, vibrant signage, and crowds of tourists.
- Be environmentally sensitive, incorporate a new ethic of social responsibility, be as "green" as possible.
- Attract retail business to its lower floors in keeping with the customer-friendliness of the new Times Square.

Each set of stakeholders, like the proverbial blind men trying to define an elephant, had a different end in mind. And each of those ends was worthwhile. It was up to the designers to actually create the elephant. How could they fulfill all these criteria? A building that's both sizzling and sedate?

The architects' answer was a monument of synergy, a collage of diverse styles that work beautifully together. Facing jazzy Times Square, the building is all platinum and curved glass with gigantic video screens worked into the façade. The retail entryway hints at New York's famous Art Deco style of long ago. On the side facing the corporate Midtown neighborhood, the building is all inlaid gray masonry with a bank-like look. The whole building is a 3rd Alternative.

But the building's most intriguing feature is invisible: it's the first "green" skyscraper ever built. Its forty-eight stories are powered in part by gigantic fuel cells that generate electricity without combustion. Heat from the cells warms water for the building. Specially designed shafts and conduits filter the air, making it 85 percent dust-free instead of the 35 percent typical for an office building. Natural-gas chillers cool the building instead of electricity-intensive air conditioning, with a 20 percent power saving. More electricity comes from the solar panels that surround the top nineteen floors.

Although 4 Times Square consumes more power than hoped, it still eats up a third less than the average New York City office building. This is the more remarkable because the power-hungry electric signs on the façade literally light up the night.[2] The most luminous of these signs is the NASDAQ

1 Kira L. Gould, *Fox & Fowle Architects: Designing for the Built Realm* (Victoria, Aust.: Images Publishing, 2005), 187.

2 Adam Hinge et al., "Moving toward Transparency and Disclosure in the Energy Performance of Green Buildings," *2006 ACEEE Summer Study on Energy Efficiency in Buildings,* http://www.sallan.org/pdf-docs/Energy-Efficiency-HPB-SummerStudy06.pdf.

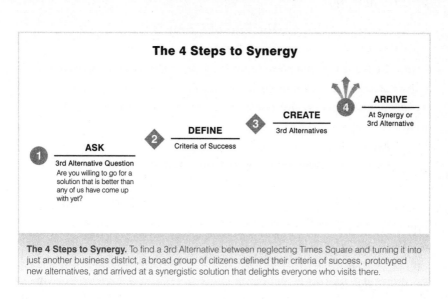

The 4 Steps to Synergy. To find a 3rd Alternative between neglecting Times Square and turning it into just another business district, a broad group of citizens defined their criteria of success, prototyped new alternatives, and arrived at a synergistic solution that delights everyone who visits there.

MarketSite, a cylindrical video screen seven stories high at the apex of the wedge of light that is today's Times Square.

After decades of renewal, the Square is now consistently listed as the top tourist attraction in the United States. Business exploded, with twenty-four thousand new jobs and $400 million in new revenues to New York City.[1] The serious crime rate plunged on the "worst block" in New York; it is now one of the best blocks. The number of felonies dropped from twenty-three hundred in 1984 (more than six assaults per day) to fewer than sixty by 1995. Overall crime dropped by 50 percent more between 2000 and 2010.[2]

The renaissance of Times Square is actually a story about people with the will and the discipline and the character necessary to transform society. The job to be done was "to turn the worst into the first," and they did it. They were incredibly diverse, including ultraconservative businessmen, liberal community activists, environmentalists, bankers, impresarios, restaurateurs, public servants partnering with private entrepreneurs. Some were pro-government, some antigovernment. In the end, though, the tired liberal-conservative ideologues had virtually nothing to contribute. The spirit of synergy infected everyone as their very diversity of views came together into one robust vision.

---

1 Roberts, *A Kind of Genius,* 251.
2 "2010 Annual Report," Times Square Alliance.

The End of Crime

Crime is a stunning, raw reality that is tightening its grip on our world. The impact of crime is very tangible and personal and real and is known all too well by policing leaders. Recent statistics reflect the sobering and oppressive scene:

- Each year, more than 1.6 million people worldwide lose their lives to criminal violence. Violence is among the leading causes of death for people fifteen to forty-four worldwide, accounting for 14 percent of deaths among males and 7 percent of deaths among females. For every person who dies as a result of violence, many more are injured and suffer from a range of physical and mental problems. Moreover, violence places a massive burden on national economies, costing countries billions of U.S. dollars each year in health care, law enforcement, and lost productivity.[1]
- More than ten thousand acts of political terror, including kidnapping, injury, and murder, occur every year around the world. Nearly sixty thousand people are killed by terrorists each year.[2]
- According to the FBI, an estimated 1.3 million violent crimes are reported each year in the United States, along with 9 million property crimes that add up to a loss of more than $15 billion.[3] Here's the crime clock: a murder occurs every 32 minutes, a sexual assault every 2 minutes, a robbery every 55 seconds, an aggravated assault every 7 seconds, and a larceny or theft every 2 seconds.[4]
- The United Nations reports that around 5 percent of the world's population between fifteen and sixty-four abuse drugs—about

---

1 World Health Organization, *World Report on Violence and Health,* 2002.
2 U.S. Department of State, *Country Reports on Terrorism 2009,* August 5, 2010, http://www.state.gov/s/ct/rls/crt/2009/140902.htm.
3 "FBI Releases 2009 Crime Statistics," *Crime in the United States,* September 13, 2010, http://www2.fbi.gov/ucr/cius2009/about/crime_summary.html. Accessed January 12, 2011.
4 *Crime Clock,* National Center for Victims of Crime, http://www.ncvc.org/ncvc/AGP.Net/Components/documentViewer/Download.aspxnz?DocumentID=33522. Accessed January 12, 2011.

200 million people. There may be as many as 38 million drug addicts in the world.[1]

- In Latin America, violence is now among the five main causes of death. It is the principal cause of death in Brazil, Colombia, Venezuela, El Salvador, and Mexico.[2]
- McAfee CEO David DeWalt reports that cybercrime has become a $105 billion business that now surpasses the value of the illegal drug trade worldwide.[3]
- In financial terms, white-collar crime dwarfs other classes of criminal behavior. No one knows the true cost, but the FBI estimates it at somewhere between $300 billion and $600 billion annually.[4]
- At the end of the twentieth century the net burden of crime in the United States exceeded $1.7 trillion per year.[5] Who knows how heavy it is now?

Of course, these statistics translate into deep emotional pain that can't be measured. The numbers go up and down a little from year to year, but there's a dispiriting inevitability about them. The cost in broken hearts, lives, and relationships is truly unfathomable. It's an acute pain, and it is chronic. We measure it statistically, we get used to it, we learn to live with it. Crime, we say, will always be with us.

Overwhelmed by the root causes, we try to treat the symptoms. For example, in the past we've tried more of the get-tough approach—a "quick fix," no messing around. In the United States the prison population has skyrocketed since 1980 from about 330,000 to more than 2 million due to nationwide crackdowns and long, mandatory prison sentences. Now the

1 United Nations Office on Drugs and Crime, "Executive Summary," *World Drug Report 2010*, 17. http://www.unodc.org/unodc/en/data-and-analysis/WDR-2010.html. Accessed January 12, 2011.
2 Roberto Briceño-León and Verónica Zubillaga, "Violence and Globalization in Latin America," *Current Sociology*, January 2002, http://csi.sagepub.com/content/50/1/19.abstract.
3 "Cybercrime Is a US$105 Billion Business Now," *Computer Crime Research Center*, September 26, 2007, http://www.crime-research.org/news/26.09.2007/2912/.
4 "White Collar Crime: An Overview," Legal Information Institute, Cornell University Law School, August 19, 2010. http://topics.law.cornell.edu/wex/White-collar_crime.
5 David Anderson, "The Aggregate Burden of Crime," *Journal of Law and Economics* 42, no. 2 (October 1999): 2, http://www.jstor.org/stable/10.1086/467436.

cost of the penal system is beginning to overwhelm the country, yet the underlying problem remains.

Does the get-tough approach actually reduce crime? According to James P. Lynch and William J. Sabol of American University, "Substantial increases in imprisonment are not associated with substantially large estimated reductions in violent crime."[1] Many experts believe that getting tough actually causes offenders to commit more crimes; it shames and stigmatizes them to the point that they feel totally alienated from society, and it destroys their potential for change. It leaves them hopeless.[2]

Opposing the tough approach is the so-called soft approach. Although no one wants to be labeled "soft on crime," the goal is to prevent crime by attacking the conditions that breed it. Of course, this makes perfect sense, but the approach proponents take doesn't disrupt those conditions. They do either too little or too much. They do things like buy back guns, which research shows makes no difference in crime rates.[3] Or they complain that nothing can be done about crime until the entire structure of society changes to eliminate poverty, illiteracy, and economic injustice. The problem is, crime happens now, and lives are destroyed now.

The get-tough approach is identified mostly with conservatives and the soft approach with liberals, but these ideological approaches just don't fit. We have to get past this 2-Alternative mentality in which most conventional thinking about the issue stops. The great criminologist Lawrence W. Sherman explains: "The debate over crime often treats 'prevention' and 'punishment' as mutually exclusive concepts, polar opposites on a continuum of 'soft' versus 'tough' responses to crime; [there is] no such dichotomy. . . . The result is policy choices made more on the basis of emotional appeal than on solid evidence of effectiveness."[4]

The acute pain of a crime-ridden society is perpetuated, not relieved, by this kind of 2-Alternative thinking, and until we change our thinking, we will get only counterproductive results. There must be 3rd Alternatives.

---

1 James P. Lynch and William J. Sabol, "Did Getting Tough on Crime Pay?," Urban Institute Research of Record, August 1, 1997, http://www.urban.org/publications/307337 .html. Accessed January 12, 2011.
2 Larry J. Siegel, *Essentials of Criminal Justice* (Florence, KY: Cengage Learning, 2008), 393.
3 See Lawrence W. Sherman et al. "Preventing Crime," n.d., http://www.ncjrs.gov/works/ wholedoc.htm.
4 Lawrence W. Sherman, *Evidence-Based Crime Prevention* (London: Routledge, 2002), 3.

3rd Alternative Policing

On June 23, 1985, Air India flight 182 from Toronto to New Delhi exploded over the Irish Sea, killing more than three hundred people. The bombs were traced to luggage someone had checked through from Vancouver International Airport. From there, investigators focused on a group of Sikh separatists living around Richmond, a Vancouver suburb. The bombing was a stroke in the ongoing war between the Indian government and Sikh extremists who wanted independence for their native land of Punjab.

That this horrendous crime should have its roots in a civil war half a world away shocked the authorities in this jewel-like city on the Pacific Coast. More than 100,000 Sikhs live in Vancouver. Analysts later concluded that if the police in Vancouver had cultivated trust with the Sikh community, they might have gained the intelligence needed to stop the attack.[1]

In not only Canada, but everywhere, the answer to crime is more than just law enforcement, catching criminals after the fact. Building a civil society is the real job to be done, a society based on strong relationships of respect and empathy. And that requires creative, 3rd Alternative thinking, the kind of thinking that Ward Clapham does. Clapham is a thirty-year veteran, now retired, of the Royal Canadian Mounted Police. A magnificent figure in his red serge coat and his immaculate hat, Ward takes pride in the "Mounties." And he should—it's the only police force I know of that has the word "proactive" in its vision statement. Their mission is primarily to "preserve the peace," which is a much larger concept than simply enforcing the law.

At the beginning of his career, as a young constable in northern Canada,

---

1 Ken McQueen and John Geddes, "Air India: After 22 Years, Now's the Time for Truth," *Macleans,* May 28, 2007.

Ward was talking one day with some aboriginal children. He asked them what they thought police officers do. They said, "You're a hunter. You wait in the bushes and take our mummies and daddies to jail."[1] Ward realized that the children feared him, and that haunted him.

Part of his work was to keep up on the files on nuisance juveniles. Reading file after file discouraged him. He knew that many of these teens would end up in jail or worse, and was disturbed that no one had any notion what to do to stop it. It was such a huge challenge. Getting tough wasn't the answer. Neither could he simply sit still while schools, churches, and governments argued over what to do. "It was like being upstream of a waterfall and watching people struggling in the water. You know what's going to happen, but you feel helpless."

When he was posted to a town in Alberta, he found the citizens indignant about out-of-control youth. One day he got an angry call about some kids who were playing a hockey game in the middle of a street and blocking traffic. He roared up in his big police cruiser, got out, and stood there while the kids looked at the ground. They had been warned before. He knew how scared they were.

In that moment, the mission to "preserve the peace" resonated in his mind. What could he do in this situation to preserve peace? Not just momentary peace, not just a false peace produced by penning in these unruly kids out of sight, but a lasting peace?

So he said, "I'll give you a choice. I can give you all a ticket, or I can play hockey with you."

Those young people were stunned. Here was a police officer grabbing a stick, chasing a puck, and laughing right alongside them in the middle of the road. His impressive hat blew off. People in the jammed traffic got upset, and he received a lot of complaints in the next few days from people who were momentarily inconvenienced, but his relationship with that town's young people was never the same after that.

Throughout his career, Ward Clapham continued to surprise both citizens and his supervisors with his proactive style of 3rd Alternative thinking. In another town, store owners were constantly being cited for selling tobacco

1 All citations from Ward Clapham are from a series of telephone interviews, October 2010 to April 2011.

to minors, and the penalties were heavy. Ward went to the magistrate and asked for a chance to try something new: to suspend the penalties if the store owners would hold antismoking classes in their stores. It sounded crazy, but the owners were eager to go along, and soon store employees and neighborhood youth were learning about the dangers of smoking. Tobacco sales to minors dropped significantly. More important to Clapham was that many young people would never get hooked on cigarettes.

Clapham has his eye on the root of the problem, not just the symptoms. He says, "We can continue to collect wrecked bodies at the foot of the waterfall or stop them upstream from going over in the first place." And that takes 3rd Alternative thinking. "We can—shame on us—just accept the fact that crime and violence are going to be the way of our lives and our children's lives. But I say, 'No, no, there is a better way.'"

In time, Clapham became chief of the RCMP Detachment in Richmond, British Columbia, at that time a city of about 175,000. You can't find the border between Richmond and Vancouver, with its vast multicultural population. In Richmond more than half the population is South Asian or East Indian, and sharp racial and economic stresses add up to a tough environment for youth. Here he found a typical urban police department, "set up for the reactive, post-incident, dial-911 style of policing." The job was to catch the bad guys and to get the kids off the streets. The kind of relationship building that could forestall crime was absent. Clapham was determined to change the mind-set, to create a new culture with the help of his fellow officers:

> Cops are trained in boot camp, and the only tool in your tool kit is law enforcement. "We enforce laws." But I started asking them to stretch their minds. I asked what it meant to be a "peace officer." We talked about Sir Robert Peel, who founded the first police force in London 150 years ago. He said it was about peace. Somehow from peace we got into law enforcement. But there's a chance to bring policing back to the whole world of peace, to get to a sustainable civil society—to get to the end of crime.

The notion of the "end of crime" is a true 3rd Alternative. Instead of waging the eternal battle over crime, we end it! We prevent it. Is it possible? Perhaps, if we can get past the idea, as Ward Clapham has, that crime prevention is a marginal job and realize that it is the *whole* job.

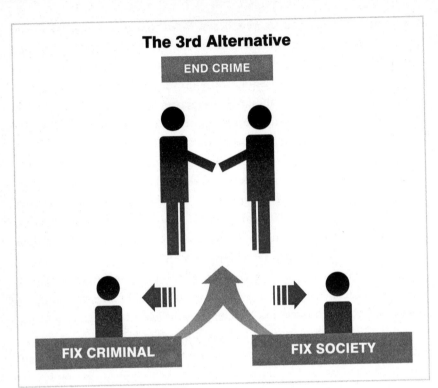

Prevention has a bad rap. To most people it means all the up-front, up-stream things that deter crime. It requires huge social changes, eradicating poverty, better parenting, great schools. No child left behind. Wouldn't all that be great? It's too big, and so police work defaults to catching troublemakers. It's not our job to keep them out of trouble.

But this is the key—it's not just what you do upstream of the waterfall, although that is crucial. What we're suggesting is that for police work, prevention is the whole continuum—upstream, midstream, and downstream.

This remarkable 3rd Alternative insight changes everything. There are things you can do—manageable things—before, during, and after trouble comes. Clapham's thinking transformed the concept of law enforcement in Richmond. Without neglecting investigation and enforcement, he was relentless in pushing for synergistic new ideas for preventing crime before it happens and preventing more crime after it happens.

Changing the paradigm of his force was a huge challenge. He took over the Richmond Detachment a few days after the terror attacks of September 11, 2001. Locally, bitter memories of Air India 182 surfaced. "The crisis threw us back to the professional model of policing more than ever," he said. "Angry people were looking for a quick fix, hard enforcement, aggressive tactics, even to giving up some of our civil rights. It put us back into that warrior mentality of us versus them."

But Clapham was determined. Quickly he set up a Talking Stick forum for the police, town leaders, and Richmond's diverse community: Muslims, Sikhs, Southeast Asians, First Nations people—everyone. The microphone was open, and the community spoke: "What are the police doing? People are calling us terrorists. We are all lumped together. We are being racially profiled. People are angry, people are scared. We are not terrorists just because of the color of our skin." Asian taxicab drivers from Vancouver International Airport complained that people would not ride with them. Shop owners were afraid of their customers. Clapham recalled, "We just let people talk about this, giving them a chance to vent, to feel that someone understood them. This big forum was a first chance to break down the whole perception. The greatest lesson I learned was to put the Talking Stick to work. And then *we* went to work to change things."

Talking Stick communication was a key tool in reorienting the thinking of Clapham's own team. Like most police departments, Richmond Detachment had their "dailies," morning briefings where the boss sits at the front,

Talking Stick

Speaker   Listener

and the officers report and wait for the boss's decisions. Clapham turned that around. The daily briefing became a Magic Theater. "What can we do differently? What haven't we tried?" he asked. "Talk about a shift. It took six months for them to feel comfortable contributing daily. We insisted on hearing each other out and making sure everyone felt heard.

"I'd mix it up. Every day I'd sit somewhere else in the room, sometimes in the corner, and let the officers lead out. We always fell back on the principle 'seek first to understand.' I have always believed that there is more than one right answer, and I liked to talk about that whenever I could because it kept communication and minds open."

This quest for ideas went beyond the police department into the community. An important goal of the RCMP was to establish partnerships with citizen groups in a community policing effort. One day an RCMP auditor came to Richmond and said, "You don't have anything on paper about your partnerships with the community." Clapham laughed and said, "Well, that would be like asking me to keep a log of every breath I take and every blink of the eye. Every one of my officers, too, because that's everything we do. It's all partnerships." So they started a log and found they were making thirty, forty, eighty partnership contacts every day.

Because of his 3rd Alternative mentality, always seeking a better way no one had thought of before, Clapham ran into heavy resistance from 2-Alternative thinkers. "If you're not hard on crime, you're soft" was the message he constantly had to confront.

> I was in direct conflict with the status quo. The status quo was loud and clear. We were expected to and rewarded for operating in a post-incident corrective model and a command-and-control model. So when you start developing all your people as leaders, introduce shared leadership, and make prevention a primary goal, you stick out like a target for the naysayers.
>
> I spent a quarter to half of every day justifying myself. They were coming at me constantly to prove me wrong, to shut me down, to make me comply with the status quo. They'd open the rule book and show me where I was violating it.

But the "tough versus soft" dilemma had no meaning for Ward Clapham. He was looking for 3rd Alternatives that would actually make a difference.

"I viewed 18,000 crimes a year as 18,000 failures. Whatever I could do to knock that number down was a success."

Positive Ticketing

Clapham's quest for 3rd Alternatives proved unexpectedly fruitful. One struck him like lightning at a seminar he attended. The leader asked this question: "What would happen if we were to catch kids doing things right?" Clapham had spent much of his career giving out citations to young people for negative behaviors. What if it were the other way around? What if they got attention when they did something right? "We give them tickets for breaking the law," he said. "What if we gave them tickets for upholding the law? For doing something helpful?" Thus was born the idea of "positive ticketing," a genuine countertype. For positive tickets, Clapham went out to his myriad partners in the community, and dozens of local businesses chipped in with fast-food coupons, free ice cream, discounts on dance clubs and sports events. The City of Richmond provided passes for swimming and skating at the community center. The positive ticket reads, "To BLANK who was caught doing something good!" Tickets are redeemed for everything from a slice of pizza to a portable music player.

One evening a Richmond teenager we'll call John was walking home when he saw a small child run into the traffic. On impulse, he snatched the child and set him safely back on the sidewalk. An RCMP officer cruising past saw it all and stopped. John must not have heard about the positive tickets, because when the officer approached him, he reacted as most teens would react. His stomach turned into a knot, his skin was clammy, and his heart started racing; he thought he was in trouble.

Later, John's foster mother said, "My foster son came to me and told me that he was stopped by the police and got a ticket. You can imagine my immediate reaction was negative. Then he said, 'No, Mom, I got a positive ticket.' I said, 'What are you talking about?'" John explained, "A little kid darted out onto the road, and I ran after him and pulled him back onto the sidewalk. A cop pulled up, got out, and asked my name—I was scared. I thought he was mad at me because he thought I hurt the little kid. The officer said that he was proud of me, that I did good, and he gave me a ticket for free swimming, free skating, and free golfing."

With tears in her eyes, the foster mother went on to relate that the positive ticket is pinned on the wall of his bedroom. She recently asked John why he had not used it. He told her, "Mom, I will never use that ticket. A police officer said I was a good kid, and I could be anything I wanted to be. Mom, I will never use that ticket."

Each year, an average of forty thousand of these positive tickets are given out to young people who are doing good things. "We are hunters," laughs Ward. "We hunt them out for the positive things they do." A policeman might stop and give a positive ticket to a boy for wearing his helmet while riding his bike. A policewoman might hand out positive tickets to a group of girls on the street who are *not* smoking or swearing. These are youths on the edge, and rewarding even small positives can reinforce big positives: using a crosswalk, coming out of a library with a book, tossing litter in a waste bin instead of on the street.

Along with the tickets, officers hand out cards about themselves. These are not business cards. They show a picture of the officer, his or her personal interests—"skiing, hang-gliding, hockey, music"—and a favorite thought about life. Clapham's own card says, "You don't need drugs to get a high out of life." It's a touch that helps the young people know them as individuals, not just as cops.

The community has seen a difference. Keith Pattinson, the director of Boys & Girls Clubs for British Columbia, says this: "When the police focus on young people's strengths, they're finding the relationship changes. Instead of getting the finger when they drive by, kids are calling them over and telling them, 'Look, there's something going down tonight. Someone's going to get hurt, maybe you guys should check it out.'"[1]

Clapham sees the same thing. "Most young people avoid the police, don't want the ticket. With positive tickets we reward young people for doing good things, so when they see the police they run to us instead of away from us." Relationships develop. The youths can turn to the police instead of fearing them. The police become a positive part of their lives; instead of impersonal enforcers of the law, they are friends who help them navigate the treacherous rapids of growing up.

Clapham also gave out the equivalent of positive tickets to his own team: small gift cards to recognize the contribution of his officers to changing the culture of Richmond. Of course, he immediately ran into trouble with

---

1 Robin Roberts, "40 Developmental Assets for Kids," *Mehfil*, September–October 2006, 37.

*the rule book: "Thou shalt not use taxpayer money to purchase gift cards
for employees to recognize their good deeds." They took my government
credit card away from me and sent me to a four-hour course, which I
refused to attend. But here's the interesting part: when I told the city leaders of Richmond about it, they asked, "How much money do you need
to continue doing what you're doing?" Then they gave me a credit card
because they saw the value of what I was doing was a thousand percent
return on their money. The rule book was just plain misaligned. I was
trusted with guns and bullets and pepper spray, but not with the tools to
transform the culture.*

*But the community loved it. When they started to see the success, they
wanted more of it. The community was the reason I kept going, because I
was driven by my passion toward my purpose—to end crime in our city.*

Positive ticketing is just one synergistic idea among many that Ward
Clapham and his unit have implemented to build the personal relationships that forestall conflict. When he wanted each of the officers to "adopt
a school" and make friends there, he knew he couldn't get funding. But his
huge network of partnerships wrote checks to make it possible. They also
started the OnSide program, which provides funding for officers to take
kids to professional sports events. One officer went rock climbing all summer with some high school dropouts and successfully coaxed them back into
school.

*We were getting a lot of complaints about kids riding their bikes in public
parks and store areas. Instead of just citing them, we got organized and
came up with a 3rd Alternative. The city donated some lots, we did all
the work ourselves along with the kids, and today we ride and race with
them in our own bike park. The connections we built with them are
priceless. Incidentally, the complaints ended.*

High-speed street races were a bane of Richmond police. When one of his
constables was killed trying to stop a street race, even Ward wanted to cut
back to hard enforcement. "But what good would it do? We'd fought it for
years and still lost four young people every year to street races, and now one
of our own." So Richmond Detachment held a synergy session on how they
could get through to the young street racers. One constable came up with a

real countertype: "If we can't get them over to our point of view, let's go to them. Let's find a MINI Cooper, put all the accessories on it that you can legally put on a car, and take it to the car shows. We'll mark it like one of ours. It'll be the coolest thing they've ever seen."

Street racers love to accessorize their cars. They go for big illegal headers, gas pedals, exhaust pipes—anything to add muscle—and they love to show off at car shows. So the police marked up a donated MINI as a police car, tricked it out, and turned it into the biggest draw at the shows. Right away they were crowded with street racers and started forming relationships, building trust with them, dialoguing about the dangers of racing on the public roads.

Of course, Clapham wasn't allowed to get away with this: "My bosses heard about it, came to the show, and ordered us to get rid of the car. Well, we could be insubordinate or give up the only tool we had to get through to the street racers." As you'd expect, they came up with a 3rd Alternative. They repainted the MINI, but they also concocted magnetic police shields and portable light bars to turn it into a police car anytime. And they kept going to the shows. "We haven't had a single street race death since 2003," he reports.

Team Izzat

Disturbed by media stereotypes of Sikh youth in Vancouver, about two dozen of Ward Clapham's officers got together to form a basketball league called Team Izzat, a word that means "respect" in Punjabi. Open to anyone, the team is mostly made up of young South Asians. Sgt. Jet Sunner, a South Asian and founder of the team, says, "With all the negative perception of South Asians, organized crime, drugs, we wanted to tell people that is just not our true image. Ninety-nine percent of the people out there in the community are good people."

Sunner is amazed at how much basketball can influence the life of a kid. Within three years, Team Izzat grew to thirty teams, coached mostly by young RCMP officers and college student volunteers. He seeks out university students because he wants his players to see them as role models. One goal he has is to bring fifty top students to talk to his teams about what constitutes real success.

Team Izzat does more than play basketball; they also sponsor youth forums for the whole community on drugs, sexual abuse, and succeeding in school. Canada's minister of public safety has officially recognized the team: "I commend Team Izzat for the exceptional work they do in equipping youth with the tools they need to make a difference in their communities. Through events like Team Izzat Youth Forum, young leaders are gaining insight into current social issues—like child exploitation and drug use—and are being challenged to help create strong and healthy neighbourhoods that are resistant to crime."[1] It makes you wonder if something like Team Izzat could have assuaged the kind of alienation and anger that produces tragedies like Air India 182.

Impressed by this zeal for helping young people, Ward Clapham made structural changes to his unit to reward officers who excelled at it: "When I came, I could see that we were perhaps not putting our best people into the youth section. Being promoted to detective was the big reward. So I said no, we're going to put our brightest and our best into working with young people. We're going to celebrate the youth section." So he turned the promotion scheme on its head. Today being selected for the youth section is a prestigious reward requiring much training and a tough application process.

Clapham has not forgotten those who are already in trouble, those who are "downstream," as he says. The focus there is intense, aimed at reintegrating offenders into society and preventing more crime. The RCMP helped create the Richmond Restorative Justice Program, which helps young offenders confront the harm they have done, but not in a punitive way. Instead of going to jail, they meet with their victims, witnesses, police officers, and a facilitator who helps them all come to an agreement that addresses the harm. It's a forum for strong empathic listening that helps the young person understand what he or she has done to others—and to be understood as well.

A young immigrant from India lied about being assaulted and shaved by a gang of white youths. When it became clear that the accusation was false, the young man was sent to the Restorative Justice Program. He heard from the people he had accused how deeply his lie had hurt them. But he was also able to vent his long-held frustration about his loneliness and the snubbing

---

1 "Public Safety Minister Toews Commends Important Work of Team Izzat Youth Forum Organizers," *Public Safety Canada,* January 15, 2011, http://www.publicsafety.gc.ca/media/nr/2011/nr20110115-eng.aspx.

and the cold prejudice he felt from those around him. It wasn't easy, but everyone got "psychological air" and the immigrant boy cleaned the slate for his crime by doing community service.

What Difference Does It Make?

Despite the innovative things he did, Superintendent Ward Clapham was not without his critics. People saw Richmond police officers "goofing around" with kids, playing ball, handing out positive tickets. "Why aren't you out arresting bad guys? What difference does all this stuff make?" they would ask. Clapham bristles at this.

> *We're making one heck of a difference. These connections with young people, the positive messages they get, influence their decision making and prevent them from getting into crime and tragedy. We recognize both the good kids and the borderline kids, to reinforce staying on the good side. We see kids who have actually been in a lot of trouble with the police change their lives. Ten years from now these young people will be adults. They will support us in what we want to do for them and their children.*

And there are plenty of hard data to show that the Richmond unit has produced excellent results:

- The juvenile crime rate dropped 41 percent in the first three years of Ward Clapham's tenure.
- The cost of processing a youth offender went down over a ten-year period from C$2,200 to about C$250—almost 90 percent.
- Recidivism rates for youth offenders under the Restorative Justice Program fell to 12 percent, compared with 61 percent outside the program.[1]
- The Richmond Detachment consistently reported the highest morale rate in the RCMP.

Most dramatically, in the months before the 2010 Olympics, the Vancouver area exploded with violence. Suppression of the drug traffic had driven

1 Christine Lyon, "Restorative Justice Gets $95K City Boost," *Richmond Review,* November 13, 2010, http://issuu.com/richmondreview/docs/11-13-10, accessed January 22, 2011.

3rd Alternative Thinking

I Synergize With You

I Seek You Out

I See Myself   I See You

the price of drugs sky high, which resulted in gang warfare in the streets.[1] But Richmond was largely untouched. The city was quiet. The Richmond Detachment of the RCMP had brought about a decade of transformation.

Over the years, Ward Clapham has been in great demand to tell his story. He has talked about positive ticketing in fifty-three countries. He's been profiled in books and magazines. I've had the privilege of traveling with him to make some of his presentations, as we did together for the senior leaders of the London Metropolitan Police and other forces in the United Kingdom.[2]

Let me share with you what I have learned from Ward Clapham.

He embodies the paradigm "I See Myself." He realized early in his career that he was not a machine made to take orders and do police work as it had always been done. He felt within himself a creative eagerness to make a great

---

1 Jeremy Hainsworth, "Ahead of 2010 Olympics, Violence Stalks Vancouver," *Seattle Times,* March 28, 2009, http://seattletimes.nwsource.com/html/nationworld/2008940523_ap canadavancouvergangs.html.

2 To see a compelling video about Ward Clapham's story of transformation, go to The3rdAlternative.com.

contribution. He saw himself as a "preserver of peace," not just a "hunter" or a "law enforcer." He listens deeply to his own conscience; he is not satisfied with a future that contains crime and broken lives.

He lives by the paradigm "I See You." The young offenders he deals with are not just statistics on the daily arrest sheet; they are individuals he wants to know and befriend, and he wants them to know and befriend him. His colleagues are not subordinates but talented people who bring distinctive gifts to be leveraged. To Ward Clapham, the solution to crime is the building of deep connections of trust among human beings.

He practices the paradigm "I Seek You Out." I have never known a person so hungry for ideas from as many diverse sources as he can find. Instead of presiding at the head of the table over his detachment, he sees himself as one of them. He sits in a different chair every day. He pleads and queries and wrings ideas out of them. He stumps the broader community for their thoughts. He reads and travels incessantly to learn from the best people. Ideas like positive ticketing would never have occurred to him without his habit of constant learning.

He believes avidly in the maxim "I Synergize With You." By synergizing with his team and town, he has engineered unheard-of solutions to the persistent problem of peacekeeping. His Magic Theater meetings are rich with 3rd Alternatives, some bizarre, some slap-on-the-head insightful, like positive ticketing or the street-racing MINI Cooper and Team Izzat. His efforts may well have produced a generation of peace in a fragmented community that had little prospect of such a future. In his work with the youth, has he created a situation where violent crime may eventually become a thing of the past? Clapham says, "I was the chief of police. But I liked to be called the Chief of Hope."

Clapham admits to being a "rule breaker" who respects rules that make sense—but pushes hard when they don't. Sometimes the rule book wins. He moves on rather than letting conventional wisdom defeat him.

I love this saying by Henry David Thoreau: "There are a thousand hacking at the branches of evil to one who is striking at the root."[1] With this insight, Thoreau captured the consequences of 2-Alternative thinking. Those

---

1 Henry David Thoreau, *Walden; or, Life in the Woods* (New York: Houghton Mifflin, 2004, 120.

who are "tough on crime" are satisfied with hacking at the branches. Those who are "soft on crime" are too often guilty of ignoring the branches. They insist nothing can be done until we get to the roots and solve the great social problems that generate crime. But if Thoreau were pressed, I think he would agree that the branches need attention too.

That's why I'm so impressed with Ward Clapham. He is perfectly aware that society's ills produce crime, but he isn't satisfied with just coping until those ills disappear. Nor does he have to prove he is tough by treating troubled young people like dirt. He is a 3rd Alternative thinker, attacking the problem both root *and* branch.

A 3rd Alternative for Preventing Crime: The Love Link

Luwana Marts is one who is striking effectively at the roots of crime. This magnificent woman calls herself a "professional nurturer," and as she travels the bayous of Louisiana helping poor young mothers give birth to and raise healthy babies, she prevents crime from ever taking root.

The roots of crime lie at the very beginning of life. Researchers can now demonstrate a clear and sizable link between the health of a pregnant woman and the likelihood that her child will become a criminal. A mother who smokes, drinks alcohol, and abuses drugs is far more likely to give birth to a future criminal than a mother who cares for her own health.[1] A registered nurse, Marts works in an area where a third of babies are born to mothers with these problems, so she is perhaps the ultimate crime preventer. As a visiting nurse, "she moves through a household, giving advice about routine building, breast-feeding, and storing shotguns out of reach."[2] She knows that if a baby can flourish during his first two years, his chances of going to prison later in life are cut in half.

Marts works along with many other nurses in a project called Nurse-Family Partnership (NFP), administered by the state of Louisiana. NFP is the creation of a true 3rd Alternative thinker, Professor David Olds. After graduating from university in 1970, Olds got his first job teaching in a Baltimore day-care center for low-income children. He found it deeply frustrating.

---

1 See Lee Ellis et al., *Handbook of Crime Correlates* (Maryland Heights, MO: Academic Press, 2009), 184–89.
2 Katherine Boo, "Swamp Nurse," *New Yorker,* February 6, 2006, 54.

Many of the children were damaged by abuse, fetal alcohol syndrome, and other parental behaviors. A four-year-old he remembers, "a fragile boy with a sweet disposition," could only bark and grunt because his mother had used drugs and alcohol while pregnant with him. Another little boy was beaten at home when he wet the bed at night, so he was terrified of falling asleep at naptime.[1]

Although the day-care center provided good early childhood education, Olds felt that much of his work was futile. He knew the pessimistic outlook for the children of dysfunctional parents. The problems seemed insoluble. At that time, the national debate was between the law-and-order types and those who believed only sweeping societal reforms would ever address the crime problem. Huge resources were being poured into education and poverty programs, but these efforts would come too late for Olds's struggling kids. He was looking for a 3rd Alternative.

Olds's great insight was to shift his focus from the born to the unborn. The roots of crime and hopelessness, he realized, lay in the womb. The mothers of more than a third of prison inmates were substance abusers, burdened with poverty and a lack of medical care. An expectant mother's addiction to alcohol and other drugs and the consequences, including fetal alcohol syndrome, can dramatically increase her child's chances of a dysfunctional life.[2] The right kind of prenatal care might be a primary deterrent to crime. There were programs for low-income pregnant women, but the mothers most at risk were the least likely to seek help. If they wouldn't come to him, David Olds decided, he would go to them.

In a rural, economically depressed part of New York State, Olds started experimenting with what he calls his "model." Registered nurses would visit the homes of young women who were pregnant for the first time. The nurses helped the moms to quit smoking, alcohol, and drugs; taught coping skills; and continued visiting through the baby's twenty-first month. Although early results looked promising, Olds wanted to make sure his model worked. For fifteen years he followed the lives of both participating and nonparticipating mothers and children. At last, he felt confident of the results: "72 per-

---

1 Andy Goodman, "The Story of David Olds and the Nurse Home Visiting Program," *Grants Results Special Report*, Robert Wood Johnson Foundation, July 2006, 7.

2 "Behind Bars II: Substance Abuse and America's Prison Population," National Center on Addiction and Substance Abuse at Columbia University, February 2010, 23, http://www .casacolumbia.org/articlefiles/575-report2010behindbars2.pdf.

cent fewer convictions of nurse-visited children at age 15."[1] Olds's model had made a huge dent in crime.

Thus was born the Nurse-Family Partnership movement. Since that first experiment, many randomized, carefully controlled trials have continued to show the remarkable power of the model. Mothers and children in more than 100,000 families around the world have flourished. Adding up savings in health and law enforcement costs, the financial return on investment in the model is about 500 percent!

Of course, this success is hard won. The women in the NFP program struggle with poverty, disease, lack of education, addiction, abuse—and they have learned distrust. Every day their amazing nurse visitors face troubles most of us can't even imagine. The distrustful "Bonnie," a typical young client, lived in a roach-infested basement with a dirt floor. Bonnie's nurse made little headway with her. She threatened to slap the nurse when she suggested Bonnie quit smoking. A drinker and smoker, she had been tortured as a child and convicted of abusing children she baby-sat. But after a few visits, Bonnie admitted, "I'm afraid I'm going to do that to my own baby."[2]

The nurse listened. An important part of the NFP's approach is "reflective," or empathic, listening; indeed empathic listening is one of the skills the nurses teach the new mothers. "The mother is the expert on her own life," one researcher observes. "Nurses do not tell her what to do, but rather they respect and encourage her to make her own decisions."[3] Once the NFP nurse had won Bonnie's trust, they made plans together. The nurse taught her what to do when a child cries uncontrollably. They arranged a new place for her to live. When the baby was born prematurely, Bonnie and her nurse managed the child's special needs. Growing up, that child avoided the pitfalls of Bonnie's young life and went on to graduate from high school.[4]

Most important of all, heroic NFP nurse visitors like Luwana Marts help young mothers—many of whom have never known love in their lives—to give love to their babies. They learn that love is about more than caring; it's about feeding, clothing, educating, and providing. From the beginning of

---

1 "Nurse Family Partnership: Overview," http://www.nursefamilypartnership.org/assets/ PDF/Fact-sheets/NFP_Overview. Accessed February 12, 2011.

2 Goodman, "The Story of David Olds and the Nurse Home Visiting Program," 11.

3 Katy Dawley and Rita Beam, "My Nurse Taught Me How to Have a Healthy Baby and Be a Good Mother," *Nursing Clinics of North America* 40 (2005): 809.

4 Goodman, "The Story of David Olds and the Nurse Home Visiting Program," 11.

life, love brings the end of crime. "The love link," Marts calls it. "It's a cycle. When there's no safe base for the baby—when you're not meeting his basic needs, satisfying his hunger, keeping him out of harm's way—there will be no trust, no foundation for love. And that's when you might just get the axe murderer."[1]

Most crime arises from the despair of the disrespected and the unloved. This fact does not excuse lawbreakers in any way, but it is still a fact. The antidote is to truly see one another, to seek to understand one another, and to create 3rd Alternative solutions to hopelessness. It's about a new paradigm of not just catching and punishing criminals but creating a partnership among the police, the health-care system, parents, schools, youth, and in particular marginalized youth, to transform a culture.

How different are Ward Clapham and Sgt. Jet Sunner and David Olds and the NFP's Luwana Marts from those who want to lock 'em up and throw away the key! How different they are from those who know that what our society is doing about crime isn't working, but can't break out of the prison of 2-Alternative thinking. Crime, we say, will always be with us. But then we meet people like these, who ask, How about a 3rd Alternative? How about an end to crime?

The Wellness of the Whole Person

The developed world is facing a nightmare scenario of exploding health costs. Our health-care system is becoming technically sophisticated and highly specialized, which drives up costs. In North America, Europe, and Japan, the number of working-age people contributing to health insurance is falling rapidly while the number of aging citizens is rising. By 2050, 40 percent of Japanese and 35 percent of Europeans and Americans will be over sixty-five. As the elderly cost more and contribute less, the burden on society of paying for their health care becomes heavier all the time.

My good friend Scott Parker, former president of the International Hospital Federation, quotes tongue in cheek the old maxim in health care: "You can have broad access, high quality, or low cost—but not all at the same time." Paradoxically, as our medical knowledge advances, we might find

---

1 Boo, "Swamp Nurse," 57.

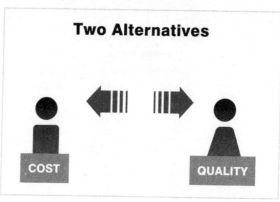

ourselves more unable than ever to apply the knowledge to everyone who needs it.

What to do about it? As usual, people line up on two sides. The liberal side argues that everyone has an inherent right to the very best health care and that society should bear the cost, whatever it is. But this thinking can lead to ruinous, growth-strangling expenditures. Many believe we will bankrupt ourselves because of it. The conservative side argues that health care is like other services; because not everyone can afford the best, they should get what they can pay for. Presumably, a free market will ultimately answer everyone's needs. But this thinking could shrink the social safety net for the elderly, the poor, and the vulnerable, who often suffer the most from health problems.

I recognize that I'm caricaturing the two sides, but those are the tendencies. The whole world is embroiled in this conflict; in America, the rival ideologies battle each other bitterly. There are intelligent, principled people on both sides, and they both have good points to make. However, they are not asking each other the crucial 3rd Alternative question: "Are you willing to look for a solution that is better than what either of us has come up with?" If they asked themselves this question, it would lead to other questions: What if our assumptions are wrong? How do we know it's not possible to give everyone the very best and still cut costs? What outcomes do we really want? Are we building a system to achieve those outcomes?

Imagine for a moment the two sides of the Great Debate coming together to synergize instead of argue. Imagine what would happen if they devoted as much time to thoughtful consideration of the real job to be done as they do trying to one-up each other. They would realize that the crisis in health care is due to a shortage not of solutions but of synergy.

The real job to be done is not to cure sickness but to prevent it. In all nations, the great health industry is actually a "sickness industry." Dr. Frank Yanowitz, who has devoted his life to wellness rather than sickness, likes to tell the old story of the medical student who is walking with his professor along a riverbank. Suddenly, they see a drowning man floating downriver. The student jumps into the water, pulls the man to the shore, performs cardiopulmonary resuscitation, and saves the man's life. Of course, the student is hoping his professor is impressed. Then, unaccountably, they see another drowning person, and the student repeats his performance. Soon the river is filled with drowning people and the breathless student is overwhelmed. "I know I'm a doctor dedicated to helping people, but I can't keep this up!" he shouts at the professor, who calls back to him, "Then why don't you go stop whoever is pushing these unfortunate people off the bridge?"

For 3rd Alternative thinkers like Yanowitz, this is the story of the health industry. We have made an exacting science of pulling sick people from the river instead of keeping them out of the river in the first place. Jordan Asher, a prominent physician and health-care executive, puts it this way:

Health care in the U.S.A. is completely backwards. We do episodic care after something bad has happened. There's no better place in the world to be if you have a heart attack, but it's the worst place to be if you want to prevent that heart attack. We're trying to stop the water by squeezing on the hose instead of figuring out where the water is coming from.[1]

Frankly, the situation in the United States is not very different from the situation everywhere. Variations on the Great Debate are universal as nations run out of resources to manage the growing flood of health problems of an aging population. Everyone is wrangling about the best way to deal with the flood instead of moving to the 3rd Alternative of stopping or at least slowing the flood.

A century ago it made sense for doctors to focus on the sick. Most people died of infectious diseases that have long since been conquered. In this century, only 2 percent of us will die from those diseases. The problem of today in the developed world is the so-called lifestyle diseases—heart disease, diabetes, and cancers—which are terribly costly in lives and money but are largely preventable by simple changes in lifestyle.

The World Health Organization defines health as "a state of complete physical, mental, and social well-being and not merely the absence of disease or infirmity."[2] This is the true definition of health: the wellness of the whole person. The 3rd Alternative to our current health-care crisis is to turn the paradigm of the "illness industry" into a paradigm of the "wellness industry."

So where are the wellness physicians? Where is the medical school for which wellness is more than just a footnote in the curriculum? Where are the 3rd Alternative thinkers who will countertype the entire industry and turn it around to an orientation that makes sense?

I can hear the voices of the medical industry protesting, "But people don't care about their health until they get ill. They won't come in for a checkup. They refuse to put in the time and effort to exercise. They won't stop smoking. They eat too much and stress out too much." All true. There's no escaping our individual responsibility for our own wellness. Ironically, a

1 Interview with Jordan Asher, February 19, 2011.
2 "Preamble to the Constitution of the World Health Organization as Adopted by the International Health Conference, New York, 19–22 June, 1946," http://www.who.int/about/definition/en/print.html.

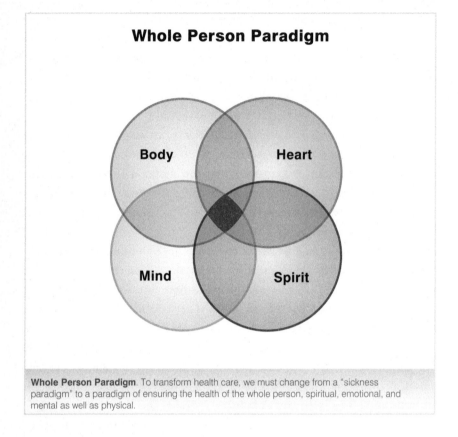

Whole Person Paradigm

Body

Heart

Mind

Spirit

Whole Person Paradigm. To transform health care, we must change from a "sickness paradigm" to a paradigm of ensuring the health of the whole person, spiritual, emotional, and mental as well as physical.

sensible diet and moderate exercise can forestall most of the lifestyle diseases. Why, then, don't we take this responsibility more seriously?

Most of us blame a lack of discipline. But it's deeper than that. I think much of the blame lies with the thick Industrial Age lens through which we view ourselves. We see our bodies as machines that can be "fixed" if something goes wrong. We see ourselves as producers who must run all the time rather than contributors who need renewal and friendship and spiritual growth to thrive. We need the brisk walk in the park as much for our spirits as for our cardio systems. We believe we need our addictions so we can keep producing, but what we really need is an authentic vision of ourselves as profoundly gifted and, as the Bible says, "fearfully and wonderfully made." We need to see ourselves whole—body, mind, heart, and spirit—and nourish and cultivate all of these priceless gifts.

It's very common to get discouraged by the cycle of setting goals to exercise, eat right, and lose weight, and then abandoning them. We beat ourselves up for laziness and lack of discipline. My experience is that the biggest problem is not the discipline; it's that we have not yet seen ourselves for who we are.

But another major reason why people don't care for themselves is, frankly, the care industry itself. The medical establishment is structured, trained, certified, and compensated not for prevention of disease but for treatment. There's simply not enough time or money to focus on prevention because it's all sucked up by the more urgent need for acute care. One thoughtful analyst of this situation says, "There is a crisis in health care resulting from the scarcity of resources and the inequitable distribution of those resources toward those most able to pay. . . . The scarcity paradigm, in which individuals must compete for scarce resources, dominates Western care and expresses and supports that crisis."[1] In other words, it is our *paradigm* that makes health care a scarce and thus expensive commodity. People with a scarcity mentality believe there is only so much of something to go around, and for medical doctors, it's time. Everyone knows that it's better to prevent a disease than to treat one, but doctors have no time to focus on prevention. They can't do a thorough annual physical on their patients because it would take too much time away from treating those same patients when they get sick. They're too busy swatting the flies to fix the hole in the screen door.

Because of the scarcity mentality, we emphasize treatment to the relative neglect of prevention, which in turn drives up costs—not to mention human pain and loss of life. Doctors are "more accustomed to the thought process used for symptomatic [i.e., sick] patients than to the thought process used for preventive care."[2] The result is long lines at hospital emergency rooms of people who shouldn't be sick in the first place.

"That's where the high costs come from," says Shawn Morris, a health-care executive in Nashville:

Emergency rooms and hospitals. Nobody wants to go there, but most people end up there anyway. You go to the doctor only when you're sick, and

---

1 Richard Katz and Niti Seth, "Synergy and Healing: A Perspective on Western Health Care," in *Prevention and Health: Directions for Policy and Practice,* ed. Alfred Hyman Katz and Robert E. Hess (New York: The Haworth Press, 1987), 109.
2 Steven H. Woolf et al., *Health Promotion and Disease Prevention in Clinical Practice* (Hagerstown, MD: Lippincott Williams & Wilkins, 2007), 9.

you're lucky if she has six minutes to spare for you. And she's frustrated with that too. It's due to the system called "fee for service," the way they're compensated. They don't get reimbursed for doing a lot of the things that would actually help the patients, so the doctors are on a treadmill. They can't stop to check if you're getting your colonoscopy or your mammogram. If you've got a cold, they're not going to pull off your shoes and do a foot exam to see if your diabetes is getting worse.

Not only does Morris understand the problem, but he and his associates are engineering a 3rd Alternative to urgency-driven care on one hand and neglect on the other. It's called the Living Well Health Center.

A New Kind of "Health Club"

In Gallatin, Tennessee, the Living Well Health Center has a southern cracker-barrel atmosphere, with rocking chairs, stone fireplace, and checkerboards; in fact, some of the people lounging in front of the fireplace are there just to play checkers. The owners call it a "patient-centered medical home," but it's more like a hangout for senior citizens in Gallatin. There's a folksy "service ambassador" to orient people to the services available or just socialize with them. There are exercise groups going on and classes in painting, flower arranging, and cooking.

But behind these scenes, the Center is dedicated to the wellness of its customers. Seniors can come in anytime, but they are carefully tracked and kept on a health-care maintenance schedule, a checklist of thirty-two risk factors. Just one item on the checklist, a regular PSA test for older men, detects prostate cancer, which has a 99.7 percent cure rate if diagnosed early. The checklist also alerts doctors to the onset of invisible killers like diabetes and heart disease. Doctors meet with patients not for six minutes (the national average!) but for as long as it takes to go through the checklist, follow up on a procedure, or just talk. These are primary-care physicians who practice what they call (ironically) "patient-centered medicine." They get to know each patient well and develop a bond of trust.

One key goal at Living Well is to keep the patients from having to make unnecessary visits to the hospital. Everything is aimed at prevention and management of chronic conditions. Because of carefully coordinated monitoring and tracking, their critical incident rate continually shrinks, meaning fewer heart attacks, cancers, and strokes and less diabetes and chronic illness.

The resulting cost savings are shared with the doctors in the form of a wellness and quality bonus. Shawn Morris says, "What we're trying to do is to change the entire paradigm of the way doctors earn money so they can spend more time with patients. Treating chronic conditions takes a lot of time, and so does preventive care. The hospital is for critical, acute conditions. People should not end up in the hospital because they can't manage routine, controllable conditions such as asthma or diabetes that are better managed in an outpatient setting." When a serious health issue arises, Living Well Health Center sends the patient offsite for specialty care. But the Center transition team brings the patient home, does home wellness checks, and works on the home environment—all to keep the patient from having to be readmitted.

By national quality measures, the Living Well Health Center performs at a level 55 percent higher than the average Medicare service provider. "We're at 90 percent, way up from the national average of 45 to 50 percent," Morris reports.[1] That translates into far healthier customers and significant cost savings both medically and socially.

The Center was created by people with a paradigm of synergy. It's the product not only of doctors and nurses, but also of cooks and personal trainers and flower arrangers, teachers, ministers, and social directors contributing to the wellness of the whole person—to fulfill physical, mental, spiritual, and social needs. This place exists not just to tend to the physical body, but also to help people learn, make friends, and have fun.

As a result, Living Well gives a whole new meaning to the term "health club." It's a meeting place, not an emergency room. It's a recreation center, not an office building with plaques covered with doctors' names and their intimidating initials. It's a refuge, not an "institution." With the buffet and the game boards and the big TVs, it has something of the feeling of a cruise ship. People actually like to just hang around. This is the genius of the people at the Living Well Health Center—instead of coaxing patients to come in for their checkups, they draw them by making it a destination that caters to the whole person.

The Center also has an ingenious solution to one of the key problems in health care: the way doctors are compensated. There are two usual methods. "Fee for service" means the doctors get paid for every procedure they do, so they have an incentive to see many patients and do lots of procedures.

---

1 Interview with Shawn Morris, Nashville, TN, October 18, 2010.

The other method, "capitation," means the doctors get paid a flat fee, so their incentive is to see no patients and do no procedures at all because they get paid whether or not they see patients. Of course, individual doctors are found all up and down this continuum. Once again, though, we confront 2-Alternative thinking, and neither alternative provides a healthy incentive.

But at the Living Well Health Center, doctors get paid for doing the job that needs to be done: helping people stay well in every aspect of their lives. The system is called "coordinated care." A primary doctor coordinates all care, making sure patients stay on top of their therapies and tests. He or she is paid for meeting quality measures for the patients, along with the wellness bonus for keeping them out of the hospital. This 3rd Alternative to the two conventional methods for compensating doctors both enhances the quality of care and lowers costs.

Clearly, places like the Living Well Health Center are 3rd Alternatives that transcend the ideological debate over systems. By starting with the job to be done, the people at Living Well have simply created a higher, better approach to health care instead of waiting for the resolution of the Great Debate.

The Norman Clinic: A 3rd Alternative Mind-set
Meanwhile, the debate grinds on, more or less fruitlessly.

> "Shouldn't everyone have the right to the best health care available?"
> "But what about the mounting cost? It would bankrupt every family and nation in the world to pay for the best for everybody."
> "So we just let people who can't afford it get sick and die?"
> "Who's going to pay for it? Me? You?"

With a little thought, you can see that these dilemmas are false. As the Living Well Health Center demonstrates, it's perfectly possible for everyone to get real health care *and* keep the costs manageable. In fact, why couldn't costs go down as quality goes up? It's just a matter of getting to a 3rd Alternative.

The real problem is neither cost nor quality. The real problem, again, is weak paradigms. The health-care establishment is sunk in 2-Alternative thinking, that strange, illogical mind-set that insists you have to choose between quality and cost-effectiveness. There is no other choice, they say.

The stunning story of the Norman Clinic disproves that.

At five o'clock on a Tuesday morning, the doors open to the Norman Parathyroid Clinic at Tampa General Hospital in Florida. Thirteen patients—from Canada, India, Latin America, and several American states—are quickly registered by smiling staff members. Each patient goes to a small room where a doctor teaches them about their condition and what to do after the surgery. He explains that they will have to take calcium pills for a while. Then they are prepped.

By noon, all thirteen have been successfully cured of a little-known but not uncommon ailment called hyperparathyroidism. We are all born with four tiny parathyroid glands, each about the size of a grain of rice. Distributed around the much larger thyroid, these glands control the level of calcium in the blood. Occasionally, one of them rages out of control and drives the body to draw more and more calcium into the bloodstream. The result is bone loss, increasing pain all over the body, depression, and exhaustion—"moans, bones, groans, and psychic overtones." Untreated, it can be totally debilitating and bring on strokes or cancer.

About one person in a thousand will develop this disease. The cause is unknown, but the cure is simple: remove the offending gland. Within hours, the patient's hormone levels return to normal as the unaffected glands kick in to compensate.

I say the cure is simple, but the surgery is not. Because the parathyroid glands are in the neck, surgeons must take care not to damage the carotid artery, the voice box, the laryngeal nerve, and other complex and delicate structures. That's why the parathyroidectomy is usually considered major surgery. Doctors often cut the patient's throat from ear to ear and take an average of nearly three hours to do the procedure. It requires several days in the hospital and weeks to recover. The typical procedure hasn't materially changed since the 1920s. The cure rate is between 88 and 94 percent, with 5 percent reporting complications. And it's costly; in the United States it can run about $30,000.

By contrast, patients at the Norman Clinic are in the operating room for an average of sixteen minutes and are out of the hospital within a couple of hours. The only trace of the surgery is a tiny one-inch incision at the base of the throat. Tampa's cure rate is 99.4 percent with near-zero complications— for about a third of the cost of the usual procedure.

Dr. Jim Norman is a man of directness and dry humor. "We don't treat this disease. We cure it," he says in his clipped voice. His near 100 percent cure rate gives him all the confidence he needs. Founder of the Norman Parathyroid Clinic, he has performed more than fourteen thousand parathyroid surgeries—far more than any other surgeon in history—and he has it down to a science. He does about forty-two operations a week, while the next most prolific endocrine surgeon in the United States might do that many in a year.

As a young surgeon, Norman specialized in the endocrine system and did all the normal kinds of surgery. He was complaining one day to his father, a car salesman, that the parathyroid procedure was awfully hard: "We're trying to get one little gland out of this six-or-eight inch hole. There's a lot of risk, lots of drainage, lots of things in your neck, complications, carotid, nerves." His dad replied, "Why don't you make a smaller hole?"

It was just the seed of an idea. In the following years, Norman experimented with smaller and smaller incisions, inventing tools he didn't have, such as a radioactive probe, until he developed an entirely new method called mini-parathyroid surgery. Through sheer focus, repetition, and thousands of hours, Jim Norman became the best, fastest, and least invasive parathyroid surgeon in the world.

At the same time, he was engineering a remarkable new business model. The staff around him are experts. He's taken on a couple of associates who are getting to be as good as he is. Scans are better because the radiologists do more than two thousand of them a year. The nurses do the same thing every day and develop a sixth sense about patients; they can see immediately if a patient is going to get better in an hour or a half hour. The doctors rarely have to ask for anything. They are constantly thinking, "How can we improve this whole experience for the patient?"

Synergies abound at the Norman Clinic. As its reputation builds, patients flock from around the world, and they need places to stay. Most patients arrive in Tampa one day, have their surgery the next day, and return home the next. So the clinic has arranged deep discounts with neighboring hotels and car services. Patients are greeted at the airport and driven to the hotel, where the staff knows all about the exceptional needs of these guests.

Mark Latham, the clinic's business manager, says, "We're trying to control the experience all the way from the patient's house back to their house. We give the hotels a lot of business, and they donate money to our foundation. We've given their staff people tours of the clinic. They understand what patients need, so they stock foods like ice cream and popsicles. You can get calcium tablets for sale right there at the hotel."

The Norman Clinic and Tampa General Hospital enjoy remarkable synergies. The high volume of operations is a win for the hospital, not only because of the revenues but also because Norman is so efficient. The clinic uses only two operating rooms, and the return on those rooms is sky high. No recovery rooms are needed; only one patient in about four thousand has to stay overnight. The hospital also benefits from predictability. Radiologists and anesthesiologists know exactly what to expect. All of the clinic's patients are already paid up and in the system before their operations. "It's true that most of our patients have to bear travel costs to Tampa," Mark Latham says. "But adding up total dollars saved on long, invasive operations, complications, and hospital stays, it is so much cheaper to go to one spot that has a true expertise. The averages are way more expensive than the total cost to our patients."

Part of the Norman Clinic's cost-saving strategy is to make sure all patients are well oriented before they come to Tampa. They use a voluminous website, cheap to maintain, to communicate with and train patients in what amounts to a planetwide practice. By design, the site is not flashy, and it's written in plain English. You can watch a video of the operation, read stories and poems written by former patients, and even see where patients come from on a world map. Using the Internet to educate patients and process records saves time and money at the clinic.

In summary, Dr. Jim Norman gives world-class service to his patients at a far lower price than they would pay elsewhere. "If the entire health-care industry took notice of us, it would be much better off," Latham says. "It's amazing to me that we're so visible. There have been so many papers written about us, so many speeches, all of the results-driven information—and yet nobody else does it. For whatever reason, nobody else."[1]

Of course, the reason "nobody else does it" is obvious. Because 2-Alternative ideology dominates the health-care debate, it doesn't occur to the ideologues that there might be a 3rd Alternative, a way for people to get increasingly great care at dramatically decreasing prices. And a 3rd Alternative is sorely needed. Think of the many synergies achieved by the Norman Clinic, the Tampa Hospital, the hotels, the patients themselves—all combining to drive down costs and drive up quality.

But formidable forces are combined *against* 3rd Alternative thinkers like

---

1 Interview with Mark Latham, November 18, 2010.

Dr. Norman. "We have only about 12 percent of the national market. Doctors won't refer patients to us. The way it normally works is that doctors and surgeons and insurers—they're all grouped together. They refer you to each other. What they call 'managed care' is like a medieval guild. They don't want us taking their business."[1] Most patients don't shop for health care; they tend to do what they're told by their doctors and insurers, who are not likely to tell their patients to break out of the system and go to Florida.

Roughly the same issue discourages patients from around the world to resort to the Norman Clinic. In most countries, such procedures are free of charge to citizens because of national health insurance, and it doesn't make much sense to pay a lot of money to go to Florida. Still, those who are educated about the outcomes and rich enough do flock there.

Which brings us back to the false dilemma of cost versus quality. In terms of the great health-care debate, zealous liberals would say that everyone should have access to Dr. Norman, and the state should raise taxes and pay for it. Zealous conservatives would say that everyone who can afford it should have access to Dr. Norman, but the state has no right to tax all of us so that some of us can go to Florida. But both positions are flawed because their assumptions are flawed, as the story of Intermountain Healthcare demonstrates.

A Model for the World

"You can have broad access, high quality, or low cost—but not all at the same time." This is the old iron rule Scott Parker learned when he was studying hospital administration at the University of Minnesota. Everyone said it, everyone nodded, and everyone knew it was true. But when in the 1970s Parker became head of one of the largest nonprofit hospital chains in America, he began to wonder about the old triple-constraint rule.

The trustees of Intermountain Healthcare (IHC), a chain of fifteen hospitals, asked Parker to lead a team to turn their system into "a model of health-care delivery for the world." That challenge both exhilarated and daunted them; it meant that IHC would have to become truly distinctive, and that the mission to make it distinctive would never end.

Of course, most hospitals wrestle over this dilemma: how to balance the quality of care with its price. Many hospitals offer a narrow set of standard

---

1 Latham interview.

services, and as long as they keep their accreditation and make a margin, they're content. They shy away from the innovative, they stay just within accepted norms for mortality and infection rates, and they try to avoid risk. Once a procedure becomes standard, they use it and don't think much about it.

So the IHC leaders asked themselves, "How can we be different? What can we do better? If we're going to become a 'model' system, what needs to change?" They weren't optimistic about the cost-versus-quality problem, so they decided at first to focus on access, the third of the triple constraints.

Hospitals will generally try to treat anyone who comes through the door. That's why emergency rooms are often crowded with patients, regardless of their ability to pay, and IHC felt a special obligation to serve those who came to them. But Parker's team wondered about those who *didn't* come to the door, those who were too poor or too far away to ask for help. IHC served a vast area of the American West, more than 100,000 square miles, and in many smaller, far-flung towns, there was no doctor at all. So IHC decided to go to them. Although it made little economic sense at the time, many new small IHC hospitals and clinics began to dot the West. As they went up, the patients came. It took a long time for these facilities to pay for themselves, but thousands of people at last had access.

Then, in the late 1980s, a Harvard-trained biostatistician and surgeon named Brent James came to see Scott Parker. He declared that it was possible to dramatically increase the quality of care to patients and reduce costs radically at the same time. Parker didn't believe him—it flew in the face of everything he thought he knew. He believed it would take heavy investments just to make small changes in patient outcomes. Ninety percent of patients came out of the hospital in good shape, and it would be prohibitively costly to boost that number even a tiny amount.

But Brent James convinced the IHC leadership team to spend a few days with him learning how to improve processes scientifically. Parker began to wonder, "Could IHC possibly become a 3rd Alternative to the old opposition of cost versus quality? Could we achieve excellence in a way no hospital ever has?" So they gave James the go-ahead to do an experiment. An IHC surgical team would be the guinea pigs. With his statistical background, James measured everything that happened with a patient in the hands of that team: diagnosis, admission, prep, anesthesia, the surgery itself, nursing, recovery, food, medications, discharge, and follow-up. Then he met with the departments involved and displayed the data, asking them, "What's your role in this? What can we do that's never been done before to improve this process?"

The room became a Magic Theater. Ideas flew from every department. Nurses saw where they could improve their prep procedure. Surgeons saw opportunities for choreographing their work to make it more efficient. They found that post-op antibiotics were given haphazardly. Even the dietitians suggested ways to get the right food to the patients. They gathered these ideas and went to work to apply them.

Each week Brent James would meet with the team and display the week's results on a distribution curve. Departments began to compete to see who could tighten the curves the most, thus achieving more and more consistency in their procedures. Impressed, Parker became a convert and asked James to turn his "science projects" into a complete system for managing care. Eventually, more than fifty crucial clinical procedures underwent the same scrutiny.

It works like this. Teams evaluate what they are already doing and then prototype tools such as checklists and guidelines to increase consistency, save time, or make more efficient use of a resource. Then they test and retest the prototypes until they can see measurable improvement.

The results have been self-evident. Hospital-acquired infections, the bane of modern hospitals, dropped significantly. Adverse drug events (over- and underdoses, allergic reactions) fell by half. More than 1.7 million Americans are hospitalized each year for pneumonia, and 14 percent of them die, but IHC has cut that rate by 40 percent. Mortality rates for heart surgery patients dropped to 1.5 percent against the national average of 3 percent. Compared to other hospitals, readmissions are rare. This translates into a savings of thousands of lives every year.

Less important but significant, it also translates into a savings of hundreds of millions of dollars. "We just started to add cost outcomes to our clinical trials and proved it true within a few months," Brent James recalls. Ironically, though, because of the way insurance reimburses hospitals, the fact that they were doing fewer procedures actually cost them money. Embarrassed by this, James found himself apologizing to IHC's executive team, but to his surprise got scolded for apologizing. "You will not apologize for better patient outcomes," said CFO Bill Nelson. "It's our job as administration to figure out how to balance the finances."[1] In the end, however, IHC hospitals now routinely charge patients across the board a full 30 percent less than does the average hospital in the United States.

Finances were only one complication. The hardest thing to do was to change the mind-set of the medical staff. Brent James explains why:

> As a doctor, to challenge my quality in some sense is challenging my competence, my professional competence, challenging me personally.... It feels very threatening to many physicians and many nurses.
>
> To make this work, physicians need to make a major shift in how they see themselves. The fact is that in the past I was an autonomous individual, accountable only to God and myself. I would tell you how good I was by my recall of how well I did for my patients. The difference is, today, we are measuring it. And we are discovering that we are not nearly so good as we thought we were relative to the outcomes that we got for our patients. And that, of course, opens doors for major improvements.[2]

Of course, this problem doesn't last long because doctors are competitive by nature. They don't want to be left behind in the race for quality results.

Now retired, Scott Parker relished being part of the quest for quality. Because he valued new ideas so much, he went everywhere he could to learn from other hospitals. He made friends with so many hospital executives, they took him up on an ingenious idea to form co-ops for purchasing supplies and insurance at deep discounts, another way to save hundreds of millions of dollars. The industry honored him by making him president of the American Hospital Association and eventually of the International Hospital Federation.[3]

In Parker's opinion, the old maxim that you can't have high quality and low costs is just plain false. By all measures, quality of care at IHC tops the national average and costs nearly one-third less than the national average. Clearly, that achievement fulfills IHC's mission as a model of health-care

---

1 Curtis P. McLaughlin and Arnold D. Kaluzny, *Continuous Quality Improvement in Health Care* (Sudbury, MA: Jones & Bartlett Learning, 2006), 458, 480.

2 Hedrick Smith, "Interview With Dr. Brent James," *Inside American Medicine*, n.d., http://www.hedricksmith.com/site_criticalcondition/program/brentJames.html.

3 Interview with Scott Parker, April 5, 2011.

delivery. Dr. John Wennberg of Dartmouth College has studied health-care systems for years and says, "It's the best model in the country of how you can actually change health care."[1] And *The Wall Street Journal* writes, "If only the rest of the country could deliver the kind of high-quality, low-cost medical care that . . . Intermountain Healthcare provides, America's health-care problems would be solved."[2]

What Jim Norman has done on a small scale, the IHC team has tried to do on a large scale. Grown to twenty-three hospitals and a half-million customers, IHC is a flourishing 3rd Alternative to the worn-out assumption that care must be rationed or costs will go through the roof. Neither Norman nor Parker is interested in the great health-care debate. Both have moved well past the ideologues because they understand the job to be done: increasing quality outcomes for patients at ever-diminishing prices. The Great Debate is a tale of lost opportunities to create 3rd Alternatives to get that job done.

But modern medicine is not a failure. Far from it. It's a miracle. And with the growing synergies between patients and health-care professionals, the future is exciting. As Brent James says, "We're not nearly as good as we're going to be."

The Wellness of the Earth

On what was once the lovely seashore of Saida, Lebanon, a vast toxic waste dump grows by the hour as garbage piles up from the nearby towns. At four stories high and a half million cubic meters in volume, the mountain regularly calves slabs of trash into the sea like icebergs from a glacier, fouling the Mediterranean, choking the native sea turtles, clogging beaches as far away as Syria and Turkey.

Everyone, from the neighbors to the nations nearby, wants this mess cleaned up.

The city says it's the national government's problem. The national government says it's the city's responsibility. There are defensible arguments on

---

1 David Leonhardt, "Making Health Care Better," *New York Times Magazine,* November 8, 2009, MM31.
2 Ron Winslow, "A Health Care Dream Team on the Hunt for the Best Treatments," *The Wall Street Journal,* December 15, 2010.

both sides, and the politics are hard to work through. But while the two sides debate, the mountain of rubbish gets bigger and poison flows from it into the water and air, killing fish and suffocating the locals, particularly children who struggle with rising levels of asthma.[1]

Saida's "trash mountain" is just one local example of the 2-Alternative thinking that has created our worldwide problem of environmental degradation. No place on Earth is immune. This is not a "liberal versus conservative" issue, and yet they wrangle over it furiously. For every society, the health of our planet is one of the most difficult challenges we face. Our Serious Challenge survey respondents chose "managing the environment" as one of their top three global concerns, as you can see from these typical remarks from every quarter of the world:

- Chile: "Most world problems stem from people not living sustainably."
- India: "We need to take care of our environment. We have abused it in ways beyond imagination."
- The Netherlands: "The Low Countries may suffer severely from our destabilizing influences on the environment."
- United States: "We cannot seriously go on this way unless we make dramatic changes to the way we live. Our natural resources are finite. There is a limit to them, and we are being overly greedy. There won't be anything left for future generations."

Of course, these statements are arguable, but they reflect the fears of people everywhere. Passions run high over the issue, as shown by the massive response to "Earth Hour," an internet phenomenon that asks people and institutions all over the globe to turn off their lights at a set hour each year. Icons like the Eiffel Tower and the Sydney Opera House, along with millions of homes, go dark to save an hour's worth of electricity. Ironically, Earth Hour is celebrated in many cities by torchlight parades, which, of course, foul the

---

1 "Mountain of Trash Blights Historic City of Saida," *News.com,* September 24, 2010, http://www.voanews.com/english/news/middle-east/Mountain-of-Trash-Blights-Historic -Lebanese-City-of-Saida-103741374.html; "Lebanon: Political Rivalries Prevent Clean-up of Toxic Rubbish Dump," IRIN, March 21, 2008, http://www.irinnews.org/Report.aspx? ReportId=77399.

air with black soot, illustrating how complicated it is even with the best intentions to do right by our shared natural environment.

The environmental debate can be bitterly polarizing at every level of society, from the most personal to the most global. It can get right down to the neighborhood level very fast. As I write, in the beautiful state of Utah, where I live, thousands of people are angry over the state's decision to demolish their homes to make way for a road rather than build it to the west, through sensitive wetlands teeming with wildlife. "Who's more important?" they cry. "My family or some rare frog?" Others retort, "You can always find another house—the frog can't!"

The issue before us is summed up in this provocative question from the writer David Pepper: "Can we achieve 'win-win' rather than 'zero-sum' solutions to development-environment conflicts? . . . Can we succeed as a global technological society in enriching the environment as we enrich ourselves?" [1]

On the global level, people are tense over indications from scientific groups that human activity might be causing our climate to change for the worse. To their credit, most scientists make a genuine effort to present their findings as objectively as possible, and they often seem less than decisive about their conclusions. That's how science should work, but it presents problems to those who do have to make decisions.

Most scientists seem to lean toward the view that our industrial technology is unnaturally warming the planet, and some are very sure about it. "Our grandchildren are in for a rough ride," says the physicist James Hansen of the NASA Institute for Space Studies. "Planet Earth is in imminent peril." He predicts that rising temperatures resulting from the mass burning of fossil fuels will cause "a loss of Arctic sea ice, melting ice sheets and glaciers," which in turn will produce climatic havoc that "threatens not only the other millions of species on the planet but also the survival of humanity itself." [2]

On the other hand are prominent scientists who believe the threat is overstated. Richard Lindzen, a meteorologist at MIT, concludes, "There is no substantive basis for predictions of sizeable global warming due to ob-

---

1 David Pepper, *Environmentalism: Critical Concepts* (Florence, KY: Taylor & Francis, 2003), 78.
2 James Hansen, *Storms of My Grandchildren* (New York: Bloomsbury USA, 2009), ix.

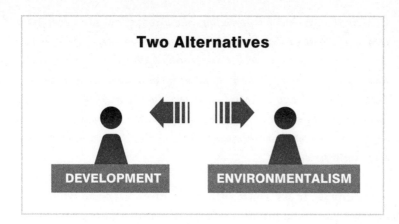

served increases in minor greenhouse gases such as carbon dioxide, methane, and chlorofluorocarbons." [1]

This would be just a mildly interesting academic discussion if so much were not at stake for our society. If the climate might change in such a way that we cannot survive on this planet, someone has to decide what to do about it—and doing nothing is just as much a decision as doing something. Unfortunately, the issue has become deeply politicized, and the 2-Alternative thinkers are busily distracting us and demonizing each other. One side denies that climate change needs a response:

> [*Environmentalists*] *want you to live on a smaller, more inconvenient, more uncomfortable, more expensive, less enjoyable, and less hopeful scale. And the greens' moral hectoring is just the beginning* [*through their*] *impatient zeal to begin dictating through force of law your mobility, diet, home energy usage, the size of your house, how far you can travel, and even how many children you can have. . . . Living green is really about someone else micro regulating you—downsizing your dreams and plugging each one of us into a brand new social order. . . . It's about you living under the green thumb.* [2]

And the other side is just as insistent that the skeptics are wrong:

---

1 "Is Global Warming a Myth?," *Scientific American,* April 8, 2009.
2 Steven Milloy, *Green Hell: How Environmentalists Plan to Control Your Life* (Washington, DC: Regnery, 2009), 2–3.

Climate change denial is spreading like a contagious disease. It exists in a sphere that cannot be reached by evidence or reasoned argument; any attempt to draw attention to scientific findings is greeted with furious invective. This sphere is expanding with astonishing speed. . . . These books and websites cater to a new literary market: people with room-temperature IQs. . . . I am constantly struck by the way in which people . . . who proclaim themselves sceptics will believe any old claptrap that suits their views.[1]

Of course, these are the voices of 2-Alternative, black-and-white thinkers who know that tossing insults back and forth gets a lot of attention. It's so easy to label the opposition as mentally sick, sinister, or stupid. According to the Gallup organization, world opinion at this writing tends to split down the middle on these questions.[2]

What Kind of Beings Are We?

Obviously, the debate over the environment is a tender area for many people who have very strong feelings. There are extremists at both left and right ends of the spectrum, but most people just want clean air and water and productive land without sacrificing the benefits of our civilization. These are competitive, perhaps contradictory goals, but as synergists, whenever we hear that there are only 2 Alternatives, we smell a false dilemma and get excited to move on to a 3rd Alternative. We also know what that requires.

We must see ourselves as more than just representatives of a point of view but as learners and problem solvers. We see others with respect and empathy. We seek them out with the intent to understand, not to engage in wearying, circular debates. Finally, we share the goal of getting to synergy, of creating a 3rd Alternative whereby the whole world wins: the land, the air, the water, the wildlife, ourselves and our families.

When teaching these principles of synergy, I often ask the question, "How many here strongly identify with the purist approach to the protection and preservation of our environment, of our water and our air?" Gener-

---

1 George Monbiot, "Climate Change Deniers Are Not Sceptics—They're Suckers," *Guardian (Manchester)*, November 3, 2009.

2 Anita Pugliese and Julie Ray, "Awareness of Climate Change and Threat Vary by Region," Gallup.com. December 11, 2009; Frank Newport, "Three Key Findings on Americans' Views of the Environment," Gallup.com, March 18, 2011.

ally about half will raise their hands. Then I ask, "How many feel that the purist approach goes simply too far and does not give enough respect to our need for progress and development?" Usually I get the other half. Then I ask for one representative from each group to join me. I ask them both, "Are you prepared to look for a solution better than the one you have in your head right now?"

If they say yes, I emphasize that their common purpose is now synergy— to find a solution that is better than what either starts with. They have to think of synergy as the fruit of their discussion. If they aren't anchored sufficiently within themselves, if they aren't secure in their integrity and respect for one another, I question whether they can get to synergy. They must not judge each other because of their deep convictions. Since they've agreed to look for a 3rd Alternative, they both have a tentative win-win attitude, but they don't know what's going to happen. A third mind has to be created.

Then I ask them to just start talking. Here's how one discussion went between a woman and a man in a session I led:

She: They're trashing our planet. We will suffer irreparably. Look at the rainforest, what they're doing. You should see our canyons. The forest, the valleys should be kept pristine so that we can enjoy them that way. I don't think we need all that progress.

He: I can appreciate that point of view, but there's a certain amount of technology and progress we do need to make.

She: But why? That's what they've said from the beginning of time, and look what they've done!

He: I understand that, but let's see if I can help us both. Don't you have synthetic clothes on?

She: No, this is from a silkworm.

He: How about the shoes? No dead animals? No leather?

She: I don't know . . .

He: I like my leather shoes.

She: Yeah, but so did the cow.

He: They're not from technology, from petroleum?

She: No, they're cotton. It's just thread.

He: Don't you think we need a reasonable amount of progress along with preservation?

She: Don't you think progress has gone too far, though?

He: Apparently *you* do. There's a certain amount of production that we do need. Some say the production machine has gone too far, that we're spoiling the environment. We ought to be cautious. We ought to be reasonable. Don't you agree?

She: That's what they always say.

Obviously there's no understanding here. The discussion gets testy fast and just goes in circles. So I taught them Talking Stick communication, the mind-set and skill-set of empathic listening. The ground rule: You can't make your point until you state the other person's point to his or her satisfaction. The other has to *feel* understood.

The woman then gave it a try. Hesitating, she looked at her partner and said, "You believe that with caution, progress can move forward and still preserve the environment. When the demand is high for production and environmental regulation is low, it's easy to let the bottom line run everything. So you're saying that if we use proper balance, we can do this with wisdom and not affect the environment so badly that my little critters will die."

It's not that she agreed. She wasn't taking his position. She was only seeking to understand. But he didn't feel satisfied that she understood yet. He felt that she was mimicking him. She had to get into his frame of reference,

Talking Stick

Speaker   **Listener**

how he saw things. But the spirit between the two of them had begun to change. It was a lot less adversarial.

Then I asked the man, "On a scale from one to ten, how well does she understand you?" He gave her a five on the ten-point scale. She gave herself a one, which didn't surprise me. Just the attempt to use Talking Stick communication helps people feel understood even when the understanding isn't there yet. When you're trying to understand someone, you're actually working on yourself. You say to yourself, "I'm not going to judge. I'm going to persist. I'm really going to get into that person's shoes and feel what he feels."

Now it was his turn to try to understand her. I asked him to go for an eight or a nine or a ten, to make *her* point as well as she did and to express the same depth of conviction. He said, "The environment is going down in quality. The animals are suffering, the landscape is suffering, the people in time will have a lower quality of life because the environment is getting worse. The children will inherit something of less quality than we have today. We are destroying the quality of life of animals and plants because of our garbage."

She gave him a seven. He gave himself something less. As for me, I thought his tone of voice, the feeling he expressed, was quite generous toward her. We were moving toward empathy.

I asked them both, "Did you find yourself preparing to reply? That your turn's coming? Or were you genuinely empathic in understanding? What about total openness to understanding with real intent?"

They agreed they were moving in the right direction, but then the man asked me, "So where are we going with this process? What purpose does this serve?"

Clearly, he had lost sight of our goal. I replied, "What is your purpose from the beginning? A synergy. A higher solution than you've thought of before. You both live on this earth. You, your families, the whole human race, all living things are interdependent." He nodded, seeming to see for the first time what we were trying to achieve together.

That was all we had time for, but I was encouraged by the empathy they had begun to show, which is essential to synergy. In the end, the two appeared to have more reverence and respect for each other. Perhaps, given time, they would be able to solve the problems of the world after all.

Ultimately, the natural environment is not separate from us. Respect and empathy for ourselves and others is not disconnected from respect and empathy for all of life. When it comes to our relationship with our environment, it's crucial to search our own hearts for our deepest motivations. Are we wasteful? Indifferent? Contemptuous and closed-minded? Narrow? Greedy? Fanatical? In the words of some thoughtful scholars, "Before answering *What is to be done?* we must first ask, *What kind of beings are we?*"[1]

The Environmental "Job to Be Done"

Ideally, synergy begins with a shared understanding of the job to be done. Without criteria of success, you don't really know what success looks like and your solution will be less than robust. That's a key reason why there must be empathy for diverse perspectives; you're not going to get to a 3rd Alternative by mocking and lobbing insults at each other. You're much more likely to get there by carefully and thoughtfully understanding the job to be done from all perspectives.

When crowds of zealous people turn off their lights to cut back the pollution from the power plant and then parade the streets with smoky torches, more thoughtful people sit back in wonder: Does anyone really understand the job to be done here? Without that understanding, we act ineffectively, producing weak or even counterproductive solutions.

For example, decades ago in the American Northwest engineers dredged out the massive, ancient logjams that had accumulated in the rivers that empty into Puget Sound. Their purpose was not only to help boat traffic but also to make it easier for spawning salmon to migrate upriver. They did all of this without the input of the Native Americans who had fished those waters for centuries and who were considered ignorant and "unscientific." Soon, however, the majestic Chinook salmon, once so plentiful in those waters, mysteriously began to disappear.

Actually, there was no mystery; the Skagit or Snoqualmie people could have told the engineers that the Chinook's favorite habitat was the deep pools around logjams that had built up over the ages. Without the pools, the Chinook was fatally displaced. But this was just the beginning of decline for

1 Michael Shellenberger and Ted Nordhaus, *Break Through: Why We Can't Leave Saving the Planet to Environmentalists* (New York: Houghton-Mifflin, 2007), 8.

the salmon in Puget Sound. For decades, massive development in the Seattle area polluted the Sound, poisoning the fish and depriving them of oxygen. Dams and overfishing further strained their numbers. Today the Pacific salmon faces a high risk of extinction. In the past century and a half, salmon stocks have dropped by 40 percent, and the trend is speeding up. They are completely gone from a third of their former habitat. Now scientists are finding that the forests and wildlife around Puget Sound are starving from the loss of a half million tons of nutrients each year. The final result could be catastrophe for the whole region. As the Seattle scientist John Lombard observes about the beautiful Puget country, "We lose our souls if we watch it degrade into a lonely, sterile, and haunted place." [1]

Of course, no one is happy about this, and fingers point in all directions: fishers blame loggers, loggers blame developers, and everyone blames the government. Some people shrug and say losing the salmon is the price of progress. Others, appalled by this point of view and depending on their biases, demand an end to logging or fishing or new building. Either fish or people have to lose. But most of us rightfully aren't satisfied with a "win-lose" *or* a "lose-win" mind-set about the environment. We need a "win-win" or we may all lose in the end.

And that's the real job to be done. "Ecology" is a word that basically describes the synergism in nature: everything is related to everything else. It's in the relationship that the creative parts are maximized. We live on an interdependent planet where the whole is far more than the sum of the parts, so we cannot treat the parts in isolation or as if they don't count. As with a work team, if the individual members don't win, the team can't win. Dr. Peter Corning warns that we must start seeing the world through the synergy paradigm:

We are constantly challenged to expand our understanding of what all of the "parts" are in our systems and to cope with the patterns of interdependency that these systems have created. There is an ever-present danger that our short-sightedness will produce unpleasant (or fatal) surprises. By the

1 David Montgomery, *The King of Fish: The Thousand Year Run of Salmon* (Boulder, CO: Westview Press, 2004),3; Ted Gresh et al., "Salmon Decline Creates Nutrient Deficit in Northwest Streams," *Inforain.org*, January 2000.

same token, we must learn to develop more sophisticated ways of under-
standing the larger, systemic consequences of our actions.[1]

The synergistic miracle of our world depends on the wellness of the
whole. We're often forced to do something about the environment only
when it gets sick. As we've seen, we treat our bodies the same way. We view
ourselves through the lens of the Industrial Age, as machines that can be
"fixed" if something goes wrong with the mechanism. We view the environment through the same lens, as a machine. It's the same mind-set that makes
health care an illness industry rather than a wellness industry.

But, as Corning says, "deterministic, machine-like models of biologi-
cal processes are fundamentally flawed."[2] The world is a living system, not
a dead machine, an interdependent reality in which the well-being of each
part is tied to the overall well-being of the whole. Among countless examples
is the African honey guide, a bird that lives on beeswax but can't break into
beehives to get it. When it finds a hive, it signals a badger-like animal called
a ratel, which scratches into the hive and eats honey while the bird feasts on
the wax. The birds can only digest the wax because of bacteria in the gut that
can break it down into nutrients. To add to the picture, the Borana people of
Kenya follow the honey guides and participate in the feast. Nomadic cattle
herders, the Borana graze their animals through the grasslands, churning
and fertilizing the grass as they go. In turn, the bees gather grass pollen and
nectar for making honey.[3]

Take one part away from this symbiotic cycle and we risk collapsing the
whole thing, from bacteria to Borana. Add one part—say, European cattle
with different grazing patterns—and we risk turning the grassland into a
desert. The wellness of the whole is extremely sensitive and requires a view
of the whole, which can come only from a broad and deep understanding
of reality.

I need to hear everyone's slice of that reality. Remember the mantra of

---

1 Peter A. Corning, "The Synergism Hypothesis," *Journal of Social and Evolutionary Systems*
   21, no. 2 (1998): 314.
2 Corning, "The Synergism Hypothesis," 293.
3 Corning, "The Synergism Hypothesis," 54, 60; A.V. Bogdan, "Grass Pollination by Bees
   in Kenya," July 18, 2008, http://onlinelibrary.wiley.com/doi/10.1111/j.1095-8312.1962
   .tb01326.x/abstract.

synergy: *As many ideas from as many people as possible as early as possible.* Before breaking the logjams in Puget Sound, I'd better listen to the Skagit people. If I want healthy grasslands in East Africa, I need to live and work and consult with the Borana. Empathy with the people is empathy with the land.

Also, I need to understand the interdependence of all life. If I'm a combative environmentalist, I risk alienating myself from the hearts of others— farmers trying to grow food, families trying to make a living. I might push actions in isolation that end up ineffective or worse, like lighting a smoky torch so I can turn off the lights. A confrontational campaign to save the Chinook by itself reveals a "fix-it" rather than a holistic mentality.

If, on the other hand, I disrespect the environmentalists, I cut out of the solution the very people with the most knowledge and energy to contribute. I can be committed to economic growth and property rights and still empathize deeply with that rare frog and those who care about it. For a 3rd Alternative thinker, it's never as simple as "either/or."

The health of Puget Sound and any other delicate environment requires, as John Lombard says, "a vision for the entire landscape, not the just the marine, or the salmon, but the whole natural heritage of the entire area draining into the Sound. . . . Restoration of Puget Sound rivers is not a fanciful daydream."[1] Lombard, for one, is working hard to promote a 3rd Alternative called "low-impact development" that recycles polluted storm water close to the source rather than discharging it into the sea. People can build *and* salmon can thrive—but it takes at least one person who believes in 3rd Alternatives, who doesn't reject out of hand the possibility of synergy, who can help create a vision of the real job to be done.

So what does success look like? We've seen how much disagreement there is on that question, but clearly for Puget Sound and the whole world, success must be holistic. It's a win-win for people *and* their natural home.

Imagine a great pine-covered mountain alive with wolves and deer. If we intervene to save the deer and kill all the wolves, the mountain now fears the deer that will multiply out of control. They will graze the mountain down to a desert, and it will erode away from wind and water. As the great ecologist

---

1 "John Lombard: Saving Puget Sound," *University of Washington Lectures,* January 23, 2007, http://www.seattlechannel.org/videos/watchVideos.asp?program=uwLectures.

The 3rd Alternative

HOLISTIC CONSERVATION

DEVELOPMENT   ENVIRONMENTALISM

Aldo Leopold said, "[We have] not learned to think like a mountain. Hence we have dustbowls, and rivers washing the future into the sea."[1]

The job to be done is to "think like the mountain," to promote the synergy of human and nature. Leopold used the term "conservation" to describe this synergy, "a genuine third alternative" to brazen exploitation on one hand and saving nature from the "destructive humans" on the other.[2]

A Landscape of 3rd Alternatives

If I have that synergistic mentality, I will think beyond the facile 2 Alternatives. I also know that getting to synergy involves, as Peter Corning says, "rigorous, disciplined, even tedious work. It runs against the grain of a hip-shooting, quick-and-dirty culture that is addicted to technological innovation, ready or not."[3] I have to pay the price for a 3rd Alternative.

---

1 Aldo Leopold, *A Sand County Almanac* (New York: Random House Digital, 1990), 140.
2 Pepper, *Environmentalism,* 78.
3 Corning, "The Synergism Hypothesis," 314.

The hip-shooters are always busy shooting each other down. Radical environmentalists in New York City rage against "big-money capitalism" that, in their view, has turned New York Harbor into a marine desert through insane urban expansion fed by greed. Insensitive business types gape back at them, asking, "What do you expect us to do? Demolish Manhattan? Give it back to the Indians?" Neither group has the respect for others, the empathy, or the discipline to move toward synergy.

But if they could couple zeal for the environment with entrepreneurial know-how, they might come up with some amazing 3rd Alternatives. A walking model of synergy is Natalie Jeremijenko, an Australian environmental activist who wants to transform New York City into an urban ecoparadise—without demolishing it. A student of aerospace engineering, biochemistry, neuroscience, and physics, Jeremijenko brings insights from all of these disciplines together in small projects designed to make a big difference.

Over the years, New York Harbor has been devastated by pollution from the great city. Much has been done to isolate the harbor from the sewage system, but when it rains, the streets shed into the water vast quantities of cadmium, neurotoxins like spilled gas and diesel fuel, and dust from millions of automobile brakes. Short of tearing out all of the asphalt in New York, there's no way to stop this—unless you're Natalie Jeremijenko.

Her idea is to plant a small garden around each fire hydrant in the city. The plants would filter the toxic load out of storm water in the gutters and dot the city with little spots of beauty. The rare emergency vehicle that parks there would only flatten a few plants, which would recover. How could this make a difference? When you realize that New York has about a quarter million fire hydrants, the tiny gardens in every block could add up to a lot of filtering.

Tragically, the marine life in the estuary is poisoned with PCBs from the many industrial plants. So Jeremijenko has floated along the shore artful fluorescing buoys that blink when fish swim around them. People can then toss the fish specially treated food that cleans out the poison.

Jeremijenko has also designed a solar chimney that vents warm air from a building, passing the air through a filter that removes carbon from CO_2. Her chimneys could capture 80 to 90 percent of the CO_2 pouring from tens of thousands of New York buildings. And the carbon black can be used to make pencils!

But Jeremijenko's most far-reaching project is urban farming. If food could be grown in the city, we could avoid the loss of nutrients and the cost of transporting food from farms. The top of a building can be an ideal place for a kitchen garden, but most roofs won't bear the weight of tons of soil. So Jeremijenko has designed an ingenious pod out of light steel and polymerized skin that sits atop a building like a spaceship with legs. Inside each pod a hydroponic garden grows in mist and light, while the legs transfer weight to the building's skeleton. An ingenious piping system helps warm and cool the building beneath, and gray waste water irrigates the plants. These larva-like silver structures could one day swarm the skyline of New York, providing the city with fresh fruit and vegetables and saving huge quantities of energy.

"A star of the alternative art world" as well as an inventive engineer, Jeremijenko easily crosses the conventional boundaries between art and technology, between natural and human creation. She sees "a view of nature where we're inside it, interacting with it, where urban forms are a part of nature and act as their own natural systems." She sees her works not as answers to our environmental problems but as provocative questions: "What are those tubes in the water? What are those shiny pods on every roof? Why are geraniums growing around every fire hydrant in town?" She wants to puzzle people into asking themselves what *they* could create. Dotting the urban landscape with 3rd Alternatives, the remarkable Natalie Jeremijenko is a rare professional practitioner of synergy.[1]

Halfway around the world from New York, air pollution in the Indian city of Delhi kills ten thousand people a year. While the authorities are struggling bravely to fight the problem, Delhi has some of the world's unhealthiest air. When Kamal Meattle, owner of a Delhi office park, found that just breathing was killing him, he couldn't wait for the battle to be won. Doing his own research, he discovered that certain plants could provide all the fresh air indoors that anyone would need. So he filled his offices with areca palm, a high-oxygen producer, and money plants that cleanse toxins

---

1 Kevin Berger, "The Artist as Mad Scientist," *Salon.com*, June 22, 2006; Natalie Jeremijenko, "The Art of the Eco-Mindshift," TED.com, October 2009, http://www.ted.com/talks/lang/eng/natalie_jeremijenko_the_art_of_the_eco_mindshift.html; Rob Goodier, "The Future of Urban Agriculture in Rooftop Farms," *Popular Mechanics*, June 3, 2010, http://www.popularmechanics.com/technology/engineering/infrastructure/future-urban-rooftop-agriculture.

from the air. To freshen the buildings at night, he introduced "mother-in-law's tongue" (so-called from its sharp leaves!), which doesn't need sunlight to change carbon dioxide into oxygen.

With enough of these three common plants, Kamal says, "you could be in a bottle with a cap on top and you would need no other source of fresh air." Tracking the results, he found that the plants reduced eye irritations by half, respiratory irritations by a third, and headaches by a quarter. "Our experience points to an amazing increase in human productivity by 20 percent and a reduction of energy requirements in buildings by 15 percent." As nearly half the world's energy is consumed ventilating, heating, and cooling buildings, the savings from the use of these plants could be staggering.[1]

In Western India a potter named Mansukh Prajapati has invented a low-cost refrigerator, the Mitti Cool, an earthen pot ingeniously designed to keep water cool, along with fruit, vegetables, and even milk, for days at a time. It costs less than $60 and needs no electricity, putting it within reach of poor people, who have bought thousands of them. In the world at large, refrigeration consumes massive amounts of power generated by burning fossil fuels, so solutions like this could save millions of tons of coal and gas and barrels of oil.[2]

The Wellness of the Land

A sobering threat to life on this planet is the loss of land. According to one scholar, "We are slowly running out of dirt. . . . Each year America's farms shed enough soil to fill a pickup truck for every family in the country. This is a phenomenal amount of dirt. . . . An estimated 24 billion tons of soil are lost annually around the world—several tons for each person on the planet. Every second, the Mississippi River dumps another truckload of topsoil into the Caribbean." As a result of modern agricultural technology, population pressures, and overgrazing, much of the world's arable land is turning to

---

1 Gigi Marino, "The Mad Hatter of Nehru Place Greens," *MIT Technology Review*, September 8, 2006, http://www.technologyreview.com/read_article.aspx?id=17442; Kemal Meattle, "How to Grow Fresh Air," TED.com, February 2009, http://www.ted.com/talks/kamal_meattle_on_how_to_grow_your_own_fresh_air.html.

2 Raja Murthy, "India's Rural Inventors Drive Change," *Asia Times*, January 29, 2010, http://www.atimes.com/atimes/South_Asia/LA29Df03.html; David Owen, "The Efficiency Dilemma," *New Yorker*, December 20, 2010, http://www.newyorker.com/reporting/2010/12/20/101220fa_fact_owen#ixzz1IxhCPA7H.

desert. About 40 percent of our land is dry, our deserts are growing, and biodiversity is shrinking. As it takes about five hundred years to produce one inch of topsoil, reviving this land is a daunting challenge. "Technology simply cannot solve the problem of consuming a resource faster than we generate it: someday we will run out of it."[1] So, do we renounce the agricultural revolution that feeds the world, or doom future generations to a sterile, starving planet?

One 3rd Alternative thinker, the Zimbabwean biologist Allan Savory, has won the Buckminster Fuller Challenge Award by rejecting that false dilemma. The annual award, which honors the great champion of synergy, goes to people who come up with "big, sweeping solutions to seemingly intractable problems."[2] Savory's big solution to regenerating the land is actually quite simple: he grazes superdense herds of livestock that break up soil with their hooves and fertilize it as they go, spawning new topsoil and vegetation in a few years instead of centuries. Where governments have tried to save soils by outlawing grazing, Savory has done the opposite and generated tens of thousands of acres of new soils.

Savory calls this countertype "holistic management" of the land. Intuitively, when you see cattle eating up all the grass, you react by wanting to rest the land, so you remove the cattle. But this is the fix-it mentality at work instead of the wellness mentality. The real job to be done, says Savory, is counterintuitive, to manage the whole natural system so you don't wreck it with reactive quick fixes while trying to save it:

> *Take noxious plant invasions—if you treat these as an isolated problem you will fail. Leaders in Montana spent over $50 million trying to kill knapweed. They may as well proclaim it the state flower because there are now more than ever. That's because it never was a problem; it's only a symptom of the loss of biodiversity. Texans have spent over $200 million chaining, poisoning, rooting up mesquite, and there's now more than ever. It never was a problem; it is a symptom of the loss of biodiversity.*[3]

---

1 David Montgomery, *Dirt: The Erosion of Civilizations* (Berkeley: University of California Press, 2008), 4, 6.

2 Cliff Kuang, "Method That Turns Wastelands Green Wins 2010 Buckminster Fuller Challenge," *Fast Company*, June 2, 2010.

3 C.J. Hadley, "The Wild Life of Allan Savory," *Range*, Fall 1999, http://www.rangemaga zine.com/archives/stories/fall99/allan_savory.htm.

Biodiversity is the mark of healthy soil. When you take a shovel and dig into good soil, you can see and smell the vigor of bacteria, molds, earthworms, abundant vegetation, the balance of birth and life and decay. Dead ground is sterile, a solemn reality when you know our human future depends on the wellness of the land. Without aeration and fertilizer, soil dies and biodiversity with it. After thirty years watching the life of the African grasslands, Allan Savory works with those principles, not against them.

Although Savory has his critics, and his method might work better in some areas than in others, he has the instinct of a synergist and a counter-typing mind, unwilling to accept conventional 2-Alternative solutions as he seeks out the simple, exciting 3rd Alternative. He sees the broad connections among human cultures and their animals, wildlife, the land, the water, and the wellness of the entire planet:

> *Holistic management of cattle and other grazing animals has the capacity to promote extremely rapid re-formation of topsoil, much of which has been lost wherever human agriculture has mucked things up. This new topsoil will, of necessity, contain vast quantities of carbon drawn out of the atmosphere, sufficient—when occurring alongside reductions in greenhouse gas emissions from fossil fuel combustion—to bring the atmosphere back to pre-industrial balance.*[1]

I don't know if Savory's 3rd Alternative would prove out or not. But I respect in people like him their freedom from 2-Alternative thinking and the banality of the Great Debate. On the one hand, they are free from an environmentalism "which seeks to constrain human ambition, aspiration, and power rather than to unleash and direct them," in the words of a thoughtful observer.[2] On the other hand, they are free from the cynical blindness of those who see in their predatory business interests no threat to our planetary home (especially when their salaries depend on *not* seeing it). Nor are they trapped in the vast middle that sees little to hope for from the Great Debate.

Our ability to produce 3rd Alternatives to ruining our planet or re-

---

1 Jonathan Teller-Elsberg, "Following up with Allan Savory on Using Cattle to Reverse Desertification and Global Warming," Chelsea Green, February 25, 2010, http://chelsea green.com/blogs/jtellerelsberg/2010/02/25/following-up-with-allan-savory-on-using -cattle-to-revsere-desertification-and-global-warming/.

2 Shellenberger and Nordhaus, *Break Through*, 17.

nouncing our way of life is limited only by our mind-set. Countertypes to our energy-hogging ways abound. As we've seen, even what look like trifling 3rd Alternatives might have enormous impacts on our environment. By unleashing the power of synergy, we can renew the glory and beauty of the world we all share.

A World Without Poverty

Perhaps the toughest problem our society faces is poverty, the root of so much crime, violence, abuse, and most other social ills. We look on the poor with anguish and too often throw up our hands. Of course, poverty is relative to culture, and those called poor in some countries would be considered staggeringly well off in others. Still, the poor suffer everywhere, and people of goodwill suffer with them. Our Serious Challenge survey respondents from around the world are deeply concerned about the effects of poverty amid incredible economic inequality:

- "Poverty is so often the catalyst that leads to the anger, hate, greed, and jealousy behind wars, terror and unemployment—solving the poverty problem has got to be the point of greatest leverage."
- "There are still so many people that haven't got the basics that so many of us take for granted."
- "No man should have to spend his life in poverty. Poverty is at the root of other global problems like poor education, environmental issues."
- "Poverty is prevalent across the globe, which is the major reason serious problems of terrorism come into play. . . . Poor uneducated people are very prone to [brainwashing]."
- "With all the money recently spent on everything—it has become obvious that the war on poverty, drugs, unemployment—was no war at all. We have and continue to be lied to and continue to pay, some with their lives—for the good of a few."
- "Our country's unemployment rate has rocketed out of control. . . . There is little or no prospect for so many of the unemployed."
- "Our country belongs to one of the poorest in Asia. This is

the battle cry . . . where the majority of our population lives in poverty classes. There is lack of employment, poor education, infrastructure facilities are hardly available, huge debt, poor governance and corruptions are rampant."

- "A better world, in my opinion, means a world without poverty."

A world without poverty would be an easy thing to achieve, say our Left and Right wings, if only we would follow their prescriptions. On few issues are the two wings more clear about their ideologies and yet more at odds than they are on what to do about poverty.

Every winter, some researchers claim, somewhere between 25,000 and 30,000 people die from cold in the United Kingdom, most of them elderly and vulnerable people, and this in one of the world's most developed countries. Justifiably outraged by this, the Left wonders why more people die from winter cold in temperate Britain than in Siberia and lay the blame on "an economic elite untouched and unmoved by the ills afflicting other people." High fuel prices penalize the poor while energy companies get rich, they argue. This is fundamentally unjust. The solution: price controls and "transferring money from richer consumers to poorer ones."[1]

From the other side, the Right asks the poor to stop depending on the state to provide for their needs. British conservatives point to the "vicious cycle" of welfare dependency from one generation to another, as the number of working-age people in workless households approaches 5 million. They say a social welfare system "that was originally designed to help support the poorest in society is now trapping them in the very condition it was supposed to alleviate," and more handouts for warmth or food or health care simply mire the poor deeper in dependency.[2]

No one can disagree with calls for more personal responsibility; on the other hand, everyone is troubled that poor, vulnerable people suffer while

---

1 George Monbiot, "Cold-Hearted," December 27, 2010, http://www.monbiot.com/2010/12/27/cold-hearted/.
2 "Tories Vow to Tackle National Scandal of Welfare Dependency," *Telegraph (London)*, August 27, 2009, http://www.telegraph.co.uk/news/politics/conservative/6098889/Tories-vow-to-tackle-national-scandal-of-welfare-dependency.html; "Reforms Will Tackle Poverty and Get Britain Working Again," U.K. Department for Work and Pensions, May 27, 2010, http://www.dwp.gov.uk/newsroom/press-releases/2010/may-2010;shdwp070-10-270510.shtml.

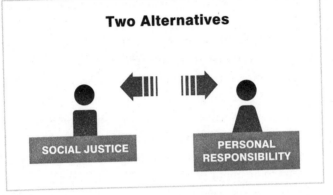

others in society are so comfortable. This is the dilemma for 2-Alternative thinkers, so they feel forced to take sides. Meanwhile the people in the Great Middle have no answers and don't really expect any: "The poor are always with us," they sigh.

I don't want to make straw men out of the Left and Right. Both sides hew to principles of personal and social responsibility, and both sides have made significant contributions to our economic prosperity, often just by counterweighting each other. But the simplistic tug-of-war between ideologues hasn't really helped break the poverty cycle. A dole makes some people dependent, and exhortations to "snap out of it and get a job" don't help much either. As synergists, we are tired of the haggling between the 2-Alternative thinkers; we wish they would join us and move on to something higher and better than narrow bipolar thinking has to offer. Our great, superordinate goal is a world without poverty.

Primary Wealth Versus Secondary Wealth

This higher, better way begins with me. Do I look at the poor with self-righteousness? Do I believe that if they were as virtuous and resourceful as I am they would not be poor? On the other hand, if I'm not as well off as I'd like, do I see myself as a victim? Do I feel somehow entitled to something from those more fortunate? In my ideological spectacles, is my Left lens stronger than my Right lens, or vice versa? Has my identity been stolen by a political party?

Neither the victimizer nor the victim is in a position to contribute to a solution.

As long as there are such things as physical, mental, or emotional disabilities—whether self-inflicted, inherited, or just bad luck—some people in our society will be dependent on the rest of us. I know of a young man, Frank, with muscular dystrophy who can do nothing but type faintly on a keyboard, earning a few dollars a week in piecework. He must be fed and cared for like a newborn baby. He has no family and no assets at all except the clothes he wears; even his wheelchair belongs to the state. I would not, however, call him poor, for he is rich in friends, in intellect, and in the gentleness of his character. When I speak of a world without poverty, I mean a world with abundant wealth of the kind Frank enjoys. A different kind of wealth.

Money is only one kind of wealth, a mark of secondary success. Primary success, as I've said before, arises from our character and is measured in terms of the contribution we make. Integrity, honesty, hard work, compassion for others—if we live by these principles, we will never be poor in primary wealth. In a world of such people, no one would be poor, not even the weak and disabled. This kind of spiritual wealth is primary wealth. Often (there's no guarantee) secondary wealth follows as a natural consequence. The assets that generally lead to material prosperity have never changed; they are character, education, skills and relationships developed over time, and patience. There are natural laws at work here, and those who live by them can be both humble and confident at the same time. It's true that some people get rich without these assets, through birth, luck, or conniving, and it's easy to get bitter over it. But if I see myself as a victim, I'll wait for society to become "fair" rather than developing those primary assets that lead to prosperity. By contrast, if I see the poor as lazy parasites, I will believe that giving them handouts is morally hazardous to them and to society. Besides, it's not fair to me that they should get something for nothing.

As synergists, however, we are not very concerned with what's fair—we want to go beyond fairness to a 3rd Alternative. We agree that primary success precedes material wealth and that the first job to be done is to promote the qualities of primary success in ourselves and in our society. At the same time, we don't agree that the poor are subnormal deviants eagerly grabbing a free ride at the expense of the rest of us. Above all people in the world, the poor need our respect and empathy. We see them in the spirit of *Ubuntu*, as irreplaceable, uniquely gifted individuals without whom we ourselves are less than human. We lift their sights so that they too can see their own worth and potential. Once they catch that vision, they will start gaining that spiritual wealth that leads to material wealth.

Like so many disadvantaged people in our society, young Weldon Long was homeless and penniless. A high school dropout at fifteen with no marketable skills, he found some solace in beer and drugs whenever he could cadge some money. He had utterly no sense of his own self-worth. By age thirty-two, he had been in and out of jail three times for robbery, had no money, no hope, and no future. "He was a garden-variety loser. He had never had a steady job. He had abandoned his three-year-old son. He had never owned a home. He had spent his entire adult life in a hopeless state of despair."[1] Weldon Long was the poorest of the poor.

Entombed in prison, he began to read idly through the library and discovered the writings of Ralph Waldo Emerson. One of the great philosopher's insights haunted him: "We become what we think about all day long." By his own account, he concentrated on those words, repeating them over and over in his mind as he glared at his image in the mirror in his cell.

> *He thought about those words intently as he gazed into his own miserable reality. He stared and wondered. Was there more to life? What would it take to find out? Was he even remotely capable of altering the course of his seemingly forged destiny by changing what he thought about "all day long"?*
>
> *Despite odds that seemed insurmountable, he decided to give it a try.*
>
> *He set out on a journey of creating transformational change in his life. He was desperate, and desperate men do desperate things. He was determined to change the course of his destiny.*

He started thinking about a "new" Weldon Long, a loving father and husband, an educated person, an honest businessman, a contributor to society. He told himself imaginary stories featuring himself in these roles. He filled his mind with these visions of primary success every day, all day. This change in thinking led to a change in his behavior. He read everything uplifting he could find: Emerson, the Bible, self-help literature. He wrote letters to his little son every week. He took every class the prison offered, eventually earning both a bachelor's degree and an MBA *summa cum laude*. ("I went to Jail, not Yale!" he jokes.)

---

1 Weldon Long, "Emerson Was Right—If You THINK He Was!," *Sources of Insight*, March 30, 2011, http://sourcesofinsight.com/2011/03/30/emerson-was-right-if-you-think-he-was/.

I came to believe that I was completely responsible for the process of chang-
ing myself. I could not control people and things around me, so taking
responsibility meant no whining and no excuses. There was no guarantee
that I would succeed in realizing my visualizations. Regardless, I had to
take responsibility . . . to do everything in my power to become a decent
human being.

By the time I was released from my third prison tour in 2003, things
had changed. I had changed. Instead of doing what I had always done—
drinking, drugging, and committing crimes—I got clean and sober. I
committed myself to achieving success and building a life based on hard
work, integrity, and personal responsibility.[1]

Out in the world a free man, Weldon faced his greatest trial of all. Would
he default back to his old life or conquer his fears and build a new life?
Fortunately, he was now in the habit of envisioning himself in new and productive roles. Finding work was tough because few employers are willing to
take a chance on a felon. At last he got a job selling heating and ventilation
equipment and broke the company sales record the first month. For the first
time in his life, he was making an honest living. Soon he started his own
equipment company that prospered due to his hard work. He now owns
beautiful homes in Colorado and Maui with his wife and son.

I know Weldon Long personally and admire him. None of this would
have happened if he had not discovered who he really was: a powerful individual with potential limited only by his own choices. Spiritual intention
drives perception, which drives behavior, which then drives results. If you
actually get people to think in terms of their contribution, it gets them immediately into a spiritual frame of mind. When you lift the hearts of poor
people, when you help them to see themselves as beings of infinite worth,
they will take their own journey out of poverty. This is the job to be done.

Anyone can do what Weldon Long did, but the shift of paradigm from
"garden-variety loser" to talented, resourceful, successful contributor to society was a fearsome leap for him. When asked, he will tell you that the
greatest obstacle to making that leap is fear: "I realized that fear had been
the major reason for all my failure. . . . My fearful thoughts had become

---

1 Weldon Long, *The Upside of Fear: How One Man Broke the Cycle of Prison, Poverty, and
Addiction* (Austin, TX: Greenleaf Books, 2009), 124.

self-fulfilling prophecies." [1] The poor face a dispiriting dilemma. Many start life with poor health and a dysfunctional home. Their education lags, and there are no good jobs without education. As years go by, the poor see before them an ever-widening gap that takes unusual strength and courage to cross. That's why so many are so afraid to try. For them, the choice is to leap and fail again and again, or to linger in deepening poverty.

Why Don't They Just Get a Job?

Of course, like most dilemmas, this one is false. Weldon Long's story shows that there is a 3rd Alternative. Still, crushing cultural forces push back at the poor who try to break out. Our society is caught between those who ask, frustrated, "Why don't they just get a job?" and those who, through a demoralizing dole, perpetuate poverty out of misguided kindness. In our time, "just getting a job" can be an overwhelming challenge for someone with meager health, education, or connections. And as for showing kindness to the poor by providing them a living without effort on their part, the great moralist C.S. Lewis wisely observed, "Love is something more stern and splendid than mere kindness." [2] Our society has a much more demanding job to do for the poor than simply to hand out food stamps and exhortations.

After thirty-two years with a major accounting firm, Dave Phillips had no intention of retiring to the golf course. For years he and his wife, Liane, had volunteered their spare time to various nonprofits and yearned to do more for their community of Cincinnati, Ohio. Astounded to learn that the poverty rate in Cincinnati had soared from 12 to 24 percent in the previous decade, they decided to devote the rest of their lives to helping the poor out of poverty.

They had no idea how to proceed, but Dave had a strong business background and both were gifted with a great capacity for empathy, so they set about learning as much as they could about the problem and how they could help. After intense study of many employment programs around the country, they gathered their ideas and launched Cincinnati Works, a nonprofit "society of members" now hailed as the "the best of the best practices for creating win-win solutions for people in poverty and for businesses that need

1 Long, *Upside of Fear*, 115.
2 C.S. Lewis, *The Problem of Pain* (New York: Harper-Collins, 2001), 32.

qualified entry-level workers." The model is spreading to cities across the United States.

Cincinnati Works (CW) is a genuine 3rd Alternative for the poor. Because they lack a strong support network, the poor usually resort to public employment agencies, most of which do their best to connect people with job opportunities, teach résumé writing, and set up interviews. They consider their job finished once the client gets a job. But this approach is far too narrow for the real job to be done. The chronically unemployed rarely keep a job once they get one; the typical retention rate after three months is an abysmal 15 to 20 percent. The real job to be done, in Liane Phillips's words, is to take "a holistic approach to the job seeker." She sees the poor person as a *whole* person who needs support not just materially but emotionally, mentally, and spiritually.

At CW, the chronically unemployed are not "clients" but "members" of a mutually supportive club whose goal is career advancement through a lifelong relationship. Most members are African American women, single mothers who struggle to work and care for their children at the same time. "They've got so many challenges," says Shirley Smith, a CW specialist. "Dropping kids off with different sitters, getting buses, trying to make their dollars stretch. . . . They need to hear over and over again, 'Yes, you can do this,' because they aren't hearing it from anybody else. Our members must feel that they are in a place of caring and commitment where we'll walk with them every step of the way on their journey out of poverty."

This reliable emotional support is crucial. In their research, the Phillipses found that 60 percent of their members suffered from chronic depression, which is true of the chronically poor not just in Cincinnati, but everywhere. The symptoms of depression are often perceived as laziness. Liane Phillips says:

> We found that perception to be resoundingly false. Most of the poor people we met were far from lazy. Every day was a struggle and required constant problem solving. Tasks that seemed automatic and simple for us required a lot of energy for them: getting to and from work without a car, finding groceries and paying for them, cashing a paycheck—if you had one—without a bank account. . . . Most striking of all, we started to grasp the depth of their despair and frustration at trying and failing repeatedly to get jobs.

An onsite mental-health specialist helps members cope medically and emotionally with the scars of poverty. A lifetime of failure and rejection fills them with fear. "It's very frightening looking for a job," says one member. "Being rejected makes me feel disappointed in myself. I wonder how and where did I go wrong." Another describes "just the fear of leaving the house, going out and getting the job, the fear of being turned down or being pushed away, the fear that they won't call you back." They agonize over their isolation and the overwhelming social message that something is wrong with them. For many, no matter how bad their lives are, it's just too painful to risk more failure.

Because of these sensitive emotional wounds, their real problem is often not to *find* employment but to *keep* it. This was a major insight for the Phillipses. Once employed, many quit if someone at work disrespects them or they miss a bus or a child gets sick. Quitting again and again discourages them and makes them more unemployable. "In the heat of the moment, or in the face of a problem—real or imagined—they quit on the spot, failing to grasp how critical job retention is to their future." With his accounting mind, Dave studied the problem and found that it took a year for the average member to stabilize in a job, and that job loss was most likely in the first three months. So CW is organized around a strict three-month regimen with frequent communication and follow-up. The mantra is "Call before you quit." Stressed-out members ring up the CW hotline for help when they run into problems.

One year on the job usually marks both material and emotional stability. A member says, "I think not having a job magnifies my depression, with isolation . . . the sense of wrongness. But when I'm working and I'm in my little rut job-wise, I feel great. I have a purpose. I have a sense of being okay. I feel like I belong, like I'm connected."

CW works hard at enriching members' mental lives as well. Workshops teach the "hidden rules" of the workplace, how to build strong relationships, how to handle a difficult boss, never to quit a job without calling first. Members learn to focus on taking the "next step" out of poverty: getting a marketable skill, a certificate or degree, or a driver's license.

The win for Cincinnati businesses who hire and mentor CW members is much higher worker retention: CW "has greatly reduced turnover for many companies—in some cases, by more than half—by placing 4,000 working poor and chronically unemployed people in jobs and then providing services that keep them there. . . . At Fifth Third Bank, 90 percent of workers hired through the program stay at least one year. Compare that with the company's one-year retention rate of 50 percent."[1] For CW as a whole, the one-year retention rate is 80 percent.

CW's impact is truly revolutionary. Where government agencies typically spend $30,000 a year in services per poor household in Cincinnati, for a one-time outlay of $1,200 CW helps one person get and keep a job. Over a decade, CW can save the community more than $100 million. "Why don't they just get a job? That's the million-dollar question when it comes to the chronically unemployed," says Liane Phillips. "That staggering amount also happens to be the minimum cost to society over the lifespan of each and every household in poverty in the United States."[2]

Too often the choice for the chronically unemployed is giving up or falling back on the overworked mechanism of public employment services. The holistic approach of Cincinnati Works is a genuine 3rd Alternative. A few, like Weldon Long, think and work themselves out of poverty; but for many of America's 37 million poor, the "stern and splendid" love of 3rd Alternative thinkers like the Phillipses can mean the beginning of self-sufficiency and the end of poverty.

Ending Poverty from the Inside Out

A world without poverty is inconceivable to most of us. Worldwide, 878 million people cannot afford the basic necessities of life, such as clean water, food, and shelter. Among these are tens of millions of street children. More than 11 million poor children will die before their fifth birthday. To people of goodwill, the challenge of alleviating these hardships is staggering.

But there is good news. Between 2005 and 2010, the number of poor people fell by nearly half a billion due to economic growth in emerging countries. Laurence Chandy of the Brookings Institution observes, "Poverty reduction of this magnitude is unparalleled in history: never before have so many people been lifted out of poverty over such a brief period of time." It

---

1 Brian Ballou and Dan L. Heitger, "Tapping a Risky Labor Pool," *Harvard Business Review*, December 2006, http://hbr.org/2006/12/tapping-a-risky-labor-pool/ar/1.

2 Liane Phillips and Echo Montgomery Garrett, *Why Don't They Just Get a Job?* (Highlands, TX: aha! Process, 2010), 31, 54, 86, 128–29, 159.

appears that the developing world is at last truly developing, and perhaps the end of absolute poverty is in sight.[1]

Tens of millions of people have followed a Weldon Long–style course of action and pulled themselves out of poverty into the marketplace. Of course, the catalyst here is the growth of global markets across Asia, Africa, and Latin America, but it's gratifying to know that faced with opportunity so many will seize it on their own initiative.

Everywhere, once-poor people are finding a 3rd Alternative to lingering in poverty or waiting for someone to save them. They are finding it within themselves. Governments and charities have made enormous contributions, but in the end the most effective approach to alleviating poverty comes from the inside out. Well-intentioned efforts from the outside world to endow people with money and resources simply don't work well until something changes on the inside. That something is respect for oneself.

People from the outside *can* help facilitate that change. Years ago, Jerry and Monique Sternin represented a charitable foundation trying to improve child nutrition in Vietnam. Healthy babies in thousands of rural villages were wasting away for lack of proper nourishment, so the Vietnamese government invited the Sternins to see what they could do on the ground. They were not the first. Many groups had come and gone, bringing milk and high-protein biscuits with them, but when the supplies and the will to help ran out, they abandoned the effort: "They came, they fed, they left, and nothing changed," Jerry Sternin relates.

"The reasons for the failure were not difficult to discern," according to Sternin. "Villagers were passive program beneficiaries, neither encouraged nor required to change any of the underlying practices that had led to their children's malnutrition." Though they brought some supplements in, the Sternins decided not to have food rain effortlessly from the sky; instead they began an empathic search for answers among the villagers themselves.[2]

First, they met with the leaders of four villages and found that no one had ever before invited their input on what was wrong with their children's health. When asked, the villagers plunged into the effort with zeal. Vol-

1 Laurence Chandy and Geoffrey Gertz, "Poverty in Numbers: The Changing State of Global Poverty 2005–2015," Brookings Institution, January 2011, http://www.brookings .edu/papers/2011/01_global_poverty_chandy.aspx.
2 Jerry Sternin, "Childhood Malnutrition in Vietnam: From Peril to Possibility," in *The Power of Positive Deviance* (Cambridge, MA: Harvard Business Press, 2010), 22.

unteers weighed every child and charted them against family income. The villagers were stunned to learn that some of the best-nourished children belonged to the poorest families. Baffled, everyone wanted to know what these families were doing differently, and so began an intense process of empathic listening. The villagers absorbed everything their neighbors had to tell them, even though they were at the bottom of the social scale.

Soon it became clear that the poorest of the poor were adding to the family rice abundant tiny shrimps and wild sweet potato greens scavenged from the rice paddies. Such sources of protein and vitamins, which most villagers considered "trash food" unsuitable for children, suddenly became highly prized. These and other discoveries that eventually saved thousands of children from malnutrition had been right in the community all the time, but the parents were blind to their own strengths due to a lack of respect for themselves. "We are a poor village," they had always said. "We have no answers. We suffer until the rich and the educated come to our aid."

As 3rd Alternative thinkers, the Sternins knew that without a paradigm shift, the village children would still be victims of the 2-Alternative thinking that plagues so many of the poor: "Others won't help us, and we can't help ourselves." The Sternins learned in Vietnam that "the traditional model for social and organizational change doesn't work. It never has. You can't bring permanent solutions in from outside."[1] But once empowered to find within themselves the solutions to their poverty, to see themselves as gifted and capable, the poor can be excellent problem solvers.

The Sternins also show how to do countertype thinking, the art of finding synergies by reversing conventional wisdom. As highly educated, technologically sophisticated experts from the West, they were invited to Vietnam to save the "primitive" villagers. But the Sternins turned everything around. They came to learn, not to teach. They listened rather than imposing their ideas. They synergized with the people rather than dictating to them. They found their richest answers among the poorest of the poor.

When it comes to 3rd Alternatives to poverty, the Magic Theater knows no boundaries of class or education. Innovation is everywhere among the poor, who often have to do the most ingenious problem solving just to get by. When we think of innovation, we think of Apple and Google and sophis-

1 David Dorsey, "Positive Deviant," *Fast Company*, November 30, 2000, http://www.fast company.com/magazine/41/sternin.html.

ticated corporate types with vast budgets and research labs, but some of the most striking innovation in the world today is flowering up from the shops and fields of the inventive poor.

Twice a year, students from the Indian Institute of Management at Ahmedabad go on a pilgrimage into the countryside for eight to ten days. On this *shodhyatra*, or foot trek, the student pilgrims are looking for 3rd Alternatives—the odd idea, the strange or new creation born of necessity in the remote villages of India. The *shodhyatris* are fascinated by the smallest positive deviation. If they find some unusual practice or device invented by a farmer or shop worker, they bring it back to be shared through the Honey Bee Network, a national organization dedicated to leveraging the new knowledge.

Professor Anil K. Gupta founded the Honey Bee Network, so called because bees and flowers and honey form a symbiosis, as a vehicle for synergy among grassroots innovators, venture capitalists, and academics. A classic countertype, the Network operates on the premise that India's greatest knowledge resource is in the countryside, not in the universities. "When we talk of India as a knowledge economy, we assume rural people will be employed only in the lowest value-adding activities and never as providers of knowledge. That is absurd," Gupta insists.

> *The developmental paradigm has been dominated for at least half a century by the idea that the role of the state or civil society is only to provide what poor people lack, i.e. material resources, opportunities for gains in skills or resources or employment. This paradigm fails to build upon a resource in which poor people often are rich: their own knowledge.*
>
> *Being economically poor does not mean being knowledge poor. But the poor who are at the bottom of the economic pyramid are often considered as being at the bottom of the knowledge pyramid as well. Nothing could be further from the truth.*[1]

Honey Bee feeds data from the treks into the National Innovation Foundation, which has catalogued more than fifty thousand innovations scouted

---

1 Sarah Rich, "Anil Gupta and the Honey Bee Network," WorldChanging.com, March 21, 2007, http://www.worldchanging.com/archives/006333.html; Raja Murthy, "India's Rural Inventors Drive Change," *Asia Times*, January 29, 2010, http://www.atimes.com/atimes/South_Asia/LA29Df03.html.

from all over India and dispersed to investors and rural people alike, anyone who can capitalize on them. The *shodhyatris* dutifully record herbal remedies, odd uses of small motors (e.g., an old Sony Walkman used to power a fan), and even local recipes for curry. They also encounter small miracles, like a child who can recite the names and uses of more than three hundred local plants.[1] Often they find truly innovative ideas that can transform the lives of the poor. One successful find was Mansukh Prajapati's "Mitti Cool" refrigerator made from an ingenious rectangular clay pot and requiring no electricity; thousands of them are in use. He has also invented a plow driven by a motorcycle and a nonstick clay pan that reportedly works as well as a Teflon pan but costs only a dollar.

Where grain mills won't accept orders from small farmers, one inventor will bring a portable wheat grinder on two wheels and take care of your harvest; it has a washing machine attachment if you want your laundry done too. The inventor of a device for climbing coconut trees is now selling his climber internationally. An herbal cream for eczema that came out of a farm village has become popular around the world. Another man invented an amphibious bicycle so he could cross the river to see his girlfriend. "I couldn't wait for the boat," he says. "I had to meet my love. My desperation made me an innovator. Even love needs help from technology." The cycle is no joke; investors are looking at it as a rescue device for flooded areas.[2]

For Professor Gupta and his Honey Bee Network, all of India is a Magic Theater for 3rd Alternatives to the conventional. The Network itself is a giant countertype, capitalizing on transformative—and lucrative—ideas from the minds of the rural poor rather than the laboratories of great corporations. To his credit, Gupta fights hard to protect the intellectual property rights of the thousands of innovators in the Honey Bee Network. "When we learn something from people, it must be shared with them," he says. And so must the economic benefits.

But more significant than economics is the spiritual worth of Gupta's work. When their knowledge is respected, when someone values the contributions they can make, the poor respond with their hearts. The rural grand-

---

1 Reports of the semiannual *shodhyatras* can be found at http://www.sristi.org/cms/shodh_yatra1. Accessed April 2011.
2 Anil Gupta, "India's Hotbeds of Invention," TED.com, November 2009, http://www.ted.com/talks/lang/eng/anil_gupta_india_s_hidden_hotbeds_of_invention.html.

mother no one has noticed for a long time suddenly becomes a precious font of knowledge about herbs as the community sits at her feet. Village children compete to show their inventions, and their pride in their accomplishments fuels their spirits.

A Grand Synergy

"Poverty does not belong in civilized human society. Its proper place is in a museum. That's where it will be," predicts the Nobel laureate Muhammad Yunus. Father of the microcredit industry—a brilliant 3rd Alternative in itself—Yunus understands that poverty is fundamentally a spiritual challenge. It involves the whole person. You cannot separate physical poverty from the mind, the heart, and the spirit. Curing poverty requires a positive internal synergy of every part of our nature. A degraded and starving body, a depressed and unvalued heart, an uneducated mind, a despairing spirit— these constitute the negative synergy we call poverty.

Yunus believes in unleashing the innate human capacities of the poor to lift themselves. In the 1970s, as an economics professor in Bangladesh, he concluded that material poverty was largely the result of 2-Alternative thinking: poor people needed credit to build up their small businesses, but banks wouldn't lend to them *because* they were poor; their loans would be too small to trouble with and they were bad risks. As a result, they were forced to depend on moneylenders who charged ruinous rates for raw materials. The poor simply couldn't escape this vicious cycle; any profit they made went back to the moneylenders.

So Yunus came up with a 3rd Alternative: a microcredit bank that lends small amounts to poor craftspeople and farmers so they can gradually get ahead and avoid the moneylenders who exploit them. He knew his people well enough to trust in their primary attributes of integrity and honesty; their rate of repayment exceeds that of most big bank customers. Today over 100 million people are climbing out of poverty with help from the micro-credit movement. Although some dishonest people have tried to pervert his concept of microcredit, it remains the hope of millions. When I had dinner with Dr. Yunus, he told me that his life's goal is to see the end of poverty.

Yunus believes that the great political debate over poverty barely touches the surface because it's all about political economics, which, "without the human side, is as hard and dry as stone." To the Hard Left wing that wants to solve poverty by simply transferring money, he says their message to the

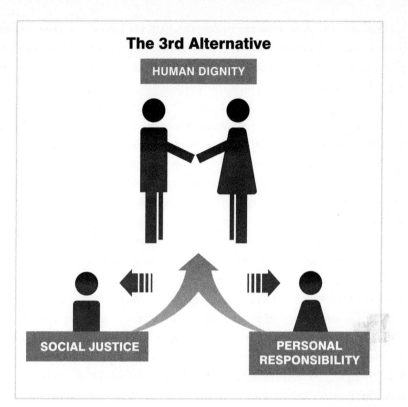

poor is debilitating: "You can't do anything, the government has to take care of you. So you become dependent." And he reminds the Hard Right wing, with its laissez-faire reliance on the free market, "Unfettered markets are not meant to solve social problems and instead may actually exacerbate poverty, disease, pollution, corruption, crime, and inequality."[1] For Muhammad Yunus, neither side sees clearly the real job to be done, which is to elevate the human dignity of the poor.

Yunus dreams of a grand synergy between the corporate world and the poor, where the power of capital connects with their aspirations to create a 3rd Alternative he calls "social business." The purpose of a social business, he says, is "to bring an end to a social problem" rather than to generate profits for shareholders. GroupeDanone, the French foods giant, has joined with him to build the nonprofit Grameen-Danone Company, which employs thousands of poor workers in Bangladesh to produce a fortified yogurt that

---

1 Muhammad Yunus, *Creating a World Without Poverty* (New York: Public Affairs, 2008), 5.

is affordable for poor children in that country. By improving child health, buying local milk in quantity, and providing jobs that build self-worth, this example of the social business model adds up to far more than the sum of its parts. It's a synergism that could transform a nation.[1]

Yunus believes that the 3rd Alternative of social business has the power to bring us a poverty-free world within a short time. That's impossible to predict. Danone investors know that the only return they will receive is "the psychological and spiritual one of helping poor people halfway around the world." Perhaps the promise of primary wealth will attract enough capital to produce that kind of change. Yunus thinks so: "A businessperson is not always someone who wants to maximize profits. Companies can also have another goal: to serve a societal purpose. We need businesspeople who are not driven by money but by their desire to contribute to society."[2]

Whether or not Yunus's vision works out, I deeply admire his 3rd Alternative mind-set that has already stirred millions of poor people to strive for a better future through their own resourcefulness and initiative. He also sees a crucial role for business and government. The combination of personal responsibility and organizations that promote social justice can elevate the human dignity of the poor and end their plight. In this book, I have tried to be a *shodhyatri*, a seeker for 3rd Alternatives in our society. They are everywhere, like campfires dotting the darkness. Each of these lights is the result of someone, somewhere, adopting the paradigms of synergy instead of the paradigms of defensiveness and attack.

I See Myself. Here is Weldon Long, the poorest of the poor, looking deeply into a mirror at his own image and realizing that poverty—moral, material, emotional—is a choice, and that he has the power to make a different choice.

I See You. Here is Anil Gupta, an urbane management professor, who sees in the eyes of poor South Asian villagers not helpless ignorance, but treasures of knowledge that can enrich the world. He says, "People may be economically poor, but they are not poor in the mind. The minds on the margin are not marginal minds."

---

1 Muhammad Yunus and Karl Weber, *Building Social Business* (New York: Public Affairs, 2010), 33–61, 95.

2 Marco Visscher, "The World Champ of Poverty Fighters," *Ode Magazine,* July–August 2005, http://www.odemagazine.com/doc/25/the_world_champ_of_poverty_fighters/.

I Seek You Out. Here is Ward Clapham, a tough police officer, a Royal Canadian Mountie, who hunts down juveniles not to arrest them but to praise them for the goodness in them, to learn from them and work with them. He sees not "delinquents" but future contributors, parents, partners in the synergistic mission of building a civil society for generations to come.

I Synergize With You. Here is Natalie Jeremijenko, who joins with artists, engineers, gardeners, and marine biologists—anyone with the mind-set of the Magic Theater—to transform the ecology of a great city through small miracles of synergy.

If I am a synergist like these amazing people, I look at our society and see its ills as opportunities for transformation, as invitations to change the game and create a future that is better than my own dreams for it. If we are both synergists, the great divides between us become dying echoes. And it makes no difference if our Circle of Influence is small or large, a little family or a whole society, because the consequences of our actions expand with time. We don't have to be paralyzed by the false dilemmas. We don't have to wait for society to change. We can consciously create our own change.

TEACH TO LEARN

The best way to learn from this book is to teach it to someone else. Everybody knows that the teacher learns far more than the student. So find someone—a co-worker, a friend, a family member—and teach him or her the insights you've gained. Ask the provocative questions here or come up with your own.

- Alan Greenspan speaks of "a general schism in our society which is becoming ever more destructive." What assumptions about society are on either side of this schism? What are the limitations of both sides?
- What is "interdependence"? Why do 3rd Alternative thinkers value interdependence in solving our social problems? In what ways might the concept of *dharma* help us as individuals confront the problems around us?
- What do we learn from the story of the Times Square renaissance about dealing with conflicts in our neighborhoods and communities? What do we learn about the value of involving diverse groups? How did they use the prototyping process to arrive at a 3rd Alternative?
- What are the limitations of the "tough" and "soft" mind-sets about crime? Why and how did Ward Clapham create a synergistic police force? In what ways are "positive ticketing" and the MINI Cooper street-racer countertypes? What is the value of a countertype?
- What are the two sides in the Great Debate about health care? Why is this debate over a false dilemma?
- What is our personal responsibility in caring for our own health? What does it mean to "care for the whole person"?
- "The great health industry is actually a 'sickness industry.'" What does this mean? What do we learn about 3rd Alternatives in health care from the stories of the Living Well Health Center, the Norman Clinic, and IHC?

- What does the account of two people discussing the environment teach us about empathic listening?
- What do we learn from Natalie Jeremijenko and Allan Savory about the potential of small-scale 3rd Alternatives to have large-scale impact?
- What is the difference between primary and secondary wealth? Why is primary wealth more fundamental than secondary wealth to our well-being?
- Weldon Long says that fear is the major obstacle when people are trying to break out of poverty. What are the sources of that fear? What does the story of Weldon Long teach us about overcoming that fear?
- What do we mean when we say the end of poverty will come "from the inside out"? What illustrations of that principle do you see in the stories of Jerry and Monique Sternin and the Honey Bee Network?

TRY IT

As you look around your own community, what social problems or opportunities do you see? Start prototyping 3rd Alternatives. Invite others to contribute. Use the "4 Steps to Synergy" tool.

4 STEPS TO SYNERGY

1 Ask the 3rd Alternative Question:

"Are you willing to go for a solution that is better than any of us have come up with yet?" If yes, go on to step 2.

2 Define Criteria of Success

List in this space the characteristics of a solution that would delight everyone. What does success look like? What is the real job to be done? What would be a "win-win" for all concerned?

3 Create 3rd Alternatives

In this space (or other spaces) create models, draw pictures, borrow ideas, turn your thinking upside down. Work quickly and creatively. Suspend all judgment until that exciting moment when you know you've arrived at synergy.

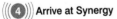 Arrive at Synergy

Describe here your 3rd Alternative and, if you want, how you intend to put it into practice.

USER GUIDE TO THE 4 STEPS TO SYNERGY TOOL

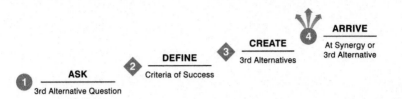

The 4 Steps to Synergy. This process helps you put the synergy principle to work. (1) Show willingness to find a 3rd Alternative. (2) Define what success looks like to everyone. (3) Experiment with solutions until you (4) arrive at synergy. Listen empathically to others throughout the process.

How to Get to Synergy

1 Ask the 3rd Alternative Question

In a conflict or creative situation, this question helps everyone move past firm positions or preconceived ideas toward developing a third position.

2 Define Criteria of Success

List characteristics or write a paragraph describing what a successful outcome would look like to everyone. Answer these questions as you go:

• Is everyone involved in setting the criteria? Are we getting as many ideas from as many people as possible?

• What outcomes do we really want? What is the real job to be done?

• What outcomes would be "wins" for everyone?

• Are we looking past our entrenched demands to something better?

3 Create 3rd Alternative

Follow these guidelines:

• Play at it. It's not "for real." Everybody knows it's a game.

• Avoid closure, premature agreement, or consensus.

• Avoid judging others' ideas—or your own.

• Make models. Draw pictures on whiteboards, sketch diagrams, build mockups, write rough drafts.

• Turn ideas on their heads. Reverse the conventional wisdom.

• Work fast. Set a time limit to keep energy and ideas flowing rapidly.

• Breed lots of ideas. You can't predict which offhand insight might lead to a 3rd Alternative.

4 Arrive at Synergy

You recognize the 3rd Alternative by the sense of excitement and inspiration in the room. The old conflict is abandoned. The new alternative meets the criteria of success. Caution: Avoid mistaking compromise for synergy. Compromise breeds satisfaction but not delight. Compromise means everyone loses something; synergy means everyone wins.

The 3rd Alternative in the World

8

The 3rd Alternative in the World

You cannot shake hands with a clenched fist.
—*Indira Gandhi*

On the way to a rare holiday at the beach near Tel Aviv, Mohammed Dajani and his family approached a long line of cars waiting to pass through an Israeli Defense Forces checkpoint. Dajani's elderly mother, who suffered from asthma, became anxious and struggled to breathe. She had forgotten to bring her inhaler with her on the outing. Suddenly she collapsed, the victim of an apparent heart attack. Trying not to panic, Dajani steeled himself to plead with the Israeli soldiers to let them quickly through the checkpoint so they could get her to a hospital.

Dajani's life reached a crisis at this moment. For years he had been subjected to these checkpoints. As a Palestinian with ancient roots in the land, he found it humiliating to be stopped and searched constantly by armed soldiers he considered aliens in his country. The Dajani family had lived in Palestine for hundreds of years. Centuries before, the sultan had honored the family with custody of King David's tomb in Jerusalem, a charge they had kept generation after generation. But then came the establishment of the State of Israel in 1948, which many Palestinian Arab families like the Dajanis viewed as *al-Nakba*, the Catastrophe, an unjust imposition of a foreign government and a foreign culture. Dajani's family was uprooted.

"For many years after that," he says, "my big dream was to rid the land of the Israelis." At university in Beirut, he discovered that he could be an articulate force for his cause. Today his office walls are covered with news photos of himself from the 1970s, speaking out to huge crowds about Palestinian liberation. Soon he became a lieutenant to Yasser Arafat, a leader of the resistance to the Jewish state. "I believed for a long time that only force was the solution."

The conflict over Israel and Palestine is too familiar to most of us. It began in the nineteenth century with the rise of Zionism, a movement to create a Jewish state in what the Jews refer to as *eretz Israel*, their ancestral homeland in Palestine. Anti-Semitism in Europe, culminating with the horrors of the Holocaust, led many world leaders to support an Israeli state, at length established by a United Nations declaration on May 14, 1948. But Palestinian Arabs, most of them Muslims, saw Zionism as gross injustice; to them, it was nothing less than the theft of *their* ancestral homeland. They rose up immediately against the new Israeli power. In the following years, both sides suffered waves of suicide bombings, rocket attacks, violent uprisings, and assassinations.

The Israeli-Palestinian conflict has long since spilled over into a source of contention between the Muslim world and the West. Grand alliances threaten war over it. Diplomatic efforts to resolve the conflict fail repeatedly. Peace seems frustratingly elusive.

As complex and ancient as it is, this bloody argument, like so many others, is at root the product of 2-Alternative thinking. Each side essentially says to the other, "My claim to the land is superior to yours. My religion is superior to yours. You must give way." The scarcity mentality reigns. It's a zero-sum game in which one side must lose or the other cannot win.

In this chapter, we expand our view to apply 3rd Alternative thinking to the world we live in, a disputatious world where the danger of catastrophic war is very real. Our Serious Challenge survey respondents listed "stopping war and terrorism" as the most important challenge facing our world today. Here are some of their thoughts:

- "Terror still is the most important challenge facing the world. It threatens to take away the liberty and progress established democracies want to serve the global citizens."

- "The toll war and terrorism take on citizens is brutal. Buildings destroyed, lives lost, and countless amounts of money spent to support the destruction, for what?"
- "The world as a whole is ravaged by war, with ever-expanding arsenals of weapons of mass destruction."
- "If there were no wars to fight and terrorism to deal with, we would be more focused on improving our economies and reducing poverty."
- "War and terrorism destroy the ability of people to have safe lives, provide for themselves and their children, and obtain a solid education."

The Israeli-Palestinian issue is only one sore point. We all have a stake in the peaceful, creative solutions that 3rd Alternative thinking can bring to our local communities, our states, and our nations. We need nothing less than a revolution in the way we debate and practice diplomacy. There are many exemplary people who are trying to get to the 3rd Alternative in the Middle East, and their efforts can teach us much about the kind of synergy that's possible in our own Circles of Influence.

Peacebuilding: The Revolutionizing of Internal Diplomacy

One of those people is Mohammed Dajani. On that desperate day at the checkpoint when his mother lay dying, he discovered something that changed his life. His only contact with Israelis to that moment had been at such checkpoints, with young soldiers carrying machine guns. But now those same soldiers fell to work to help his stricken mother. They had two ambulances in place in minutes. They transported his mother to an Israeli army hospital because it was the closest facility. "That afternoon I watched my enemy trying to save my mother. It was a very important event in my life. For me it was one of many turning points from 'us or them' to 'us *and* them.'" [1]

---

1 Interview with Mohammed Dajani, Wasatia Headquarters, Beit-Hanina, Israel, January 12, 2010.

Professor Mohammed Dajani of al-Quds University is now one of the leading exponents of the 3rd Alternative in Palestine, an "us *and* them" paradigm. His remarkable change of heart led him to found an organization called Wasatia to educate young Palestinians specifically against 2-Alternative thinking. The name of the organization comes from a verse in the Qur'an: "We have made you a *wasatan* community." Variously translated, the term *wasatia* means something like "the midpoint between two extremes." Thus Wasatia is dedicated to moving beyond extremes toward a higher, more balanced approach to all of life.

Professor Dajani says, "The roots of the problem lie in the fact that Palestinian youth are growing up learning two lessons: that the only way to resolve conflict or differences is through a win-lose formula; and that Muslims, Christians, and Jews are not meant to coexist, let alone thrive together."[1] Of course, this is classic 2-Alternative thinking.

My impression of the Islamic concept of *wasatia* is that it is very close to the notion of the 3rd Alternative. It is a repudiation of 2-Alternative thinking that imprisons people in what Dajani calls "zealous partisanship, tribal solidarities, fanaticism, racism, bigotry, and intolerance . . . the tendencies which drive man to become the mortal enemy of man."[2] Those who embrace *wasatia* seek a higher, better way, beyond the compromise of mere coexistence toward a 3rd Alternative of thriving together in the same land.

What led Dajani to start this influential movement among his fellow Palestinians? Largely, it was the Israeli soldiers' demonstration of empathy that made the difference. This impression was reinforced when Dajani's father was treated for cancer at an Israeli hospital. "The staff laughed and joked with him and didn't treat him as an Arab—that was an eye-opener for me," says Dajani.

Rabbi Ron Kronish, director of the Interreligious Coordinating Council in Israel (ICCI), dedicates his life to providing opportunities for Israelis and Palestinians to listen empathically to one another. It is the absolute precondition for a peaceful 3rd Alternative in that troubled land—or anywhere else.

---

1 Mohammed Dajani, "The Wasatia Movement—An Alternative to Radical Islam," *Worldpress.org*, June 21, 2007, http://www.worldpress.org/Mideast/2832.cfm.
2 Mohammed S. Dajani Daoudi, *Wasatia: Centrism and Moderation in Islam*, n.d., 17, http://www.ptwf.org/Downloads/Wasatia.pdf.

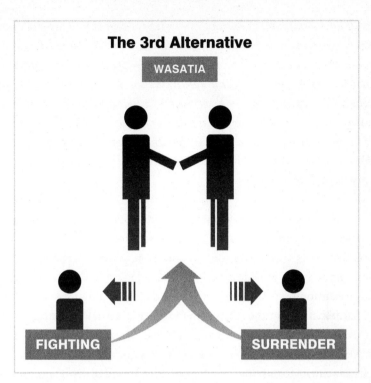

"Palestinians and Israelis rarely meet one another in daily life," says Rabbi Kronish. "We are flooded with terrible media stereotypes of each other. Palestinians meet Jews mostly at checkpoints. They see the Jews there as soldiers who are part of an occupying army. To Jews, Palestinians are perceived as terrorists and Islam is considered to be a religion of death, which encourages suicide bombers." Yet these are the people he convenes together regularly in long-term systematic, substantive, and sensitive encounters, to meet one another—women, youth, young adults, educators, religious leaders—people who can be multipliers in their communities and societies. "What do we do at ICCI? We bring people into dialogue, to change their hearts and minds about the possibilities and benefits of peaceful coexistence, now and for the long-term future."

It's a radical surprise to people who enter into serious dialogue with the other—who is also the enemy—to find that the others are actually human and that each person has a unique story, which is usually also related to the larger religious and political conflict. In addition, when they study

a bit about each other's religion, they discover that their religions share
similar humanistic values at their core. The Jews in the groups have never
opened the Quran, and the same in reverse—the Palestinian Muslims
and Christians know very little about Judaism. In one group, a Muslim
religious leader heard for the first time the Talmudic verse "If you save one
human life, it's as if you save a whole world" and exclaimed, "We have
the same verse in the Quran!" Through study of each other's sacred texts,
Jews, Christians, and Muslims in Israel and the region develop trust as
they learn from each other.

ICCI is creating the environment for individuals embroiled in this conflict to deliberately seek each other out and listen to one another. Dr. Kronish
reports that "they share their feelings about the issues. Occasionally, things
get hot enough that we think maybe we should stop—but the participants
insist on continuing." Although the ICCI dialogues are often very difficult,
most participants stay the course since a deep need for empathic listening
takes over. These people *want* to understand one another and to see how
they can learn to live together. One of the Jewish participants recently said,
"I read something troubling in the news, and in my dialogue group I want
to hear what my friend and colleague—whether Palestinian Muslim or
Christian—is feeling and thinking. What does he *really* think?" They bring
large national issues to the table in a *personal* way.

To reach young people, ICCI is one of the international partners with
Auburn Theological Seminary of New York in a year-long dialogue process
that includes a summer camp for Palestinian and Israeli students as well as
high school students from South Africa, Northern Ireland, and parts of the
United States. At the "Face to Face/Faith to Faith" camp, held in Upstate
New York each summer, they eat kosher, halal, and vegetarian food; they
bunk together; they argue; and they cry when they leave one another, just
like at any other camp.[1]

Working alongside Rabbi Kronish at the ICCI is Margaret Karram, a
Palestinian Arab. She says, "My identity is complex. I am an Israeli Catholic
Christian Arab Palestinian." As a child, she suffered when she had to face
the Jewish children in her neighborhood on the slopes of Mt. Carmel. As if
reflecting what the adults were doing, they threw stones and hurled names

---

1 Interview with Dr. Ron Kronish, Hebrew University of Jerusalem, January 7, 2011.

at each other. "I was always crying," she remembers. One day after such a fight, she came limping home. Her extraordinary mother, who was baking, told her to invite the Jewish children into the kitchen, where she gave each of them Arab bread to take home to their families. The Jews would come to thank her, and soon they were attending each other's feasts. A profound relationship started to grow up in that little neighborhood of Haifa.

At the age of fifteen, Karram encountered the Focolare Movement, a worldwide Catholic movement whose aim is to work toward fostering dialogue at all levels and between different peoples and religions. Following her mother's example, and nourished by the spiritual values of the Focolare Movement, Karram came to love her Jewish friends and, as a Christian, wanted to learn more about them. She went to Los Angeles for Jewish studies at the University of Judaism. "I didn't open my mouth for six months," she says. The other students assumed she was a Jew, but eventually they found out who she was. They were stunned that they had been studying the Torah and Talmud alongside a Palestinian Arab. She explained to them that she was there to help close the chasm between them and her people. "To do that, I have to know you," she said. After five years of empathic listening, she graduated and returned to her homeland, an Arab with a college degree in understanding the Jewish people.

Now Margaret Karram lectures on Jewish-Christian-Arab relations, doing her best to build bridges. She invests her life in creating dialogue and promoting empathy. "I can't make a lot of difference," she says, "only stone by stone."[1]

I think Margaret underestimates her influence. As they talk together, people like Margaret Karram and members of groups like ICCI and Wasatia come to trust and feel genuine affection for one another. They know that dialogue is not enough, but it is the first and essential step toward creating new possibilities. And that explains, in my opinion, why so many formal diplomatic efforts fail to resolve conflicts like the one in the Middle East. By neglecting the opportunity to create the empathic connection people need from each other, standard diplomacy does not allow for "psychological air."

The conventional approach to peacemaking is rational negotiation among the people the great political scientist Samuel P. Huntington calls

---

1 Interview with Margaret Karram, Wasatia Headquarters, Beit-Hanina, Israel, January 12, 2011.

"the Davos culture." Each year the world's top government and business elites convene a summit meeting in luxurious surroundings in Davos, Switzerland. They know each other well and form a kind of "transnational consensus of the jet set, who control virtually all international institutions, many of the world's governments, and the bulk of the world's economic and military capabilities."[1] But the rarefied atmosphere of Davos supplies no psychological air to the millions who are actually hurting.

For example, the Oslo Accords of 1993 were hailed as a "Davos-style" breakthrough that would change everything. Representatives of Israel and the Palestinians agreed to recognize each other's "right to self-determination" and to share territory. The delegates beamed as they spoke of an end to the conflict, that everything was worked out in principle and the details would be left to the lawyers.

How did such firm antagonists get to this breakthrough? Because the negotiations were not actually the typical formal encounters between diplomats. They were "back channel" discussions, kept quiet and away from the media. The delegates lived together for weeks in the same house near Oslo, ate at the same table, and took long walks together in the woods of Norway. During this time they came to know each other well, and a good deal of Talking Stick communication took place. To the surprise of the official diplomats, the two sides came to a working agreement they could all support.

Unfortunately, the same empathic process was not followed in actually carrying out the agreement. People on the ground who had to execute it did *not* get psychological air. Despite the official signatures on official papers, many years went by with no progress on implementing the Oslo Accords.

Dr. Marc Gopin, a distinguished scholar and practitioner of peace efforts in the Middle East, understands the importance of the emotional, personal connection that must be made if there is to be a creative solution. Formal agreements are not enough. "Conflict resolution as a field is in a very primitive stage of development," he says. "Its theoreticians seem not very adept at facing their own feelings and inadequacies. The diplomats have no sense of the trauma that will happen. They run away from it." The rationalism of the negotiators leaves no space for truly seeing one another.

Much of the good achieved at the Oslo meetings was undone at the 1999 Camp David conference between the Israeli leaders and the formidable Palestinian chief Yasser Arafat. Although he was celebrated by his own people, many Israelis viewed him as a vicious terrorist. The Israeli delegation treated Arafat with incredible disrespect. They kept him waiting for hours and then entered the room with a written plan all worked out. Throwing it on the table, they told him what he was to say and what they would say in response. So Arafat got out of his chair, left the room, and never met with the Israelis again. The Camp David meeting ended in failure. After that, Arafat denied that the Jews had any history at all in Palestine and no claim whatever to their "so-called Holy Land."

Ironically, at Camp David twenty years before, Israeli Prime Minister Menachem Begin and Egyptian President Anwar Sadat had faced each other across the same conference table, also deadlocked over a peace agreement. As a third party, President Jimmy Carter had worked hard to build a warm relationship with both men, and Sadat was ready to sign. But Carter found Begin unwilling to give on the final agreement. On the thirteenth day, when the conference seemed a failure, Carter ordered his secretary to find out the names of all of Begin's grandchildren. He then had photos of the three leaders produced and autographed a photo with a personal message to each grandchild. Those who were there say, "Begin was visibly moved at seeing each grandchild's name on the photos. A short time later, Begin agreed to remove the last obstacle to the peace accord." [1]

Was Carter's empathic gesture the tipping point that brought about peace between Israel and Egypt? Did Prime Minister Begin see the faces of his grandchildren as he looked at their names and wonder what kind of world he was creating for them? No one knows. But we do know that Carter had labored at this relationship. The two leaders had held long personal talks. President and Mrs. Carter had dined privately with Begin and his wife and heard how Begin had lost his parents and brother in the Nazi Holocaust. Begin knew that Carter had given him psychological air. Can anyone doubt that something happened in this man's heart when he trembled at the sight of his grandchildren's names, when he quietly spoke each name as he looked at those photos?

1 Joyce Neu, "Interpersonal Dynamics in International Conflict Mediation," in *Natural Conflict Resolution*, ed. Filippo Aureli (Berkeley: University of California Press, 2000), 66.

Marc Gopin believes that empathic gestures like this are essential to the search for a 3rd Alternative. At one of the worst moments of the Israel-Palestine conflict, Gopin had an opportunity to meet face to face with Arafat and make such a gesture.

Bridging the Unbridgeable Gap

In the spring of 2002, the Israeli army and Palestinians were fighting terrible battles in the streets of the West Bank. Innocent civilians were being targeted for death. The Israelis had quarantined Arafat, imprisoning him in his compound. Appalled at the killing, Marc Gopin decided on his own to try to get through the blockade and talk with Arafat personally. It was a frightening moment, fraught with inner turmoil for Gopin, who wondered, "Should I embrace him? Give him a gift?" Gopin had to decide if he himself was able to look beyond his own prejudices and fears and sit down with the mortal enemy of his people.

> *When I sat with him, it was the first time I touched a person who had killed a lot of Jews, who was still giving orders to kill Jews. But I thought, "If this can save one life, then it's worth it." That's what we were facing. Every day there were killings, and he was a major player in this cycle of endless violence. If only he could just say a few words to calm things down.*
>
> *So I looked into his eyes as if he were a nice old man and expressed sincere sorrow for all the Palestinian children who had died. I told him there's a* mitzvah *[commandment] in Judaism to comfort the mourning. I told him that in Jewish and Islamic tradition, it's a sacred act to share texts with others. It's a sacred bond. Now, there's a text in the Talmud that says the world stands on three things: truth, peace, and justice. Rabbi Muna said that where there is no justice, there will never be peace.*
>
> *Arafat knew that I was acknowledging his people's need for justice, but that I was also criticizing his methods for attaining justice. Mostly he was silent. Then he looked at me deeply and said, "You know, when I was a boy, I prayed at the Wall. You know . . . the Wall. With the old men. And they said their prayers and I said my prayers."*
>
> *I was stunned. His coterie were stunned. You have to understand the*

subtleties here. What was he saying to me? He was acknowledging that the Western Wall in Jerusalem was indeed a Jewish holy place, that Jews and Muslims could worship side by side. This was the same man who at Camp David had denied that there had ever been a Jewish presence in Jerusalem. He blew up the Camp David conference on that basis.

The day after Gopin's visit, Arafat issued an official communiqué to his forces to stop attacking Israeli civilians.

Gopin observes, "Now, Arafat was dark. He was corrupt, had millions of dollars hidden, and had sponsored terror. But the point of my story is to exemplify the power of gestures of respect. Sometimes they matter more than anything else. That moment between Carter and Begin and Sadat, when Carter appealed to Begin's grandchildren—where is that in international-relations theory?"[1]

Diplomatic rationalists and negotiators are absolutely unprepared for making gestures like this, but it's the first step in resolving any conflict sustainably.

During the 2003 uprising in Palestine, the streets of Jerusalem were deserted. No tourists, few business people. Gopin describes being one of the few guests in a major Jerusalem hotel. He walked out in the evening to take a taxi. There were five empty cabs on his side of the street and one cab all alone on the other side of the street. One of the five drivers came up to him and said, "Don't go with that cab over there. He's an Arab." So Gopin, being the bridge builder that he is, walked across the street and got into the Arab's cab.

He was sitting there alone, burning. He knew I was Jewish. He knew I came over to him on purpose. He was quiet. I said ten words to him: "This must be very hard for you and your family." Of course, all the cab drivers were starving because there was no business. Amazingly, he started speaking a torrent of things that could've gotten him in serious trouble with some of his Palestinian compatriots. "That man Arafat, he's destroyed everything. We were getting along before he came. He caused all of this." Now, that unburdening of his was a remarkable gift to me, but

---

1 Interview with Marc Gopin, Hebrew University of Jerusalem, January 10, 2011. See also Marc Gopin, *Healing the Heart of Conflict* (Emmaus, PA: Rodale, 2004), 187–88.

it came only because I had shown him a little empathy. He knew I had gone against my own people when I took his cab.

That's what happens when you're willing to step out. These gestures of respect and empathy are very contagious, just like anger is very contagious. I heard more honest conversation from him that night than I had heard in all the stupid diplomatic dialogues where everyone is acting a part and saying nothing. Real conflict resolution starts with single personal relationships.[1]

A Symphony of Synergy

Israel and Palestine came together one day in a London hotel in one of those singular personal relationships Gopin talks about. The great Israeli pianist and conductor Daniel Barenboim was sitting in the hotel lobby and said hello to a man in the armchair next to him. The man introduced himself as Edward Said, a Palestinian Arab who was also a renowned professor of literature at Columbia University. That evening these two men who should have been poles apart in their political positions started a conversation that went on for years.

Barenboim and Said became the closest of friends. After the death of his friend in 2003, Barenboim said of him, "Edward Said did not fit into any single category. He was the very essence of human nature because he understood its contradictions. . . . He fought for Palestinian rights while understanding Jewish suffering, and did not see this position as a paradox." In our terms, Said was a 3rd Alternative thinker: "He always looked for the 'beyond' in the idea, the 'unseen' by the eye, the 'unheard by the ear.'"

For his part, Said made these observations about Barenboim: "He is a complex figure . . . a challenge and even an affront to the usually docile majority." Arguably one of the greatest musicians in history, Barenboim has directed the Chicago Symphony and the Berlin Opera, recorded more classical music than any other individual performer, and serves as an outspoken advocate for peace in the Middle East. He was the first and most prominent Israeli musician ever invited to perform in the Palestinian West Bank (the

---

1 Gopin interview.

invitation was arranged by Said), and his empathy for both peoples is legendary.

In their years-long conversation about the unfolding crisis in the Middle East, neither Said nor Barenboim had much confidence that peace would arise from the stiff, formal contacts at governmental levels. They concluded that the root of the problem was the Israelis' and Palestinians' utter ignorance of one another: "Ignorance is not an adequate political strategy for a people, and there, each in his own way must understand and know the forbidden 'other,'" Said wrote.

When people are unwilling to know one another, they oversimplify one another—the consequence of what I have called the "I See Only My Side" paradigm. If, when I look in the mirror, I see myself only in terms of the group I belong to—my party, my country, my gender, my religion, my ethnic group—I will never see clearly see into my own complex and rich identity, nor into that of the people on the other side. Speaking as an Arab, Said concludes:

> *For Arabs, it has been a foolish and wasteful policy for so many years to . . . refuse to understand and analyze Israel on the grounds that their existence must be denied because they caused the Palestinian nakba. History is a dynamic thing, and if we expect Israeli Jews not to use the Holocaust to justify appalling human rights abuses of the Palestinian people, we too have to go beyond such idiocies as saying that the Holocaust never took place, and that Israelis are all, man, woman, and child, doomed to our eternal enmity and hostility.*

In their disillusionment with the fading peace process, Barenboim and Said wondered what they could do as a 3rd Alternative to help the two sides come to know one another. They hit on the idea of forming an orchestra of young Palestinian and Israeli musicians. Said recalled, "The idea was to see what would happen if you brought these people together to play in an orchestra." To begin with, they sent out invitations to a workshop to be held in Weimar, Germany, wondering if anyone at all would respond. They were flooded with applicants. Like most 3rd Alternative experiments, it was exciting, risky, and unpredictable. The project soon became "the most important thing" in the lives of both Barenboim and Said.

Barenboim led rehearsals every day and Said hosted a discussion every evening "about music, culture, politics. . . . No one felt under any pressure to hold back anything." There were Jewish students from Israel, Russia, and Albania and Arab students from Syria, Lebanon, and Palestine. Said started the discussion by asking, "So what do people feel about this whole thing?" Immediately a Jewish musician complained that he was being discriminated against because the Arabs wouldn't let him learn to play Arabic music in their jam sessions after hours. "They said to me, 'You can't play Arabic music. Only Arabs can play Arabic music.'"

Barenboim insisted that they were not there to repress their feelings but to express them to each other. He told the players, "It is not that we say we're all musicians and isn't it lovely to play music and forget about everything else. On the contrary, it is a project where everyone has the possibility, the right, and in fact the duty to express exactly his opinion."[1]

After a few weeks of tension and psychological airing of grievances, things began to change. "The same kid who had claimed that only Arabs can play Arabic music was teaching Yo-Yo Ma how to tune his cello to the Arabic scale. So, obviously, he thought Chinese people could play Arabic music. Gradually the circle extended and they were all playing the Beethoven Seventh. It was quite an extraordinary event."[2]

Out of this workshop came a full-fledged youth orchestra, the West-Eastern Divan, with musicians from Egypt, Iran, Israel, Jordan, Palestine, and Syria. The name of the orchestra comes from the title of Goethe's book of poems in which he celebrates the beautiful connections between Eastern and Western culture. Since 1999, hundreds of the most gifted young people in the Middle East have connected with each other in this way. The award-winning orchestra has played in dozens of countries and in both Israel and the Palestinian territories, and not without danger. When the Divan played in New York's Carnegie Hall, concertgoers had to pass through metal detectors to get in.[3] Daniel Barenboim says:

---

1 "Barenboim's Music: A Bridge across Palestinian-Israeli Divide." *AFP*, http://www.youtube.com/watch?v=GpGS1gVcU-k&NR=1.

2 Daniel Barenboim and Edward Said, *Parallels and Paradoxes: Explorations in Music and Society*, ed. Ara Guzelimian (New York: Vintage Books, 2002), ix–xi, 8–9, 181.

3 Anthony Tommasini, "Barenboim Seeks Harmony, and More Than One Type," *The New York Times*, December 21, 2006.

The Divan was conceived as a project against ignorance. . . . It is absolutely essential for people to get to know the other, to understand what the other thinks and feels without necessarily agreeing with it. I'm not trying to convert the Arab members of the Divan to the Israeli point of view, and I'm not trying to convince the Israelis to the Arab point of view. But I want to create a platform where the two sides can disagree and not resort to knives.[1]

There are still many thousands of Israelis who go to bed at night dreaming that when they wake up in the morning the Palestinians will not be there anymore, and the same on the other side. . . . They come with such total ignorance that they look at each other as a monster. But when they have played a Beethoven symphony together, days and weeks trying to play the same notes with the same expression, it doesn't solve the political problem, but I think it influences the way they see the other.[2]

Has the Divan Orchestra influenced its musicians? One Israeli performer says this about the experience:

The major problem is that everyone is surrounded by his own world, enveloped with his own world. We know nothing about them, and they know nothing about us, and whether we like it or not, we're going to be living next to each other forever. . . . We should start to learn how to live together, we have to break the wall that is in our minds and we have to start to understand each other.[3]

The Israeli cellist Noa Chorin says, "When I am playing next to Dana from Syria, I don't think 'she's from Syria,' I think 'that's my friend.'" After they played in a Palestinian town, Chorin remembers, "One girl said we were the

1 Ed Vulliamy, "Bridging the Gap, Part Two," *Guardian* (Manchester), July 18, 2008, http://www.guardian.co.uk/music/2008/jul/13/classicalmusicandopera.culture. Accessed October 21, 2010.
2 "Palestinian-Israeli Orchestra Marks 10th Anniversary," *Al-Jazeera English,* August 21, 2009, http://www.youtube.com/watch?v=gDJui5-zoeg. Accessed October 20, 2010.
3 *Knowledge Is the Beginning: A Film by Paul Smaczny,* 2005.

first Israelis she had ever seen that were not soldiers. And when it came to say goodbye, and go our different ways, people were crying."[1]

Two gifted pianists who played with the Divan, Shai Wosner from Israel and Saleem Abboud Ashkar from Palestine, quickly became close friends. Barenboim recalls, "They wanted to play together rather than coach with me individually and they began to prepare Mozart's Double Piano Concerto. It was incredibly refined when they played together. Their music making was full of understanding and feeling for each other's playing and style. . . . It was also a very symbolic move, and it was a wonderful occasion for all of us."[2] Barenboim loves this symbolism: "When I see little Karim at the piano, a Palestinian from Jordan and Inbal, from Israel with her cello, it is a source of unbelievable joy for me."

Barenboim downplays his own role in this small miracle. Through the vehicle of the Divan Orchestra, he has succeeded in bringing many talented young people in the Middle East to the threshold of 3rd Alternative thinking. He has, in the words of Carl Rogers, created "a situation in which each of the different parties come to understand the other from the *other's* point of view. This has been achieved, in practice, even when feelings run high, by the influence of a person who is willing to understand each point of view empathically."[3]

Like any other courageous seeker after 3rd Alternatives, Barenboim has critics. Pro-Palestinian activists charge him with creating a "utopian alibi" for Israeli aggression and maintaining an unjust status quo.[4] At the same time, many of his fellow Israelis distrust him for empathizing and consorting with Arabs, "the enemies of Israel."

But Barenboim has no illusions about the Divan Orchestra. He knows it will not by itself bring peace to the region, nor does he believe Israelis and Palestinians are somehow equally to blame for the situation. He is openly

1 Vulliamy, "Bridging the Gap, Part Two."
2 Daniel Barenboim, *A Life in Music* (New York: Arcade Publishing, 2003), 188.
3 Carl Rogers, "Communication: Its Blocking and Its Facilitation," n.d., http://www.red woods.edu/instruct/jjohnston/English1A/readings/rhetoricandthinking/communication itsblockingitsfacilitation.htm. Accessed October 20, 2010.
4 Raymond Deane, "Utopia as Alibi: Said, Barenboim, and the Divan Orchestra," *Irish Left Review,* December 9, 2009, http://www.irishleftreview.org/2009/12/09/utopia-alibi -barenboim-divan-orchestra/. Accessed October 21, 2010.

critical of his own government. Nevertheless the orchestra gives people from both sides the chance to know and at least begin to understand one another.

In 2004 Daniel Barenboim won the Wolf Prize for distinguished achievement in the arts. At the awards ceremony before the Israeli Parliament, he described his 3rd Alternative for promoting peace in his homeland:

> *A solution must be found. I ask myself: Why should I wait until such a solution materializes? This is why, together with my late lamented friend Edward Said, I have established a musical workshop for young musicians from all countries of the Middle East, Jewish and Arab alike. By its very nature, music can elevate the feelings and the imaginations of Israelis and Palestinians to new unimaginable spheres.*[1]

Then, in 2008, after playing a piano recital for charity in Ramallah, Barenboim was presented with a Palestinian passport. This makes him the first and perhaps the only person in the world to hold both Israeli and Palestinian passports. Expressing his pleasure, he said the passport "symbolizes the everlasting bond between the Israeli and Palestinian people."[2]

The dual passports make Daniel Barenboim a living, breathing 3rd Alternative. In this respect, he is unlike anyone else in the world. Where 2-Alternative thinking has dehumanized so many others in the region, Barenboim allows neither side to define him. As a moral imperative he feels deeply, he sees beyond the two sides to a rich third possibility: to be a citizen of *both* great cultures.

The Peacebuilding Paradigm

In the work of these exemplary people, do we see the prospects of a 3rd Alternative that will transcend the deadly wrangle in the Middle East and bring peace? No one can tell. Synergy is nothing if not unpredictable. What

---

1 Daniel Barenboim, in Smaczny, *Knowledge Is the Beginning.*
2 Kate Connolly, "Barenboim Becomes First to Hold Israeli and Palestinian Passports," *Guardian (Manchester)*, January 15, 2008, http://www.guardian.co.uk/world/2008/jan/15/musicnews.classicalmusic. Accessed July 14, 2010.

we do know is that synergy works; it's a correct principle. Although the 3rd Alternative thinkers I've described cannot control the paradigms of others, they have found ways to create synergy within their own Circles of Influence.

It may be that the intense positive synergy produced by Muslims like Mohammed Dajani and Christians like Margaret Karram and Jews like Daniel Barenboim will contribute to a grand solution. If so, it will happen because they have laid a foundation of empathy. They have instilled in the minds and hearts of many people the fundamental paradigms "I See Myself" and "I See You." They have worked at helping opponents adopt the paradigm "I Seek You Out" in search of understanding. As history has shown, all the diplomatic conferences and truce documents in the world will make little difference in the absence of these paradigms.

What do we learn from our examination of these pioneers of peace in the Middle East? What can we apply from their experience that we can use in the worlds we live in?

First, we learn the absolute necessity of the paradigm "I See Myself." Each of these individuals has gone through the essential self-examination required of

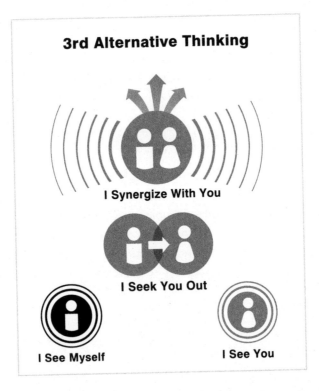

those who would truly seek the 3rd Alternative. Instead of unreflectively accepting the narrow self-definitions that so many of their coreligionists would impose on them, they question those definitions. They refuse to be defined by the extreme and marginal voices that threaten what is generous and loving about their religion.

Reflecting on how his fellow workers for peace differ from other people, Marc Gopin says, "We are deeply focused on the internal. I've found in my work with peacemakers, these true practitioners of the wisdom of peacemaking, they are a very special group of people on this planet. Invariably, they are working on themselves. They always ask themselves, 'Why did I do that? What do I do next?'"

In the history of any religion, as Gopin points out, the most amorphous things—love, compassion, justice—are always the most important things, but they are neglected because they are so general. The particulars—rituals, rules about clothing or food or the calendar—are actually very easy to observe by comparison. Love my enemies? How am I supposed to live that way? So I strain at gnats and swallow camels. It's far easier to have my ritual and feel good about myself.

"Love thy neighbor as thyself," according to Jews, is the whole of the Torah and, according to Christians, is the great commandment. But how do I love my neighbor? Even the one who's coming at me with an axe? The general rule is powerful, but it requires hard introspection to live up to.

That kind of introspection is actually basic to every great religion, including those that collide in the Middle East. For the Jews, it's called *cheshbon ha-nefesh,* the examination of the soul. The term *cheshbon* means "calculation." When impatience, fear, or anger threatens to overwhelm me, I must pause and calculate: What is happening? How should I respond? What are the consequences? How am I doing? What is or isn't going right with me?

In Islam, the term is *musahabah,* "to assess and adjudge ourselves": "It is the assessment of our own actions with total honesty, which requires of us genuine (and frequent) meditations."[1]

Says Gopin, "That moment in which you calculate is the salvation of your mind. If you're stunned by anger, the moment you say, 'I'm going to sit

---

1 Abdul Aziz Ahmed, "Al-Muhasabah: On Being Honest with Oneself," *Al-Jumuah: Your Guide to an Islamic Life,* n.d., http://www.aljumuah.com/straight-talk/40-al-muhasabah -on-being-honest-with-oneself. Accessed January 20, 2011.

here and think about my anger,' the brain changes. For the great Muslim and Jewish thinkers, as for the Dalai Lama, this is fundamental."[1]

Between any stimulus and our response to it is a mental space. This is what makes us human. We are not animals driven by instinct; we have the power to choose our response to any given situation, person, thought, or event. We have a built-in pause button we can engage to think about who we really are and what our conscience is telling us before we act. I have always believed that this is the first and fundamental habit of highly effective people. It is also the foundation of peacemaking.

The second lesson we learn is the absolute necessity of the paradigm "I See You," when you can see past the simple—and simple-minded—stereotype to connect with another real human being who happens to differ from you.

At five o'clock one spring morning in 1990, five Arab brothers were asleep in their home in East Jerusalem. Israeli soldiers broke down the door. Pointing their guns, they shouted, "Have you been throwing stones?" They

---

1 Gopin interview.

dragged the oldest brother, eighteen-year-old Tayseer, out of bed. By this time, their mother was awake, pleading with the soldiers, but they took Tayseer with them. He was beaten for two weeks until he finally admitted throwing stones at Israeli cars. For nearly a year after that, Tayseer was imprisoned without trial. He was at last released, desperately ill and vomiting blood. Three weeks later he was dead.

This is the story according to Aziz, his ten-year-old brother, who recalls, "I became extremely bitter and angry. . . . I grew up with anger burning in my heart. I wanted justice. I wanted revenge." Aziz became a journalist, writing a flood of articles "to spread hatred." "However," he says, "the more I wrote the more empty and angry I became." Aziz knew that to get a good job in Jerusalem, he would have to learn Hebrew. He had refused to learn the "enemy's language," but now he enrolled in a Hebrew school.

It was the first time I had sat in a room of Jews who were not superior to me. It was the first time I had seen faces different from the soldiers at the checkpoints. Those soldiers had taken my brother; these students were the same as me. I found myself confused, thinking "How can they be normal human beings, just like me?" I was amazed that I could build friendship with these students and share their struggles. We went out for coffee together. We studied together. For me, this was a turning point in my life.

I came to understand that unfortunate things happen in our lives which are out of our control. A ten-year-old could not control the soldiers who took his brother. But now as an adult, I could control my response to these hurts. They had acted unjustly and murdered Tayseer, but I had the choice, and I still have the choice, of whether to follow in the same direction.[1]

Today Aziz Abu Sarah is a respected journalist and director of Middle East projects at George Mason University in the United States. He has spoken on Israeli-Palestinian reconciliation before the European Parliament and the United Nations and is Marc Gopin's associate at the Institute for Conflict Analysis and Resolution.

1 Aziz Abu Sarah, "A Conflict Close to Home," *Aziz Abu Sarah: A Blog for Peace in Israel-Palestine,* May 6, 2009, http://azizabusarah.wordpress.com/2009/05/06/a-conflict-close-to-home/. Accessed January 20, 2011.

When Aziz connected with his "enemy"—with the normality and the struggles and the hopes of the "other side"—he began working from the paradigm "I See You." It's hard enough for us in the ordinary routine of life to live by this paradigm. But when we consider how people like Aziz and Mohammed Dajani have met their agonizing challenges, we realize that we must make the conscious decision to really see people and not reduce them to sides.

I cannot overemphasize the importance of these personal connections. Marc Gopin says, "I don't care if there's one state or two states or three states. Aziz and I aren't interested in that anymore. For us everything is relationships. The rational discussions can come later. Nobody has *any* control over the political situation; only in personal relationships do we have control."

While some use religion as a pretext for hostility, people like Gopin and Aziz find in their differing faiths a strong foundation for human love, generosity, and inclusiveness—all the characteristics of the "I See You" paradigm.

For Gopin, the overwhelming message of Judaism is to "love the *ger*— the stranger—among you." Although, as he says, this commandment is repeated thirty-seven times in the Bible, the animosity of the outside world has led many Jews to redefine the word *ger* to include only their fellow Jews. This is a tragic paradigm shift, but it's important to understand that warfare and generations of abuse have brought it about.[1]

Likewise, Palestinian Arabs have good historical reasons for their reflexive anger against Israel. Still, according to another much-loved Islamic peace activist in Jerusalem, Sheikh Abdul Aziz Bukhari, "No one can be a Muslim without love in his heart for all men." Bukhari is well known for interpreting the Islamic concept of *jihad* as the everyday human struggle to overcome anger. He pleads with Jews and his fellow Muslims to stop fighting "over the three percent of their scriptures which differ while ignoring the other 97 percent which they have in common."[2]

The task, to paraphrase Sheikh Bukhari, is to rehumanize those we have dehumanized.

For the peace activists in Jerusalem, religion is not a wall between people

---

1 Gopin interview.
2 "Sheikh Abdul Aziz Bukhari," Jerusalem Academy, http://www.jerusalem-academy.org/ sheikh-aziz-bukhari.html. Accessed January 20, 2011.

3rd Alternative Thinking

I Synergize With You

I Seek You Out

I See Myself   I See You

but a bridge to understanding. Far from rebelling against or rejecting their own religious traditions, they have found within those traditions the governing paradigm "I See You": I respect you, I include you, I value your difference from me.

The third lesson we learn is the absolute necessity of the paradigm "I Seek You Out," the mind-set that says, "You disagree with me? I need to listen to you." And mean it.

Most of the efforts of the peace pioneers we have met in these pages have been aimed at creating this mind-set. More than three hundred different organizations are trying to promote interreligious dialogue between Israelis and Palestinians. Although their work is piecemeal, little recognized, and underfunded, they are actively bringing into dialogue students, community leaders, rabbis, imams, mothers—in short, anyone who is willing.

You can't underestimate the emotional difficulty of these dialogues, but they are unbelievably productive in changing people's paradigms. Marc Gopin says:

If you want to make a paradigm shift with somebody's feelings, you have to confuse them by actually listening to them. I'm going to take all the stuff they can throw. I'm going to listen to outrageous things, some things that are true and some things that are ridiculous—total demonization of me and my people, escaping from their own crimes. I am so wanting to say things back.

But he doesn't. He has trained himself to seek first to understand. And he has learned that there is a tremendous return on this investment. "Remarkably, people in the Middle East have very warm hearts, they are very passionate. Respect and care in the right moments can totally change things in the Middle East, *and in the Middle East in particular.*"[1]

On the Islamic side, Sheikh Bukhari also learned the value of understanding the full passion and energy of the Other. "The stronger one is the one who can absorb the violence and anger from the other and change it to love and understanding. It is not easy; it is a lot of work. . . . But this is the real jihad."[2]

A fourth lesson we learn is the absolute necessity of the paradigm "I Synergize With You." This is the paradigm that asks, "Are you willing to look for a 3rd Alternative?" It takes people with this paradigm—people like Daniel Barenboim and Edward Said—to confront each other with that question and find that willingness. Still, until a critical mass of Israelis and Arabs concede each other's need for respect and empathy, no 3rd Alternative is likely.

That's why Mohammed Dajani, Ron Kronish, and others no longer talk in terms of "peacemaking." Fed up with the stifling politics of the region, they now speak of "peacebuilding," a 3rd Alternative to the stubborn cycle of 2-Alternative thinking that has led nowhere. Conventional peacemaking, they say, is about negotiating a settlement. By contrast, peacebuilding is not about negotiating anything. It's about synergy—it's about growing a thriving community organically through the proliferating of personal relationships. That's why they call themselves "peacebuilders."

The peacebuilding mind-set thinks beyond the treaty making that too

---

1 Gopin interview.

2 Abdul Aziz Bukhari, "Two Wrongs Don't Make a Right," *Global Oneness Project,* http://www.globalonenessproject.org/interviewee/sheikh-abdul-aziz-bukhari. Accessed January 20, 2011.

3rd Alternative Thinking

I Synergize With You

I Seek You Out

I See Myself   I See You

often papers over the passions generated by conflict. "I've watched twenty-seven years of treaties fail completely because there is no engagement with the issues of honor and respect that people feel deeply about," says Marc Gopin.

> *There's a blind spot about the violent gestures—for example, the check-points in Israel. You have ironclad prevention of movement, checkpoints manned by teens with machine guns. They produce horrible memories for Palestinians. Why couldn't there be a welcoming corps instead, dem-onstrating a lot of respect? Why couldn't they say, "Welcome, we just need to check your bags"? There's this constant idolization of the negotiated contract over gestures and deeds that can defuse things.*

The notion of a "welcoming corps" exemplifies the kind of 3rd Alternative thinking that leaders in Israel and Palestine need to do. Instead, because they lock themselves into 2-Alternative thinking, they doom their peoples to the negative synergy of warfare.

Negative synergy works like this. First, I dehumanize you and set you up as my enemy. As the historian Samuel P. Huntington notes, "People are always tempted to divide people into us and them, the ingroup and the other, our civilization and those barbarians. Scholars have analyzed the world in terms of the Orient and the Occident. . . . Muslims have traditionally divided the world into Dar al-Islam and Dar al-Harb, the abode of peace and the abode of war."[1] As a barbarian, you must be controlled. And if my group can't control yours, then I must attack you in hopes of bringing about a new synergy, a perverse, negative 3rd Alternative that cancels out your humanity, that denies you and your story any dignity at all. So many Arabs and Israelis dream that they will wake up and the "other ones" will be gone. They delude themselves that this destructive 3rd Alternative will be better than the status quo.

This is the reactive cycle that drives all warfare. The ancient Greek historian Thucydides described the Peloponnesian wars among the Greeks of his time as a kind of cyclical disease wherein one battle was answered by another, ending in the death of the glorious Golden Age of the Greeks. The same unthinking cycle drove the devastation of World War I: reactive decisions in Vienna, Berlin, London, and St. Petersburg. The First World War led inexorably to the Second because of the humiliating and vengeful terms imposed on the vanquished, who eventually struck back with insane fury. You hit me, I hit you back. Things will be better if I can hit you hard enough and knock you out of the picture. War is the ultimate expression of the zero-sum mentality.

By contrast, positive synergy is the opposite of war. It's proactive, not reactive. It's abundant, not scarce. It means deliberately going for the 3rd Alternative: "The maintenance of peace requires an aggressive commitment to imaginative diplomacy . . . not spasms of despair and the clash of military action in the hope for something better. Something better is almost always something worse."[2] Of course, imaginative diplomacy is harder than unimaginative diplomacy.

One of the most imaginative strokes of diplomacy in history was the

---

1 Samuel P. Huntington, *The Clash of Civilizations and the Remaking of World Order* (New York: Simon & Schuster, 1997), 32.
2 Robert I. Rotberg, Theodore K. Rabb, and Robert Gilpin, *The Origin and Prevention of Major Wars* (Cambridge, UK: Cambridge University Press, 1989), 248.

Marshall Plan, truly a 3rd Alternative to ongoing European war. With every major city on the Continent in ruins, with millions freezing and starving, the U.S. Congress voted to donate $13 billion to feed, house, and rebuild the infrastructure of their former enemies. (If you think that doesn't sound like much money, in terms of the 1948 American gross domestic product, it was one dollar in twenty—a vast outlay.) The Marshall Plan was the abundance mentality in action, the mind-set that says I can help my enemy, I can share, we can build together a plentiful future. The resulting revival broke the cycle of centuries of violence in Europe.

I might mention my experience with the Leadership Group on U.S.-Muslim Engagement. This was a meeting of Christians, Jews, and Muslims whose purpose was to build a better relationship between the United States and the world Islamic community. In that room were some of the world's most eminent scholars, diplomats, and practitioners of peace, including former U.S. secretary of state Madeleine Albright; Imam Faisal Abdul Rauf, head of the American Society for Muslim Advancement; and Dr. Marc Gopin. They allowed me to teach Talking Stick communication the night the conference opened, and for two days not one person spoke without the Talking Stick.

I could see that this distinguished group was totally transformed. People who were on different sides of almost every issue—cultural, social, religious—came to understand each other, respect each other, and love each

Talking Stick

Speaker   Listener

other. I watched this happen. Madeleine Albright told me she had never seen anything so powerful, and that it could totally revolutionize international diplomacy. She explained to me that most diplomacy consists of figuring out who has the power and what compromises can be made with them. The only alternative in most people's minds is compromise. Meeting each other halfway is the best they hope for, rather than getting really creative and producing a 3rd Alternative.

I have read the Qur'an and the Old and New Testaments; they are all inspiring, uplifting books. I believe the Muslims, Jews, and Christians of the Middle East can discover rich 3rd Alternatives to war in their own faith traditions.

One of the key recommendations of this group was to establish a vigorous interfaith dialogue so people can understand one another and find in their common beliefs a bridge to the future. Most important is the building of deep personal relationships across the dividing lines, networks of thousands who come to know and trust one another. These exchanges can be far more effective than the work of Davos-style conferences. When people feel empathically understood, their hearts are satisfied and their minds become open. When enough of these transformations take place, you can't stop 3rd Alternatives from flowing. You reach a tipping point where people will no longer accept the unacceptable and instead move forward to an abundant future together.

The key is the heart. Until we understand people's hearts, not just their minds and ideologies, nothing can happen. That's why it's absolutely essential to create opportunities for people to listen to each other with the heart, mind, and spirit. Only then can people move past the old destructive ways to "the better thing."

Archbishop Desmond Tutu understands the power of the 3rd Alternative as "the better thing":

Now and again we catch a glimpse of the better thing . . . when the world is galvanized by a spirit of compassion and an amazing outpouring of generosity; when for a little while we are bound together by bonds of a caring humanity, a universal sense of Ubuntu, when victorious powers set up a Marshall Plan to help in the reconstruction of their devastated former adversaries.

If the protagonists in the world's conflicts began to make symbolic ges-

tures for peace, changed the way they described their enemies, and began talking to them, their actions might change too.

What a wonderful gift to the world, especially as we enter a new millennium, if true peace would come in the land of those who say salama, or shalom, in the land of the Prince of Peace.[1]

A Nation That Should Not Be

When people ask me to explain my philosophy of the 3rd Alternative, I can answer with one word: "Switzerland." Often they have some idea of what I mean.

Most of us think of Switzerland as a peaceful, prosperous land with pretty mountains and great chocolate. But this country of 7 million people is far more than that—it's a marvelous example of 3rd Alternative thinking on a national scale.

Synergy is the hallmark of Swiss thinking. If you walk midday into the cafeteria of a great pharmaceutical company in Basel, with windows overlooking the Rhine, you'll see people from all over the world having lunch together. You'll hear a hundred languages spoken. You can eavesdrop on countless energetic discussions about science and medicine and the art and business of healing. Innovative new products for curing disease simply flow out of this place. You get the feeling that these are the brightest people on the planet.

What draws them here?

As a nation, Switzerland is an unquestioned success story. Swiss workers lead the world in efficiency. The Swiss per capita income is on top of the rankings. The Swiss government is "among the most effective and transparent in the world." And, according to the World Economic Forum, Switzerland has seized the top spot as the most globally competitive nation on the planet. It enjoys "an excellent capacity for innovation. . . . Its scientific research institutions are among the world's best, and the strong collaboration between the academic and business sectors, combined with high company spending on R&D, ensures that much of this research is translated into mar-

---

1 Desmond Tutu, *No Future Without Forgiveness* (New York: Doubleday, 1999), 264, 280–81.

ketable products and processes."[1] The World Database of Happiness Project reports that Switzerland is only a fraction below Denmark as the happiest country on earth.[2]

But Switzerland shouldn't even *be* a nation.

Nothing about Switzerland is favorable to nationhood. Geography is against it: the Swiss live on different sides of the massive Alps, enjoy few natural resources, and have no access to the sea. Language is against it: French is spoken in the west, German in the north and east, and Italian in the south. Religion is against it, with a long history of a Protestant-Catholic divide. Historians wonder at it: "Imagine trying to unite these different communities of aggressively independent farmers and merchants, especially when ties of religion, language, and power were often tempting them to turn outside."[3]

The history of Switzerland isn't as happy as people think. Subjugated, fought over, and divided many times, the twenty-two cantons, or counties, of Switzerland clashed relentlessly with each other for a thousand years. The cantons jealously guarded their rights and their boundaries. For centuries, commerce bypassed the country: "A piece of cloth, cheese, or other item passing through . . . was liable to some 400 taxes on the transport of goods." Money was a mess. As each canton issued its own currency, there were more than seven hundred different types of coinage.[4]

But the most serious concern was religion. "From the intra-Catholic disputes of the Middle Ages through the strife of the Reformation," Switzerland did not escape the religious fury that tore Europe apart. By 1845, cantons were forming into Protestant and Catholic leagues, and civil war broke out between them in 1847. Foreseeing complete breakdown, Austria, France, and Germany were poised to divide among themselves a ruptured Switzerland.

The Swiss government forces had the good fortune to be led by Gen. Guillaume-Henri Dufour. A multitalented soldier engineer, Dufour had

---

1 Klaus Schwab, ed., *The Global Competitiveness Report 2010–2011*, World Economic Forum, 14, http://www3.weforum.org/docs/WEF_GlobalCompetitivenessReport _2010–11.pdf.

2 R. Veenhoven, *Average Happiness in 146 Nations 2000–2009*, World Database of Happiness, Rank report Average Happiness, http://worlddatabaseofhappiness.eur.nl/hap_nat/ findingreports/RankReport_AverageHappiness.php.

3 George A. Fossedal and Alfred R. Berkeley III, *Direct Democracy in Switzerland* (Piscataway, NJ: Transaction Publishers, 2005), 30.

4 Fossedal and Berkeley, *Direct Democracy in Switzerland*, 31.

The 3rd Alternative in the World   405

fought in the Napoleonic wars and designed the world's first permanent suspension bridge at Geneva. But he was also a man of peace who was pained by war. It was said of him, "He is a soldier, but he draws the human being out in the soldier. He wages war, but he transforms it into a prelude to peace."[1]

When Dufour took command of the Swiss army, he issued to his soldiers a memorable order that "deserves to be remembered for its noble humanitarian tone": "As you cross the boundary, leave your anger behind, and think only of fulfilling the duties your native country imposes on you. . . . As soon as victory is decided in our favor, forget every feeling of revenge; act like generous soldiers, for you will thus prove your real courage. . . . Take all the defenceless under your protection; do not allow them to be insulted or maltreated. Do not destroy anything unnecessarily; waste nothing; in a word, conduct yourselves in such a manner as to win respect."[2] The Confederation troops showed "great forbearance" in the war, and historians believe the credit for this goes to Dufour.

Mostly through parleys and truces, Dufour skillfully brought the war to a close in twenty-six days. Few actual battles were fought, and only 128 soldiers died. (By contrast, eight years later, 618,000 had died in the American Civil War.) Dufour's extraordinary care for wounded enemy soldiers and his generous terms won the admiration of the rebels and helped reunite Switzerland.[3] And this was not the end of Dufour's contribution; in 1863 he presided over the first Geneva Convention, which created the International Red Cross.

The 1847 civil war pitted liberal, industrial Protestant Swiss against conservative, rural Catholic Swiss. The Switzerland of today is a 3rd Alternative to that political, economic, and religious conflict. The writer Michael Porter says, "A poor nation as late as the nineteenth century, [Switzerland's] major export was emigrating citizens. By the early decades of the twentieth century, Switzerland had emerged as an industrial nation of importance far beyond its small size."[4]

1 "Guillaume-Henri Dufour—A Man of Peace," *International Review of the Red Cross,* September–October 1987, 107. http://www.loc.gov/rr/frd/Military_Law/pdf/RC_Sep -Oct-1987.pdf. Accessed February 1, 2012.

2 William D. McCrackan, *The Rise of the Swiss Republic* (Boston: Arena Publishing Co., 1892), 330.

3 Fossedal and Berkeley, *Direct Democracy in Switzerland,* 18, 33, 37–38.

4 Michael E. Porter, *The Competitive Advantage of Nations* (New York: Free Press, 1990), 20.

How did this happen? How did Switzerland go from near-fatal fragmentation to arguably the most successful nation-state on the planet?

A good deal of credit goes to Dufour's leadership, the generosity and charity and attitude of forgiveness he showed to his opponents. Hatred between Protestant and Catholic had persisted since the Reformation, as each side wronged the other in a long round of retributions. W.H. Auden wrote, "I and the public know what all schoolchildren learn, / Those to whom evil is done do evil in return." [1]

Yet after their civil war, something changed. The Swiss engineered a national government unlike any other in the world. To break the cycle of enmity that had led to the war, they adopted a system of direct democracy through the Constitution of 1848. Although laws are made by the legislature, any citizen can challenge any law through a petitioning process. Then the entire electorate votes on the issue. These "votations" now occur about four times a year. "After votations it is customary to say that 'the sovereign has spoken.'" According to analysts, the system educates the public, encourages power sharing and respect for minorities, and motivates policymakers to be moderate and consensual. [2] Of course, lapses do occur, and if human rights are not respected, the Federal Supreme Court can strike down a law.

Somehow this 3rd Alternative form of government helped to end the wrangling among the Swiss cantons. When all the Swiss people at last felt their voices would be heard, a remarkable transformation overtook the country. The patchwork of tolls and coinages and the cobweb of laws disappeared. Peace became a governing principle; in the following century, Switzerland completely avoided the ravages of two world wars.

Still, although their democracy helps account for Switzerland's "unity in diversity," that's not a sufficient explanation. Other contributing factors include the educational system, which actively emphasizes the creative unity they share and de-emphasizes old resentments. Additionally, the law recognizes no ethnic group identity, only individuals. According to Professor Carol L. Schmid, "This attitude, which implies respect for minorities, means that it is not the numerical strength of the group that should be decisive,

---

1 W.H. Auden, "September 1, 1939," http://www.poemdujour.com/Sept1.1939.html.
2 Clive H. Church, *The Politics and Government of Switzerland* (Basingstoke, UK: Palgrave Macmillan, 2004), 143.

with an individual being placed at a disadvantage merely because he is a member of a minority group." At heart, the success of Switzerland is due to what I've called "the ethic of respect." In her study of countries with major ethnic divides, Schmid observes that "successful ethnic coexistence is dependent on a significant amount of equality between groups. . . . Tensions are likely to be aggravated by an awareness of significant inequalities among ethnic groups." This awareness is the great barrier to synergy. Ethnic conflict, says Schmid, is almost always the result of the arrogance of an elite group. "Violent societies show considerable economic and political inequality."[1]

Diverse yet unified, practicing many religions and speaking many languages, Switzerland shows the world how to build a 3rd Alternative culture. The ancient cultures of the cantons are revered. All individuals, religions, and languages are respected; German, French, and Italian have equal status, "a principle of equality before the law which was to illuminate the future." As the Swiss made these gestures of respect toward each other, "barbaric prejudices broke down, which make men rivals, then enemies, and finally slaves." The result has been a synergistic "marriage of German profundity with French elegance and Italian taste," wrote Frédéric La Harpe, one of the framers of the Swiss Constitution.[2] People who honor the ethic of respect, who deliberately seek to benefit from the rich variety around them, cannot be kept from synergy.

Could the land tensely divided between Israelis and Palestinians become another Switzerland? Only if they decide to adopt the 3rd Alternative mindset of mutual respect and valuing differences. It is not, as some people say, an insoluble conflict. There are no insoluble conflicts. The success of Switzerland was not an accident. The Germans, French, and Italians of Switzerland, bloodied for generations by ethnic and religious rifts, *chose* to change. Scholars know that "Switzerland came about because human ingenuity was able, at critical times, to surmount large difficulties."[3] In other words, Switzerland was a *choice*.

There is no reason at all that others could not make the same choice.

---

1 Carol L. Schmid, *Conflict and Consensus in Switzerland* (Berkeley: University of California Press, 1985), 155–56.
2 Schmid, *Conflict and Consensus in Switzerland*, 3.
3 Fossedal and Berkeley, *Direct Democracy in Switzerland*, 30.

What many call the Holy Land could become another Switzerland. Imagine the 3rd Alternatives that could be achieved by a marriage of Arab energy and Israeli ingenuity! This is not a naïve dream. Andrew Reding of the World Policy Institute has suggested Switzerland as a model for an Israeli-Palestinian federation.[1] In 2010 Alvaro Vargas Llosa, the vigorous Latin American writer, toured homes and businesses and street markets across the region. What he saw galvanized him: "Israel's economy is booming and the Palestinian territories [of the West Bank] are experiencing a free-market bonanza. . . . The economic élan of the Palestinian territories, and Israel's mesmerizing entrepreneurship all demonstrated to us the wonders these two societies could achieve together. What is sad is not how distant reality is from that but how easy it is to imagine it."[2]

Still, I am optimistic that the world is trending overall toward peace. There are discouraging zones of conflict, but they are diminishing. There are psychopaths who can take monstrous measures, but they are more and more isolated. I believe that global commerce and democratization will continue. We see young, educated people in emerging nations from Morocco to Indonesia taking control of their future from the constraining forces of the past.

The journalist Robert Wright speaks of the fascinating role of 3rd Alternative thinking in the history of human conflict. He points out that our life on this planet has been through many zero-sum phases, in which scarcity rules and there's always a winner and a loser. A conqueror comes along, turns people into slaves, and is eventually conquered by another. But Wright argues that the direction of history is always toward "non-zero-sum" phases, in which abundance rules and everyone wins: "Have you ever thought when you buy a car, how many people on how many different continents contributed to the manufacture of that car? Those are people in effect you're playing a non-zero-sum game with." Human synergy can lead to the end of conflict between peoples and states as they become so deeply interconnected in cre-

1 Andrew Reding, "Call It Israel-Palestine: Try a Federal Solution in the Middle East," World Policy Institute, June 25, 2002, http://news.pacificnews.org/news/view_article.html?article_id=601. Accessed February 1, 2011.
2 Alvaro Vargas Llosa, "Postcard from Hebron," Washington Post Writers Group, June 2, 2010. http://www.postwritersgroup.com/archives/varg100602.htm. Accessed December 12, 2010.

ating the future. As our interest shifts toward contributing to our global society, old hatreds wither away. I see wisdom in Wright's conclusions:

> *On balance, I think history is a net positive in the non-zero-sum game. And a testament to this is the thing that most amazes me, most impresses me, and most uplifts me—that there is a moral dimension to history, there is a moral arrow. We have seen moral progress over time.*[1]

1 "Robert Wright on Optimism," TED.com, February 2006, http://www.ted.com/talks/lang/eng/robert_wright_on_optimism.html.

TEACH TO LEARN

The best way to learn from this book is to teach it to someone else. Everybody knows that the teacher learns far more than the student. So find someone—a co-worker, a friend, a family member—and teach him or her the insights you've gained. Ask the provocative questions here or come up with your own.

- What do we learn from the story of Mohammed Dajani about the moral power of 3rd Alternative thinking?
- Margaret Karram says of attending a Jewish college, "I did not open my mouth for the first six months." Why do you think she was silent? What does her example teach us about the value of empathy?
- How did the Oslo Accords of 1993 come about? What do we learn about the synergy process from this story?
- How did Jimmy Carter bring about the Camp David Accords? How is this story an example of the importance of giving people "psychological air"?
- What role do "empathic gestures" play in resolving conflict, according to Marc Gopin?
- In what ways is Daniel Barenboim a "walking 3rd Alternative"?
- What role do you think the Divan Orchestra is playing in the quest for peace in the Middle East? What insights do you gain from the musicians in the orchestra?
- Explain the importance of each of the synergy paradigms in the quest for peace.
- According to both Jewish and Muslim tradition, what is the role of self-awareness and introspection in resolving conflict?
- "That moment in which you calculate is the salvation of your mind," says Marc Gopin. What does he mean by this? Why is that moment so important in resolving conflict?
- "If you want to make a paradigm shift with somebody's feelings

you have to confuse them by actually listening to them." What is the role of empathic listening in the quest for peace?

- Explain the difference between peacemaking and peacebuilding. What does it mean to say "Peacebuilding is about synergy"?
- Explain why positive synergy is the opposite of war.
- Why do scholars say Switzerland shouldn't even *be* a nation? What do we learn by comparing the story of Switzerland to the story of the Israeli-Palestinian conflict?
- What is there about the direction of history that should make us optimistic?

TRY IT

As you consider your own relationships, neighborhood, or community, are there serious conflicts you could help resolve? Start prototyping 3rd Alternatives. Invite others to contribute. Use the "4 Steps to Synergy" tool.

4 STEPS TO SYNERGY

1 Ask the 3rd Alternative Question:

"Are you willing to go for a solution that is better than any of us have come up with yet?" If yes, go on to step 2.

2 Define Criteria of Success

List in this space the characteristics of a solution that would delight everyone. What does success look like? What is the real job to be done? What would be a "win-win" for all concerned?

3 Create 3rd Alternatives

In this space (or other spaces) create models, draw pictures, borrow ideas, turn your thinking upside down. Work quickly and creatively. Suspend all judgment until that exciting moment when you know you've arrived at synergy.

 **Arrive at Synergy**

Describe here your 3rd Alternative and, if you want, how you intend to put it into practice.

USER GUIDE TO THE 4 STEPS TO SYNERGY TOOL

The 4 Steps to Synergy. This process helps you put the synergy principle to work. (1) Show willingness to find a 3rd Alternative. (2) Define what success looks like to everyone. (3) Experiment with solutions until you (4) arrive at synergy. Listen empathically to others throughout the process.

How to Get to Synergy

① Ask the 3rd Alternative Question

In a conflict or creative situation, this question helps everyone move past firm positions or preconceived ideas toward developing a third position.

② Define Criteria of Success	③ Create 3rd Alternative
List characteristics or write a paragraph describing what a successful outcome would look like to everyone. Answer these questions as you go: • Is everyone involved in setting the criteria? Are we getting as many ideas from as many people as possible? • What outcomes do we really want? What is the real job to be done? • What outcomes would be "wins" for everyone? • Are we looking past our entrenched demands to something better?	Follow these guidelines: • Play at it. It's not "for real." Everybody knows it's a game. • Avoid closure, premature agreement, or consensus. • Avoid judging others' ideas—or your own. • Make models. Draw pictures on whiteboards, sketch diagrams, build mockups, write rough drafts. • Turn ideas on their heads. Reverse the conventional wisdom. • Work fast. Set a time limit to keep energy and ideas flowing rapidly. • Breed lots of ideas. You can't predict which offhand insight might lead to a 3rd Alternative.

((④)) Arrive at Synergy

You recognize the 3rd Alternative by the sense of excitement and inspiration in the room. The old conflict is abandoned. The new alternative meets the criteria of success. Caution: Avoid mistaking compromise for synergy. Compromise breeds satisfaction but not delight. Compromise means everyone loses something; synergy means everyone wins.

The 3rd Alternative in Life

9

A 3rd Alternative Life

It is not more vacation we need—it is more vocation.

—Eleanor Roosevelt

In the town of Ceiba, Puerto Rico, you'll find a house known locally as "The Manger," where the great cellist Pablo Casals spent his last twenty years before his death in 1973. Nearly a century before, in his native Spain, he had heard his first cello, and it conquered him before he conquered it. As a boy, he did little else but practice the Bach cello suites from a worn-out copy his mother gave him, and when a prominent composer heard him and invited him to play for the Spanish royal family, his career soared. At twenty-three, he performed for Queen Victoria, and at eighty-five for President John F. Kennedy at the White House.

The six decades between were a long crescendo upward in the world of music. Casals starred with the great orchestras, won every possible honor, and was acclaimed the greatest cellist on the planet and perhaps in history. He was so beloved in Spain that when he played before the king, listeners pointed to the royal box and shouted, "This is our king, but Pablo is our emperor!"

In the great man's last years, his neighbors in Ceiba would listen to the sound of the Bach suites coming from the windows of The Manger. One day, when he was ninety-three, one of them asked him why he continued to practice the cello three hours every day. Casals replied, "I'm beginning to notice some improvement. . . . I notice myself getting better at this."

Living in Crescendo

Pablo Casals never stopped playing his music until the day he laid down his bow for the last time at age ninety-seven. He built his capacity, improved his powers, and contributed the best that was in him right to his last breath. When others wondered why he didn't slow down as he approached the end of his long life, he would tell them, "To retire is to die." Casals could have explained to them that when the music dies down, it's called a *diminuendo*, and when the music swells to life and grows in grandeur, it's called a *crescendo*. He was determined that his life would not slip into *diminuendo*. He lived in *crescendo*.

Of all the ideas I share in my professional work, I know of no greater one that ignites and empowers others more than my personal motto: *Live Life in Crescendo! Your Most Important Work Is Always Ahead of You.*

I once taught this idea to a large professional group, and afterward a judge came up to me with fire in his eyes. He explained that he had planned on retiring soon, at the typical age, but after hearing about living in crescendo, he realized he still had an intense passion for his work and could contribute to solving problems in his city. He decided to postpone retirement indefinitely.

Always believe your most important work is ahead of you, never behind you. It's essential to live with that thought. Regardless of what you have or haven't accomplished, you have important contributions to make. You may do different work than you have done in the past; it may be significant in different ways; but it is important work nevertheless, especially if you can positively impact the lives of others. We should avoid the temptation to keep looking over our shoulder in the rearview mirror at what we have done and instead look ahead with optimism.

No matter what our age or position in life, we 3rd Alternative thinkers are never finished contributing. It's the nature of a 3rd Alternative mentality always to be seeking something higher and better from life. We may get satisfaction from past accomplishments, but the next great contribution is always on the horizon. As this book shows, there are challenges everywhere that require the creative influence of a synergist. We have relationships to build, communities to serve, families to strengthen, problems to solve, knowledge to gain, and great works to create.

In my case, I am now past the typical retirement age, but I am still actively writing, teaching, consulting, and traveling for my profession. The happiness and personal growth of my children and grandchildren are vital to me. With all these exciting challenges before me, I'm more than ever a seeker of 3rd Alternatives. As the comedian George Burns said when he was ninety-nine, "I can't retire now, I'm booked!"

One of my daughters asked me if I would ever again write anything with the impact of *The 7 Habits of Highly Effective People.* I think I startled her with my answer: "Are you kidding? My best stuff is yet to come! I have ten books in my head right now!" This is not to overvalue myself—I truly *believe* my best work is ahead of me. Why shouldn't I feel that way? What motivation would I have to get up every day if I thought I had already given my best and had nothing of value left to share? I agree with the statement by Ernest T. Trigg, "The man who has accomplished all that he thinks worthwhile has begun to die"—no matter how old he is!

Too many of us live a kind of 2-Alternative existence: we work or we play. Many people work *in order* to play. We put in long days at work with no particular end or goal in mind except to get through it as quickly and as hassle-free as possible so we can relax. We hear it all the time:

"Well, another Monday."
"I'll be glad when this week is over."
"If I can just get through this day . . ."
"It's almost the weekend."
"Thank goodness it's Friday."

And so we wish our days, weeks, years, and lives away. Each day is a dichotomy between "brain on" and "brain off." We see ourselves through the lens of the Industrial Age, as machines that perform a certain function until we're no longer needed. We switch off every night until the switch goes on again the next morning—and at last a day comes when the switch is turned off for good. What then?

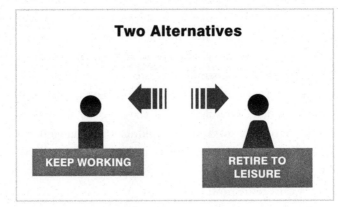

We go on the shelf. We retire to leisure, to play for the rest of our days. And that's exactly what many of us want because we have been brainwashed to see our whole lives in terms of these 2 Alternatives.

But this is a false dichotomy imposed by a society with an Industrial Age mind-set. We are conditioned to believe there are only two choices: *keep working* or *retire*. We think that someday when we are no longer "machines," we'll be happy. *Then* life will be meaningful. But for many, as the poet William Butler Yeats wrote, "Life is a long preparation for something that never happens." Their lives slip into diminuendo, and the decline can be long and futile.

I believe that the 3rd Alternative is by far the best. *Make a contribution.* It can encompass the first 2 Alternatives. You can keep going with your life's work well past the "golden age" of sixty-five and continue to make a strong contribution. Or you can retire from your career and start a second career of making meaningful contributions to your family and to society, responding to the great needs you see around you.

Of course, if you have the paradigm of contribution, both your working years and your retirement years will be meaningful.

I propose a drastic paradigm shift in our thinking about our work and our retirement. According to demographic reports on developed countries, between 33 and 40 percent of men over fifty-five no longer work for a living. While only a generation or two ago our forebears died exhausted at this age, most of us can look forward to a full "second adulthood" in our later years. The question of how to spend that second adulthood will preoccupy a lot of people in the next few decades, as the over-sixty-five population doubles to more than 25 percent. The average European or American will live to

The 3rd Alternative

CONTRIBUTE

KEEP WORKING

RETIRE TO LEISURE

about seventy-nine, the average Japanese to about eighty-two. Every day of the past century, the life expectancy of Americans increased by seven hours; that translates into more than twenty-five additional years for each of us! The bad news is some of us don't know what to do with this time and may miss invaluable opportunities to make a difference in the lives of so many.

Will we squander those years doing nothing much, or make them count?

The contribution paradigm can actually save your life. I have observed that people who retire to leisure often decline mentally and physically almost at once, unless they get busy making a meaningful contribution. According to the noted expert on stress, Dr. Hans Selye:

With advancing years, most people require increasingly more rest, but the process of aging does not progress at the same speed in everybody. Many a valuable person who could still have given several years of useful work to society, has been made physically ill and prematurely senile by the enforced retirement at an age when his requirements and abilities for activity were still high. This psychosomatic illness is so common that it has been given a name: retirement disease.[1]

The author Chuck Blakeman describes retirement disease this way: "I'll wait until I'm 65 to live significantly. I'll go through the motions for the first 65 so I can get there. Until then I'm just marking time."[2]

By contrast, a mission-driven life is rejuvenating. Meaningful contribution keeps our immune system strong and the regenerative forces of the body working. My own sense of mission is swelling inside of me, not shrinking, and that's why every new day excites me. I don't sense myself as just growing older; as Carl Rogers said, "I sense myself as older and growing."[3]

The notion of quitting meaningful work at a certain time of life is a relatively new concept. If you look back, you will realize that the great men and women of history never ceased in their desire to discover new paths along life's journey. To me, the whole concept of retirement is a flawed notion, a culturally misaligned relic of the Industrial Age.

Look around and you'll see plenty of older people who still work as engineers, CEOs, coaches, educators, lawyers, entrepreneurs, inventors, ministers, scientists, business owners, doctors, who don't buy into society's notion of retirement and continue to contribute significantly year after year. Others totally redefine their roles and make unexpected contributions. They live in crescendo.

3rd Alternative Lives

In 1981, when President Jimmy Carter and his wife, Rosalynn, returned home to Plains, Georgia, they wondered, "Is there life after the White House?" They had been so vitally engaged in the state senate, the governorship, and at last the highest office in the land, where would they go from here? Discouraged and involuntarily retired, they felt empty, fearing that their lives would drop into diminuendo.

---

1 Hans Selye, *The Stress of Life* (New York: McGraw-Hill, 1948), 413.
2 Chuck Blakeman, "Business Diseases of the Industrial Age," http://chuckblakeman.com/2011/2/texts/business-diseases-of-the-industrial-age.
3 Carl Rogers, *A Way of Being* (New York: Houghton Mifflin, 1995), 95.

Of course, they enjoyed the unaccustomed time spent with family and friends and their church. Still, something was missing from their lives. They certainly were not going to frolic on the golf course forever. Nor did they want to settle for what was expected of a former president, writing memoirs and building up a presidential library. Carter wanted to leave behind more than a book and a building as his monuments. Then, one night, he awoke with a vision of a 3rd Alternative life. He realized he was now free to do things he could never do in the White House: he could still use his status as a former president of the United States to help solve some of the world's toughest problems.

His vision was to become a catalyst for change, an agent of peace and healing. He went to work furiously on his first project, establishing a refuge where people from all over the world could meet and talk and explore creative alternatives to their problems. This project, which eventually became the Carter Center, excited his wife as well. It was then they realized what had been missing from their lives: the opportunity to make greater, even more meaningful contributions than ever before.

Although serving as president of the United States is a pinnacle of human achievement, the Carters felt they could achieve higher things. "Who knows?" they asked themselves. "If we set our objectives high, we might even be able to do more than if we had won the election in 1980." It was an empowering insight that invigorated them both. "What could possibly be beyond the White House?" we might ask ourselves. The Carters are the answer to that question.

They are living in crescendo. They are busier than they have ever been. They work with the Carter Center to resolve conflicts and advance democracy and human rights everywhere. As part of a coalition of seventy countries, they sponsor public-health projects such as eradicating the guinea worm disease that once painfully disfigured millions in Africa. They promote Habitat for Humanity, volunteering to build homes for needy people; a familiar picture is Jimmy Carter, hammer and nails in hand, working alongside others raising a house. He is almost universally acknowledged as the most productive former president in history.

How could Jimmy and Rosalynn Carter have known on leaving the White House that perhaps their most important work still lay ahead of them? They have not retired from life, and they challenge us to join in synergy with others to answer the needs of humanity:

Involvement in promoting good for others has made a tremendous dif-
ference in our lives in recent years. There are serious needs everywhere
for volunteers who want to help those who are hungry, homeless, blind,
crippled, addicted to drugs or alcohol, illiterate, mentally ill, elderly, im-
prisoned, or just friendless and lonely. There is clearly much left to be
done, and whatever else we are going to do, we had better get on with it.[1]

One of those who is "getting on with it" is Harris Rosen, a hotelier based in Orlando, Florida. Growing up poor in Hell's Kitchen in New York City, he continually heard from his parents that "a good education will get you out." Applying their advice, Harris was the first in his family to graduate from college. He paid his dues from the bottom up in the hotel business and eventually owned seven hotels in the blossoming Orlando area. He could well afford to sit back and enjoy the fruits of his labors.

However, he couldn't ignore nearby Tangelo Park, a short distance from one of his luxury hotels on International Drive, but worlds apart in fear and poverty, infested with crime, drugs, joblessness, and an alarming 25 percent high school dropout rate. Driven to contribute a good education for the kids of Tangelo Park, he stood up unexpectedly at a school meeting and told the stunned crowd, "I promise to send every Tangelo Park high school student who graduates to college for free!" People could hardly believe it, but Rosen's initiative went ahead. And he did more: he funded preschools so small children would enter grade school without an educational deficit, and established a family resource center where parents could get counseling and skills to strengthen their families.

"This is an amazing story," says Professor Charles Dziuban of the University of South Florida and a member of the Tangelo Park Program advisory board. The results of this infusion of hope were almost immediate: crime dropped by 66 percent and the dropout rate went from 25 to 6 percent. An incredible 75 percent now go on to college.[2]

Rosen was more than repaid when one day he was having a prescription filled, and the young pharmacist recognized him. "Mr. Rosen, I went

---

1 Jimmy and Rosalynn Carter, *Everything to Gain: Making the Most of the Rest of Your Life* (Fayetteville: University of Arkansas Press, 1987), 171.
2 DeWayne Wickham, "An Amazing Story of Giving That Could Change Our World," *USA Today,* March 20, 2007. http://www.usatoday.com/news/opinion/2007-03-19 -opcom_N.htm.

through the Tangelo Park program you established and graduated from college. I am a pharmacist today because of you!" Another young graduate of the program became "Teacher of the Year" in Orange County. This fine teacher can afford to live anywhere, but chooses to live in Tangelo Park and raise his family close to the students he wants to influence.

In his seventies, Harris Rosen could have a lavish Florida retirement. Or he could keep working, minding his own business, head down and oblivious to the suffering across the street. But he rejects both those alternatives. His passion is a 3rd Alternative—the total renewal of this problem-plagued, impoverished neighborhood. He challenges other wealthy people to follow his model, believing it can transform society.

Now I can hear you say, "But I'm not a former president or a wealthy executive." By now you should know my answer: it doesn't matter. Within our own Circles of Influence, we can have proportionally the same impact as do the Carters or Harris Rosen.

At the farthest possible other end of the celebrity spectrum is "Jackie," whose true name I don't even know. Jackie lives in a one-room house that measures twelve feet by twelve feet. I have no idea where this house is, other than somewhere in the American South. And I ask you not to go looking for her.

We get to know Jackie through the remarkable writings of William Powers, an environmental journalist from New York. Powers sought her out and received permission to tell her story because it might contribute important insights to the rest of us on how to live a truly sustainable lifestyle.

To her neighbors, Jackie is known as a "wisdomkeeper" in a tradition that goes back to Native Americans. "They're elder women who inspire us to dig more deeply into life." Under the laws of Jackie's state, a building twelve by twelve feet or less is not a house but a shed, so she can stay completely "off the grid" of codes and public utilities: no gas, no electricity, no running water, no sewer, no phone. To the bureaucratic world, Powers says, Jackie is "invisible."

A medical doctor, Jackie felt her connection to the pace and chaos of urban life weakening, and she longed to connect to a quieter world. After raising her family and approaching her later years, she downsized her job and found a wild patch of ground where she has redefined herself as a "permaculture farmer" devoted to living in stable harmony with the land. In permaculture, inputs equal outputs; that is, nothing external comes into the system, and all wastes are reused so that nothing leaves the system.

Jackie's life might sound rough, but it's actually idyllic. Powers describes his first meeting with Jackie:

> She was partly obscured by the tea bushes. At a distance, all I could see was part of her face and a ponytail of salt-and-pepper hair. . . .
>
> With a little pull on my hand, Jackie led me over to some rainwater pooled by the tea bushes. We crouched there, and a bee flew off my arm and landed beside the pool. Above us sat a bee box. Jackie told me her Italian bees produced forty pounds of honey a year, enough to give to friends. "Listen to how quiet the bees are," she said. . . .
>
> A slight buzz mingled with the murmur of the creek. We were surrounded by Juneberries, figs, hazelnuts, and sourwood. The bee that had been on my forearm was now sipping from the pool. Jackie reached down and stroked its wings as it drank. "Sometimes I wake up in the morning out here in the silence, and I get tears of joy."

Jackie describes permaculture as "the things your grandparents knew and your parents forgot." More complex than it seems, her woodland acre is laid out in zones, some protected by hedges from wild deer and rabbits. Besides her vegetable garden, she cultivates native berries, pecans, heirloom apples, and mango-like pawpaws. In the forest, she harvests shiitake mushrooms. Her tiny house is cedar-fragrant and "surprisingly roomy. . . . By scaling down to this speck of human space, Jackie had been enveloped by nature. No electrical wires, no plumbing."

Still, Jackie is no hermit. She tends to patients, enjoys her family, and travels—very cheaply—to work with peace and environmental groups. Her way of life is a 3rd Alternative to the two sicknesses of her generation: enthusiastic materialism and vague purposelessness. Powers draws a forceful contrast between Jackie and an acquaintance who "retired from financial planning at forty-eight and, with her third husband, bought a house with an ocean view. There, she'd been living for the past few years, neither happy nor unhappy . . . [on] a 'permanent vacation,' pina coladas accompanying every sunset."[1]

---

1 William Powers, *Twelve by Twelve: A One-Room Cabin off the Grid and Beyond the American Dream* (Novato, CA: New World Library, 2010), xiv, 15–17, 75.

A Permanent Vacation or a Permanent Mission?

I recognize that many people love the idea of a permanent vacation. Some long for it throughout their working years. We get so battle-scarred and beaten up in our Industrial Age jobs that it's only natural to dream about an endless cruise through the tropics or a limitless green fairway. We *should* unwind when we need it—there's everything right about a beautiful day on the links or an exotic trip—but we delude ourselves if we think escape will make us happy. It is against the nature of things. No matter where we are in life, we can get addicted to waste: mindless TV, fixating on social media, constant gaming and club hopping, dumb novels, obsessing over medications, sleeping the hours away. These things can diminish anyone, but retired people are especially at risk of turning their lives into scrap.

My Grandfather Richards taught me "Life is a mission and not a career." He might have added "and not a vacation." Think carefully about the contrasting lives of those who are on a permanent vacation and those who are on a permanent mission.

One man on a permanent mission is James Kim, who as a fifteen-year-old South Korean soldier lay wounded and perhaps dying on a battlefield of the brutal Korean War. A deeply devout and humble boy, he asked his God to spare his life so that he could "return love to my enemies," the armies of North Korea and China.

He survived the war, and from then on everything he did was to fulfill the vow he made to help his neighbors to the north, "to save their lives, not to kill them." An ordinary young man without much education and no money, he had no idea at first what he could do to help his former enemies, whose borders were shut tight against him in any case. But he knew he would need resources, so he went to America to make some money.

Kim became a U.S. citizen, started a business importing Korean wigs and, over time, built up a little wealth—but only as a means to accomplish his end in mind. He knew that a U.S. passport would help him penetrate the then closed societies of North Korea and China. In the 1980s he was ready to carry out his mission. The job to be done, he felt, was to help educate young people and open their minds to learning. It was the best gift to his old enemies that he could think of.

Invited to give a speech at a Beijing business conference, he used the opportunity to announce that he would fund a small college at Yanji on the North Korean border. Skeptical but intrigued, the Chinese authorities decided the school might support their strategy of opening up to the West. A few years later, Kim and his wife, Grace, moved into the dormitory, where he could live with and befriend the students of the new Yanbian University of Science and Technology. To give back, the students would do volunteer work in local schools and hospitals along with their studies. The college prospered, attracting gifted teachers from around the world.

Then in 1998, hearing of food shortages in North Korea, Kim volunteered to cross the border with supplies and was promptly arrested. Accused of spying, he was jailed and interrogated every day for a month and a half:

> *"When I was detained, I was very calm. I wrote that I was not afraid to die, because I knew I would go to a better place. And I wrote that if I did die, I would donate my organs for medical research in North Korea. I told them I was at peace." What he heard back, Kim says, is that the Dear Leader was touched by that sentiment.*[1]

Released at last, Kim continued to petition the North Koreans to let him build a university for them. By 2001 he had convinced the government, and preparations began for the new Pyongyang University of Science and Technology, funded by Kim's savings and donors he recruited. It took nine years to build, but on October 25, 2010, the school opened its doors and welcomed the first 160 of the most brilliant students in the country. Kim believes that it will help North Koreans connect with the world of information technology and ultimately break down barriers.[2]

Many of his beneficiaries are baffled by Kim's generosity. "Ask Kim about where he finds his inspiration, and he'll always say, 'Love.' The cheerful professor sees love as a force that stretches across borders, with education as a toolbox to apply it." When his North Korean and Chinese hosts asked him

1 Bill Powell, "The Capitalist Who Loves North Korea," *Fortune*, September 15, 2009, http://money.cnn.com/2009/09/14/magazines/fortune/pyongyang_university_north _korea.fortune/index.htm.
2 Richard Stone, "PUST Update," *North Korean Economy Watch*, November 1, 2010, http://www.nkeconwatch.com/category/dprk-organizations/state-offices/pyongyang -university-of-science-and-technology/.

if he would call himself a capitalist or a communist, he recalls, "I told them I was simply a 'love-ist.' " [1]

I would call James Kim a "walking countertype." Where the wounds of war embitter some, Kim's wounds softened his heart toward his enemies. Where many would be pleased to see the last of their enemies, Kim virtually beat down the doors to help his. Now in his advanced years, at a time when so many are in diminuendo, he is still living in crescendo. He could be relaxing somewhere on a beach, or he could have forgotten his youthful, impractical vow and still be running his business in Florida. Either alternative is perfectly justifiable.

But not for Kim. He has chosen a 3rd Alternative. Is it a higher and better thing to be on a permanent vacation or a permanent mission? That's a question you'll have to answer for yourself.

You might be asking, "But after a long life of labor, don't I deserve to slow down, sit back, and take things easier? What if I just don't feel strong enough? What if my health has failed?"

I would be less than empathic if I didn't understand those feelings. Although I get tired more easily, need more sleep, and find it much harder to travel than in earlier years, I am grateful that my own health is pretty good, but my wife, Sandra, has had a series of back surgeries that changed her life entirely. She is confined to a wheelchair and depends on the help of others even for simple tasks. It has been difficult for both of us to adjust to this new lifestyle, and our whole family has suffered through this difficult experience along with her.

Of course, Sandra wishes for the freedom to walk again and do what she wants without restraints, but for now it's not to be. Despite those difficulties, her attitude has been remarkable and inspiring: she is doing what she can with what she has. Her motto is the Latin phrase *Carpe diem!* "Seize the day!" She stays engaged with her family, friends, and the causes that are important to her. She is acting within her Circle of Influence, constantly enlarging each day despite her challenges. She is involved in her book club and lunch group with friends, teaches a class at our church, serves on a university board, wraps up St. Patrick's Day cookies for the neighbors, plays tricks on her family on April Fool's Day. She showers her grandkids with cards, phone

1 Geoffrey Cain, "Former Prisoner of North Korea Builds University for His Former Captors," *Christian Science Monitor*, February 16, 2010.

calls, and visits. She reads voraciously, stays active politically, and supports an arts center for which she raised much of the funding herself. Not too bad for being in a wheelchair! As they say, "Don't 'dis' on disability!"

Though Sandra's life has changed radically, she still lives in crescendo by contributing as much as she's able. The philosopher Friedrich Nietzsche said, "He who has a *why* to live can bear almost any *how*."

I believe we also have a responsibility to help others live in crescendo. Regardless of age or infirmity, every person is valuable and capable of contributing. I have a friend who is under great pressure at work and has a heavy schedule. Recently his aged mother came to a point in her life where she could no longer live independently, and the family debated about what would be best for her: to stay in her home with hired help, move to assisted living, or move in with her son. My friend had a lot on his mind and wasn't sure he had the space in his life to accommodate caring for his mother. Fortunately, his splendid and capable wife was not so reluctant, and she welcomed her mother-in-law into the home. Tiny, frail, mostly blind and deaf, the elderly lady was truly disoriented by the move. It was like having a dependent child in the house; they had to do most things for her, washing, feeding, getting her up in the morning and to bed at night. Impatient, yet feeling guilty about it, my friend wondered if this arrangement was really going to work.

Then one evening he found himself watching his mother next to him at the dinner table and his wife across from him. His mother was telling her a little story about her childhood on the family farm, how they would gather beans together and bottle them for the winter. My friend realized that the television was off, the house was quiet, and the sunset light falling on his mother's face made her look quite young. He felt an unfamiliar contentment in a connection he hadn't sensed for a long time. To his surprise, he was taking the time to really *see* his mother, to listen to her, and to enjoy her calm influence. She was so thankful for everything, so courteous and gentle, that she seemed to come from another world and time. His wife smiled, resting her hand on her chin, listening to the mother's stories as if she had all evening.

Gradually, the geography of my friend's life changed. He and his wife took his mother on brief, extremely slow walks. They listened to music together. They recorded her telling stories about her life. She taught them old tips about baking, and under her supervision they shakily reproduced a loaf of her homemade bread. In the evenings they would watch ancient black-and-white movies, mostly comedies from the 1930s that she barely remembered, and her son would repeat in her ear the funny lines that she couldn't hear.

In time, my friend realized how raw and unfinished his life had been before. Though his mother was past her ninetieth birthday, unable to see or hear or work in the usual sense, this late contribution she was making to her son enriched him in ways he had never anticipated. He, who was so used to walking fast through life, learned to walk more slowly, to linger over a restful dinner, to enjoy an old story, and to sit contentedly next to his mother just holding her hand. To the end, her life was lived in a gentle crescendo.

I credit my friend with the sensitivity to enable his mother to contribute meaningfully in her last days. "She did us a favor by coming to live with us," he says. "We were the ones who benefited." He could have put her in a rest home, and she would have enjoyed her associations there and been well cared for. But *he* would have missed something that transformed his life: the quiet rewards of love and service.

In our headlong search for secondary success—money and social status— we run a very serious risk of missing entirely the far deeper satisfactions of primary success: the love, trust, and gratitude of those we serve.

It is my personal belief that we are on this earth to serve others, that God expects us to do His work by helping our fellow men and women. We may be the answer to another's prayer for help. Through the gift of conscience, God inspires us to bless His children in ways both material and spiritual. I believe service is the key to lasting happiness and is the *measure of true success in this life*.

Some, like machines, will continue their dull, daily grind without much sense of this kind of success until death switches them off. Others will escape and amuse themselves to death. Yet others will choose a 3rd Alternative and strive as long as they live to make higher and better contributions to the hap- piness of their fellow beings. This is the ultimate "job to be done."

Will you choose the 3rd Alternative to make a contribution and live your life in crescendo? Or will you allow your life to diminish as you age? What will your legacy be? Don't look back. What else do you have to contribute? What exciting adventure is ahead? What will you build that will be last- ing? What will you do when you have more time to offer those around you and you have knowledge and experience on your side? What key relationship do you need to build or repair? Is your greatest work still ahead of you? Those around you will be waiting and hoping you can answer the daunting challenges of our world. And as you answer with a synergy of mind and heart, you will be blessed with a life of meaning and purpose as well.

In his great poem "Ulysses," Tennyson imagines the hero of Troy as an "idle king" sitting on his throne long after his epic odyssey is over, surrounded by banquet tables and tedious games, growing old and useless with self-indulgence. He reflects on his past deeds, on his struggles with storms and giants, on the challenges he faced and surmounted against titanic odds—and he realizes he cannot die where he is. Not like this.

No longer the young hero but still driven toward something higher and better, Ulysses rises from his chair and orders his ship made ready. His old companions feel as he does, and, as they set sail together, they know their greatest adventures still lie ahead.

> *I cannot rest from travel: I will drink*
> *Life to the lees: all times I have enjoyed*
> *Greatly, have suffered greatly, both with those*
> *That loved me, and alone. . . .*
> *How dull it is to pause, to make an end,*
> *To rust unburnished, not to shine in use!*
> *As though to breathe were life. Life piled on life*
> *Were all too little. . . .*
>
> *. . . Though*
> *We are not now that strength which in old days*
> *Moved earth and heaven; that which we are, we are;*
> *One equal temper of heroic hearts,*
> *Made weak by time and fate, but strong in will*
> *To strive, to seek, to find, and not to yield.*

TEACH TO LEARN

The best way to learn from this book is to teach it to someone else. Everybody knows that the teacher learns far more than the student. So find someone—a co-worker, a friend, a family member—and teach him or her the insights you've gained. Ask the provocative questions here or come up with your own.

- What does it mean to live life in crescendo? What does it mean to live in diminuendo?
- Too many of us live a kind of 2 Alternative existence. How would you describe those 2 Alternatives? What are the limitations of each alternative to a person seeking to live a full life? What is the 3rd Alternative?
- The contribution paradigm can actually save your life. What natural processes make this true?
- What were the 2 Alternatives facing Jimmy and Rosalynn Carter after their White House years? In what way do the Carters live a 3rd Alternative life?
- The 3rd Alternative lives of Harris Rosen and "Jackie" are virtually opposite in the size of their Circles of Influence, yet both are making contributions. What do we learn from them about the scale of our contributions in life?
- We delude ourselves if we think happiness is a "permanent vacation." Why is it against the nature of things?
- What is so liberating about the idea of being on a "permanent mission"? What does the story of James Kim teach us about that?
- I would call James Kim a "walking countertype." In what ways is Kim's life a countertype?
- Nietzsche said, "He who has a *why* to live can bear almost any *how*." How does the example of Sandra Covey exemplify this insight? In what ways does this insight help you as you consider your own limitations?
- What do we learn about living in crescendo from the story of

my friend and his mother? Why do we have a responsibility to help others live in crescendo? Who might you help to live in crescendo?

- What do these lines from Tennyson's poem "Ulysses" mean to you? "How dull it is to pause, to make an end, / To rust unburnished, not to shine in use!"

TRY IT

How will you "live in crescendo"? What are your own criteria of success? What 3rd Alternative might transform your life? Start prototyping 3rd Alternatives. Invite others to contribute. Use the "4 Steps to Synergy" tool.

4 STEPS TO SYNERGY

① Ask the 3rd Alternative Question:

"Are you willing to go for a solution that is better than any of us have come up with yet?" If yes, go on to step 2.

② Define Criteria of Success

List in this space the characteristics of a solution that would delight everyone. What does success look like? What is the real job to be done? What would be a "win-win" for all concerned?

```


```

③ Create 3rd Alternatives

In this space (or other spaces) create models, draw pictures, borrow ideas, turn your thinking upside down. Work quickly and creatively. Suspend all judgment until that exciting moment when you know you've arrived at synergy.

```


```

((④)) Arrive at Synergy

Describe here your 3rd Alternative and, if you want, how you intend to put it into practice.

```


```

USER GUIDE TO THE 4 STEPS TO SYNERGY TOOL

ARRIVE
At Synergy or
3rd Alternative

CREATE
3rd Alternatives

DEFINE
Criteria of Success

ASK
3rd Alternative Question

The 4 Steps to Synergy. This process helps you put the synergy principle to work. (1) Show willingness to find a 3rd Alternative. (2) Define what success looks like to everyone. (3) Experiment with solutions until you (4) arrive at synergy. Listen empathically to others throughout the process.

How to Get to Synergy

❶ Ask the 3rd Alternative Question

In a conflict or creative situation, this question helps everyone move past firm positions or preconceived ideas toward developing a third position.

❷ Define Criteria of Success	❸ Create 3rd Alternative
List characteristics or write a paragraph describing what a successful outcome would look like to everyone. Answer these questions as you go: • Is everyone involved in setting the criteria? Are we getting as many ideas from as many people as possible? • What outcomes do we really want? What is the real job to be done? • What outcomes would be "wins" for everyone? • Are we looking past our entrenched demands to something better?	Follow these guidelines: • Play at it. It's not "for real." Everybody knows it's a game. • Avoid closure, premature agreement, or consensus. • Avoid judging others' ideas—or your own. • Make models. Draw pictures on whiteboards, sketch diagrams, build mockups, write rough drafts. • Turn ideas on their heads. Reverse the conventional wisdom. • Work fast. Set a time limit to keep energy and ideas flowing rapidly. • Breed lots of ideas. You can't predict which offhand insight might lead to a 3rd Alternative.

(((❹))) Arrive at Synergy

You recognize the 3rd Alternative by the sense of excitement and inspiration in the room. The old conflict is abandoned. The new alternative meets the criteria of success. Caution: Avoid mistaking compromise for synergy. Compromise breeds satisfaction but not delight. Compromise means everyone loses something; synergy means everyone wins.

10

Inside Out

One summer many, many years ago I was leading a group of young people on an outdoor survival camp. The purpose was to teach them how to survive in the wilderness with very few provisions, living mostly off the land. Near the end of the week, we were showing them how to cross a river with a simple, heavy rope strung tightly between large trees on both sides of the river. I was to demonstrate to the teenagers how to cross—holding tightly to the rope with hands and legs and moving hand over hand to the other side. About half way I decided to have some fun and show off by swinging wildly on the rope. The river was deep and slow-moving, so in this case, there was little danger below. The kids loved it. Laughing away, I even started taunting them, "I'll bet *you* won't look this good when *you* cross!" The problem was, I expended so much energy monkeying around, that when I got back to the task of crossing, I felt my muscles start to cramp and lose their strength. I mustered all my willpower and was determined to make it the rest of the way. Within moments, however, I couldn't make another move. I hung there for a few seconds. Muscles gave way. I went splashing into the water below. I struggled to the bank, climbed out soaking wet, and endured the teasing I deserved the rest of the week!

I learned a great lesson, one that I've never forgotten. You see, the body, like most things in nature, teaches us the law of the harvest—you reap what you sow. There are natural laws. They ultimately govern all of life. No matter how much I psyched myself up and willed my way across the rest of the river,

I was ultimately subject to the condition, strength, and endurance capacity of my muscles. Without strength inside myself, I could not expect to succeed outside myself.

You will face this same reality as you attempt to create 3rd Alternative solutions to your toughest problems and challenges. Despite all your best desires and efforts, I guarantee you will find yourself falling short and experiencing what feels like failure as you attempt to resolve a tough difference with a friend, colleague, or family member and it doesn't turn out as you hoped. It may even seem to make matters worse.

I come up against these limits all the time. I lose my patience. I overreact. I find it really hard to listen at times . . . especially when I KNOW I'm right! And since I've taught these principles to my now grown children so often over the years, they don't hesitate to call me on it when I'm not listening. So I've learned to smile, take a deep breath, apologize quickly, and then say, "Okay, help me understand." And to be honest, sometimes it takes me a while to get there.

We may start off with great intentions, but in the struggle find ourselves becoming defensive, hurt, reactive, or falling back into old patterns of "fight or flight" communication. These things need not indicate failure at all, but rather that we need to do more work inside our souls and develop greater strength in the "muscle" of our character.

The more we care, the more we attempt to live with a 3rd Alternative mind-set in every great challenge and opportunity in life, the more we desire to take on the big, important issues we face, the more inner strength it will require. The greater the problem, the more important the relationship or issue, the greater the need for inner security, abundant win-win thinking, patience, love, respect, courage, empathy, tenacious determination, and creativity. The broader the river, the more internal strength it takes to cross.

How do we develop this inner character strength? This is one of the truly great questions of life. It's at the heart of what I tried to get at when I wrote *The 7 Habits of Highly Effective People.* The original subtitle was "Restoring the Character Ethic." So I suggest you either read or re-read *The 7 Habits* book. I do so without reservation because it is a book of timeless, universal, self-evident principles of human effectiveness. They belong to every enduringly prosperous culture, society, religion, family, and organization. I did not invent them; I simply sequenced and organized them into a framework that gives people personal access to them. I believe these universal principles come from God and are a manifestation of His love for us and desire for our happiness. I also recognize and have the deepest of respect for the many who may not share this belief, yet who live principled lives of great service and contribution.

Your success as a 3rd Alternative thinker will come from the inside out. I recommend twenty things that I've found to be very helpful in developing the inner strength and security to create 3rd Alternative solutions:

1. Beware of pride. Let go of needing always to be "right." Your grasp on reality is always partial anyway. Allow yourself to achieve the important breakthroughs in relationships and creative solutions that will never likely be realized if you stubbornly hold on to being "right."

2. Learn to say "I'm sorry." Do it quickly once you realize you've fallen short or hurt someone. Be sincere and don't hold back. And don't go just half way. Apologize fully, take responsibility, and express your desire to understand.

3. Be quick to forgive perceived slights. Remember, you choose whether or not to be offended. If you feel offended, let it go.

4. Make and keep very small promises to yourself and others. Take baby steps. As you create a pattern of doing so, make and keep bigger promises. Your own integrity will become your greatest source of security and strength.

5. Spend time in nature. Go on long walks. Create space in your life every day for reflection on the synergies of the world around you.

6. Read widely—it's one of the best ways to make mental connections and get insights that can lead to 3rd Alternatives.

7. Exercise often, each day if possible; and eat healthy food, with balance and moderation. The body is the instrument of the mind and spirit.

8. Get enough sleep, at least 7 to 8 hours daily. Science tells us that the brain grows new connections during sleep, which is why we often awake with sparkling new ideas. And you'll find yourself so much more able to give the emotional, mental, and spiritual energy needed to create 3rd Alternatives.

9. Study inspiring or sacred literature. Ponder, meditate, or pray. Insights will come.

10. Make quiet time for yourself to think through creative 3rd Alternative solutions to your challenges.

11. Express love and appreciation to those with whom you associate. Listen empathically to them. Devote time to learning about them, what is important to them, what is their story.

12. You have two ears and one mouth: use them proportionally.

13. Practice being generous with others—with your time, your heart, your forgiveness, and your affirmation. Be wise and generous in sharing your resources with those in need. Be generous with and forgive yourself. We all have weakness. We all have strength. Look to the future and move on. All these things will cultivate within you a spirit of abundance.

14. Avoid comparing yourself to others. Just don't. You are unique. You are of infinite worth and have great potential. Define your own exceptional mission in life. Just be true to it, be yourself, and serve others and the world simply and magnificently!

15. Be grateful. Express it.

16. Learn to become enthusiastically relentless about discovering how to create great wins for others—wins that increase their peace, their happiness, and their prosperity. It will become infectious, and you may often find others seeking the same for you. This is the key to producing remarkable synergies.

17. When things aren't going well, take a break, take a walk around the block, get a good night's sleep, and come back at it with the freshness and perspective of a new day.

18. If you truly can't reach win-win, remember that "no deal" in some cases is the best alternative.

19. When it comes to other people, their reactions, their weaknesses, and peculiarities, just smile a lot. And when it comes to your teenagers, remind yourself, "This, too, shall pass."

20. Never stop believing in the possibility of the 3rd Alternative.

By winning these Private Victories, you will find that your Public Victories will follow.

In closing, I express to you my love, my belief in you and in your potential, and my confidence that as you choose to walk the path of a 3rd Alternative life, you will bring about great good in the world. You're so needed. God bless you.

—Stephen R. Covey

Acknowledgments

I thankfully acknowledge the many wonderful people who have contributed to this book. To friends, colleagues, clients, and "trim-tabbers" around the world who exemplify the 3rd Alternative—whether featured in this book or not—I say you inspire me with deep gratitude. Thank you for sharing your stories and lives so willingly.

Thanks to my colleagues at FranklinCovey: Sam Bracken, who ably managed the project with infectious passion and commitment; Dr. Dean Collinwood, who conducted our Serious Challenge survey around the world; Jody Karr, whose talented team designed the graphics; Terry Lyon, who collected hundreds of permissions; and Debra Lund, my make-it-happen publicist, whose loyalty and dedication have contributed in countless ways to the reach and impact of my books and work; likewise, Janita Andersen, who has magnificently done so in the international arena. The work was immeasurably improved by valuable insights from the reviewers and contributors Annie Oswald, Michael Ockey, and my son Sean Covey.

My special thanks go to Boyd Craig, my business partner, friend, and colleague for over two decades, who originally proposed this book idea and framework to me, bringing together years of synergistic work we've done on many of the core dimensions of this book. He is one of the most extraordinary 3rd Alternative leaders I know, and one of the most courageous, wise models of 3rd Alternative thinking, creating, teaching, and problem solving I've worked with. The fruit of his work and character is manifested throughout this book and in so much of my professional life's work.

I thank my assistants: Julie Gillman and Darla Salin; Boyd's assistant, Victoria Marrott; and all my assistants and associates over the years who have been so important and enabling to my work. Their unseen, tireless devotion has blessed me in ways I'm sure that no one will ever fully know.

I also gratefully acknowledge Bob Whitman, FranklinCovey's chairman and CEO, my colleagues on our board of directors, our executive team, and all our associates worldwide who provide inspiring leadership and committed service every day. I love and appreciate you.

For the design, production, marketing, and publishing of the book, I acknowledge the fine work of our friends at Simon & Schuster/Free Press, including Carolyn Reidy, Martha Levin, Dominick Anfuso, Maura O'Brien, Suzanne Donahue, and Carisa Hays. Thanks also to my dear friend Jan Miller and her associate Shannon Miser-Marven for their superb representation.

To my wife, Sandra, my children, Cynthia, Maria, Stephen, Sean, David, Catherine, Colleen, Jenny, Joshua, and their remarkable spouses, who contributed many experiences to enrich the book, I express my love and thanks. Our children, grandchildren, great-grandchildren, and posterity yet to come are the light and hope of our lives and will ultimately be the realization and manifestation of my lifelong desire to "live life in crescendo." In particular, I am grateful to my daughter Cynthia Covey Haller, who is largely responsible for the chapter "A 3rd Alternative Life."

I pay tribute to my parents and grandparents who blessed me with inner security and who loved, affirmed, and raised me with an abundance mentality—the foundations of 3rd Alternative thinking. I also thank my dear sisters and especially my brother John, who has been the most loyal and true of friends my entire life, and who contributed extensively to the chapter "The 3rd Alternative at Home." His leadership of FranklinCovey's Marriage, Home, and Family work around the world is leaving a legacy that will be felt for generations.

I am especially indebted to my old friend Judge Larry M. Boyle of the United States District Court system, who coauthored with me the chapter "The 3rd Alternative and the Law." An example of 3rd Alternative thinking at the highest levels of the judiciary, Larry has given us in this book the benefit of his unique experience in synergistically resolving the most difficult conflicts. I also wish to acknowledge and express appreciation to Brian L. Boyle, a skilled lawyer with a 3rd Alternative mind, whose insightful contributions to the law chapter provide a perspective of today's legal practitioner. Thanks also to legal research assistants Brandon Karpen, Kristin Fortin Lewnes, Michael Miles, Mark Shaffer, and Rebecca Symbrowski.

Special acknowledgement also goes to Ward Clapham, whose life and principle-centered leadership in the world of policing are ending crime, strengthening young people, and sowing seeds of civil society wherever he goes. I'm grateful to him for his significant contributions to the chapter "The 3rd Alternative in Society."

Finally and foremost, I thank Breck England, FranklinCovey's chief writer, for his hundreds of hours of research and writing that made this book possible. His was a zealous and whole-souled contribution as he ranged around the world in search of the best thinking about synergy. Like all of my colleagues, he typifies the mission of FranklinCovey: to enable greatness in people, organizations, and societies everywhere.

Index

About the Author

Stephen R. Covey, one of *Time* magazine's twenty-five most influential Americans, has dedicated his life to demonstrating with profound yet straightforward guidance how every person can control his or her destiny. He is an internationally respected leadership authority, family expert, teacher, organizational consultant, and author. He has sold over 20 million books (in thirty-eight languages), and *The 7 Habits of Highly Effective People* was named the #1 Most Influential Business Book of the 20th Century. His other bestselling books include *Principle-Centered Leadership, First Things First, The 7 Habits of Highly Effective Families, The 8th Habit: From Effectiveness to Greatness,* and *The Leader in Me: How Schools and Parents Around the World Are Inspiring Greatness One Child at a Time.* He is the cofounder of FranklinCovey, a leading global education and training firm with offices in 147 countries. Dr. Covey is a tenured professor in the Huntsman School of Business, Utah State University, where he holds the Jon M. Huntsman Presidential Chair in Leadership. He lives with his wife and family in Utah.

Dr. Breck England is chief writer for FranklinCovey Co. and has collaborated with Dr. Covey on several books, including *Predictable Results in Unpredictable Times* and *Great Work, Great Career*. In more than two decades of consulting experience, he has helped some of the world's largest corporations improve their leadership and communication processes. He has directed such projects for the Fortune 50, and from Switzerland to Saudi Arabia. A Ph.D. in English, he taught organizational communication for seven years in the Marriott School at B.Y.U. He and his wife live on a mountainside in northern Utah.

LEARN MORE

Want to learn more about how to reach 3rd Alternatives in your life and your business?

Visit us on the Web at www.The3rdAlternative.com

The 7 Habits®

Based on the best-selling book *The 7 Habits of Highly Effective People*, FranklinCovey's *7 Habits Training Solutions* help employees apply timeless principles of effectiveness to improve interpersonal communication, take initiative, establish greater trust, strengthen relationships, increase influence, and balance key priorities.

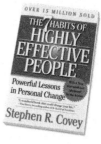

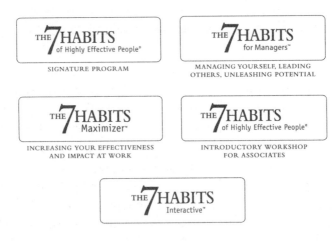

webinar workshops

The *3rd Alternative* Training Workshops

Experience world-class training for the 3rd Alternative exclusively through Franklin-Covey LiveClicks webinar workshops. Available as open-enrollment workshops or as exclusive training for your team, you will be taught live by a certified instructor who will help you truly learn how to live the 3rd Alternative. Or bring the content to your organization by becoming certified to teach it yourself through the Franklin-Covey LiveClicks platform.

- **3rd Alternative Problem Solving**
- **3rd Alternative Decision Making**
- **3rd Alternative Conflict Resolution**
- **3rd Alternative Innovation**
- **3rd Alternative Negotiation Skills**

For more info, visit www.franklincovey.com/liveclicks/the3rdalternative

---

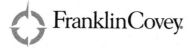

FranklinCovey is the global consulting and training leader in the areas of strategy execution, customer loyalty, leadership, and individual effectiveness. Clients include 90 percent of the Fortune 100, more than 75 percent of the Fortune 500, and thousands of small and mid-sized businesses, as well as numerous government entities and educational institutions. FranklinCovey (www.franklincovey.com) has 46 direct and licensee offices providing professional services in 147 countries.

www.franklincovey.com